Investing for Social Impact, Economic Justice, and Racial Equity

Dorcas R. Gilmore, Lisa Green Hall, and Susan R. Jones

ABA
AMERICAN BAR ASSOCIATION
Business Law Section

Cover design by Catherine Zaccarine.

Printed in the United States of America.

27 26 25 24 23   5 4 3 2 1

ISBN: 978-1-63905-209-7

Discounts are available for books ordered in bulk. Special consideration is given to state bars, CLE programs, and other bar-related organizations. Inquire at Book Publishing, ABA Publishing, American Bar Association, 321 N. Clark Street, Chicago, Illinois 60654-7598.

www.shopABA.org

Contents

Acknowledgments

Dorcas R. Gilmore

I am grateful to the Gilmore Khandhar, LLC team, who supported me from the book concept through the final drafts—Barbara Bezdek, Jhenna El-Sawaf, Nisha Jain, Parag Khandhar, and Trey McKinney. Your encouragement, review of drafts, research assistance, and steadfast support were invaluable. The University of Maryland Carey School of Law provided early research assistance and support. I appreciate my co-editors, Susan R. Jones and Lisa Green Hall, for contributing their depth of knowledge and wisdom in community development and social impact investing to this book. All of the book contributors generously provided their experiences and expertise to make this a useful resource to the field.

The love of my family inspires and grounds me. Thank you to my husband, Chad E. Harris; daughter, Carolyn Ella Gilmore-Harris; my mother, Ella J. Gilmore; my sister, Tabitha Gilmore-Curtis; brother-in-law, Kwame Curtis; and niece, Kaelynn Ella Curtis. The memory and experiences of my father, Ray Gilmore, propel me in this work.

Lisa Green Hall

I want to thank the incredible team at Georgetown University's Beeck Center for Social Impact and Innovation for their early support of this book and my editing work. Sonal Shah, former Executive Director of the Center, has been and continues to be a guiding light for me and so many others in the field of impact investing and social justice. I am also grateful for the many mentors I have had over the years, especially, Jamie Gorelick, who has been an amazing friend, coach, and supporter professionally and personally for more than twenty years. I am also deeply appreciative of my co-editors Susan Jones Johnson and Dorcas Gilmore who recruited me to this project and have been such wonderful partners in the editing of this book, which we hope will contribute to the field and be a guide for both students and lawyers alike.

Last but most importantly, I would like to thank my daughter, Lee, who is my biggest fan and my heartbeat. She is my staunchest advocate and without her patience and resilience, this project would not have come to fruition.

Susan R. Jones

I extend a heartfelt thanks to the George Washington University for summer writing support; to Tiffany Robson, GW Law Business & Finance Law Librarian, for excellent research help; and to Gabriella Joseph, GW Law 2022, an incoming junior associate at Venable LLP's NY Office who provided invaluable research assistance. I also offer my sincere thanks to Dorcas Gilmore for her visionary leadership in conceptualizing this edited book and inviting me to participate. We could not have anticipated the challenges associated with producing this book during the COVID-19 pandemic, and I commend our collective perseverance.

As always, I am grateful for the love and support of my husband, G. H. Abasi Johnson; my mother, Dr. Shirley J. Jones; my brother, Sande R. Jones, Jr.; my sister-in-law, Stefana Frank Jones; and my nephew, Sande R. Jones III, the apple of my eye. Because of you all, I am fueled beyond measure.

Introduction

The Current Moment and the Need for Investment that Directly Addresses Social, Economic, and Racial Inequities

As the book goes to press, the COVID-19 pandemic, beginning in 2020, is highlighting long-standing social and economic inequities worldwide alongside the necessity for equitable treatment of people of color and underserved communities.[1] In the United States, those inequities permeate every aspect of society, including health, wealth, life expectancy, income, and employment. From the killing of George Floyd, an unarmed Black man killed by on-duty police officer Derek Chauvin, who was subsequently criminally convicted of his murder,[2] to the January 2021 attack on the U.S. Capitol by white nationalists aimed at disrupting a peaceful transfer of democratic power, and bold efforts to deny Americans the right to vote, America, a divided nation, is at a crossroads.

1. John Elflein, *Distribution of Covid-19 Deaths in the United States as of February 2, 2022, by Race*, Statista (Feb. 7, 2022), https://www.statista.com/statistics/1122369/covid-deaths-distribution-by-race-us/.
2. Since 2020, there have been eighteen unarmed black men and women who have been killed at the hands of the police. David Fallis and Danielle Rindler, *1,021 People Have Been Shot and Killed by Police in the Past Year*, Wash. Post (Feb. 9, 2022), https://www.washingtonpost.com/graphics/investigations/police-shootings-database/.

This moment requires renewed attention to social, economic, and racial divisions and their root causes: social, economic, and racial inequities. Long before the COVID-19 pandemic, investors concerned with combating inequities and community economic development practitioners (called "practitioners" in this book) were heeding low-income communities and communities of color's calls to urgent action that both stems the social and economic losses and builds fair and just economic systems.

Growing Field of Impact Investment

A range of interrelated environmental, social, and economic global trends are driving growth in social enterprises and impact investing. These trends include accelerating climate changes and the impacts of more severe weather events such as floods and hurricanes, growing economic inequality, shifting demographics, deepening political tensions from the erosion of public trust in democratic institutions, declining social cohesion and social unrest in the United States and worldwide. When the US SIF: The Forum for Social and Responsible Investment, began measuring "the size of the U.S. sustainable investment universe" in 1995 it was $639 billion.[3] Significantly, by 2020, there was $17.1 trillion in professionally managed sustainable investments—investments that consider environmental, social, and governance (ESG) factors.[4]

Investment priorities of financial institutions, foundations, and high-net-worth individuals are shifting to address these global ESG challenges. One of the principal drivers in the United States for this shift is and will continue to be the investment priorities of Millennials born between 1981 and 1996[5] and Generation Z, those born after 1996.[6] "Today's millennials and Gen Z have more economic power than any generation that preceded them . . . Not only are millennials the largest workforce in U.S. history . . . When they deploy that capital, they are investing with a different set of expectations than their parents: 95% say they want to use their financial capital for socially responsible investing."[7] The investment decisions of Millennials and Gen Z will influence the field of social enterprise and impact investment for the foreseeable future.

Lawyers' Roles in Stemming Economic and Social Losses and Remaking the Economy

These shifts in investment priorities of individual and institutional (public and private) investors toward socially responsible investments take many forms and require lawyers to have a range of skills. To meet the current moment's charge to stem the economic losses in

---

3. *Report on US Sustainable and Impact Investing Trends 2020*, US SIF Foundation, https://www.ussif.org/files/US%20SIF%20Trends%20Report%202020%20Executive%20Summary.pdf.
4. *Id.*
5. Richard Fry, *Millennials Overtake Baby Boomers as America's Largest Generation*, Pew Research Center (Apr. 28, 2020), https://www.pewresearch.org/fact-tank/2020/04/28/millennials-overtake-baby-boomers-as-americas-largest-generation/.
6. Kim Parker & Ruth Igielnik, *On the Cusp of Adulthood and Facing an Uncertain Future: What We Know about Gen Z So Far*, Pew Research Center (May 14, 2020), https://www.pewresearch.org/social-trends/2020/05/14/on-the-cusp-of-adulthood-and-facing-an-uncertain-future-what-we-know-about-gen-z-so-far-2/.
7. Jean Case, *Millennials and Gen Z Are a Growing Force in Investing. The Market Needs to Catch Up*, Fortune (Nov. 18, 2021), https://fortune.com/2021/11/18/millennials-genz-investing-markets-wealth-transfer/.

communities and build new, more just economic systems, lawyers must be prepared with the skills to achieve both goals.

Over ten chapters, *Investing for Social Impact, Economic Justice, and Racial Equity* provides lawyers with an understanding of current U.S. private and public investment strategies, legal tools, and checklists created by lawyers and practitioners serving both investors and investees. These experts examine community stakeholders' needs, lawyers' roles in impact investment deals, and practice tips for a range of legal issues in developing and executing diverse investment strategies.

This premier book shows the range of strategies being deployed in communities to address the present social and economic challenges and strategies to undo inequitable systems. The first half of the book uplifts strategies to reduce the economic and social losses in communities. Some of these traditional economic development strategies have been scrutinized for privileging investor interests over the interests of low-income communities and communities of color. To illustrate, the Opportunity Zone program offers clear financial boon to Opportunity Zone investors funding activities in underserved neighborhoods. At the same time underestimated and underrepresented communities strive to craft innovative ways to benefit from this existing tax program. Another vehicle with possible unequal investor versus community benefits, is social impact bonds (SIBs), contractually negotiated social services provided by social service organizations with proven track records, perhaps enabling greater community participation.

The second half of the book focuses on strategies aimed at shifting the underlying policies and practices of the inequitable economy. The work of building a new economy is broad and deep—from regenerative finance, a concept at the intersection of impact investing and ESG investments aimed at using capital to solve problems and support healthy communities,[8] to nonextractive finance that requires a lender's return on investment and the cost of capital to never exceed the wealth created by the borrower.[9]

Given impact investing's international roots, chapter 1, *Global Impact on Domestic Investment Landscape*, explores international lessons and models that can be brought to the United States from addressing the world's most pressing problems. It also explores the distinctions between global and U.S. investing impact models and tools, and strategies for blended finance.

Demonstrating the overlap of community economic development (CED) and impact investing, chapter 2, *The Intersection of Community Economic Development and Impact Investing: History and Key Terms*, integrates a brief history of the CED movement and the rise in impact investing. It will be especially useful to readers new to these fields and those seeking a deeper understanding of their essential interrelationship. The chapter includes key concepts and definitions, including public sector community investment approaches, the role of philanthropy, the importance of Community Development Financial Institutions

8. Regenerative Finance refers to using money as a tool to solve systemic problems and to regenerate communities and natural environments. Jasper van Brakel, *Regenerative Finance Is No Longer the Future—It Has Arrived*, Impact Entrepreneur (Nov. 15, 2021), https://impactentrepreneur.com/regenerative-finance-is-no-longer-the-future-it-has-arrived/.

9. In non-extractive finance deals, the "returns of the lender" will not ever exceed "the wealth created by the borrower using the capital." *Our Model of Finance*, Seed Commons, https://seedcommons.org/about-seed-commons/seed-commons-approach-to-non-extractive-finance/.

(CDFIs), and the range of investor strategies, as well as stages and types of investment capital.

Chapters 3 and 4 discuss current CED and impact investing tools that utilize public–private partnerships. Chapter 3, *Opportunity Zones: The Promise and the Potential for Peril*, explores a specific, controversial community investment tool, "Opportunity Zones," enacted into law in 2017 and designed to drive billions of dollars into low-income communities while providing tax breaks for the wealthy. This chapter explains how the tax incentive works, as well as the potential for a shared impact model embracing principles of community engagement, equity, transparency, measurement, and outcomes for community benefit alongside the challenges of the Opportunity Zone program.

Chapter 4, *Social Impact Bonds: Overview and Lessons Learned*, discusses the purpose and structure of Social Impact Bonds (SIBs), the parties to a SIB contract, the roles of the participants, and an analysis of various contract provisions. It provides examples of SIBs that address pressing social problems of mental health, employment of veterans, and homelessness for families with children. Chapter 5, *Green Capitalism: The Case of the Environmental Impact Bond*, contextualizes and situates Environmental Impact Bonds (EIBs) as a specialized SIB, which is likely to expand given the rise in environmental and climate disruptions.

Chapter 6, *State and Local Policies for Social Impact Investing*, highlights ways the policies of state and local governments support directing capital to meet the needs of underserved communities and offers possibilities for new investments.

Chapter 7, *Community Capital Raising Strategies*, addresses the importance of community driven financing tools, the role of individual investors in shaping strong local communities, and the U.S. Securities and Exchange Commission's laws and regulations governing community capital raising.

Chapters 8 and 9 illuminate the importance of people-powered local interventions. Chapter 8, *Role of Philanthropy in "Place-based" Community Investment Strategies*, focuses on philanthropic investors using grantmaking and program-related investments that are guided by community participation. Chapter 9, *"Place-based" Cooperative Finance and Governance Models*, describes strategies for community ownership that shift governance and ownership to low-income communities and communities of color.

Through interviews with impact investing changemakers from eight individual or institutional investor organizations, chapter 10, *Beyond Impact: Shifting the Field of Impact Investment to Achieve Economic Justice and Racial Equity*, provides concrete recommendations to investors and their lawyers to accelerate transformative finance work.

The long-term disruptions caused by the COVID-19 pandemic and its lingering economic effects remain to be seen, but by many accounts, transformation is afoot. We hope those will be positive changes leading to a world and a nation that is just and equitable for all, and that this book can serve as an inspiration for that transformation.

Chapter 1
Global Impact on Domestic Investment Landscape

Deborah Burand and Chintan Panchal

Introduction

Twenty years ago, C. K. Prahalad and Stuart Hart pointed out an untapped market that was hiding in plain sight—the four billion people living at the bottom of the pyramid.[1] Their groundbreaking assertion that the world's poor could become profitable customers of businesses, not just passive beneficiaries of international development assistance, grabbed the attention and imagination of corporations, policymakers, and investors around the world. Today, while Prahalad and Hart's fortune at the bottom of the pyramid has not reached its full promise, a growing number of organizations are working in emerging markets to develop financially sustainable business models for delivering essential goods and services to low-income and underserved populations. As these organizations grow, so too do their capital needs.

This chapter looks at the global impact investment landscape to find models and learnings that could be brought back to the United States. It focuses in particular on emerging markets because, while emerging markets can present significant financial and political risks, these markets also provide opportunities to conduct meaningful impactful investments that

1. "Collectively, we have only begun to scratch the surface of what is the biggest potential market opportunity in the history of commerce. Those in the private sector who commit their companies to a more inclusive capitalism have the opportunity to prosper and share their prosperity with those who are less fortunate. In a very real sense, the fortune at the bottom of the pyramid represents the loftiest of our global goals." C. K. Prahalad and Stuart L. Hart, *The Fortune at the Bottom of the Pyramid*, 26 Strategy + Business at 14 (Booz Allen Hamilton, Inc., 2002).

address some of the world's most pressing problems—poverty, financial exclusion, environmental degradation, food insecurity, and inadequate housing, to name just a few.[2] Moreover, these high-risk, impact-rich markets offer lessons about how lawyers in the United States and elsewhere can structure and document impact investment transactions to improve financial risk/return profiles while maximizing positive social/environmental impacts.

Before turning to examples of impact investments being made in emerging markets, however, it is worth highlighting how impact investing in emerging markets can differ from impact investing in developed markets like the United States. The Global Impact Investing Network's (GIIN) annual survey of impact investors as to their impact investment assets under management at the end of 2018 provides several insights into these differences.[3] Here are several that can be observed among the GIIN's survey respondents. Sectoral allocations differ depending on the geographic focus of impact investors.[4] The stage of the investee[5] and, therefore, the form/instrument[6] used in impact investing also differs according to the geographic focus of the investor. So too do impact return[7] and financial return

2. Another reason to look at what is happening in emerging markets is that this is where many impact investments are being made. The Global Impact Investing Network (GIIN) surveyed 262 impact investors about their impact investments as of end-2018. The GIIN's surveyed respondents transacted 14,416 impact investments in 2018, totaling $60 billion. These surveyed respondents also reported that they held $239.1 billion in impact investment assets under management (AUM) as of end-2018. The amount of these impact investments was distributed nearly equally between emerging markets and developed markets with about half (47 percent) invested in each. Abhilash Mudaliar et al., ANNUAL IMPACT INVESTOR SURVEY 2019 (9th ed.) at 16 (GIIN: June 2019; available at the GIIN website, https://thegiin.org/research/publication/impinv-survey-2019; hereafter "GIIN 2019 Investor Survey").

3. The GIIN's annual investor surveys do not reflect all impact investments made in the surveyed year, yet discernible trends are captured by these annual surveys, particularly among repeat survey respondents. (The GIIN estimated in early 2019 that the amount of impact investment assets under management globally to be $502 billion. See GIIN 2019 Investor Survey at 10.)

4. For example, surveyed investors who focused on emerging markets allocated a much larger amount of their capital to making impact investments in financial services and microfinance (45 percent combined) than did investors focused on developed markets (3 percent). In contrast, surveyed investors that focused on developed markets allocated a larger amount of their capital to impact investments in housing (13 percent) and forestry (11 percent) than did investors that focused on emerging markets (1 and 0.4 percent, respectively). *Id.* at 20.

5. Surveyed impact investors that focused on emerging markets allocated proportionately twice as much capital into growth stage companies than did investors focused on developed markets, whereas surveyed investors that focused on developed markets allocated much more of their capital to mature, public companies than did those focused on emerging markets (47 percent by investors with developed market focus as compared to 8 percent by investors with emerging market focus). *Id.* at 25.

6. Among the surveyed investors, emerging market-focused investors allocated a much greater share of their capital to private debt (39 percent) than did developed market-focused investors (14 percent). On the other hand, developed market-focused investors allocated much more capital to public equity (30 percent) and real assets (26 percent) than did emerging market-focused investors (0.2 percent for each). *Id.* at 23.

7. Just over half of both groups of surveyed impact investors target both social and environmental objectives (55 percent of emerging market-focused investors and 52 percent of developed market-focused investors). But among surveyed investors that only target social or only target environmental objectives, differences emerge. Namely, among surveyed impact investors with an emerging market focus, 44 percent target only social objectives and 1 percent target only environmental objectives. Among developed market-focused investors, 35 percent target only social objectives and 13 percent target only environmental objectives. *Id.* at 26. The differences in impact objectives do not stop there. With respect to the United Nations' Sustainable Development Goals (SDGs), the GIIN 2019 survey found that emerging market-focused investors are more likely to track performance against the SDGs for *all* their investments than do developed market-focused investors (54 vs. 28 percent). *Id.* at 30. Furthermore, impact investors that focus on emerging markets are more likely to target as impact objectives the SDGs of "no poverty," "gender equality," and "decent work and economic growth." Developed market-focused investors, on the other hand, are more likely to target as impact objectives the SDGs of "sustainable cities and communities," "climate action," and "peace, justice and strong institutions." *Id.* at 27.

expectations.[8] Yet, even with these observable differences between impact investing in emerging markets versus developed markets like the United States, there are transferable lessons to be gleaned.

This chapter examines the role of blended finance in general, and the use of third-party guarantees more specifically, in increasing the size, diversity of capital, and likelihood of success of three impact investments taking place in emerging markets. These investments illustrate the extent to which the global impact investing landscape can inform impact investing in the United States.

Case Examples: Blended Finance—Using Third-Party Guarantees to Mitigate Financial Risks in Impact Investments and Crowd in Additional Sources of Capital

Blended Finance

Blended finance is a new buzzword in impact investing.[9] Behind the excitement being generated around blended finance is a simple and not so new idea, namely that, ". . . [I]f you bring multiple actors—across the public and private sectors—together in the same structure to attack a problem, then maybe one plus one is a whole lot more than two."[10]

So, what is blended finance? Not unlike the definitional issues that surround impact investing and social entrepreneurship, the term "blended finance" also has many definitions and uses.[11] Here are two. The GIIN defines blended finance as "a strategy that combines capital with different levels of risk in order to catalyze risk-adjusted, market-rate-seeking capital into impact investments."[12] The Organization for Economic Cooperation and Development (OECD) adds specific impact goals (sustainable development goals (SDGs)) and also geographic boundaries (developing countries) to reach a relatively narrower definition of blended finance, saying blended finance is "the strategic use of development finance for the mobilization of additional finance towards the SDGs

8. For example, impact investors focused on emerging markets generally have higher expectations for financial returns than do investors that focus on making investments in developed markets. *Id.* 34–35.

9. Between 2012 and 2015, blended finance transactions mobilized $81 billion from the private sector. Since 2000, more than 160 blended finance facilities have been launched around the world. See Barbara Scola, Louise Moretto, & Estelle Lahaye, *Navigating the Next Wave of Blended Finance for Financial Inclusion* (CGAP Brief, Aug. 2018) (citing OECD 2018 described in Footnote 11).

10. John Crabb, *Rhino Bonds: Firms Collaborate on Blended Finance Solution to Conservation*, INT'L FIN. L. REV. (Aug. 28, 2019) (describing a blended finance approach to saving black rhinos through the use of an impact bond that attracted multiple types of investors and capital).

11. *See, generally*, OECD, "Making Blended Finance Work for the Sustainable Development Goals" at 49–50 (Paris: OECD Publishing, 2018), available at https://read.oecd-ilibrary.org/development/making-blended-finance-work-for-the-sustainable-development-goals_9789264288768-en#page1 (hereafter referred to as "OECD 2018") (provides a sampling of ten definitions used for blended finance).

12. Abhilash Mudaliar, Rachel Bass, & Hannah Dithrich, *2018 Annual Impact Investor Survey* at 19 (GIIN: June 2018), available at https://thegiin.org/assets/2018_GIIN_Annual_Impact_Investor_Survey_webfile.pdf (hereafter referred to as "GIIN 2018 Impact Investor Survey").

in developing countries."[13] Despite their differences, both of these definitions describe blended finance as a strategy, not as a particular type of financial instrument nor an asset class.

If thought of as an investment strategy, rather than a particular form or instrument of investment, blended finance transactions can take many shapes and structures. What blended finance transactions hold in common is that they intentionally include investors with a range of risk/return appetites. To do so, they typically employ financial instruments that shift the return/risk profile of investment opportunities so as to crowd in investors who otherwise might not invest at all or would only invest on financial terms commensurate with a highly risky environment.[14] The financial instruments used for this transfer or mitigation of risks can vary, including traditional instruments such as equity, debt, mezzanine finance, insurance, hedges, and guarantees. Grants and other forms of philanthropic capital, such as targeted technical assistance facilities, can also be used to de-risk blended finance transactions so that other sources of capital might be more inclined to participate.[15]

It is worth pausing here to consider the important role to be played by the public or official sector in blended finance transactions. In emerging markets, development finance providers, such as multilateral development banks (MDBs), international finance institutions (IFIs), and bilateral development institutions (which include bilateral development banks and bilateral development finance institutions (DFIs)), "[p]lay a key and critical role in blended finance, providing the public or private development finance that mobilises [*sic*] the private sector to engage."[16] Not surprisingly, the role of development finance providers is particularly pronounced in countries where there are few alternative sources of finance.[17]

This public sector role is not without controversy, however. At issue is a long-standing debate over whether providers of development finance are crowding in or crowding out private sector sources of funding. Related are questions about whether development finance providers are assuming appropriate levels of financial risk given their broader social mandates and where concessional finance is best placed in a blended finance approach.

Answering questions like these is not an academic exercise. In recent years, a group of MDBs and DFIs have worked to align their blended financing approaches, particularly when considering how or if to blend concessional finance into their private sector

---

13. OECD 2018 at 13–14. To understand this OECD definition, two other terms need clarification—development finance and additional finance. In this context, "development finance" means both public and private finance so long as they are being deployed with a development mandate. So, for example, private philanthropic capital would count as development finance for this purpose. (Private philanthropy is becoming an important source of development finance, according to the OECD. Between 2013 and 2015, the philanthropic giving of 130 foundations for development objectives averaged in total $7.8 billion a year. *Id.* at 72.) As used by the OECD, "additional finance" means commercial finance that does not have an explicit development mandate nor is primarily targeted at spurring development outcomes in developing countries.

14. *Id.* at 79.

15. *Id.* at 84 (citing role that grants and technical assistance can play in strengthening a project's capacity and noting broad range of activities that can constitute technical assistance, ranging from project preparation to capacity building to awareness raising).

16. *Id.* at 63.

17. *Id.* at 68–69.

operations.[18] Together, this working group has created (and updated annually their progress in implementing) guiding principles to align their activities around the following topics: (1) developing an additionality rationale for using blended finance to address market failures; (2) crowding in private sector resources/ensuring minimum use of concessional resources; (3) advancing commercial sustainability of clients; (4) reinforcing, not distorting, markets; and (5) promoting high standards of conduct by clients (such as corporate governance, environmental impact, social inclusion, transparency, integrity, and disclosure).[19]

Description of the Investment Tool/Strategy Approach

The following section describes three approaches that specific impact investment structures took as they endeavored to blend financing from a variety of sources with a variety of financial return expectations in order to expand the scale and related impact of their investments. What they have in common is that each of these three approaches makes use of a third-party guarantee to help unleash and catalyze other parties' capital.

For readers well-versed in community development investing in the United States, the use of third-party guarantees to bring other sources of capital to the table will come as no surprise. Similarly, the providers of these guarantees—philanthropic and public sector players—also will look familiar.[20] Furthermore, although the risks present in transactions taking place in the United States may differ in scope, prevalence, and kind from those taking place in emerging markets, the primary impact motivations driving third-party guarantors that are active in U.S. community development investing are quite similar to those found in the three structures described below. First, some of these third-party guarantors aim to leverage private capital into transactions where "the economics do not provide a commercially attractive risk-return profile."[21] Second, other third-party guarantors are helping investors gain comfort with a new sector or business model. In this second scenario,

---

18. The DFI Working Group on Blended Concessional Finance for Private Sector Projects is composed of multilateral development banks and development finance institutions, including the International Finance Corporation (IFC; which operates as the chair of this DFI Working Group), African Development Bank (AfDB), Asian Development Bank (AsDB), Asian Infrastructure Investment Bank (AIIB), European Bank for Reconstruction and Development (EBRD), European Development Finance Institutions (EDFI), European Investment Bank (EIB), Inter-American Development Bank Group (IDBG), and Islamic Corporation for the Development of the Private Sector (ICD). Established in 2013, this DFI Working Group has continued to update its principles, most recently in 2017, and to provide annual updates on its progress. See DFI Working Group on Blended Concessional Finance for Private Sector Projects: Joint Report, October 2019 Update, at 7 (hereafter referred to as "DFI Working Group 2019 Update"; available at https://www.adb.org/sites/default/files/institutional-document/532646/dfi-blended-concessional-finance-joint-report-2019.pdf) (defining blended concessional finance as "[c]ombining concessional finance from donors or third parties alongside DFIs' normal own account finance and/or commercial finance from other investors, to develop private sector markets, address the Sustainable Development Goals (SDGs), and mobilize private resources").

19. *Id.* at 8.

20. In a survey of fifty-eight community development investments, foundations and government agencies (federal and local) were the most common sources of third-party guarantees used to support U.S. community development investments, followed by guarantees provided by high net-worth individuals and nonprofit organizations. Hannah Schiff & Hannah Dithrich, *Scaling the Use of Guarantees in U.S. Community Investing*, at 8 (GIIN Issue Brief, Apr. 25, 2017; available at https://thegiin.org/research/publication/guarantees-issue-brief) (hereafter referred to as "Schiff and Dithrich").

21. *Id.* at 9.

the guarantors hope to eventually work themselves out of a job, providing guarantees only until investors become familiar enough with the sector or business model to develop underwriting guidelines.[22]

Guaranteeing Financial Inclusion—Grameen Foundation's Growth Guarantee Program

In 2004, when the venture capitalist John Doerr convened a small group of entrepreneurs at his home for a weekend to brainstorm about creating scalable solutions to poverty alleviation, they ended up seeding a blended financing—although they might have not articulated it as such at the time. In short, the entrepreneurs gathered at Doerr's home devised a plan to use U.S. philanthropic capital to unlock local sources of capital to increase the poor's access to finance. More specifically, they focused on how best to finance the growth of microfinance institutions (MFIs) operating in emerging markets that targeted their financial products to those living at the base of the economic pyramid.

Microfinance at the time was proving to be a viable and even profitable way to increase poor and underserved populations' access to financial services. But MFIs around the world were facing funding constraints. Lack of access to appropriate funding was limiting many MFIs' abilities to grow the number and size of microcredits made to people living at the bottom of the pyramid.

In particular, many MFIs were having problems accessing funding that was denominated in local currency. As a result, these MFIs were facing a significant currency mismatch across their liabilities and assets and, hence, were assuming a troubling amount of foreign exchange risk. Their own borrowings (liabilities) were often denominated in foreign currencies such as U.S. dollars or Euros, while their loans to microcredit customers (assets) were denominated in local currencies such as pesos, manats, or rupees.[23]

In retrospect, the microfinance sector was facing what we in the United States sometimes characterize as a Wall Street/Main Street problem. In essence, those financial institutions that were most physically proximate to (and presumably knowledgeable about) borrowers were least likely to lend to them. In this context, global financial institutions were willing to invest in MFIs operating in emerging markets, but local banks operating in these same markets were not—even if the MFI seeking additional loan capital had a strong track record of performance.[24]

There were a number of factors—regulatory, cultural, and political—shaping local banks' lending behaviors in their respective emerging markets. But one stumbling block was common to many local banks—their limited appetite for financial risk. Many local banks were reluctant to lend to MFIs because they thought the business of providing financial services

---

22. *Id.*

23. According to the Grameen Foundation, in 2006, 86 percent of funding available to MFIs was denominated in foreign currency. By 2011, 69 percent of the funding available to MFIs was denominated in foreign currency. See *Growth Guarantees: 2005-2015*, at 2, available at https://grameenfoundation.app.box.com/v/GrowthGuarantees 2005-2015.

24. This reluctance to lend to MFIs was not limited to the microfinance sector, however. Local banks often were not investing in small or medium-sized enterprises—no matter their sector or individual track record. What finance was available locally in many emerging markets was more likely to be flowing to large and politically well-connected corporations.

to poor and underserved populations was just too risky, no matter the potential financial or social returns.

This was the problem that Doerr and his fellow entrepreneurs determined to tackle. That is, how could philanthropic capital reduce the financial risks (perceived or otherwise) that local banks faced when lending to MFIs in their local markets? The stakes were high. If this problem was not solved, growth of the microfinance sector was likely to stall due to a lack of appropriate loan capital. On the other hand, if the group could find a way to make it easier for MFIs to tap local banks for access to local currency denominated funding, this would reduce foreign exchange risk while providing MFIs with a more stable source of future funding and, importantly, eventually integrating MFIs more fully into their local financial sectors.[25]

Before the weekend at Doerr's home ended, an idea had hatched for a blended financing—a credit enhancement that would transfer some (not all) of the risk associated with lending to MFIs from local banks to U.S. philanthropists in the form of donor guarantees. Nine of the individuals who participated in the brainstorming session at Doerr's home that weekend in 2004 agreed to act as donor guarantors to pilot a guarantee structure aimed at de-risking loans made by local banks to MFIs. Together, they committed approximately $30 million in the form of pledges or guarantees to a guarantee program to be administered and managed by the Grameen Foundation, a nonprofit organization organized in the United States with deep roots in the pioneering work of Dr. Yunus who spearheaded the start of microfinance by founding the Grameen Bank in Bangladesh.[26]

Over the next ten years, the Grameen Foundation nearly doubled the original amount of donor guarantees to reach a guarantee pool of $59.6 million.[27] From 2005–2015, the guarantee program leveraged, on average, nearly four times that amount in local currency, generating a total of $235.1 million of local currency financing for MFIs globally.[28]

The guarantee program, as structured by the Grameen Foundation, used standby letters of credit (SBLCs) issued by Citibank, N.A. to local banks as credit enhancements for their loans to MFIs. Each of these Citibank SBLCs was, in turn, backstopped by a set of SBLCs that were issued by the donor guarantors' banks and collateralized with donor assets. Under this back-to-back SBLC structure, in the unlikely event that an MFI defaulted on its loan to the local bank,[29] the local bank could draw on the SBLC issued by Citibank, and Citibank then would turn to the backstopped SBLCs to be made whole. When there was a draw on donor assets supporting the backstopped SBLCs, the donor guarantor could realize a charitable contribution to the Grameen Foundation with respect to his or her drawn assets. So, in the event of an MFI default and draw on the backstopped SBLC, while the donor guarantor would lose a part of its pledged assets, the donor guarantor still could claim a charitable contribution deduction for the amount of drawn assets to the extent permitted by U.S. tax law (see Annex A for Grameen's growth guarantee structure).

25. Growth Guarantees: 2005-2015 at 3.

26. Two years later, Dr. Muhammad Yunus and the Grameen Bank that he founded in Bangladesh won the 2006 Nobel Peace Prize.

27. Growth Guarantees: 2005-2015 at 3–4.

28. *Id.* at 4.

29. Only 0.3 percent of the MFIs benefitting from the Grameen guarantee program defaulted on their local bank loans during the period 2005–2015. *Growth Guarantees 2005-2015* at 2.

But this story does not end with Grameen's guarantee program. Over the following decade and beyond, versions of this donor guarantee structure would be used by others, not only to unlock local currency financing for MFIs from their local banks but also to expand the funding available from U.S. banks, accredited investors, and DFIs to provide much-needed capital to MFIs and small and growing businesses around the world.

Guaranteeing Adequate Housing—Habitat for Humanity International's MicroBuild Fund

Like other blended finance approaches that aspire to be replicated, the Grameen guarantee program has since been adopted by other nonprofit organizations based in the United States and, where necessary, adapted to suit their needs and developmental goals. One prominent example of this replication is the decision by Habitat for Humanity International, another U.S. nonprofit organization, to use a donor guarantee pool to support the impact investment fund it launched in 2012.[30] Called the MicroBuild Fund, this impact investment fund has secured $100 million in funding, most of which is in the form of debt borrowed from the U.S. government's DFI, then called the Overseas Private Investment Corporation (OPIC) and now called the U.S. International Development Finance Corporation (DFC).[31] The MicroBuild Fund is a demonstration fund, the first impact investment fund of its kind to be dedicated to financing housing microfinance products for the poor and underserved.

From the start, the MicroBuild Fund had grand ambitions. Over 1.5 billion people in the world do not have adequate shelter, and this number is only expected to increase given trends toward global urbanization.[32] With the growth of microfinance around the world, Habitat for Humanity saw an opportunity to improve housing for millions of poor families. As noted by Patrick Kelley of Habitat for Humanity, "[e]stimates showed that housing products comprised about 2 percent of microfinance portfolios worldwide. If we could work to raise that to 10 percent, an estimated 15 million families would gain access to over $4 billion of capital for housing."[33]

The challenge that the MicroBuild Fund sought to address was that most microcredits at the time were designed as working capital loans, even though there was increasing evidence that the poor were diverting as much as 40 percent of their microcredits to finance incremental housing improvements rather than to grow their businesses.[34] By offering MFIs a combination of loan capital and targeted technical assistance, the MicroBuild Fund aimed

---

30. For background on the launch of the MicroBuild Fund, see Grunin Center's Launching the MicroBuild Fund Case Study (2019) (available at https://cases.grunin.law.nyu.edu/product/launching-the-microbuild-fund/; hereafter referred to as the "MicroBuild Fund Case Study").

31. OPIC, pursuant to the Better Utilization of Investment Leading to Development (Build) Act of 2018, was merged in early 2020 with the U.S. Agency for International Development's (USAID) Development Credit Authority (DCA). The merged entity is called the U.S. International Development Finance Corporation (DFC).

32. Sashi Selvendran et al., *Inclusive Finance for Housing: Exploring Viable Business Models* at 1 (SEEP 2014), available at https://www.habitat.org/sites/default/files/cisf-inclusive-finance-case-studies.pdf (hereafter referred to as "Inclusive Finance for Housing").

33. *See* Patrick Kelley & Steven Evers, "The MicroBuild Fund Story: Habitat for Humanity and Triple Jump on forming the first investment fund for housing microfinance" (European Microfinance Platform), available at http://www.e-mfp.eu/blog/microbuild-fund-story-habitat-humanity-and-triple-jump-forming-first-investment-fund-housing.

34. Inclusive Finance for Housing at 1.

to help MFIs create and launch housing microfinance products that were better suited to funding the housing needs of their microfinance clients.

To leverage funding from OPIC, Habitat adopted the Grameen guarantee program. Back-to-back SBLCs were used to support the MicroBuild Fund's borrowings from OPIC, the loan proceeds of which were then onlent to MFIs for use in financing housing improvements initiated by their customers. As with the Grameen Foundation's guarantee program, a pool of donor guarantees collateralized the SBLCs that backstop the SBLC issued to OPIC (see Annex B for MicroBuild Fund's donor guarantee structure).

In addition to these donor guarantees, Habitat also de-risked its loan portfolio by providing donor-funded, technical assistance support to those MFIs borrowing from the MicroBuild Fund to launch housing microfinance loan products and also to support the end-borrowers of those MFIs, thereby blending in yet another form of philanthropic capital into the overall fund structure.

OPIC so valued the creation and maintenance of this technical assistance facility that the facility's establishment was a condition to OPIC's loan disbursements and the facility's maintenance is an ongoing loan covenant.[35] This technical assistance facility serves dual purposes. First, it serves as a risk mitigant by helping to ensure that MFIs borrowing from the MicroBuild Fund are able to deploy these loan funds into well-designed and targeted housing microfinance products and, therefore, improve the likelihood that they are able to repay their loans to the MicroBuild Fund. Second, and perhaps even more importantly, it also may shift MFI behavior in ways that last long beyond the life of the MicroBuild Fund itself as MFIs learn how to make housing microfinance a viable and enduring part of their loan portfolios.[36]

Guaranteeing a Cleaner Ocean—Circulate Capital's The Ocean Fund

Circulate Capital also turned to a blended finance solution, bringing together public and private sector capital, to reduce marine plastic pollution. The harmful effects of plastic waste and its leakage into the world's oceans have only recently started to be grasped, and more is still to be learned. We know that more than 800 species of marine life have been impacted by plastic waste. We also know that people are being impacted, as research has found plastic particles not only the fish we consume, but also in our drinking water.[37] The long-term effects of this exposure are still being determined.

A disproportionate amount of the world's marine plastic pollution is coming from countries in South and Southeast Asia due to the ineffective and undeveloped, integrated waste management systems located there. Although the major source of this pollution is known, there are relatively few investors actively investing in solid waste management and recycling in the South/Southeast Asia region.[38]

---

35. *See* OPIC Loan Agreement and Habitat Undertaking Letter (attached as exhibits to the MicroBuild Fund Case Study).
36. Burand interview with Bruce Cameron, OPIC (June 2019) (videotaped excerpt attached to the MicroBuild Fund Case Study).
37. *See, generally*, Investing to Reduce Plastic Pollution in South and Southeast Asia: A Handbook for Action (published by Circulate Capital, 2019).
38. *Id.* at 7–11.

This was the issue that Circulate Capital faced as it worked to unlock significant amounts of capital to finance market-based solutions to the growing problem of ocean plastics.[39] Rob Kaplan, founder of Circulate Capital, recognized that in order to make significant progress toward solving such a complex and persistent global problem, a holistic, multi-pronged approach was required. As he has put it, "Philanthropic and investment capital are often thought of as operating in entirely separate spheres. But when it comes to addressing some of the world's biggest social and environmental challenges—like ocean plastic—they actually need to work together."[40]

The cornerstone of Circulate Capital's strategy is The Ocean Fund, a Singapore-based investment fund, launched in 2019 to make venture-style debt, equity, and quasi-equity investments into Southeast Asian companies and technologies that aim to reduce the leakage of plastics into the ocean. In order to maximize the effectiveness of The Ocean Fund, Circulate Capital involved a variety of stakeholders with often disparate motivations, return expectations, and investment criteria.

To raise the capital to be invested by The Ocean Fund, Circulate Capital turned to large, multinational, consumer product companies as founding investors, including PepsiCo, Procter & Gamble, Dow, Danone, Unilever, and The Coca-Cola Company, among others.[41] In October 2019, Chevron Phillips Chemical Company LLC also joined these founder investors, bringing the total amount of committed capital to The Ocean Fund to over $100 million.[42]

While these corporate investors are not your typical "impact" investors, Circulate Capital secured their commitment to invest in The Ocean Fund on a substantially risk-adjusted basis because of their unique connection to, and concern for, the issue of ocean plastics. Kaplan explains that a motivation for many of The Ocean Fund's corporate investors is a growing recognition that "too much of their packaging is polluting the environment. They lack access to the recycled content to put back into their products. They are constantly getting accused of being bad actors and face a huge 'license to operate' risk."[43] Some of these investors invested funds from corporate foundations, some from on-balance sheet funds available for investment, and others from corporate funds available for research and development and similar endeavors.

In addition to their investment commitments to The Ocean Fund, Circulate Capital's investors have provided funding for incubation and technical assistance facilities as well as critical field-building, including studies, research, education, media, and awareness around the ocean plastics issue generally. These initiatives are expected to substantially increase the

39. Among these challenges were (1) the very early stage and undeveloped nature of certain of the technologies and enterprises, (2) the underdeveloped capital markets in the developing economies where many of these technologies and enterprises are based, and (3) the high level of risk involved in investing in these technologies and enterprises.

40. Robert Kaplan, We Need the World's Ocean Philanthropies to Join the Fight Against Ocean Plastic, Forbes Online (Oct. 9, 2019).

41. *See* Press Release, "Circulate Capital Announces $90 Million in Expected Funding to Combat Ocean Plastic" (Oct. 25, 2018).

42. *See* Press Release, "Circulate Capital Announces Additional US$15 Million in Expected Funding to Combat Ocean Plastic in South and Southeast Asia" (Oct. 23, 2019).

43. Plastic Waste Is a Global Crisis. Investing to Prevent Plastic Waste Is an Investment Opportunity, Impact Alpha (June 17, 2019).

pool of investment opportunities for The Ocean Fund as well as for other future investors that may follow The Ocean Fund into this sector.

In order to further de-risk investments made into the portfolio companies of The Ocean Fund, Circulate Capital also sought to involve a public sector, development-oriented entity as a risk sharing partner. The Development Credit Authority (DCA), originally administered by U.S. Agency for International Development (USAID) and now administered by the DFC,[44] agreed to make available a $35 million guarantee facility that would cover 50 percent of the principal losses from qualifying loans made by The Ocean Fund to its portfolio companies.[45] Over time, it is hoped that guarantees of this sort will not be necessary as investors become more comfortable with the credit risks of lending to such portfolio companies. As noted by a representative of USAID, "USAID wants to work ourselves out of a job as quickly as possible. Eventually, we want the market to say, 'We no longer need a guarantor in this structure.'"[46]

Finally, in order to significantly supplement and expand on the technical assistance and field-building work being done by Circulate Capital, the Circulate Capital team also launched The Circulate Initiative, an independent, tax-exempt, charitable organization. The Circulate Initiative is focused on promoting technical assistance and field-building through programmatic activities using grant funds provided by philanthropic funders.

In sum, Circulate Capital turned to an array of existing financial and corporate tools to solve a complex problem, including an investment fund, a partial guarantee by the U.S. government's foreign assistance agency, a technical assistance facility, and philanthropic grant capital (see Annex C for The Ocean Fund's structure, including the DCA guarantee).

Legal Questions and Issues Related to the Investment Tool/Strategy/Approach and the Lawyers' Roles

Any lawyer engaged in structuring and documenting an impact investment that takes a blended financing approach will likely be confronted by the challenge of weaving together a variety of financial instruments, while also attempting to harmonize and address the often disparate mission objectives, financial return expectations, and other motivations and requirements of a range of stakeholders. Just how wide a range of financial instruments and stakeholders might be involved? As a thought experiment, try listing all of the forms of capital involved and all the stakeholders involved in the three blended financing structures described above that were launched by the Grameen Foundation, Habitat for Humanity, and Circulate Capital. On your list you will likely find capital in the form of debt, equity, guarantees, and pledges of collateral as well as concessional capital in the form of grants and technical assistance facilities. As for stakeholders, you will likely list high net-worth philanthropists and family foundations, nonprofit organizations, DFIs, bilateral foreign assistance organizations (like USAID), multinational corporations, local enterprises and their consumers/customers, and a variety of financial institutions (ranging from local and foreign commercial banks to MFIs).

Daunting as coordinating and aligning these disparate forms of capital and stakeholder interests may appear to be, it is worth noting the obvious. None of the above blended

44. As noted above in footnote 31, the DCA guarantee program has since been merged with OPIC into the U.S. government's new International Development Finance Corporation.
45. Circulate Capital and USAID Team Up to Fight Ocean Plastic Pollution, Asian Scientist (June 11, 2019).
46. Plastic Waste Is a Global Crisis. Investing to Prevent Plastic Waste Is an Investment Opportunity, Impact Alpha (June 17, 2019).

finance structures employed a novel financial instrument. Similarly, no new regulations or changes to existing laws were required.[47] In short, the novelty present in the impact investment transactions described above came instead from how very traditional financial instruments and structures—in this case, third-party guarantees (such as SBLCs supported by high net-worth individuals and family foundations, and a preexisting, government-sponsored, guarantee program), loans, grants/charitable contributions, and investment fund vehicles—were combined together to crowd in additional sources of capital from a variety of funders with a variety of objectives.

This insight should be heartening to transactional lawyers seeking to practice in this area as many will already have familiarity with documenting credit enhancements, loans, and fund structures. What might be unusual, however, is doing so with different types of capital supplied by differently motivated investors—all in the same transaction. That is where even the most seasoned transactional attorney may flounder.

So, how is a lawyer to prepare herself for negotiating and documenting an impact investment that takes a blended finance approach? A first step is to know what you don't know. Put differently, it is unlikely that any single attorney will be steeped in the nuances of bank finance, fund formation, nonprofit law, and that elusive, but important, understanding of the rules by which DFIs (or other public sector parties) operate. Accordingly, these transactions are likely to be undertaken by teams of lawyers, often representing many different interests, and bringing legal expertise from many different practice areas and, if operating internationally, from many different jurisdictions.

Related, presumptions about the parties' motivations and capacities (operational and regulatory) can often cause missteps. So, while it may sound like just old-fashioned, common-sense, it is worth reminding any lawyer working in this field that her first and perhaps most important responsibility is to listen carefully to her client and to the other parties at the table. Only then can she identify the risks that need to be addressed,[48] as well as the financial and social/environmental returns that need to be generated, for the transaction to be successful.

---

47. Even the Grameen growth guarantee program did not require any change in law or regulations to make this guarantee program (and its variations) more appealing to donor guarantors. Rather, the guarantee program made use of existing rules in the United States regarding charitable contributions deductions to assure donor guarantors that they could likely avail themselves of a charitable deduction to the extent that their guarantees were called.

48. *See, e.g.*, the 2018 Banana Skins Report about financial inclusion. Different actors involved in financial inclusion were surveyed to learn their perceptions of the most pressing risks confronting financial inclusion in 2018. Besides the observation that technology risk was the highest ranked risk on everyone's list, the other risks and their relative ranking as issues of concern varied across these actors. Those *investing* in financial inclusion in 2018 identified the following as their top five risks of concern: (1) Technology risk, (2) Risk management practices (or lack thereof), (3) Credit risk, (4) Political risk, and (5) Competition risk (from new providers of finance and their influence in driving standards down). In comparison, those *providing* financial inclusion services had a slightly different take on the key risks to watch and prioritized them differently than do the investors: (1) Technology risk, (2) Political risk, (3) Credit risk, (4) Strategy risk, and (5) Risk management practices. Yet a third perspective can be found in those *supporting* financial inclusion providers as networks, associations, or *through grants and technical assistance*, which listed the following as the top five risks to financial inclusion: (1) Technology risk, (2) Regulation, (3) Strategy, (4) Talent, and (5) Credit risk. Keyur Patel and David Lascelles, "Finance for All: Wedded to Fintech, for Better or Worse: A CSFI 'Banana Skins' survey of the risks in financial inclusion," at 10–12 (Centre for the Study of Financial Innovation: 2018), available at https://static1.squarespace.com/static/54d620fce4b049bf4cd5be9b/t/5b7c1f2d562fa704995d02d7/1534861133477/Banana+Skins_08-18_v5.pdf.

Given the risks in making an impact investment[49] no matter where it is located—in Kampala, Uganda or in Indianapolis, Indiana—the use of credit enhancements is likely to be key to encouraging "the flow of capital to these [impact] investment opportunities by improving their risk-return profiles and, thus, incenting more investors to invest."[50] Yet, studies suggest that credit enhancements in the impact investment market have been underutilized.[51]

This is again where a lawyer's knowledge of the risk mitigants that are used in more commercially oriented investments can prove helpful. There may be no need to invent (and thus increase the time and costs of transacting) new "wheels" to address the financial risks present in impact investments. The two checklists provided at the end of this chapter provide considerations that can inform impact investment structures that make use of blended finance, and the role that third-party guarantees can play as a form of credit enhancement in such financings.

Conclusion

As noted before, blended finance is a strategy, not an instrument. The most successful blended financings are likely to make use of time-tested and rather conventional financial instruments, not unlike the SBLCs that provided the foundation for the donor guarantee programs used by the Grameen Foundation and Habitat's MicroBuild Fund or the DCA guarantee used by The Ocean Fund. Indeed, introducing novelty into risk-mitigation can be counterproductive as relatively untested instruments may be viewed by some investors as increasing, not reducing, risk. But it is also because the costs in time, money, and complexity that come with creating and deploying new risk mitigants may well overwhelm the impact investments that they are intended to serve. Lawyers who understand how to repurpose existing tools and instruments for use in blended financings can introduce significant savings into these transactions.

This is not to suggest, however, that there is little creative room for lawyers in impact investing. That is far from the case. Rather, it is a caution to not rush after the shiny new object, when there may be perfectly serviceable tools at hand that a lawyer can turn to when structuring and documenting impact investments that adopt a blended financing strategy.

Right sizing legal advice and support is never an easy task. And it is likely to be of even greater importance to clients intent on maximizing desired social and environmental impacts of their investments—be it in emerging markets or, for those operating in developed markets like the United States, closer to home. As the stories of the three impact investment structures described in this chapter illustrate, the stakes are high and the needs are urgent. Accordingly, if we are to reach those billions of people identified by Prahalad and Hart who are living at the bottom of the economic pyramid, the intellectual capital and talents of the legal profession need to be harnessed. Sharing knowledge and experiences within our growing legal community of practice in structuring and documenting impact investments that can attract significant amounts of capital is an important step in that direction.

---

49. The GIIN's 2018 Impact Investor Survey asked impact investors to identify the risks that they saw as most important when negotiating an impact investment. Survey respondents cited "business model execution and management risk" as severe (29 percent), followed by "country and currency risks" and "liquidity and exit risk" (22 percent each). See 2018 Impact Investor Survey at XV.

50. *Catalytic First-Loss Capital*, at 3 (GIIN Issue Brief, Oct. 2013).

51. *Id.* at 2.

Exhibit A

Blended Finance Checklist: Issues to Consider before Contract Drafting Starts

The following are questions to consider when structuring a blended finance approach to impact investing that aims to catalyze a range of sources of capital. Following this line of inquiry usually leads to a small handful of possible structures. Stress test them, assume folks act in their own self-interest and play out the scenarios. Then, assume irrational action and see where the structures can break down. These fault lines can point to areas to focus on when guiding and advising the client.

(1) What is the client trying to accomplish? Why?

- (a) What are the drivers and what is the desired outcome? In most instances, this is the most important question. Push back here to keep digging to uncover the fundamental drivers. Focus on impact outcomes as well as outputs (i.e., key performance indicators).[52]
- (b) What does success look like? How will we know when it has been achieved?

(2) What are the impediments (legal, structural, economic, political, and practical) to achieving the desired outcome(s) and output(s)?

(3) Are there alternative routes to achieving some or all of these objectives? Try to move toward the simplest and most straightforward of them.

(4) Who are the other stakeholders in and around the transaction or structure? Consider counterparties, partners, customers/clients, employees, competitors, regulators/government actors, and the broader community.

- (a) Are there societal and/or environmental drivers at play? Think especially about "impact" here. Also think about environmental, societal, and governance (ESG) considerations. These questions can also help uncover other stakeholders who might be valuable partners, supporters, investors, beneficiaries, customers, etc.
- (b) What are the objectives and perspectives of each of these folks?

(5) Identify alignments and misalignments with the client's motivations. Look for overlooked or hidden benefits, motivations, and challenges.

(6) Can incentives be harmonized or disincentives be neutralized? Can they be priced into the deal?

(7) When structuring, are there any obvious or typical structures available to solve the challenge? If not, are there other situations that present similar challenges? If so, what are the solutions often used in those situations? Can those be applied here? Why or why not (test the idea)?

(8) How does the proposed solution affect the other stakeholders? Look for ways to align interests and objectives. Try to confirm buy-in from key stakeholders and counterparties. A term sheet discussion/negotiation is often helpful here.

---

52. For a discussion of the differences between "outcomes" and "outputs," see Deborah Mills-Scofield, *It's Not Just Semantics: Managing Outcomes vs. Outputs*, Harvard Business Review (2012), available at https://hbr.org/2012/11/its-not-just-semantics-managing-outcomes.

(9) How can transaction risks best be addressed? Consider structural solutions first, then contractual provisions, and, finally, leverage dynamics (i.e., coercive power).

(a) Relatedly, how complete or incomplete should the contractual relationships be among the parties? Are the transaction/negotiation costs of addressing possible points of contention likely to overwhelm the size of the transaction? Consider which risks need to be addressed by the parties ex ante, and which are better left to be addressed by the parties ex post.

(b) If responses to issues are deliberately left to be determined in the future, what is the most appropriate decision-making process (when is this process triggered, whose views should be consulted, who should have decision-making authority, etc.)?

(10) Where the client is relying on others to contribute to the desired end-result, pay special attention to the other side's motivations. Try to align interests so that the other party's self-interest drives it to the same place your client wants to go. If this can't be done, what kind of accountability can be built into the relationship? Does accountability run in both directions?

(11) What is the client's desired "legacy" from its impact investing activities?

(a) What actions need to be encouraged (or conversely discouraged) during the life of the transaction that enhance the chances that these legacy goals will be achieved?

(b) Can technical assistance or other forms of grants/concessional finance be used (as is being done in the MicroBuild Fund and The Ocean Fund) to build markets and change actors' behavior beyond the life of the transaction at hand?

(12) What does a responsible exit from investments look like such that the portfolio companies individually, and the market/sector as a whole, are stronger because of this investment?

Exhibit B

Checklist for Using Third-Party Guarantees in Impact Investments that Make Use of Blended Financing

As the cases in this chapter illustrate, impact investing that takes a blended finance approach often makes use of credit enhancements. These credit enhancements can be structural (such as where the investment sits relative to others in the capital stack of the investee) or contractual (such as a pledge of collateral as security for a debt). The following are general considerations when using a third-party guarantee as a credit enhancement to catalyze funding from others.

In the debt context, a third-party guarantee substitutes a third party's creditworthiness (the issuer/provider of the guarantee) for that of the borrower. The impact investments described in this chapter made use of two common types of third-party guarantees: standby letters of credit[53] (used by Grameen Foundation and Habitat for Humanity's MicroBuild Fund) and a contractual guarantee agreement (used by Circulate Capital's The Ocean Fund). Depending on the objectives and motivations of the issuer/guarantor as well as the laws of the jurisdiction that govern the guarantee, third-party guarantees also may include a reimbursement agreement between the borrower and the issuer/guarantor.

- Key Stakeholder Considerations for Using a Third-Party Guarantee in a Blended Finance Structure[54]
    - What is the risk that the guarantor needs to mitigate so as to catalyze other sources of capital?
        - Lack of creditworthiness of investee
            - Political risks, foreign exchange risks, climate change risks, or other exogenous risks of lending to investee
        - Misperceived risk of investee
        - Unproven business model/sector of investee
        - Other?
    - How does provision of this guarantee mitigate that risk?
    - Who is the guarantor?
        - How creditworthy is the guarantor?
        - What are the motivations of the guarantor?
            - Will the guarantor impose any requirements on the investee or beneficiaries of the guarantee to ensure those motivations are addressed satisfactorily?
            - How long is the guarantor likely to participate in the transaction? (Working itself out of a job? Staying for duration?)
    - What is the minimum amount of coverage required by guarantee in order to attract additional capital?
        - If a guarantee facility, what investments are to be covered?
            - All investments?
            - Only qualifying investments?
            - Transaction by transaction approvals required?
        - What will be covered by the guarantee?
        - Who will be covered by the guarantee?
            - All investors? Only senior investors? Only debt investors? Others?

53. A Standby Letter of Credit (SBLC) is an instrument that substitutes a third party's creditworthiness (the issuer of the SBLC) for that of the borrower (the applicant) in which the issuer promises to pay a specified amount to the recipient of the SBLC (the beneficiary) when the beneficiary presents a document to the issuer stating the conditions (such as payment default) specified in the SBLC have been met. Typically, the SBLC is fully collateralized by applicant with deposit of cash or other financial instruments in an account maintained at the issuer (bank) of the SBLC. In the United States, banks cannot provide guarantees as a third-party guarantor. So, instead, they may issue a standby letter of credit.

54. Many of these considerations are drawn from A Resource for Structuring Blended Finance Vehicles: Utilizing Junior Equity, Subordinated Debt, First-Loss Capital, Guarantees, or Technical Assistance (GIIN: Oct. 2018).

        - How long will the guarantee be in place?
            - Life of guaranteed transaction? Life of fund? Rolling? Other?
            - If not permanent, when will guarantee coverage cease/decrease?
                - Automatically?
                - Upon reaching pre-agreed milestones?
                    - Financial or impact milestones?
                - Other?
    - Amount of desired leverage: How much additional capital is the guarantee expected to generate?
        - At what point is leverage too low (suggesting guarantee is not valued by others)?
        - At what point is leverage too high (suggesting guarantee is not necessary)?
    - Pricing
        - How much does this guarantee cost the investee relative to the improved terms/increased amount of capital the guarantee leverages?
        - To what extent is pricing concessionary relative to risks?
    - Additional capital
        - If additional funding is subsequently raised, will the guarantee cover additional amount/investors?

- Key Contractual Considerations for a Third-Party Guarantee of a Debt Investment
    - What does the lender require in ascertaining creditworthiness of the guarantor? Does the lender impose any ongoing reporting or other requirements on financial condition or otherwise of the guarantor?
    - What fee is to be paid by borrower to the guarantor for the guarantee (annual or initial)?
    - Does the guarantor require collateral as security for reimbursement obligation of the borrower for amounts paid under the guarantee?
    - Does the guarantor impose any restrictions on how proceeds of underlying loan are used or other limitations on the borrower's behavior during term of guarantee?
    - Does the guarantor require its approval for any amendments to underlying loan agreement?
    - Does the guarantor require its approval for an assignment of guaranteed loan by the lender to others?
    - What are procedures to trigger a guarantee payment?
        - If a contractual guarantee, is it a guarantee of payment or collection?
        - Does the guarantor have any defenses (by contract or by law) to avoid making a payment of the guaranteed amount?
    - If the guarantee is triggered, what claims/rights does the guarantor have against the borrower (subrogation, rights specified in a reimbursement agreement, other)?
        - Where do the guarantor's claims/rights stand vis-à-vis other existing funders of the borrower (subordinated, collateral sharing, other)?

- What does the guaranteed amount cover?
  - Complete?
  - Partial?
    - Interest?
    - Principal?
      - All?
      - Partial?
        - Specified percentage of loan amount?
        - Specific principal installments?

Expanding Your Toolkit

This resource, Sandra M. Rocks, PROVISIONS OF STANDARD COMMERCIAL GUARANTEE AGREEMENTS: TECHNICAL GUIDE (CGAP: 2010) (available at https://www.cgap.org/sites/default/files/CGAP-Technical-Guide-Provisions-of-Standard-Commercial-Guarantee-Agreements-Oct-2010.pdf), contains an annotated third-party guarantee agreement and reimbursement agreement. Its annotations highlight issues that are likely to be negotiated and offer general guidance and tips for drafting and negotiating standard clauses often found in guarantees. Its annotations provide descriptions, in plain English, of the purpose of various provisions commonly found in third-party guarantee agreements. Drafted for a microfinance audience, much of the guidance found in this resource nonetheless is applicable to other sectors and users of third-party guarantees.

This resource, prepared by Cleary, Gottlieb, Steen, & Hamilton for CGAP, FOREIGN EXCHANGE RISK MITIGATION TECHNIQUES: STRUCTURE AND DOCUMENTATION—A TECHNICAL GUIDE FOR MICROFINANCE INSTITUTIONS (CGAP: 2006) (available at https://www.cgap.org/sites/default/files/CGAP-Technical-Guide-Foreign-Exchange-Risk-Mitigation-Techniques-Structure-and-Documentation-Oct-2006.pdf), contains an annotated SBLC and reimbursement agreement. Its annotations also provide general guidance and tips for drafting and negotiating the standard clauses often found in SBLCs.

ANNEX A—Grameen Foundation's Growth Guarantee Structure

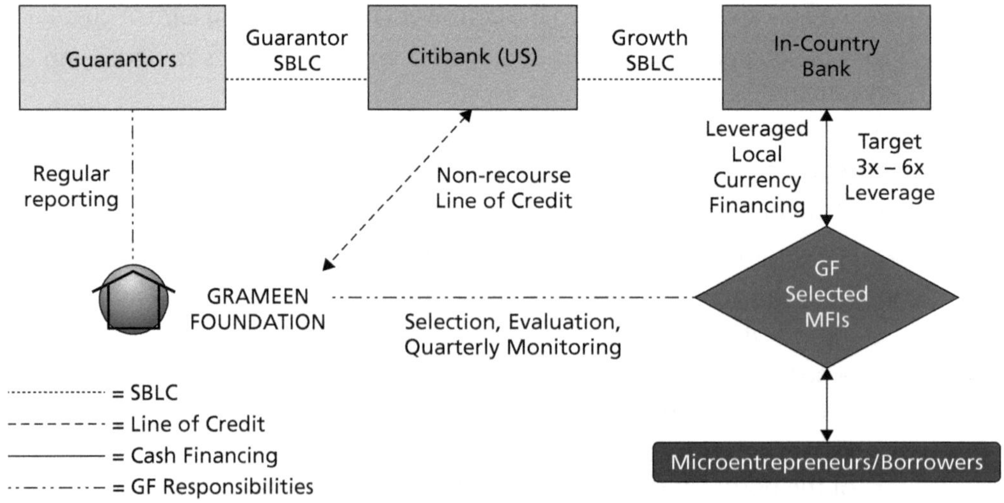

ANNEX B—Habitat's MicroBuild Fund—SBLC Donor Guarantee Structure

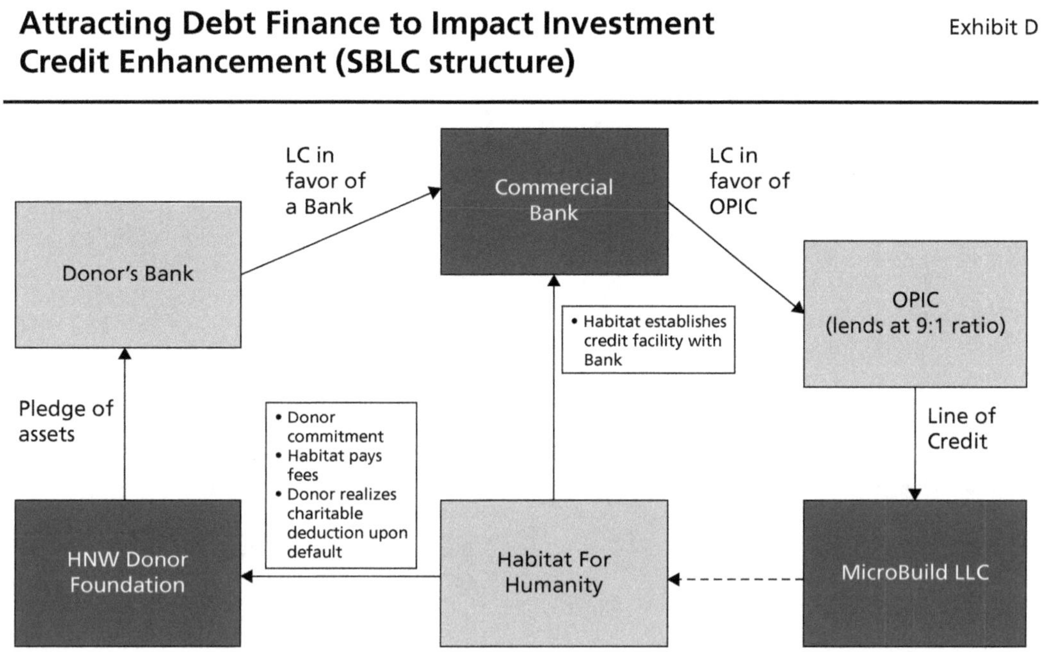

ANNEX C—Circulate Capital's The Ocean Fund—DCA Guarantee Structure

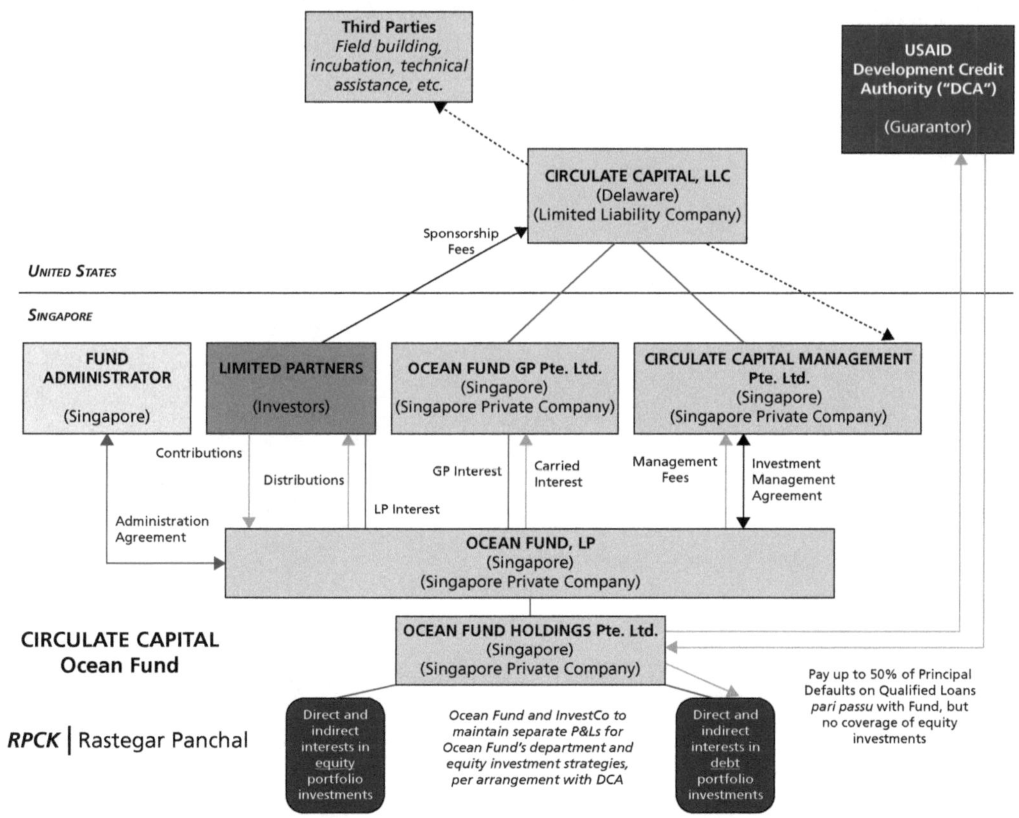

Chapter 2
The Intersection of Community Economic Development and Impact Investing: History and Key Terms

Lisa Green Hall, Susan R. Jones, and Dorcas R. Gilmore[1]

A necessary foundation for the succeeding chapters of this book is the intersection between "impact investing" and its predecessor practices in the field of community economic development (CED), strategies for improving underserved communities, firmly rooted in social justice and racial equity. Viewing them together reveals the longer arc for the assessment of capital flows to redress the effects of exclusionary investment practices and the creation of impactful systemic change. Importantly, the challenges associated with the COVID-19 pandemic, structural racism, and climate change, alongside other societal challenges, call for new and innovative approaches appropriate for this historic, transformative moment. This history of CED and impact investing rests on long-standing principles and practices of cooperation and collective action aligned with the centuries-old quest for Black liberation.

1. With contributions from Amanda Spratley.

Present-day approaches to correct racial and economic inequities in marginalized communities reignite calls to reallocate, rethink investment risks, and ultimately rethink the economy.

For Black communities, racial equity has always been at the forefront of investing for social impact and economic equity, reflecting the central role of race in American social, legal, and economic history.[2] As Chapter 1 explained, investing for social and economic impact plays a key role in the modern global economy. CED is an approach to local economic development that is driven by a community's social, environmental, and economic priorities, shaped by those who live, work, and run businesses, often aided by community serving nonprofits. This chapter explores the intersection of CED as the field has evolved in the United States alongside the rise of impact investing. It presents brief histories of both movements, provides an overview of the primary approaches to impact investing, and finally, relates key terms used in the overlapping fields with a brief glossary.

The Rise of Community Economic Development

The U.S. community economic development (CED) movement can be characterized broadly into four major phases. The first took root post-slavery and Reconstruction, part of the long rich history of Black people in America to practice self-help and economic cooperation in the face of racial discrimination and market exclusion. The second occurred during the 1960s War on Poverty, which saw substantial federal government funding for social programs; while the third phase, privatization, promoted in the 1980s and 1990s, is distinguished by market-based CED approaches. The fourth and current phase of the CED movement, still underway, has been influenced by Community Development Financial Institutions (CDFIs), solidarity economies,[3] technological advancements, climate change, and most recently by mutual aid practices spurred by the COVID-19 pandemic.[4]

Scholars and practitioners identify the roots of what is now called community investing or impact investing and of the CED movement in the 1900s Progressive Era and the historical dialogue between influential Black leaders such as Booker T. Washington, founder of the Tuskegee Institute and Black economic self-sufficiency advocate; W. E. B Du Bois, a proponent of the talented tenth philosophy of cultivating college-educated Black leaders; and Marcus Garvey, founder of the United Negro Improvement Association and Back to Africa Movement.[5] These leaders advocated for a range of localized economic self-help approaches, federal economic intervention and investment, and mutual aid and cooperative approaches to address racial inequities.

CED is both a movement and an approach to building healthy communities addressing all aspects of daily life for low-income, underrepresented, and marginalized communities. Community-driven CED projects include: developing safe, affordable, and attractive housing;

2. Nikole Hannah-Jones, *Our Democracy's Founding Ideals Were False When They Were Written. Black Americans Have Fought to Make Them True*, N.Y. TIMES (Aug. 14, 2019), https://www.nytimes.com/interactive/2019/08/14/magazine/black-history-american-democracy.html.

3. Renee Hatcher, *Solidarity Economy Lawyering*, 8:1 TENN. J. OF RACE, GENDER, & SOC. JUST. 23 (2019).

4. *See, generally*, Clifford N. Rosenthal, Democratizing Finance: Origins of the Community Development Financial Institutions Movement (2018); Jessica Gordon Nembhard, Collective Courage: A History of African American Cooperative Economic Thought and Practice (2014).

5. Roger A. Clay Jr. & Susan R. Jones, Building Healthy Communities: A Guide to Community Economic Development for Advocates, Lawyers, and Policymakers 5–6 (2009).

developing good, well-paying jobs; financing small business development; ensuring environmental safety; and providing broadband internet access to communities neglected by private markets. The CED movement advanced during President Lyndon B. Johnson's "War on Poverty" and the various urban renewal and community action campaigns that emerged during the 1960s and 1970s. An early exemplar of the CED movement and of the community development corporation (CDC) is the Bedford Stuyvesant Restoration Corporation,[6] dedicated since 1964 to creating prosperity and community health in Central Brooklyn. There are 4,600 CDCs throughout the United States.[7]

CED practice at its best is driven by a vision for equity and inclusion in places that have traditionally been overlooked and underestimated by mainstream investors and capital providers.[8] During the 1980s and 1990s, government support for the CED movement shifted to market-based economic development strategies and governmental policy emphasized privatization of critical government services. The federal government created tax credit programs such as Low-Income Housing Tax Credits (LIHTCs) to increase affordable housing units and New Markets Tax Credits (NMTCs) to increase capital inflows in underinvested communities.

Writ large, CED requires private and public sector strategies and policies advanced by government and the philanthropic sector. The economic boom following the 2007–2009 Great Recession did not reach all communities and households. Poverty in fact increased in both urban and rural areas across the United States, approaching 20 percent in larger cities and 20 percent in rural areas.[9] Following the unprecedented global coronavirus pandemic of 2020, poverty continues to grow. At the same time, wages for working-class people remained stagnant. The average U.S. real wage adjusted for inflation remains the same as it was in 1964.[10] And this number is expected to fall more in the immediate aftermath of the pandemic.[11]

Strategies for combating economic inequality have evolved over time and are no longer limited to philanthropic grantmaking and public sector programs like the Community Development Block Grant (CDBG) and Tax Increment Financing (TIF). Traditional public community development efforts are now supplemented by private sector investment strategies that include the programs mentioned earlier alongside social impact bonds (SIBs), program-related investments (PRIs), and mission-driven investments (MDIs).

---

6. *History*, RESTORATION, https://live-restorationwp.pantheonsite.io/about/history/ (last visited Apr. 26, 2022).
7. *Overview: Community Development Corporations (CDCs)*, COMMUNITY-WEALTH.ORG, https://community-wealth.org/strategies/panel/cdcs/index.html (last visited Apr. 26, 2022).
8. Todd Bishop, *"Underestimated": How Venture Capitalist Arlan Hamilton Is Turning Inequality into Opportunity*, GeekWire (Dec. 19, 2018), https://www.geekwire.com/2018/underestimated-venture-capitalist-arlan-hamilton-turning-inequality-opportunity/.
9. Elizabeth Kneebone, *The Changing Geography of U.S. Poverty*, BROOKINGS (Feb. 15, 2017), https://www.brookings.edu/testimonies/the-changing-geography-of-us-poverty/; Elizabeth A. Dobis et al., *Rural America at a Glance*, USDA Economic Research Service (Nov. 2021), https://www.ers.usda.gov/webdocs/publications/102576/eib-230.pdf.
10. Drew DeSilver, *For Most U.S. Workers, Real Wages Have Barely Budged in Decades*, PEW RESEARCH CENTER (Aug. 7, 2018), https://www.pewresearch.org/fact-tank/2018/08/07/for-most-us-workers-real-wages-have-barely-budged-for-decades/.
11. Cecilia Rouse & Martha Gimbel, *The Pandemic's Effect on Measured Wage Growth*, WHITE HOUSE BLOG (Apr. 19, 2021), https://www.whitehouse.gov/cea/blog/2021/04/19/the-pandemics-effect-on-measured-wage-growth/.

The Importance of CDFIs: Pivot to Capital

Given the central role of CDFIs in modern CED practice and directing resources to underrepresented American communities, the proliferation of CDFIs deserves special attention. The early CDFI movement and present-day industry can trace their roots to the 1860s post–Civil War, abolitionist supported, racial participation efforts of newly freed African Americans. The Freedman's Savings and Trust Company, a private savings bank chartered by the U.S. Congress in 1865, was created to collect deposits from newly emancipated African Americans.[12] In their contemporary form, CDFIs are private financial institutions with the social purpose to deliver responsible, affordable lending to low-income, low-wealth, and disadvantaged people and communities to facilitate participation in the economic mainstream. They aim to foster economic growth at the community level, by financing small, minority-owned businesses, microenterprises, affordable housing, nonprofit and volunteer organizations, and services essential to revitalizing low-income neighborhoods. Their goal is to support wealth-building in underrepresented and overlooked communities and communities of color by supporting economic growth through community redevelopment.

An extension and core component of CED, the Community Development Finance field grew alongside CED in the 1960s. The 1970s witnessed the enactment of the Community Reinvestment Act in 1977[13] to encourage financial institutions to meet the needs of low- to moderate-income people. This period is also characterized by the growth of grassroots community development organizations (CDOs), CDCs, and community development credit unions (CDCUs).[14] The famed South Shore Bank of Chicago, founded in 1973, became the nation's first Community Development Bank.[15] The Institute for Community Economics was founded in 1979 as a revolving loan fund for nonprofit housing organizations.[16]

The 1980s ushered in a new chapter for the CDFI movement, as large foundations like Ford and MacArthur, as well as faith-based organizations invested in CDOs and CDFIs. The Community Development Financial Coalition was created in 1992 and remains the "unified voice of community development financial institutions" numbering more than 1,000 throughout the fifty states.[17]

In 1994, the U.S. Congress established the CDFI Fund to provide direct funding to CDFI programs (CDFIs) as a way to leverage private investment and foster local economic development and financing. The CDFI Fund invests in, trains, and supports CDFIs. It has spurred the rapid expansion of CDFIs from the 1990s to the present.[18] There are over 1,000 CDFIs certified by the CDFI Fund, and numerous charitable organizations doing similar work around the country. The CDFI Fund is also responsible for aspects of the New Markets Tax

12. Clifford N. Rosenthal, Democratizing Finance: Origins of the Community Development Financial Institutions Movement, 6–11 (Friesen Press Canada 2018).
13. 12 U.S.C. § 2901 (2020).
14. Rosenthal, *supra* note 12, at 23–77.
15. *Id.* at 40–47.
16. *Institute for Community Economics*, Community-Wealth.Org, https://community-wealth.org/content/institute-community-economics (last visited Apr. 26, 2022).
17. Cdfi Coalition, https://cdfi.org/.
18. *About Us*, CDFI Fund, https://www.cdfifund.gov/about (last visited Apr. 26, 2022).

Credit Program (NMTC)[19] which was created to increase private investment in low and moderate communities through qualified private investment in Community Development Entities (CDEs). Specifically, the CDFI Fund makes tax credit allocations through a competitive award process to CDEs. Investors are allotted a credit of up to 39 percent of the CDE investment which must be claimed over seven years.[20] Some of the earliest CDFIs have established "families" of funds, significant networks of affiliates and partnerships, and have aggregated billions of dollars in capital, with which they make loans, as well as provide grants and equity, to under-resourced communities. A few of the intermediaries and leaders in the field include Enterprise Community Investments,[21] Local Initiative Support Corporation (LISC),[22] Capital Impact Partners,[23] and Calvert Impact Capital.[24]

The Emergence of Impact Investing

In 2007, the term *Impact Investing* emerged among practitioners to express an intentional approach to investing in businesses, social enterprises, and funds that generate measurable social returns alongside financial returns.[25] Publication of the report "Investing for Social and Environmental Impact" in 2009 is generally recognized as the foundational report describing the initial landscape of the impact investing field and key objectives for its continued development.[26] While impact investing has become a "term of art," it is sometimes referred to more broadly as community investing or socially responsible investing (SRI). Socially responsible investing started largely in the public markets, accessed through SRI mutual funds. These funds commonly use value screening and exclusion to avoid investments in companies that might have negative social or environmental exposures, such as tobacco or firearms. A similar development has been the rise of "ESG investment strategies." ESG refers to the use of a set of criteria used to evaluate a company's environmental, social, and governance risks and practices, to help investors consider risks to sustainability.[27] Both SRI and ESG investment approaches aim to recognize the materiality of risks that lie beyond the typical financial statement analysis. By contrast, impact investing is seeking positive impactful investment attributes rather than screening out perceived negative attributes. ESG and SRI each offer a framework for evaluating companies, whereas intentional impact investment targets selected types of investments.

19. H.R.5662—106th Congress (1999–2000): Community Renewal Tax Relief Act of 2000, H.R.5662, 106th Cong. (2000), https://www.congress.gov/bill/106th-congress/house-bill/5662. NMTC is part of the Community Renewal Act of 2000, contained within the Consolidated Appropriations Act 2001 (P.L. 106-554). *Id.*

20. *CDFI Fund Announces $5 Billion in New Markets Tax Credits*, U.S. Dep't of the Treasury (Sept. 1, 2021), https://home.treasury.gov/news/press-releases/jy0340.

21. Enterprise Community Investments, https://www.enterprisecommunity.org/.

22. LISC, https://www.lisc.org/.

23. Capital Impact Partners, https://www.capitalimpact.org/.

24. Calvert Impact Capital, https://calvertimpactcapital.org/.

25. *What You Need to Know about Impact Investing*, Glob. Impact Investing Network, https://thegiin.org/impact-investing/need-to-know/#what-is-impact-investing.

26. *See* Jessica Freireich & Katherine Fulton, *Investing for Social & Environmental Impact: A Design for Catalyzing an Emerging Industry*, Monitor Inst. (2009), https://www2.deloitte.com/content/dam/Deloitte/global/Documents/Financial-Services/gx-fsi-monitor-Investing-for-Social-and-Environmental-Impact-2009.pdf.

27. Blog: What is ESG?, Pitchbook (Jan. 18, 2022), https://pitchbook.com/blog/what-is-esg.

Approaches to Impact Investing

Impact investors may select among multiple fundamental investment approaches in the impact investing landscape, which are continually developed and refined. The broad array facilitates strategic decision making in how investors and socially minded businesses identify and structure impact investments, as well as how investors choose to value, measure, and evaluate the success of impact investments. The next section provides an overview of key investor strategies based on type of investment and stage of business life cycle, as well as the roles of intermediaries and various means of outcome measurement.

Investor Strategies for Impact Investing

Investors approaching impact investing typically start with a clear idea of their particular investment goals and a vision of what they will deem a successful and impactful investment. Core attributes include the following:

Return

Examples of possible investment strategies include Market Rate with Impact, indicating a goal to achieve market rate financial returns but with the additional benefit of resulting positive social impacts. In a Blended Strategy, the investor may view positive social impact as a form of expected beneficial return, and so may be willing to accept lower than market rate financial returns for a significant combined financial and social return in line with their desired expectations. A Sector-Focused investment strategy values the potential for early investments in an emerging field to yield further investment opportunities as part of the desired return, and an Impact Alpha strategy prioritizes impact with the belief that a differentiation between financial and social return is unnecessary because higher impact investments will ultimately succeed on both measures.[28]

Sectoral Focus and Diversification

Impact investors also generally consider traditional investment factors such as diversification as a risk mitigation action. Diversification within impact investing may occur with respect to investing across multiple sectors, asset classes, or geographic areas. Examples of multiple sectors within the impact investing field include:

- Community development
- Small business finance
- Health and wellness
- Education
- Microfinance and financial inclusion
- Sustainable consumer products and fair trade

---

28. Sean Greene, *A Short Guide to Impact Investing*, The Case Found. 28–29 (Sept. 2014), https://casefoundation.org/wp-content/uploads/2014/11/ShortGuideToImpactInvesting-2014.pdf.

- Natural resources and conservation
- Renewable energy and climate change
- Sustainable agriculture and development[29]

Thematic Focus

More recently, impact investors have begun to examine investments around thematic lenses such as gender,[30] racial equity,[31] creative,[32] and nonextractive finance, which prioritizes community-defined approaches to lending that will not leave communities less wealthy (nonextractive financing is discussed in chapter 9). Impact investors may also choose to focus their investments within a particular geographic area, multiple targeted geographic areas, or investments with a broad generalized geographic focus as a means to diversify or tailor their investments.[33] The terms place-based and place conscious, discussed in chapters 8 and 9, are often used to describe this work. Investors may also consider balancing their investments between emerging markets versus developed economies in diversifying and structuring their investment strategies, as well as assessing their desired investment in structured/fund versus direct/custom investing opportunities.[34]

Asset Class

Depending on an investor's objectives, an impact investor may choose to diversify across or specialize within particular asset classes or stages of business development. The multiple asset classes within impact investing include cash, fixed income, public equities, private equity/venture capital, and real assets.[35] Further discussion of considerations for types and stages of investment capital is below.

Types and Stages of Investment Capital

Impact investors may invest in different ways and at different stages in the life cycle of an impact investment initiative or business, depending on the unique objectives and strategy of the investor and the particular needs of the investment vehicle. Impact investing has typically taken the form of private equity, private debt, and real assets.[36] In recent years, impact investment has seen a rapid development of impact investment funds and other intermediaries to help coordinate and support access to and further expansion of impact investment opportunities.

---

29. *Id.* at 18.
30. Slyvia Kwen, *What's Gender-Lens Investing and Why Is It Important?*, Ellevest (Nov. 27, 2018), https://www.ellevest.com/magazine/impact-investing/gender-lens-investing; Joseph Quinlan & Jackie Vanderbrug, *Gender Lens Investing: Uncovering Opportunities for Growth, Returns, and Impact*, Stan. Soc. Innovation Rev. (Apr. 3, 2017), https://ssir.org/books/excerpts/entry/gender_lens_investing_uncovering_opportunities_for_growth_returns_and_impac; Gender Smart, https://www.gendersmartinvesting.com/.
31. *Racial Equity & Impact Investing*, Mission Invs. Exch., https://missioninvestors.org/racial-equity-impact-investing.
32. Upstart Co-Lab, https://www.upstartco-lab.org/.
33. Sean Greene, *A Short Guide to Impact Investing*, The Case Found. 20 (Sept. 2014), https://casefoundation.org/wp-content/uploads/2014/11/ShortGuideToImpactInvesting-2014.pdf.
34. Id.
35. Id.
36. *Roadmap for the Future of Impact Investing: Reshaping Financial Markets*, Glob. Impact Investing Network 50 (2018), https://thegiin.org/research/publication/giin-roadmap.

Key investor considerations include whether to engage in early-stage investments, invest in established businesses, or a combination of both. Businesses must similarly evaluate at which stages of the life cycle of the business they will seek investment and what opportunities will most likely attract investors. Investors must also assess different types of investment capital. Key among these decisions are whether to invest in equity or debt, and whether to seek public or private investment opportunities. These and additional stages and types of impact investment capital are explored next.

(1) Private Equity

Impact investing in the form of private equity can occur at multiple stages of the target company's life cycle and take various forms. Types of private equity capital investment include venture capital, angel investments, seed capital, and late-stage equity.

(a) Venture Capital & Angel Investment

Popular sources of private equity investment include those made by venture capital firms and angel investors. Increasingly, venture capital investments will come from firms specializing in social impact investments or those that have developed a practice area dedicated to social impact investing. Traditional venture firms will similarly consider social impact goals in their investments; however, adequate understanding of the unique considerations relevant to impact investing and a willingness to pursue substantial impact initiatives is still underdeveloped.[37] Individual or small groups of angel investors may be more willing to pursue financially risky or uncertain investments that align with their social impact objectives; however, these efforts currently do not create the collective ecosystem and broad-based structural coordination important for transformative change and long-term sustainable support for the impact investing field.[38] While both venture capital and angel investments are essential to the impact investing field, further development of these avenues is important and necessary for the continued growth of the field.

(b) Seed Capital and Early-Stage versus Late-Stage Investment

Early in the business life cycle, an impact investor may contribute seed capital to help establish and launch the company. Some investors may shy away from investing in the early stages of a business due to the increased uncertainty and risk about whether the business will be successful and whether investment objectives will be achieved. Nonetheless, some investors specifically seek this early-stage impact and heightened return.

Early-stage investment can be critical for generating greater investment opportunities within new untapped spaces and for addressing under-supported pressing social issues.[39] Given the relatively recent emergence

37. Investment Guide: Angel & Impact Investors, Energy Catalyst (June 2020), https://energycatalyst.community/developer/wp-content/uploads/2020/12/Investment-guide-Angel-impact-investors.pdf.

38. Id.

39. Eva Yazhari, *Making the Case for Early-Stage Impact Investing*, Next Billion (June 15, 2018), https://nextbillion.net/the-case-for-early-stage-impact-investing/.

of social enterprise and social entrepreneurship as focus areas for business activity and innovation, many socially focused businesses seeking to create positive impacts require early investment for their survival.[40] Similarly, many founders of impact-focused businesses may trend younger and lack adequate financial resources, contacts, and track records of experience to establish these businesses without early-stage investment. Early investment is often critical for the creation and early viability of these impact-focused businesses, and consequently important for the future of impact investment to continue to encourage impact-driven innovation and business creation.[41]

Some investment funds form explicitly for the purpose of engaging in early-stage impact investing, such as Beyond Capital.[42] Investing seed capital to support the creation of impact investment opportunities and providing related early rounds of funding may constitute an investor's entire investment focus, or part of an investor's diversified plan to balance the potential risk of early-stage investment with more established and predictable investment opportunities. An investor's personal risk exposure will vary based upon the investor's particular investment objectives. A high likelihood of achieving a desired positive impact may mitigate or outweigh attendant financial risk. Investors may also hold different timelines, evaluating the investment against shorter or longer expected investment time frames.[43]

(2) Private Debt and Real Assets

Impact investing through private debt may take many forms, including convertible debt, community development notes, and a variety of different types of bonds such as green bonds or environmental bonds. Private debt is discussed in chapter 9 as an impact strategy to maintain ownership and control in communities.

Additionally, one of the most common avenues for impact investing through real assets is by investing in Real Estate Investment Trusts.[44]

(3) Public Equity

In addition to private equity investment, some impact investors seek opportunities to invest in public equity. This frequently takes the form of utilizing ESG screens to ensure that the target investment companies pursue initiatives that align with the investor's impact objectives.[45]

Measuring Impact and Outcomes

With the increased focus on impact investment, there has also been more interest in understanding what differentiates impact investing from traditional forms of investing and how investors can seek and maintain investments that actually make an impact. Therefore,

---

40. *Id.*

41. Id.

42. Beyond Cap. Fund, https://www.beyondcapitalfund.org.

43. Beyond Cap. Fund, https://www.beyondcapitalfund.org/. Beyond Capital is an impact investment fund that invests in early-stage, for-profit social enterprises serving low-resourced communities in India and East Africa. *Id.*

44. *See A Strategy for Investing in Sustainable Reits*, Principles for Responsible Inv., https://www.unpri.org/download?ac=6411.

45. Brian Deese et al., *The Case for Impact Investing in Public Equities*, BlackRock (Sept. 30, 2020), https://www.blackrock.com/us/individual/insights/public-equities-impact-investing.

measurable impact has emerged as a defining characteristic of impact investing.[46] Impact investments seek measurable indicia of the desired positive social impact in addition to measurable financial returns. The challenge arises in determining how to reliably measure social impact and outcomes. Measuring social impact is complex.[47] A full exploration of measuring impact and outcomes is beyond the scope of this book; however, it is worth addressing the important role that measurement plays in this field and in connection to determining an impact investing strategy.

Notably, it is important for investors to independently assess how they define impact, and then examine how impact is measured by the investees (companies and initiatives). Different investors, businesses, other investment initiatives, and communities may define and measure desired impact differently. Although the impact investing field is moving toward greater standardization of measurement techniques, investors and businesses must still remain attune to what they choose to measure and what defines success.

Organizations have emerged to support further standardization and coordination of social impact evaluation and measurement within the field. The Impact Management Project is an initiative that seeks to create a forum for building global consensus on how to manage and measure impact in social impact investing.[48] This effort stems from a recognized need to enhance consistency and standardization in evaluating social impact in order to continue to scale and grow the field. Multiple frameworks and guiding principles have emerged to provide tools and promote consistent standards for measuring and evaluating social impact. An introduction to some of these resources follows.

(1) Social Impact Certifications and Ratings Systems

In recent years, many companies have decided to initially adopt or convert their existing business structure to a hybrid organizational form to signal to the public and both internal and external stakeholders the company's commitment to social impact objectives. A popular organizational form for this purpose has been the Benefit Corporation, which is distinguished from the traditional business corporation by state statute and governing documents mandating one or more public benefit purposes, as well as internal and external accountability for impacts on stakeholders such as community members and, the environment.[49] Benefit Corporations must assess their performance against a recognized independent third-party standard of their choice to ensure compliance with objectives.[50]

A number of organizations have emerged to provide an independent third-party standard against which Benefit Corporations and other social enterprise organizations can reliably measure their performance toward operating for social

46. *What You Need to Know about Impact Investing*, Glob. Impact Investing Network, https://thegiin.org/impact-investing/need-to-know/ (last visited Apr. 26, 2022).

47. *See* Gwendolyn Reynolds et al., *A Playbook for Designing Social Impact Measurement*, Stan. Soc. Innovation Rev. (Dec. 21, 2018), https://ssir.org/articles/entry/a_playbook_for_designing_social_impact_measurement#; Hans Rawhouser et al., *Social Impact Measurement: Current Approaches and Future Directions for Social Entrepreneurship Research*, 43 Entrepreneurship Theory and Prac. 82 (2019), https://journals.sagepub.com/doi/pdf/10.1177/1042258717727718.

48. Impact Mgmt. Project, https://impactmanagementproject.com/.

49. *See What Is a Benefit Corporation?*, Benefit Corp., https://benefitcorp.net/ (last visited Apr. 26, 2022).

50. J. Haskell Murray, Understanding and Improving Benefit Corporation Reporting, https://www.americanbar.org/groups/business_law/publications/blt/2016/07/04_murray/.

good. These third-party standard organizations often provide guidance and recommendations for best practices among social enterprises, as well as providing certification and rating systems enabling qualifying organizations to demonstrate and promote their recognized compliance to the public.[51]

(a) B-Corp Certifications

One of the most popular third party certification organizations is the B-Corp Certification awarded by B Lab. B Lab seeks to shift the culture of business to reimagine it as a driver for positive social change.[52] It does this in large part by verifying the credibility of businesses pursuing positive impact through its certification process, identifying these businesses as role models and leaders to others in the field, and endeavoring to build supporting infrastructure and incentives to grow the field and achieve "an inclusive, equitable and regenerative economic system for all people and the planet."[53]

(b) Aeris Ratings System

The Aeris Ratings System is another system providing guidelines for and verification of satisfactory social impact–focused initiatives.[54] Aeris has rated over 150 CDFIs managing more than $19 billion in loan capital.[55]

(2) Impact Frameworks (For-Profit)

In addition to the public and nonprofit initiatives to support the impact investment field previously described, multiple for-profit impact frameworks exist, providing external expert guidance, specialized investment knowledge, and recommended benchmarks for assessing and evaluating impact investments. Below are a few examples of these venture capital firms or investment companies specializing or providing a niche practice catering to impact investing.

(a) The Rise Fund

The Rise Fund works exclusively with mission-driven companies driving measurable social and environmental impact.[56] With $5 billion under management, the Rise Fund focuses its investments in growth-stage, high potential companies.[57]

(b) Rock Creek Group

Rock Creek Group is a global investment management firm committed to supporting MDIs that promote sustainability, inclusion, and creation of long-term value.[58] It has directed investments in sectors such as education, clean energy, fossil fuel divestment, and affordable housing.[59]

---

51. *See, e.g.*, Food All. Certified, http://foodalliance.org/. Food Alliance provides comprehensive third-party certification for social and environmental responsibility in agriculture and the food industry.
52. *About B Lab*, B Lab, https://www.bcorporation.net/en-us/movement/about-b-lab.
53. Id.
54. *Inside Aeris Ratings for CDFIs & Other Loan Funds*, Aeris Insight (2018), https://www.aerisinsight.com/wp-content/uploads/2018/10/Inside-Aeris-Ratings-2018.pdf.
55. *About Aeris*, Aeris, https://www.aerisinsight.com/about/.
56. The Rise Fund, https://therisefund.com.
57. Id.
58. RockCreek Grp., https://therockcreekgroup.com.
59. Id.

(c) CapRock
CapRock is an investment advising company that specializes in providing guidance and serving as an advocate for family businesses regarding their financial decisions, with a focus on protecting and building wealth for individuals and families lacking the expertise and resources to confidently navigate these decisions independently.[60] The company has a specific practice area dedicated to impact investing with approximately $1 billion of impact investments across all asset classes.[61]

(d) Core Innovation Capital
Core Innovation Capital is a venture capital fund dedicated to democratizing prosperity and facilitating upward economic mobility for everyday Americans through investments in early-stage, high-growth financial services companies.[62] It leverages its partnerships and technology to create efficient, scalable, MDI opportunities, such as reducing fees and barriers to access in the banking industry through investment in the digital economy.[63]

(e) Learn Capital
Learn Capital LLC is a venture capital firm with a commitment to "transforming how the world learns" by focusing exclusively on funding entrepreneurs seeking to effect positive impact linked to learning initiatives.[64] These investments recognize the potential for the funding of innovation, technology, and services in education to promote long-term positive societal impact.

The measurement of impact is critical to ensuring these investments meet their intended goals. The tools and frameworks highlighted above facilitate the transparency and accountability that are vital to the field.

Intermediaries for Outcomes Finance

A financial intermediary serves as a middleman between parties in a financial transaction.[65] For example, Social Finance is a nonprofit organization that forms public–private partnerships with a variety of government and private partners to facilitate investment initiatives seeking to achieve measurable positive social impact. These partnerships effectively shift risk away from the public sector to the private sector, expecting partners experienced in social impact work to effectively evaluate and manage the unique risk and operational considerations presented by these investments. Social Finance acts as an intermediary to focus on delivering positive outcomes that create actual positive social change that can

60. CapRock, https://www.caprock.com.
61. Id.
62. Core Innovation Cap., http://corevc.com; LA Venture Podcast: *Arjan Schütte of Core Innovation Capital*, dot.LA (Nov. 19, 2020), https://dot.la/core-innovation-capital-2648972980.html; *Core Innovation Capital*, PitchBook, https://pitchbook.com/profiles/investor/51001-03#overview.
63. LA Venture Podcast: *Arjan Schütte of Core Innovation Capital*, dot.LA (Nov. 19, 2020), https://dot.la/core-innovation-capital-2648972980.html.
64. Learn Cap. LLC, https://learncapital.com; *Learn Capital*, Crunchbase, www.crunchbase.com/organization/learncapital.
65. James Chen, *Financial Intermediary*, Investopedia (Sept. 23, 2020), https://www.investopedia.com/terms/f/financialintermediary.asp.

be measured and keep partners accountable to achieving the social impact objectives of the investment. As an intermediary, Social Finance connects a broad base of investors and partners and aggregates substantial sums of investment money to create the substantial and sustainable positive impact sought to address the complex and challenging social issues often ignored or neglected.

Social Finance has mobilized nearly half a billion dollars to accomplish its social impact investments. It pursues investment strategies in accordance with five principles: (1) clearly defined outcomes, (2) data-driven decision making, (3) cross-sector partnership, (4) strong governance and accountability, and (5) catalytic capital for impact. Social Finance refers to its broad set of outcomes-based financing strategies as "Pay for Success." These strategies include SIBs, Career Impact Bonds, Environmental Impact Bonds (EIBs), Development Impact Bonds (DIBs), and Outcomes Rate Card. The "bond" terminology refers to the public–private contract nature of these initiatives, rather than a type of financial instrument as it may be thought of in the traditional banking sense.[66] See more about Social Finance's work in chapter 4. Other examples of intermediaries for social finance include Third Sector Capital[67] and Maycomb Capital.[68]

Glossary of Key Concepts and Terms

Community investing, the term used in this book to characterize the intersection of CED and impact investing, is filled with concepts, terms, definitions, and acronyms that create a common language for investments for social and economic impact. The word impact itself is a proxy for social and economic outcomes that mission-driven investors are seeking to achieve. Social scientists define impact as a longer term sustainable change attributable to a specific definition.[69] In contrast, in the social impact context, outcomes are typically viewed as shorter term effects or influences. Regardless of the exact definition used, investing for social and economic impact (or outcomes) is an approach employed by the public, private, and social, nonprofit sector (or third sector) as explained throughout this book.

The terms and definitions below provide a broader context for the work that is considered impact investing and situate impact investing within the larger field of CED. While a few of the terms are not specifically discussed in this book, they are important to CED and, more broadly, development finance.

Community Investment Tax Approaches

The public sector plays a critical role in community investing through tax incentives, municipal finance, zoning and permitting, and public subsidies. A variety of tax tools are used to drive private sector incentives for social and economic impact. These incentives are briefly discussed below.

66. *See* Soc. Fin., socialfinance.org.
67. Third Sector Cap., thirdsectorcap.org.
68. Maycomb Cap., maycombcapital.com.
69. A Question About Impact, By Whom, For Whom & Definitions (2013) https://www.impact.upenn.edu/a_question_about_impact/.

(1) Tax Increment Financing (TIF)
TIFs pay for present real estate improvement costs of targeted redevelopment areas from future tax revenue pledged to finance improvements or development. Effectively, it is a method of betting on an increase in property tax revenue that will result when a project is finished.[70]

(2) Tax Abatements
Tax Abatements or relief of a taxpayer's liability are used to incentivize businesses and investors to invest in communities in exchange for a tax break like a property tax reduction.[71]

(3) Opportunity Zones
Opportunity Zones, discussed in chapter 3, are low-income census tracts where new investments, derived from capital gains on the sale of assets, are eligible for preferential tax treatment and a deferral and/or reduction of tax on the prior gains.[72]

(4) New Markets Tax Credits Program
New Markets Tax Credits (NMTCs) attract private capital into low-income communities by permitting individual and corporate investors to receive a tax credit against their federal income tax in exchange for making equity investments in Community Development Entities. The credits are allocated by the CDFI Fund.[73]

(5) Low-Income Housing Tax Credit Program
Low-Income Housing Tax Credit Program gives state agencies the authority to issue tax credits for the acquisition, rehabilitation, or new construction of rental housing targeted to lower income households. These credits permit individuals and corporate investors to receive a tax credit against their federal income tax in exchange for making equity investments.[74]

Direct Public Subsidy

Although there are a myriad of direct public subsidies employed to facilitate and catalyze community investments, three critical CED programs, commonly used in CED parlance, are briefly described below.

(1) Community Development Block Grant Program (CDBG)
CDBG authorized under Title 1 of the Housing and Community Development Act of 1974[75] provides annual grants on a formula basis to states, cities, and counties in urban areas to provide affordable housing and expand economic opportunities

70. *Tax Increment Finance Resource Center*, Council of Dev. Fin. Agencies, https://www.cdfa.net/cdfa/cdfaweb.nsf/resourcecenters/tif.html.

71. *See* Code of District of Columbia § 47-857.07.

72. *Opportunity Zones*, Internal Revenue Serv. (Aug. 6, 2021), https://www.irs.gov/credits-deductions/businesses/opportunity-zones.

73. *New Markets Tax Credit Program*, U.S. Dep't of Treasury Cmty Dev. Fin. Insts Fund, https://www.cdfifund.gov/programs-training/programs/new-markets-tax-credit.

74. *Low-Income Housing Tax Credits*, Nat'l Hous. L. Project, https://www.nhlp.org/resource-center/low-income-housing-tax-credits/.

75. 12 U.S.C. § 1706e.

in low- and moderate-income areas.[76] The program is important because 95 percent of yearly allocated CDBG funding goes to public facilities, housing rehabilitation, municipal infrastructures, economic development, and related community development efforts.[77] Two important CDBG programs are the Disaster Recovery Program, providing flexible grants for presidentially-declared disasters like the COVID-19 pandemic, and the Neighborhood Stabilization Program to assist communities suffering in the wake of property foreclosure and abandonment.[78]

(2) Section 8 Rental Assistance
The Housing and Community Development Act of 1974 created the Section 8 rental assistance program, a federally funded program that pays private landlords the difference between what a low-income household can contribute, or afford to pay, and the fair market rent.[79] It enables 5.2 million low-income households and 10.2 million people to afford basic housing.[80]

(3) Community Health Centers
Section 330 of the Public Health Services Act created and authorized the Health Center Program and authority to make grant awards to eligible health centers serving low- and moderate-income individuals and households.[81] This program is important, especially in the wake of the COVID-19 pandemic, because community health centers are located in high need rural and urban areas and serve, without regard to insurance, over 29 million people living in poverty.[82]

Other Approaches to Public Investments

Other approaches to public investments include municipal finance, real estate zoning, and permitting, all briefly explained below.

(1) Municipal Finance
Municipal finance is a broad field governing the revenue and expenditures of municipal governments and a major source of capital for investing in communities. Municipal government revenues include an array of taxes—property,

76. Id.
77. Community Development Block Grant Program: Guide to National Objectives & Eligible Activities for Entitlement Communities, U.S. Department of Housing and Urban Development Office of Community Planning and Development, https://files.hudexchange.info/resources/documents/CDBG_Guide_National_Objectives_Eligible_Activities.pdf.
78. Community Development Block Grant Disaster Recovery Program, Legal Aid Disaster Resource Center (Nov. 2020), https://www.ladrc.org/wp-content/uploads/2020/11/CDBG-DR-Overview-A_Final-dated.pdf; *Neighborhood Stabilization Program*, U.S. Dept. of Housing and Urban Development, https://www.hud.gov/program_offices/comm_planning/nsp (last visited Apr. 26, 2022).
79. 42 U.S.C. § 1437f.
80. *Federal Rental Assistance Fact Sheets*, Center on Budget and Policy Priorities (last updated Jan. 19, 2022), https://www.cbpp.org/research/housing/federal-rental-assistance-fact-sheets#US.
81. *330 Statute*, National Association of Community Health Centers, https://www.nachc.org/focus-areas/policy-matters/health-center-funding/330-program-requirements/#:~:text=Section%20330%20of%20the%20Public%20Health%20Service%20Act,in%20order%20to%20be%20eligible%20for%20these%20awards (last visited Sept.5, 2022).
82. Community Health Center Chartbook 2020, Nat'l Assn. of Community Health Centers (2020), https://www.nachc.org/wp-content/uploads/2020/01/Chartbook-2020-Final.pdf.

income, sales, and excise—as well as proceeds from bonds issued by state and local development finance agencies. These bonds can be for specific uses, including housing, infrastructure, water and sewer, roads and tollways, education, and health facilities.[83]

(2) Zoning and Permitting

The governance of land through zoning and permitting is another important public sector investment tool. Indeed, local governments use inclusionary zoning, in particular, to require developers to build, for example, a certain number of low- and or middle-income units in new real estate developments. These units are "below market rate" in the sense that the developer would otherwise be able to rent or sell these units at a market rate. Most inclusionary zoning programs are mandatory and in some cases are viewed as controversial because they require the construction of below market rate units in locations where luxury or above market rate units can be easily sold or rented.[84]

Philanthropy & Foundations

The philanthropic sector plays an important role in seeding and growing investments for social and economic impact. Some philanthropic tools are described below.

(1) Program Related Investments (PRIs)

PRIs are a very specific type of investment made by charitable organizations, specifically private foundations, to achieve their charitable purpose. PRIs must meet three requirements as defined by the IRS:

- The primary purpose is to accomplish one or more of the foundation's exempt purposes,
- Production of income or appreciation of property is not a significant purpose, and
- Influencing legislation or taking part in political campaigns on behalf of candidates is not a purpose.[85]

Types of PRIs include below market loans, subordinate loans, and even equity in social purpose, for-profit organizations. Many large foundations like the Bill and Melinda Gates Foundation[86] and the Ford Foundation have dedicated significant amounts of their assets to PRIs. There are also numerous networks and

83. *Guide to Municipal Finance*, UN-Habitat (2009), https://www.local2030.org/library/65/Guide-to-Municipal-Finance.pdf.
84. Amy Armstrong et al., The Effects of Inclusionary Zoning on Local Housing Markets: Lessons from the San Francisco, Washington DC and Suburban Boston Areas, Ctr. for Hous. Pol'y 2 (Mar. 2008), https://www.seattle.gov/documents/Departments/SeattlePlanningCommission/MinutesAndAgendas/IZPolicyBrief.pdf.
85. *Program-Related Investments*, Internal Revenue Serv. (Feb. 2, 2021), https://www.irs.gov/charities-non-profits/private-foundations/program-related-investments.
86. Paul Brest, *Investing for Impact with Program-Related Investments,* Stan. Soc. Innovation Rev. (2016), https://ssir.org/articles/entry/investing_for_impact_with_program_related_investments.

platforms like the Mission Investors Exchange[87] and Confluence Philanthropy,[88] which support their members in making PRIs, as well as Mission Driven Investments (MDIs) described below.

(2) Mission Driven Investments (MDIs) or Mission Related Investment (MRIs)
MDIs refer to a host of practices that harmonize a charitable organization's mission for social or environmental impact with the management and investment of assets while sustaining long-term financial return. Generally, MRIs refer to market rate investments that are mission-driven.

There has been a movement to shift larger amounts and in some cases 100 percent of foundation endowments into MRIs to achieve complete alignment between the foundation's mission and all of its assets. Examples of foundations that have announced commitments to 100 percent alignment of their assets with mission include Nathan Cummings Foundation[89] and F. B. Heron Foundation,[90] a pioneer in community investing.

Impact Investment Terms

(1) Sustainable and Responsible Investing (SRI)
SRI is a type of investing which seeks to consider both financial return alongside social and environmental positive social change missions. SRI can include impact investing, MRIs (or MDIs), and ESG investing or a combination of all three approaches to investing.[91]

(2) Environmental, Social and Governance (ESG)—Negative and Positive Screens
Typically, ESG investing refers to an analysis of publicly held companies around environmental, social, and governance issues.[92] However, ESG criteria may be applied to any asset class, including private equity. ESG strategies may be aimed at companies committed to specific ESG practices (i.e., positive screens) or screening for companies that minimize negative impacts (i.e., negative screens).[93]

(3) Green Bonds/Sustainable Bonds
A green bond is a bond used to fund environmentally friendly projects.[94] Green bonds can be issued by investors and corporations. For example, the World Bank

87. Mission Investors, https://missioninvestors.org/.

88. Confluence Philanthropy, https://www.confluencephilanthropy.org/.

89. *NCF Commits to 100 Percent*, The Nathan Cummings Foundation (Mar. 12, 2018), https://nathancummings.org/ncf-commits-to-100-percent/.

90. *About Us*, Heron, https://www.heron.org/about-us/.

91. Michelle Zhou, *ESG, SRI, and Impact Investing: What's the Difference?*, Investopedia (June 20, 2021), https://www.investopedia.com/financial-advisor/esg-sri-impact-investing-explaining-difference-clients/.

92. Catherine Brock, *What Is ESG Investing & What Are ESG Stocks?*, The Motley Fool (June 29, 2021), https://www.fool.com/investing/stock-market/types-of-stocks/esg-investing/.

93. *Investor Alerts and Bulletins: Environmental, Social and Governance (ESG) Funds—Investor Bulletin*, SEC (Feb. 26, 2021), https://www.sec.gov/oiea/investor-alerts-and-bulletins/environmental-social-and-governance-esg-funds-investor-bulletin.

94. Lyubov Pronina, *What Are Green Bonds and How "Green" Is Green?*, Bloomberg Businessweek (Mar. 24, 2019), https://www.bloomberg.com/news/articles/2019-03-24/what-are-green-bonds-and-how-green-is-green-quicktake.

Green Bonds, now more than a decade old, connect investors to climate change projects.[95]

(4) Pay for Success

Pay for Success (discussed in chapter 4) is a movement that began more than ten years ago in the United Kingdom with the development of the world's first SIB. Today, Pay for Success has expanded to include more than SIBs and now encompasses career impact bonds enabling career training for persons facing barriers to training, employment, and education.

Pay for Success describes a broad range of financial innovations fueling social programs based on four core principles: (1) clearly defined outcomes, (2) data-driven decision making, (3) outcomes-based payment, and (4) strong governance and accountability. Applied in the public, private, and nonprofit sectors, it can help governments better allocate tax dollars for social programs by leveraging funds from impact investors designed to scale a variety of social programs. Examples of the various social issues addressed by Pay for Success include criminal justice reforms, housing, and economic mobility.[96]

(5) Development Impact Bonds (DIBs)

Development Impact Bonds (also called Global Impact Bonds (GIBs)) build on SIBs to spur innovation and local problem solving by funding positive social outcomes and a return on investment to investors. DIB principles are aligned with the Pay for Success core principles, but the interventions are global in areas such as sustainable development and finance, government and development, migration, displacement and humanitarian concerns, and climate, energy, and environment.[97]

(6) Environmental Impact Bonds (EIBs)

Another innovative financing tool, Environmental Impact Bonds (EIBs) (discussed in chapter 5), use a Pay for Success approach to deploying private investor capital for environmental projects. EIBs use new approaches to addressing environmental issues or scaling impactful projects.[98]

Categories of Mission-Driven Private Investors

Mission-Driven Investors

Mission-driven investors, also called socially responsible investors, come in many forms. Below are the most common.

(1) Faith-Based Investors

Faith-based investors are diverse and have a long history of socially responsible investing, recognizing that investment decisions can include commitments

95. *IBRD Funding Program*, The World Bank (May 16, 2021), https://treasury.worldbank.org/en/about/unit/treasury/ibrd/ibrd-green-bonds.

96. *What Is Pay for Success?*, Soc. Fin., https://socialfinance.org/what-is-pfs/.

97. *FAQ's: Investing in Social Outcomes: Development Impact Bonds*, Center for Global Development, https://www.cgdev.org/page/investing-social-outcomes-development-impact-bonds-0 (last visited Apr. 26, 2022).

98. Quantified Ventures, https://www.quantifiedventures.com.

in many areas like climate change and good governance.[99] Globally, faith-based investments represent trillions of assets under management.[100] Faith-based investor goals can support efforts like the United Nations Sustainable Development Goals (SDGs), including poverty elimination, decent work, and economic growth and quality education.[101]

(2) Pension Funds

Pension funds have historically been considered Economically Targeted Investments (ETIs), which share aspects of impact investments, but they are different in prioritizing financial returns above social, environmental, and related impact investment criteria. For example, New York City allocates two percent of pension assets for teachers, police, and firefighters to ETIs with a goal of promoting economic development while generating risk-adjusted market rate returns. $3.9 billion has been invested since the inception of the New York ETI program.[102]

Guidance from the U.S. Department of Labor allow pension funds to make ETIs, so long as the investments are prudent.[103] Pension fund assets in the thirty-eight member countries of the Organization for Economic Co-Operation and Development (OECD)[104] are worth over $38 trillion.[105]

(3) Insurance Companies

Insurance companies are uniquely suited to impact investing because insurers have a long view of investment, patience, and flexibility to address social and environmental issues. They also have extensive investment expertise in evaluating nonfinancial outcomes alongside experience with ESG. Through their history of community investing, corporate giving, and volunteer programs, insurance companies have engaged in practices aligned with impact investing.[106]

---

99. Community Investing Toolkit for the Faith Community, Social Investment Forum Foundation, https://community-wealth.org/sites/clone.community-wealth.org/files/downloads/tool-SIF-faith-based-cmty-invest.pdf.

100. Engaging Faith-Based Investors in Impact Investing, Global Impact Investing Network (GIIN) (Jan. 2020), https://thegiin.org/assets/Engaging%20Faith-Based%20Investors%20in%20Impact%20Investing_FINAL.pdf#:~:text=The%20Global%20Impact%20Investing%20Network%20%28GIIN%29%20is%20the,the%20development%20of%20a%20coherent%20impact%20investing%20industry.

101. *The 17 Goals*, United Nations Department of Economic and Social Affairs, https://sdgs.un.org/goals (last visited Apr. 26, 2022).

102. *Pension / Investment Management: Initiatives: Economically Targeted Investments*, New York City Comptroller, https://comptroller.nyc.gov/services/financial-matters/pension/initiatives/economically-targeted-investments/.

103. Tom Woelfel & Lauren F. Dixon, *A Catalog of Economically Targeted Investments by Pension Funds: Trends, Analysis, and Reflections*, Accelerating Impact Investing Initiative (AI3) (Oct. 2016), https://www.pacificcommunityventures.org/wp-content/uploads/sites/6/2016/10/AI3-Pension-Fund-ETI-Catalog.pdf.

104. *OECD Welcomes Costa Rica as Its 38th Member*, OECD (May 25, 2021), https://www.oecd.org/newsroom/oecd-welcomes-costa-rica-as-its-38th-member.htm. "The OECD's 38 members are: Austria, Australia, Belgium, Canada, Chile, Colombia, Costa Rica, Czech Republic, Denmark, Estonia, Finland, France, Germany, Greece, Hungary, Iceland, Ireland, Israel, Italy, Japan, Korea, Latvia, Lithuania, Luxembourg, Mexico, the Netherlands, New Zealand, Norway, Poland, Portugal, Slovak Republic, Slovenia, Spain, Sweden, Switzerland, Turkey, the United Kingdom and the United States." *Id.*

105. *Housing Finance: Investment Opportunities for Pension Funds*, World Bank Grp. (2018), https://documents1.worldbank.org/curated/en/405421551711776551/pdf/128295-REVISED-Housing-Finance-Investment-Opportunities-for-Pension-Funds-FINAL.pdf.

106. Pauliina Swartz, *Insurance Companies and Impact Investing*, Bos. Univ. Inst. for Sustainable Energy (Jan. 29, 2021), https://www.bu.edu/ise/2021/01/19/insurance-companies-and-impact-investing/.

To address the racial wealth gap, in 2021, New York Life, America's largest mutual life insurance company, announced a $1 billion, three-year, impact investment initiative to help undercapitalized and underserved communities. The insurance company will partner with CDFIs and other mission-driven organizations to support community development, small businesses, and affordable housing.[107]

(4) High-Net-Worth Individuals

Impact investing and sustainability have become priorities as younger generations of high-net-worth individuals take leadership of family businesses.[108] One report found that 27 percent of investors with over $1 million in investible assets had an interest in sustainability while 40 percent of ultra-high-net-worth investors with over $30 million of investible assets were interested in sustainability.[109]

(5) Family Offices

The U.S. Securities and Exchange Commission defines family offices as "entities established by wealthy families to manage their wealth and provide other services to families, such as tax and estate planning services."[110] The UBS Global Family Office Report found that one-fourth of family offices make impact investments and 81 percent of these investments met or exceeded investment goals. Common areas of impact included energy, agriculture, and education.[111] Impact investing is a natural fit for family offices because they can engage in creative financing, be flexible in making investment decisions, do not have the financial return constraints placed on institutional investors like venture capital firms, and have leaner structures for decision making. Examples of family offices making impact investments include Omidyar Network (Pierre Omidyar Single Family Office) and Blue Haven Initiative (Simmons Single Family Office).

(6) Foundations

Broadly stated, a foundation provides grants to 501(c)(3) public charities, but some foundations may also actively direct nonprofit charitable and educational programs, as private operating foundations.[112]

Federal law requires endowed foundations to spend at least 5 percent of their assets a year on grantmaking and most foundations meet this requirement and no more, through earnings on their investments. This leaves 95 percent or up to 100 percent of foundation assets in place with an intention for these assets to remain in perpetuity.

---

107. *New York Life launches $1 billion impact investment initiative to address racial wealth gap by investing in underserved and undercapitalized communities over next three years*, N.Y. Life (Apr. 27, 2021), https://www.newyorklife.com/newsroom/2021/impact-investment-initiative.

108. Zircon Group, *Meeting the Changing Expectations of High-Net-Worth Individuals*, Forbes (June 1, 2021), https://www.forbes.com/sites/zircongroup/2021/06/01/meeting-the-changing-expectations-of-high-net-worth-individuals/?sh=125492893001.

109. Id.

110. *Family Office: A Small Entity Compliance Guide*, U.S. Sec. and Exch. Comm'n, https://www.sec.gov/rules/final/2011/ia-3220-secg.htm.

111. Anne Field, *Why Impact Investing Is a Natural Fit for Family Offices*, Impactivate (June 30, 2020), https://www.theimpactivate.com/why-impact-investing-is-a-natural-fit-for-family-offices/.

112. *Foundation Basics*, Council on Foundations, https://www.cof.org/content/foundation-basics (last visited Apr. 26, 2022).

Foundations make grants and contributions to projects or organizations with no expectation of repayment and in exchange for a tax break. Grantmaking 501(c)(3)s are also generally not taxed on any profit they generate. There are numerous restrictions and requirements for maintaining this tax exempt status. The Internal Revenue Service distinguishes private foundations from public charities, and there are strict requirements for each. A private foundation is generally created by a single individual, a small group of individuals, or a business while a public charity receives direct support for its initiatives through publicly collected funds.[113]

It is noteworthy that some foundations recognize the importance and urgency of MDIs to further racial equity. By 2050, people of color will comprise half the U.S. population and half of them will be working age. They also recognize a clear reality: racial equity in all forms—economic, educational, political, and social—will be required.[114]

(7) Endowments

A financial endowment is a donation of money to a nonprofit in which the investment income is used for a specific purpose as determined by the donor.[115] Private foundations with endowments can use their endowments as vehicles for impact investing.

(8) Corporations

Some large corporations that are not Benefit Corporations organized under state corporate laws may be mission-driven. For example, Warby Parker, the U.S.-based eyeglasses retailer, is a publicly traded company, with B-Corp Certification but its business strategy of "buy a pair-give a pair" supports its mission "to inspire and impact the world with vision, purpose, and style (without charging a premium for it)."[116] Other large corporations may brand themselves as mission-driven through corporate social responsibility departments.[117]

---

113. *Public Charities*, Internal Revenue Serv. (July 1, 2021), https://www.irs.gov/charities-non-profits/charitable-organizations/public-charities.

114. *Mission Driven Investments*, W.K. Kellogg Found., https://www.wkkf.org/what-we-do/mission-driven-investments.

115. James Chen, *Endowment Fund*, Investopedia (June 3, 2021), https://www.investopedia.com/terms/e/endowment-fund.asp.

116. Gennaro Cuifano, *How Does Warby Parker Make Money? Warby Parker Business Model in a Nutshell*, FourWeekMBA (Oct. 10, 2021), https://fourweekmba.com/warby-parker-business-model/.

117. Digital Marketing Institute, *16 Brands Doing Corporate Social Responsibility Successfully*, Digital Marketing Institute (Sept. 1, 2021), https://digitalmarketinginstitute.com/blog/corporate-16-brands-doing-corporate-social-responsibility-successfully.

Chapter 3
Opportunity Zones: The Promise and the Potential for Peril

Lisa Green Hall, Perry Teicher, and Carolyn Kim Allwin

Introduction

Opportunity Zones are one of the most controversial community investment tools of the twenty-first century, serving as a tool to drive billions of dollars of capital to low-income communities and as a tax windfall for the wealthy. According to the Economic Innovation Group's analysis, more than 6 trillion dollars[1] in unrealized capital gains were cited as available for Opportunity Zone investments. This amount has no doubt been impacted by COVID and the election of President Biden in the years since the program started. But even at a lower amount, the potential capital that could be allocated to this program makes it one of the most significant programs attempting to catalyze capital for low-income communities in a generation. Analysts from across the ideological and nonpartisan spectrum estimate that between $85 billion and $100 billion of new capital investment could be generated as a result of this program, a dramatic pass-through of potential capital being driven into low-income neighborhoods.

1. *Opportunity Zones: Tapping into a $6 Trillion Market*, Economic Innovation Group Blog (Mar. 21, 2018), https://eig.org/news/opportunity-zones-tapping-6-trillion-market.

While the anticipated financial impact is likely to be powerful, a key outstanding question is "who benefits?" Will communities themselves, largely communities of color and historically marginalized populations and geographies, see the economic, social, and environmental benefits or will the program be yet another wealth transfer on the backs of these communities, stripping assets while clothed under a cloak of doing good?

Background and Original Intention

Enacted as part of the 2017 Tax Cuts and Jobs Act (the "Jobs Act"), the Opportunity Zone provisions empowered governors (and corresponding executives) across all fifty states, the District of Columbia, and territories to designate low-income census tracts as "Opportunity Zones," designed to provide an incentive structure for U.S. taxpayers to invest capital gains into these distressed areas in exchange for a tax deferral. Opportunity Zones stand on the tradition of other community development strategies, including New Market, Low-Income Housing, Historic Tax Credits, and other local incentivization strategies. While not solely framed as community development strategy, based on legislative history and related development of the concept, Opportunity Zones are intended as an additional—and particularly powerful—tool in the movement for effective and scalable community impact across the United States.

As part of the Jobs Act, Opportunity Zones were a tool intended to promote economic recovery in low-income communities by driving long-term investment capital into designated low-income areas across the United States. Specifically, investing in Opportunity Zones results in tax deferments, and for long-term investments, an elimination of taxes to investors in designated low-income census tracts. Investors who realize capital gains on currently held assets and invest those gains in a "Qualified Opportunity Zone" (QOZ) receive a deferral and reduction of taxes on these gains and an elimination of taxes on further gains on their investments over a ten-year holding period. The benefit can be combined with existing tax programs like the New Markets Tax Credit and Low-Income Housing Tax Credits, and local policy tools like Tax Increment Districts and Tax Abatement programs.[2] Rarely does the tax code offer such an opportunity to reduce and eliminate taxes on an otherwise taxable event.

The Opportunity Zone legislation can be traced back to a bipartisan proposal by Senator Corey Booker (D-NJ), Senator Tim Scott (R-SC), Congressmen Pat Tiberi (R-OH), and Ron Kind (D-WI), who introduced the Investing in Opportunity Act in April 2016[3] to help revitalize economically distressed communities which suffer from a lack of investment and business growth. A major difference between the enacted policy and the original proposal was the stripping of required social outcome reporting, including a requirement to collect and report on employment data. The conceptual genesis emerged from the Economic Innovation Group, a bipartisan public policy group dedicated to advancing solutions that empower entrepreneurs and investors to forge a more dynamic economy throughout America. And the idea of special treatment for capital gains in low-income communities dates back more than thirty years ago to 1998 when Senators J. C. Watts (R-OK), Jim Talent

2. Novogradac & Company LLP, Novogradac Special Reports: Low-Income Housing Tax Credit Showcase, https://www.novoco.com/sites/default/files/atoms/files/novogradac_lihtc_showcase_0.pdf.
3. Investing in Opportunity Act, S. 2868, 114th Cong. (2016).

(R-MO), and Danny Davis (D-IL) proposed the idea of American Renewal Communities which would have a tax exemption for capital gains. The development and implementation of Opportunity Zones in the Jobs Act was part of a multiyear approach, stemming from a recognition of historical disinvestment in certain communities, lack of effective government or private investment to ameliorate challenges, and substantial, "hidden" capital gains.

The inclusion of Opportunity Zones in the Jobs Act was unanticipated but welcome by most community development advocates. However, in the process of moving to a final bill, the original language from the Investing in Opportunity Act which required data collection and reporting on social benefits, such as employment metrics, was removed from the final statutory language. Policy makers hope for a technical corrections bill to address the desire of the original sponsors to include impact reporting requirements. Since the Jobs Act passed in 2017, there have been a series of subsequent bills intended to provide additional reporting requirements, including the IMPACT Act,[4] intended to provide "robust and granular analysis" of outcomes, the Opportunity Zone Reporting and Reform Act, and the Opportunity Zone Accountability and Transparency Act, each of which takes a slightly different approach in providing additional reporting and transparency for outcomes.[5] There was also a bill, HR 6890, introduced in September 2018 by Mark Meadows (R-NC) to allow for the designation of Opportunity Zones every ten years, effectively perpetually renewing the incentive that was part of the original tax reform legislation.

Designation of Opportunity Zones

The tax legislation authorized governors to nominate 25 percent of their states' low-income census tracts for designation as Opportunity Zones by March 21, 2018, or to submit a one-month extension to April 21, 2018. Low-income census tracts are defined by one of two criteria: median incomes that are less than 50 percent of area median income or a poverty rate of 20 percent or more. All fifty states plus the District of Columbia and all territories met these deadlines; 100 percent of low-income census tracts in Puerto Rico were automatically designated as Opportunity Zones, in recognition of the need for reinvestment there following Hurricane Maria. In total, 42,176 low-income census tracts across the nation were eligible to be designated, including the designation of contiguous census tracts. By June 14, 2018, the Internal Revenue Service had certified approximately 8,762 census tracts as Opportunity Zones in all fifty states, the District of Columbia, and five U.S. territories.[6] The existing legislation does not provide for any new census tracts to be designated as Opportunity Zones. However, there is no limit on the amount of equity capital that can be invested so long as the money was generated from the sale of an appreciated asset. In contrast, a program like the New Markets Tax Credit has a fixed, limited allocation on an annual basis and any type of equity capital can be invested.

---

4. *Scott, Grassley, Colleagues Introduce Expanded Bill on Opportunity Zone Reporting Requirements*, Tim Scott: Press Release (Dec. 6, 2019), https://www.scott.senate.gov/media-center/press-releases/scott-grassley-colleagues-introduce-expanded-bill-on-opportunity-zone-reporting-requirements.

5. *Why the Newly Introduced Opportunity Zone Reporting Bills Are a Win for Transparency*, NES Financial Blog (Nov. 7, 2019), https://nesfinancial.com/why-the-newly-introduced-opportunity-zone-reporting-bills-are-a-win-for-transparency.

6. *See Treasury, IRS Announce Final Round of Opportunity Zone Designations*, U.S. Dep't. of Treasury, https://home.treasury.gov/news/press-releases/sm0414 (last visited Apr. 5, 2021).

The Demographics of Opportunity Zones[7]

The intention of the original Opportunity Zone legislation was to empower states by delegating the responsibility for selecting zones to governors, acknowledging that local officials closest to the ground know what is best for their own communities in each of their states. The goal was to limit federal regulation of Opportunity Zones and eliminate the potential for intervention by federal officials, in order to encourage free market behavior and activity. States were not only empowered in the selection of Opportunity Zones but also have full responsibility and authority for how Opportunity Zones will be implemented on a local level. Some states view the new tax provision as an unfunded mandate which they must manage without additional resources. However, most states have taken on the challenge of implementation as a chance to attract new private investment capital to areas and communities that have been underserved and underinvested for years.

Although the IRS was responsible for certifying the nominations made by states, the final result for designated Opportunity Zones matched closely with the states' selections. Not surprisingly, designated tracts have higher poverty rates, higher unemployment, higher percentage of people of color, and lower income than the United States overall. A total of 8,762 zones were designated and of these, 8,532 (97 percent) were low-income communities. The remaining 3 percent comprise adjacent communities. Within the zones, 39.57 percent of residents identify as white, 24.04 percent as Black, 29.93 percent as Hispanic, and 2.92 percent as Asian American and Pacific Islander; 23.60 percent of residents are below the age of eighteen and 13.61 percent are above the age of sixty-four. More than three-quarters of designated census tracts fall within metropolitan areas, but Opportunity Zones are split between urban zip codes and rural ones.

Governors prioritized selecting the most economically distressed communities. Designated Opportunity Zones have an average poverty rate of 31 percent, which is higher than originally envisioned by the 20 percent eligibility threshold.[8] The average median family income is also lower than the requisite 80 percent,[9] with a median household income averaging $33,345. A similar indication that governors skewed their designations to high-need areas is the overall poverty rate of 31.75 percent which far exceeds the minimum of 20 percent needed to be considered an eligible census tract for designation. With an unemployment rate of 13.41 percent, more than four times the national unemployment rate of 3.7 percent, areas designated as Opportunity Zones stand to benefit immensely from newly mobilized equity.[10]

The designated Opportunity Zones as a whole are also ripe for sustainable growth, with more than 1.5 million existing places of businesses and 24 million jobs; 75 percent of Opportunity Zones are located in zip codes that experienced at least some level of

7. *See Metropolitan Housing and Communities Policy Center*, Urban Institute, https://www.urban.org/policy-centers/metropolitan-housing-and-communities-policy-center/projects/opportunity-zones (last visited Apr. 2, 2021). *See also* Enterprise Community Partner's 360Partners: Opportunity microsite360, https://www.enterprisecommunity.org/opportunity360 (last visited Apr. 2, 2021).

8. *Opportunity Zones*, U.S. Congressman PatrickMcHenry, https://mchenry.house.gov/constituentservices/opportunity-zones.htm.

9. Source: *Opportunity Zones: The Map Comes into Focus*, Economic Innovation Group Blog (June 15, 2018), https://eig.org/news/opportunity-zones-map-comes-focus.

10. *Investing for Impact: Real Estate Convening on Opportunity Zones*, Georgetown University: The Beeck Center (Nov. 8, 2018), https://beeckcenter.georgetown.edu/investing-impact-real-estate-convening-opportunity-zones/.

post-recession employment growth from 2011 to 2015.[11] In states such as Minnesota and Alaska, governors included set-asides for tribal areas to be designated as Opportunity Zones. It is difficult to identify all the tribal areas that were selected; however, some have suggested that somewhere between 300 and 400 census tracts are located within (or contiguous to) tribal jurisdictional areas and have been designated as Opportunity Zones.[12] Opportunity Zone designations represent a substantial opportunity for a significant cross-section of Indian Country which have been historically underinvested and distressed communities.

A Special Case for Puerto Rico: Almost the entirety of Puerto Rico is an Opportunity Zone. As outlined in the Jobs Act, 100 percent of low-income census tracts in Puerto Rico are designated as Opportunity Zones. Like many jurisdictions, Puerto Rico has a complex dynamic with regard to Opportunity Zones. On one hand, the influx of capital could provide substantial and meaningful infrastructure improvements. On the other hand, Puerto Rico does not just have a lack of capital but rather a disconnected financial ecosystem that flows capital and proceeds to investors outside of Puerto Rico rather than the community itself. While a number of projects have aimed to support the island's economic ecosystem, given the substantial debt load, legal challenges with regard to restructuring, and political realities, these initiatives have not yet resulted in the robust entrepreneurial ecosystem many would envision. With this framing, Opportunity Zones, rather than catalyzing a regenerative, circular ecosystem on the island, have the potential to create redundant, extractive financial systems.[13] While this is not a given, Opportunity Zones need to address these issues in Puerto Rico (as well as similarly situated areas).

The Mechanics of the Tax Incentive

Overview

The first step in any Opportunity Zone investment is the realization and recognition of a capital gain. This gain may come from the sale of stock, real estate partnership interests, or other property. The Proposed Regulations released by the U.S. Treasury on October 19, 2018, clarified that the Opportunity Zone incentive applies to capital gains specifically versus other types of gains. Eligible taxpayers who can defer taxation on these capital gains under the Opportunity Zone statute include:

- Individuals
- Corporations
- Real Estate Investment Trusts (REITs)
- Partnerships
- Trusts and estates

---

11. *Source: Opportunity Zones: The Map Comes into Focus*, Economic Innovation Group Blog (June 15, 2018), https://eig.org/news/opportunity-zones-map-comes-focus.

12. *Source:* Nancy Pindus and Brady Meixell, "Why Opportunity Zones Are Important for Indian Country" (June 7, 2018), *Why Opportunity Zones Are Important for Indian Country*, Urban Institute Blog: Urban Wire: Economic Growth and Productivity (June 7, 2018), https://www.urban.org/urban-wire/why-opportunity-zones-are-important-indian-country.

13. Luis Gallardo, *Why Puerto Ricans Fear Opportunity Zones*, Next City (July 2, 2020), https://nextcity.org/daily/entry/why-puerto-ricans-fear-opportunity-zones.

- Common trust funds under Section 584
- Qualified settlement funds
- Disputed ownership funds
- Other entities taxable under Section 1.4688

It is perhaps obvious, but important to note that entities that do not pay U.S. taxes are not eligible to receive any tax benefit from investing in Opportunity Zones. These organizations include municipalities (states, cities, towns, and counties), nonprofit organizations with 501(c)(3) tax-exempt status, pension funds, private foundations, public charities, and community foundations.

In order to receive the benefit under the legislation, once a taxpayer has recognized a capital gain, the taxpayer must invest the gain in a "Qualified Opportunity Fund" (QOF) within 180 days of the recognition (or "realization") event. A QOF is an investment vehicle that is set up either as a partnership or corporation for investing in eligible property that is located in a QOF. A QOF can be any corporate or partnership form used for federal income tax purposes, including a limited liability company, a limited liability partnership, and an REIT. A QOF must be created or organized in one of the fifty U.S. states, Washington, DC, or a U.S. possession.

A taxpayer cannot invest directly in a property, even if it is in a QOZ. In order to receive a deferral of tax on the realized capital gains, the taxpayer must invest in QOF which in turn invests in a business or property located in a QOZ (such business or property, a "QOZB"). The QOF self-certifies and is not required to disclose its existence, other than when it completes the Form 8996, the QOF Form, for its federal income tax return. There is no minimum or maximum amount for an investment in a QOF. There are prohibitions against investment in traditional federal "sin businesses": gaming, including a racetrack or other facility used for gambling, private or commercial golf course, country club, massage parlor, hot tub facility, suntan facility, or any store the principal business of which is the sale of alcoholic beverages for consumption off premises.

A QOF then makes an equity investment in a QOZB. The regulations clarify that only equity investments are permissible investments. However, in addition to common stock, investments in QOFs include preferred stock, profits interest, or partnership interests with special allocations. A QOF must hold 90 percent of its assets in a QOZB. Failure to comply results in a penalty.

A QOZB may also not have more than 5 percent of its assets in the form of nonqualified financial property, which effectively includes debt instruments or loans. The intent of this provision was to exclude conventional financial institutions, like traditional commercial and investment banks, or market-rate investment vehicles, like hedge funds or payday lenders, that can be highly profitable without a subsidy, from benefitting from federal tax incentives. Unfortunately, this provision also excludes "Community Development Financial Institutions" ("CDFI"), which in order to be financially viable are subsidized by operating support from the U.S. Treasury through the CDFI Fund and fees from programs like the New Markets Tax Credit Program. There are some advocates who believe that CDFIs should not be included in this exclusion for what is considered a QOZB.[14]

14. Opportunity Zones, Milken Institute: Center for Financial Markets, https://assets1c.milkeninstitute.org/assets/Events/Forum/2016/Image/FINAL-Milken-Institute-Opportunity-Zone-Overview-and-Recommendations.pdf (last visited Apr. 2, 2021).

If a taxpayer holds its investment in a QOF for ten or more years, the taxpayer is permanently exempt from capital gains from the sale of his or her interest in the QOF. However, taxes must still be paid on the original capital gain and are only deferred, depending on how long the taxpayer is invested in the QOF. If the investment is held for five years, then the capital gains liability on the original investment will be reduced by 10 percent; if it is held for seven years, then the capital gains liability will be reduced by 15 percent after seven years. After ten years, the taxes on any new capital gains generated from the Opportunity Fund investment are reduced to zero.

Using Public Subsidies and Tax Credits in Opportunity Zones

Investments structured as Opportunity Zones are eligible to receive and take part in other tax credit programs on a municipal, state, and federal level. In particular, certain states have developed various initiative programs to further catalyze investments in Opportunity Zones and regions adjacent to Opportunity Zones. Importantly, a number of states and regions have recognized that real estate investments in themselves are not sufficient to create the outcomes which local communities are often seeking. Instead, while operating within the Opportunity Zone framework, municipalities have recognized that additional support is often necessary to focus investments in a more meaningful manner. For example, although not a part of the Jobs Act itself, various cities are attempting to support community ownership models and strategies to share wealth creation opportunities beyond investors. This could include models of land trusts, community ownership trusts, and other mechanisms.[15]

Regulatory Clarifications

Initial Regulations

Since the Jobs Act was passed and the initial Proposed Regulations were released, the regulations went through the standard rulemaking process. On October 19, 2018, Proposed Regulations were released by the U.S. Treasury clarifying many questions raised by investors and community stakeholders in numerous comment letters.[16]

In response to the initial set of Proposed Regulations, many more formal comment letters were submitted by the deadline of December 28, 2018, and a hearing, postponed by the 2018 government shutdown, was eventually held by the IRS on February 14, 2019, with a standing room only audience.[17] Over the course of the regulatory development, at least 175 comment letters were provided by interested parties.[18]

The proposed regulation clarified a number of issues which were making it difficult for investors to proceed with the creation of Opportunity Funds and actual investments. The primary issues covered by the regulations are outlined herein. The regulations were well

---

15. Ben Bartlett & Matt Napoli, *A Community Blueprint for Opportunity Zones*, Meeting of the Minds (Aug. 8, 2019), https://meetingoftheminds.org/a-community-blueprint-for-opportunity-zones-30896.
16. *Treasury, IRS Issue Proposed Regulations on New Opportunity Zone Tax Incentive*, IRS (Oct. 19, 2018), https://www.irs.gov/newsroom/treasury-irs-issue-proposed-regulations-on-new-opportunity-zone-tax-incentive.
17. Jimmy Atkinson, *Recap of Feb 14 IRS Public Hearing on Opportunity Zones*, The Opportunity Zones Database (Feb. 16, 2019), https://opportunitydb.com/2019/02/recap-of-feb-14-irs-public-hearing-on-opportunity-zones/.
18. *Opportunity Zone Comment Letters*, CRE Models, https://www.cremodels.com/opportunity-zone-comment-letters/ (last visited Apr. 2, 2021).

received by real estate investors in particular, many of whom proceeded with plans to invest in Opportunity Zones based on this guidance.

(1) For an investment vehicle to be qualified as a QOF, at least 90 percent of assets must be invested in Opportunity Zone business property which can include an investment in an Opportunity Zone business that owns such property or a direct investment in such property. This means that up to 10 percent of a fund may invest outside of an Opportunity Zone, in contiguous or noncontiguous property or even in intangible assets. This leaves open interesting possibilities for investment in supporting entities, like CDFIs, many of which are located in Opportunity Zones, but cannot be considered Opportunity Zone business due to the 5 percent limit on financial assets.

(2) QOFs must "substantially improve" a property in the amount of its basis (roughly the acquisition cost) in order for an investment in an Opportunity Zone property to be a permissible investment. The Proposed Regulations clarify that land may be excluded from the basis in calculating substantial improvement. The result of this regulation is that it will be easier for developers to meet a substantial improvement test, especially for new construction and in high-cost areas. This test will be hard to meet, however, when applied to moderate rehabilitation projects, or even some gut rehabilitation projects, especially in high-cost areas.

(3) The Proposed Regulations also allow for a working capital safe harbor of up to thirty-one months for the QOF to invest in businesses that acquire, construct, or rehabilitate tangible business property, which will be particularly helpful for construction and gut rehabilitation transactions. This provision also requires that the intended uses are designated in writing, there is a reasonable written schedule, and the working capital is used consistent with the designated uses.

Tranche II Regulations

On May 1, 2019, the IRS released another set of regulations meant to clarify how investments can be made in operating businesses in Opportunity Zones.

Final Regulations

The changes introduced in the Final Regulations were intended to encourage investment in operating business and commingled funds, which have long been a focus on furthering the intersection of Opportunity Zones and community investment.[19]

The Final Regulations included more flexible qualifying rules, which could lead to investments in operating businesses.

A QOZB is a trade or business that meets each of the following requirements: At least 70 percent (i.e., "substantially all") of the tangible property owned or leased in connection with the QOZB's trade or business must be QOZB Property. This 70 percent requirement is intended to provide an incentive for QOFs to invest in QOZBs rather than directly into QOZP,

19. Subsequent section supported from Richard Chirls et al., *Final Tax Regulations Offer More Certainty to Opportunity Zone Fund Managers and Investors*, Orrick (Feb. 4, 2020), https://www.orrick.com/en/Insights/2020/02/Final-Tax-Regulations-Offer-More-Certainty-to-Opportunity-Zone-Fund-Managers-and-Investors.

as all of a QOF's investment in QOZP must otherwise qualify (not just 70 percent). In addition, under the Final Regulations, if entered into at market rates and valued pursuant to the Final Regulations, leased property can now qualify as QOZB Property (unless the lessor is a state, city, or tribal nation, where market rates are not required).

Tangible property held in connection with a QOZB must either be "original use" or if not original use, "substantially improved" (i.e., improvements equal in value to the tax basis of the tangible property must be made by the QOZB). This "substantial improvement" test can be satisfied on an aggregate basis rather than on an asset-by-asset basis if the assets (1) are in the same QOZ, (2) are used in the same trade or business, and (3) improve the functionality of the property to be improved. Brownfields and land vacant for at least one year are generally exempted from the "substantial improvement" test and treated as original use. However, property that becomes vacant in a designated QOZ must be vacant for three years in order to be treated as original use property. This looser interpretation of the substantial improvement rules may provide more comfort to operating businesses, in terms of measuring this requiring and managing vacant property.

The Final Regulations also loosed certain operating tests, required by the QOZB:

(1) At least half of the QOZB's total gross income must be derived from the active conduct of the trade or business in the QOZ. This test can be satisfied based on the location of (a) employees (including independent contractors), based on hours worked or compensation; (b) management; (c) key tangible assets; or on a more general set of facts and circumstances. This broader set of tests provides an opportunity for a broader set of businesses, including operating, early-stage, and manufacturing operations to be capitalized through an OZ investment.

(2) At least 40 percent (i.e., a "substantial portion") of the QOZB's intangible property must be used in the active conduct of the trade or business in the QOZ. Intangible property is treated as used in an active trade or business if the use is normal, usual, or customary in the conduct of the trade or business and the intangible property is used by the business to generate gross income in the QOZ.

(3) Less than 5 percent of the average of the QOZB's aggregate unadjusted bases of the property must be attributable to nonqualified financial property (e.g., cash and cash equivalents). Clarifying the business plan safe harbor set forth in the Proposed Regulations, the Final Regulations explained that the thirty-one-month spending period can be applied to a start-up operating business and that, if the investment includes capital contributions over multiple tranches, this period can be extended to sixty-two months.

While a QOZB cannot be a "sin business," such as a massage parlor, tanning salon, tattoo parlor, liquor store, or golf course, the Final Regulations permit a small portion of assets (i.e., less than 5 percent) to be allocated to these activities, if a part of a larger development. For example, a hotel development could include a tanning salon as part of the spa facilities.

Clarity for Commingled Funds and Multitiered Investment Strategies

The approach set forth in the Proposed Regulations—requiring that a QOF investor could only elect, after a ten-year holding period, to exclude gains from the sale of qualifying investments or capital gain property sold by a QOF operating in partnership or S corporation form, but not property sold by its QOZB—limited the formation of commingled funds invested in multiple properties or businesses, due to the challenge of planning a tax-free exit by the QOF for multiple assets at the same time at a future point. The Final Regulations provide a more effective structure, allowing capital gains from the sale of property by a QOZB that is held by such a QOF to be excluded from income as long as the investor's qualifying investment in the QOF has been held for ten years. The amount of gain from such QOF's or its QOZB's asset sales that an investor in the QOF may elect to exclude each year will reduce the amount of the investor's interest in the QOF that remains a qualifying QOF investment eligible for further QOF tax benefits.

Disposition by QOF Investors of Stakes in Multi-Asset Funds

The Proposed Regulations made the tax exemption available only upon disposition by a QOF after the ten-year holding period. However, in a typical QOF sale, a portion of the gain would not be capital gain and thereby would potentially reduce the QOZ tax benefits as compared to a sale by the QOF investor of its interests in the QOF. This could lead to structuring issues for a QOF with multiple properties or QOZBs. The Final Regulations expand the proposed rules by providing for gain exclusion for asset sales. In particular, a taxpayer that invests in a QOF partnership or S corporation is permitted to make an election for each taxable year to exclude a QOF's gains and losses from all sales or exchanges in the taxable year, rather than just capital gains or losses. Thus, the Final Regulations more appropriately align the QOZ tax benefits on a sale by a QOF with the benefits on a sale by the QOF investor of its QOF interests, providing more flexibility for multi-asset QOFs to sell underlying assets, businesses, and real estate projects.

Distributions

To the extent an investor's basis has been stepped up in an amount sufficient to cover certain distributions (such as partnership tax allocations of profit and loss, allocations of leverage, or payment of 2026 deferred tax), certain distributions by a QOF to its investors may qualify for the exemption, and certain interim distributions offered prior to the end of the ten-year holding period may be made tax-free.

Multitier Investment; Investment by Members of a Consolidated Group

Any U.S. taxpayer, including any member of a corporate consolidated group, seeking to obtain the tax benefits offered by the OZ program must invest directly into a QOF rather than through an intermediary such as a Fund of Funds that might act to aggregate investors' capital gains for the purpose of investment in QOFs.

Although the Final Regulations provided a guidance generally favorable to promoting a broader swatch of OZ investment strategies, issues such as integration of partnership tax accounting rules with OZ accounting, Foreign Investment in Real Property Tax Act (FIRPTA) withholding tax, compliance, and violations of the tests remain not fully resolved and subject to further development based on practice and potential further IRS clarification.

The Potential for a Shared Impact Framework for Opportunity Zones

The Opportunity Zone Framework

Opportunity Zones represent a unique chance to build out shared impact frameworks that could be applied to all placed-based impact investing. A collaboration between the Beeck Center at Georgetown University, the U.S. Impact Investing Alliance, and the Federal Reserve Bank of New York resulted in a gathering of impact management professionals in July 2018. The convening focused on transparency as a hallmark of any healthy marketplace. Participants advocated for collection of baseline data which led to creation of the proposed shared impact framework. There has also been a call to action around authentic engagement with communities about their needs, strengths, and impact objectives.

The work which began at this convening resulted in the release of Guiding Principles and a Reporting Framework in February 2019.[20] The Principles and Reporting Framework has been well received by investors and community stakeholders.[21]

The five principles outlined in the framework are as follows:

(1) *Community Engagement:* Opportunity Fund investors should request that fund managers integrate the needs of local communities into the formation and implementation of the funds, reaching low-income and underinvested communities with attention to diversity.

(2) *Equity:* Opportunity Fund investments should seek to generate equitable community benefits, leverage other incentives, and aim for responsible exits.

(3) *Transparency:* Opportunity Fund investors should be transparent and hold themselves accountable, with processes and practices that remain fair and clear.

(4) *Measurement:* Opportunity Fund investors should voluntarily monitor, measure, and track progress against specific impact objectives, identifying key outcome measures and allowing for continuous improvement.

(5) *Outcomes:* Opportunity Fund metrics should track real change, with an understanding that both quantitative and qualitative measures are valuable indicators of progress.

Potential for a Legislative Fix

Recognizing that not all Opportunity Funds will choose to incorporate impact into their investment strategy, some Opportunity Funds are setting impact objectives prior to deploying funds. The original authors of the Opportunity Zone legislation intended for the tax incentive to be married with a minimally viable level of impact reporting. At hearings held by the Joint Economic Committee of Congress, both Senator Scott and Senator Booker

---

20. *See about*: *The OZ Reporting Framework*, OZ Framework, https://ozframework.org/about-index (last visited Apr. 2, 2021). *See also* Beeck Center, Prioritizing and Achieving Impact in Opportunity Zones, https://static1.squarespace.com/static/5c5484d70b77bd4a9a0e8c34/t/5d1144358bc6b10001a5af3f/1561412661497/Opportunity+Zones+Reporting+Framework+-+June+2019.pdf (last visited Apr. 2, 2021).

21. *Id.*

spoke about their original vision for the bill which was known in initial form as the Investing in Opportunity Act.[22]

At the hearing, the Senators along with leading impact investing experts advocated for transparency to ensure accountability around impact. At a minimum, funds should go beyond self-certification and disclose to communities if they are operating in an Opportunity Zone. All the testimony at the hearing encouraged funds to report transaction-level information, such as where funds have invested, how much they have invested, and what types of investments they have made.

If the incentive is to be viewed as a success, there will need to be data demonstrating the results of investments. Any chance of extending the Opportunity Zone legislation will almost certainly require some proof of concept around impact. Some even envision that technical corrections could be made to the existing bill which would require Opportunity Funds to share the type of data encouraged by and utilized by community development practitioners. In the meantime, mission-driven investors along with public sector players in Opportunity Zone Funds demand information from Opportunity Funds about their impact management and measurement. Accordingly, Opportunity Funds that want to access capital from the growing impact investing marketplace will benefit from having an impact framework in place.

Practical Application for Opportunity Zones

Early Movers in Opportunity Zone Investments

Real Estate

Real estate investors lined up early on to begin realizing capital gains and re-investing their profits into Opportunity Funds. In many cases, as early as the end of 2017, developers created single asset Opportunity Funds to capitalize on the tax incentive for projects already in their pipeline that were shovel-ready. In this sense, the Opportunity Zone benefit did not immediately catalyze new projects that would not have already happened without the legislation. However, since 2018, there have been an increasing number of real estate funds and real estate developers focused on Opportunity Zones that expanded their capital raise or shifted their investment strategies based on the legislation. COVID and the change in the U.S. presidential administration have delayed some of these efforts, and the first movers and fund managers also found the initial set of regulations to be limiting for multi-asset vehicles.

Nonetheless, the real estate community has been an early adopter for several reasons:

(1) To maximize the benefit of the tax incentive, Opportunity Funds must be invested in Zones for ten years. As a long-term asset class, real estate is uniquely suited for the expected tenor of an investment in an Opportunity Zone.

(2) Real estate is a fixed asset and cannot be moved out of an Opportunity Zone, thus limiting concerns about asset mobility and increasing the life span of these projects so that they can best serve their respective communities.

---

22. *The Promise of Opportunity Zones: Hearing before the J. Econ. Comm.*, 115th Cong. (2018) (statement of Hon. Tim Scott, U.S. Sen. S.C., et al.).

(3) There is an extensive network of tax accountants and attorneys, who for decades have supported other real-estate-based tax programs in low-income communities, including the New Markets Tax Credit, the Historic Tax Credit, and the Low-Income Housing Tax Credits. These professionals rallied quickly to assist their clients in real estate to mobilize and utilize the Opportunity Zone incentive.

A list of Opportunity Funds being tracked by Novogradac, a leading tax accounting firm, can be found on the firm's website.[23]

Catalyst Opportunity Funds was among the first to launch a fund, led by a thought leader in the Opportunity Zone fund legislation, Jeremy Keele, and seeded by Utah entrepreneur and philanthropist Jim Sorenson. Catalyst Opportunity Funds is a double bottom-line private equity firm focused on making high-impact Opportunity Zone investments in small and midsize markets throughout the United States. Catalyst raised $125 million to invest in underutilized real estate into high-impact office, residential, and retail spaces within neighborhoods that offer potential but lack capital investment and quality development.

Early movers like Catalyst recognized the need to efficiently launch within the OZ regulations' time constraints and to partner with real estate developers that had shovel-ready projects and "community curation."[24] Catalyst uniquely recognized upfront that to make the impact real estate investments successful, it would be essential to involve all community leaders. They established the notion of a "community curation" leader, well respected and integrated into the community for decades, who could act as a spokesperson and a voice for the community's needs and make recommendations to the developers. Notably, such a community curator could even prior to project development have a list of prospective tenants such as a barbershop, interactive art spaces for children, tech incubators for African American entrepreneurs—curating what will be well received by the community.

Given the fund's deep roots and relationships in the state, Utah was the natural starting point for Catalyst to start breaking ground on its first two projects: "INDUSTRY SLC" and "Pickle and Hide." Both of these properties are located in blighted, industrial neighborhoods near downtown Salt Lake City. INDUSTRY SLC will offer office spaces and an entrepreneurial ecosystem, consisting of community and event space, amenity areas for local businesses, and residential workforce housing. Pickle and Hide will create an impact and innovation campus with office and retail spaces, social centers, outdoor gardens, and community event areas.[25]

As a more environmentally friendly approach, Catalyst prioritized converting existing buildings rather than building ground-up.[26] The projects involved repurposing dilapidated industrial buildings into creative office, retail space, and affordable housing. Their goal is to catalyze and anchor additional growth and investment in the neighborhood in the coming years—working with local developers who have been lauded for their responsible use of land.

---

23. *Opportunity Zones Resource Center: Opportunity Funds List*, Novogradac, https://www.novoco.com/resource-centers/opportunity-zone-resource-center/opportunity-zone-funds-listing.

24. Interview with Jeremy Keele by P. Teicher and C. Allwin November with Jeremy Keele (Nov. 9, 2020).

25. *Catalyst Opportunity Funds Kicks Off 2020 with High-Impact Opportunity Zone Investments*, BusinessWire (Jan. 29, 2020), https://www.businesswire.com/news/home/20200129005056/en/Catalyst-Opportunity-Funds-Kicks-Off-2020-With-High-Impact-Opportunity-Zone-Investments%C2%A0.

26. Interview with Jeremy Keele by P. Teicher and C. Allwin (Nov. 9, 2020).

Another early mover launching into Opportunity Zones was Enterprise Community Partners, a traditional impact-driven real estate player. With more than forty years of experience and thousands of local partners, Enterprise has built and preserved 662,000 affordable homes, invested $53 billion in communities, and changed millions of lives. As a result of their substantial experiences in Opportunity Zones in which they were already working, Enterprise understood the markets better than many other nascent Opportunity Zone players. Enterprise was guided by its past experience in affordable housing development when Opportunity Zones first came into existence in the absence of a preexisting marketplace. Based on their experiences in impact-driven real estate, Enterprise could apply those lessons outside the Opportunity Zone context into the Opportunity Zone context.[27]

Enterprise had a good sense of the floor and the ceiling of investors' impact investing risk-adjusted return expectations for Opportunity Zone funds versus other funds. Ultimately, they were well positioned to anticipate where the investors would align to raise Opportunity Zone capital from investors quickly. Enterprise raised $100 million across four funds to invest in affordable housing across Opportunity Zones.[28]

Operating Businesses

Although the original intent behind the creation of Opportunity Zones was to fuel investment in both businesses and real estate, there has been less initial traction among private equity investors launching funds dedicated to Opportunity Zones or with a focus on Opportunity Zones. In the early days of the marketplace, there has been some confusion around whether or not Opportunity Zone investments can practically be made into new businesses. The Proposed Regulations have gone a long way toward resolving these concerns; however, investors were reluctant to move forward until the regulations were finalized.

Even though start-ups and operating businesses had the opportunity to take on Opportunity Zone capital as per the regulations, unfortunately, this opportunity has fallen short. As of April 2021, Novogradac reported that more than 1,000 Opportunity Funds had raised more than $16.34 billion with only 2.8 percent of those funds targeting operating businesses, a percentage which has hovered between 2.6 and 4.1 percent.[29] QOFs with a sole focus on operating businesses have raised $140.0 million and those with at least a partial focus on operating businesses have raised $354.5 million—or 3.5 percent of the total.[30]

Private equity and venture capital firms found the first set of regulations limiting; it was not until the Final Regulations clarifying how the 50 percent test could be satisfied that most investors felt comfortable with the risk associated with this uncertainty. It was not until the safe harbor allowing a more practical application in the operating business context arose that these investors could contemplate investing in small businesses and start-ups

---

27. Interview with Julia Shin by P. Teicher and C. Allwin (Nov. 9, 2020).

28. Id.

29. This figure has hovered between 2.6 and 4.1 percent since Novogradac began tracking the information nearly two years ago. https://www.novoco.com/notes-from-novogradac/novogradac-tracked-oz-investment-exceeds-16-billion-qofs-surpass-1000-mark.

30. Michael Novogradac, *Opportunity Zones Resource Center: Novogradac Opportunity Funds List Surpasses $10 Billion in Investment*, Novogradac (Apr. 29, 2020), https://www.novoco.com/notes-from-novogradac/novogradac-opportunity-funds-list-surpasses-10-billion-investment.

with Opportunity Zone capital. Ultimately, despite the hype, most of the investments in this sector have been at the intersection of real estate deals. With increased awareness, education, and guidelines in this sector from tax advisors, we may see an increase in investments flow into Opportunity Zone businesses.

There are a few success stories amid the lack of larger investment activity in operating businesses.

The Pearl Fund was ranked one of the top ten Opportunity Zone funds by Forbes[31] and was among the first movers in Opportunity Zone venture capital. As a pre-seed/seed tech investor targeting start-ups, the Pearl Fund focuses on high-potential businesses delivering Internet infrastructure, cellular coverage, and green tech that can yield a 10X+ tax-free return along with positive social and economic impact in Opportunity Zone communities. These businesses are already located in or can relocate into Opportunity Zones and are not located in areas where most venture capitalists congregate (e.g., the Bay Area, Boston, NYC). A preference is given to start-ups founded and/or run by women and people of color. Most recently, the Pearl Fund led a $3 million Opportunity Zone Investment round for Micronic Technologies for its sustainable water purification technology which includes a "zero liquid discharge" technology to treat wastewater from industries and municipal landfills.[32] Based in Southwest Virginia, Micronic Technologies is a woman-led and co-founded small business.[33]

Galen Robotics is another notable example; Galen brings robotics to microsurgeries, invented at the Laboratory of Computational Sensing and Robotics at Johns Hopkins Labs. Galen Robotics expanded in Baltimore by employing local talent—and received investment that will support the local job growth via College Park, Maryland-based Verte Opportunity Fund,[34] which draws on the Opportunity Zone program to invest in operating businesses.[35] The Baltimore Development Corporation (BDC) was instrumental in helping to use Opportunity Zone incentives to bring Galen Robotics to Baltimore from Silicon Valley.

SoLa Impact was selected as a top Opportunity Zone Fund by Forbes Magazine and Sorenson Impact Center. SoLa Impact targets the critical issues of homelessness, access to higher education, and living-wage jobs across Los Angeles' OZ tracts; 85 percent of SoLa's tenants come from disadvantaged backgrounds, 53 percent were formerly homeless, 33 percent are survivors of domestic violence, and 60 percent live below the poverty line.

31. Steven Bertoni, *Meet the Forbes OZ 20: The Top Players Investing for Lasting Impact*, Forbes (Dec. 12, 2019), https://www.forbes.com/sites/stevenbertoni/2019/12/12/meet-the-forbes-oz-20-the-top-players-investing-for-lasting-impact/amp//.

32. *CIT GAP Funds and the Pearl Fund Lead $3M Opportunity Zone Investment in Micronic Technologies*, CIT: Center for Innovative Technology (Oct. 21, 2020), https://www.globenewswire.com/news-release/2020/10/21/2111991/0/en/CIT-GAP-Funds-and-The-Pearl-Fund-Lead-3M-Opportunity-Zone-Investment-in-Micronic-Technologies.html.

33. *Id.*

34. As of August 2020, after warehousing five opportunity zone businesses (QOZBs) deals, Verte OZ Fund was raising a Series A round of $10 million: *Early Access for Accredited & Capital Gain Investment into Next Generation High Growth and Social Impact Startups via the Verte OZ Opportunity Zone Fund*, Cision PR Web (Aug. 31, 2020), http://www.prweb.com/releases/early_access_for_accredited_capital_gain_investment_into_next_generation_high_growth_and_social_impact_startups_via_the_verte_oz_opportunity_zone_fund/prweb17326496.htm. As of August 2020, after warehousing five opportunity zone businesses (QOZBs) deals, Verte OZ Fund was raising a Series A round of $10 million. *Id.*

35. The amount was not disclosed. *Galen Robotics Investment Shows How the Opportunity Zone Program Can Fund Startups*, Technical.ly (Nov. 11, 2019), https://technical.ly/baltimore/2019/11/11/galen-robotics-verte-investment-opportunity-zone-fund-startups//. The amount of investment was not disclosed. *Id.*

Their $165 million[36] Opportunity Zone fund was intended to develop high-quality affordable housing and commercial centers in designated OZs in South Central Los Angeles, Watts, Compton, and other historically disadvantaged communities. In September 2019, SoLa Impact announced the launch of "The Beehive," a 92,000-square-foot-campus for start-ups, creatives, and established Opportunity Zone businesses.[37] The Beehive will launch special incentives for local and nonlocal companies, minority-owned businesses, and women-owned businesses.[38]

Finally, Catalyst Opportunity Fund has invested in a few businesses, including a modular home construction company, which offers sustainable and affordable home options to customers while creating well-paid job opportunities within the community and a SaaS (software as a service) platform with a public service component.

In addition to these case studies, one of the goals of the Final Regulations was to decrease the regulatory uncertainty around what could qualify as a legitimate and viable OZ investment into a business. To this end, the Final Regulations introduced more flexible qualifying rules for OZ investments into operating businesses.[39] A combined effort between the Final Regulations and the track record of these early investments de-risk the OZ investment thesis and should pave the path for future OZ investments into operating businesses.

Community Catalysts

State & Municipal Initiatives and Partnerships

There are several states, like Colorado, and cities, like Baltimore, that have identified personnel to serve at least part-time, if not full-time, as a dedicated resource on Opportunity Zones. Cities and states that appointed central leaders to spearhead initiatives successfully brought more projects to fruition. BDC, for example, is a great success story and was named among the Forbes OZ Top 20: Top Players Investing for Lasting Impact for its efforts.[40] The BDC and grants from local foundations funded a role for an Opportunity Zone Coordinator at the BDC for Ben Seigel,[41] whose role was primarily to connect investors with Baltimore's Opportunity Zones.

Working together, the BDC and Ben Seigel connected investors with Baltimore's Opportunity Zones to tackle social entrepreneurs' challenges and prioritize job growth. BDC connected private and public organizations to bring transformative investment to Baltimore's OZ communities. The program used OZ incentives to convince surgical robotics maker, Galen Robotics, to move to Baltimore from Silicon Valley.[42]

---

36. Bertoni, *supra* note 30.
37. *Martin Muito's SoLa Impact Selected as Top Opportunity Zone Fund by Forbes Magazine & Sorenson Impact Center*, Cision PR Web (Feb. 5, 2020, 3:11 p.m.), https://www.prnewswire.com/news-releases/sola-impact-selected-as-top-opportunity-zone-fund-by-forbes-magazine--sorenson-impact-center-300999740.html.
38. *Martin Muito's SoLa Impact Fund Investments in Housing and South LA Business Center Undaunted by Covid-19*, The Planning Report (May 4, 2020), https://www.planningreport.com/2020/05/04/martin-muoto-s-sola-impact-fund-investments-housing-and-south-la-business-center.
39. Subsequent section supported from Richard Chirls, *Final Tax Regulations Offer More Certainty to Opportunity Zone Fund Managers and Investors*, Orrick (Feb. 4, 2020), https://www.orrick.com/en/Insights/2020/02/Final-Tax-Regulations-Offer-More-Certainty-to-Opportunity-Zone-Fund-Managers-and-Investors.
40. Bertoni, *supra* note 30.
41. The BDC is a nonprofit, quasi-public organization, which serves as the economic development agency for the City of Baltimore.
42. Bertoni, *supra* note 30.

The BDC brought new stakeholders to projects and new investors who may know Baltimore but have never looked at specific neighborhoods as investment opportunities. BDC led monthly investment pipeline meetings to review local and state-level initiatives, compare notes, set priorities, and unlock subsidies from state and municipal agencies[43] previously unallocated. Through this coordination, process deals could come together faster. In a city like Baltimore, margins are so thin that projects could sit incomplete for years without such coordination. Many of these projects would have relied on Low-Income Housing Tax Credits or New Market Tax Credits. Only a limited allocation of such credits exist; thus, if projects were denied, they would have to sit idly for a year before re-applying the following year.

Statewide initiatives bringing a diverse group of stakeholders to the table including leaders within the OZ communities, investors, entrepreneurs, banks, universities, and development organizations have been instrumental in garnering OZ capital. Initiatives such as Opportunity Alabama (OPAL) is a nonprofit dedicated to connecting investors with investable assets in Alabama's Opportunity Zones.[44] Founded by Alex Flachsbart, with support from Alabama's corporate philanthropic community, the organization is building programs that educate communities on OZ policy and measure the social impact of projects across Alabama's 158 OZ communities. At the time of publication, OPAL facilitated connections to capital and technical assistance necessary to spur over $300 million on over a dozen real estate and operating business investments across Alabama. These projects range from a $12 million senior care facility in an abandoned high school in Heflin, Alabama, to a $20 million workforce housing project, fueled by a local nonprofit organization in downtown Birmingham, and providing free living space.[45]

OPAL introduced national community development finance institutions to opportunities in Alabama.[46] With this impact motivated capital, OPAL launched the Rural Recovery Accelerator (RRA) to ensure continued development of quality projects in the state's most underserved areas. The RRA supports a pipeline of projects in rural areas by helping communities identify their top two to three investable projects and provides support and infrastructure necessary to bring those deals to fruition. The first two RRA cohorts graduated in December 2020. OPAL has also partnered with Blueprint Local to facilitate more consistent access to capital for its statewide network of investment opportunities. OPAL partnered with Blueprint Local to support its work on Opportunity Zone–based projects across the state of Alabama. Blueprint Local, a joint venture between Brown Advisory and a group of national investors committed to strengthening underserved parts of the country, invests in entrepreneurs and real estate opportunities in economically distressed areas across the country. Blueprint Local aims to change the way communities connect with capital—bringing together investors, landowners, developers, and community members to collaborate in

43. *See, e.g.*, Baltimore City Department of Housing & Community Development; https://dhcd.baltimorecity.gov (last visited Apr. 2); Neighborhood Impact Investment Fund, https://www.baltimoreniif.org (last visited Apr. 2, 2021).
44. *See* Opportunity Alabama, http://opportunityalabama.com/ (last visited Apr. 2, 2021).
45. *Opportunity Alabama Partners with Blueprint Local on Opportunity Zone-Based Work in Alabama*, Opportunity Alabama (July 16, 2020), https://opportunityalabama.com/2020/07/16/opportunity-alabama-partners-with-blueprint-local-on-opportunity-zone-based-work-in-alabama//.
46. *See also* "The organization is helping national community development finance institutions like *Reinvestment Fund* and *Hope Credit Union* establish their footprints in Alabama." https://impactalpha.com/alex-flachsbart-opportunity-alabama/

revitalizing their neighborhoods. With Blueprint Local, the OPAL Fund raised $13 million from local foundations, family offices, individuals, and corporations.[47]

In a separate initiative, in Baltimore, Blueprint Local partnered with local developers, municipal leaders, and community constituents in Baltimore to redevelop historic Penn Station.[48] This transformational project had stalled for twenty years. Blueprint Local funds made it possible for developer Penn Station Partners to convert the historic train station into a modern facility with new retail, restaurants, and office space. This upgrade will be complemented by Amtrak's $90 million funding for new passenger loading platforms and the addition of another platform area to accommodate a new fleet of high-speed Acela trains.[49,50] According to Governor Larry Hogan, this Amtrak project "harnesses the strength of the public and private sectors, it builds on the partnership at the federal, state and local levels, and the job creation potential and associated economic and transit benefits are an absolute game-changer for Baltimore City and the region."[51]

The Role of Philanthropy in Opportunity Zones

Most philanthropic organizations are tax-exempt and therefore cannot take direct advantage of the Opportunity Zone benefit. However, philanthropy can play an important role as a catalyst, a source of technical assistance and capacity building capital and as a thought leader in this emerging marketplace. Grant providers can also fund training and educational efforts to increase awareness and philanthropy. Foundations can also provide subsidy or guarantees for transactions in markets where it is necessary to prime the pump to attract the private capital which will benefit from the tax incentive.

Program-related investments (PRIs) are a very specific type of impact investment provided for in the federal tax code and made by foundations. Three main criteria for PRIs include the following: The primary purpose of the investment is to accomplish one or more of the foundation's exempt purposes,[52] the investment's significant purpose is not for the

---

47. *Opportunity Alabama Is Combining Community and Capital to Fulfill the Potential of Opportunity Zones*, ImpactAlpha (Apr. 29, 2021), https://impactalpha.com/opportunity-alabama-is-combining-community-and-capital-to-fulfill-the-potential-of-opportunity-zones/.

48. Melody Simmons, *Baltimore Development Corp. "Inundated" With Opportunity Zone Questions*, Baltimore Business Journal (Jan. 13, 2020), https://www.bizjournals.com/baltimore/news/2020/01/13/baltimore-development-corp-inundated-with.html.

49. Melody Simmons, *Penn Station Redevelopment Gets Opportunity Zone Funding from Local Investor*. Baltimore Business Journal, https://www.bizjournals.com/baltimore/news/2020/02/05/penn-station-redevelopment-gets-opportunity-zone.html (last updated Feb. 5, 2020).

50. *Amtrak and Penn Station Partners to Break Ground for Baltimore Penn Station Redevelopment Project*, Amtrak (Oct. 22, 2021), https://media.amtrak.com/2021/10/amtrak-and-penn-station-partners-to-break-ground-for-baltimore-penn-station-redevelopment-project/. In October 2021, local politicians, Amtrak, and developers hosted a groundbreaking ceremony to mark the commencement of the redevelopment of Penn Station. *Id. See also Amtrak and Developers Push Ahead with Multimillion-Dollar Transformation of Baltimore's Penn Station*, The Baltimore Sun (Mar. 18, 2021), https://www.baltimoresun.com/business/bs-bz-penn-station-redevelopment-20210318-fuen4cjidvh6reaozmsr3sttoi-story.html.

51. *Amtrak and Penn Station Partners to Break Ground for Baltimore Penn Station Redevelopment Project*, Amtrak (Oct. 22, 2021), https://media.amtrak.com/2021/10/amtrak-and-penn-station-partners-to-break-ground-for-baltimore-penn-station-redevelopment-project/.

52. IRC §26 U.S.C. § 170(c)(2)(B).

production of income or appreciation of property, and the funds are not being made to influence legislation or as a campaign donation.[53,54]

Examples of PRIs include the following: low-interest or interest-free loans to students in need, high-risk investments in nonprofit low-income housing projects, low-interest loans to small businesses owned by members of economically disadvantaged groups, where commercial funds at reasonable interest rates are not readily available, investments in businesses in low-income areas under a plan to improve the economy of the area by providing employment or training for unemployed residents, and investments in nonprofit organizations combating community deterioration.[55] These examples are predominantly those of fixed income instruments, but elements of equity without debt do not necessarily disqualify the investment from qualifying as a PRI.[56] The regulations provide a plethora of examples but have not fully unlocked the potential of PRI capital.

PRI makers could become significant players in the Opportunity Zone marketplace by providing companion financing that helps support private investment in the capital stack. This type of blended finance is common in impact investing where a project or investment fund intends to meet specific social objectives, like the provision of affordable housing. The recent Proposed Regulations also explicitly allow for funds to be co-mingled in a single special purpose vehicle, which makes it possible for Opportunity Zones to raise capital from investors, who will not benefit from the tax incentive. Foundations, therefore, can play a critical role for Opportunity Funds by providing capital that will help bridge the return requirements for projects that are critical to community well-being but where margins may be thin like early childhood development facilities, schools, and health clinics.

Foundations can also provide guarantees for investment funds. In June 2018, Kresge Foundation and Rockefeller Foundation released a call for letters of inquiry from potential Opportunity Zone fund managers.[57] Twenty of the one hundred forty-one applicants[58] to Kresge and Rockefeller were chosen to potentially receive grant-funded packages of technical support that include advisory services on legal, accounting, reporting, and capital raising. The vast majority put forward state or local funds. The inquiries spanned asset classes, including real estate, venture capital, small business, private equity, green energy, infrastructure, and more.[59]

From this pool of applicants, in March 2019, Kresge Foundation pledged $22 million as a guaranty of first loss to Arctaris Impact and Community Capital Management after the managers agreed to a level of transparency, accountability, and disclosure surpassing other

53. IRC §26 U.S.C. § 170(c)(2)(D).

54. *Program-Related Investments*, IRS, https://www.irs.gov/charities-non-profits/private-foundations/program-related-investments (last visited Apr. 2, 2021).

55. *Id.*

56. Treas. Reg. § 53.4944-3 (as amended in 2016).

57. *Press Releases: Nearly 150 Letters of Inquiry on Opportunity Zones Pour into Kresge, Rockefeller Foundations*, The Rockefeller Foundation (Sept. 14, 2018), https://www.rockefellerfoundation.org/news/nearly-150-letters-inquiry-opportunity-zones-pour-kresge-rockefeller-foundations//.

58. Id.

59. *Kresge and Rockefeller Identify Opportunity Fund Managers for Grants and Support*, Impact Alpha (Sept. 16, 2018), https://impactalpha.com/kresge-and-rockefeller-foundations-narrow-pipeline-for-opportunity-fund-support//.

Opportunity Zone Funds.[60] The fund managers agreed to include covenants to prioritize development of affordable housing units, prevent displacement, expand investments into living-wage jobs, and impose restrictions on nonproductive investments (e.g., self-storage units).[61]

To support Opportunity Zone businesses, foundations can deploy PRI capital to support training of local entrepreneurs and/or the re-skilling of local workers.[62] For example, in Wisconsin, the Incourage Community Foundation (https://incouragecf.org/) partnered with the chamber of commerce to launch more than twenty programs, including an entrepreneurial boot camp, which supported the launch of more than forty businesses.[63] This collaboration also led venture funds supporting and funding programs to create additional workforce training opportunities.

CDFIs

CDFIs and, in particular, nonprofit community loan funds have been instrumental in improving the conditions in low-income communities for decades since the passage of the Community Development and Regulatory Improvement Act of 1994, a bipartisan initiative, which established the CDFI Fund. Some CDFIs predated this legislation and have been operating for as long as forty and fifty years. As fund managers for New Markets Tax Credits and Low-Income Housing Tax Credits, these organizations have successful track records of investing in communities which mirror the characteristics of Opportunity Zones.

Blended Capital Stacks

One benefits of the Opportunity Zone program has been to bring stakeholders to the table to create unique blended capital stacks that would not have otherwise been created outside of this legislative opportunity.

Innovative financing opportunities emerged from philanthropic, municipal, and state support. Arctaris Opportunity Zone Fund, for example, employed first-loss guarantees and other forms of principal protection via grants and investments from leading philanthropic, government, and community partners to leverage a multiple of those amounts with private capital investment. Concluding a competitive review process by Kresge and Rockefeller Foundations of more 150 fund managers, the Arctaris Opportunity Zone Fund was awarded a $15 million principal-protection guaranty commitment.[64] In prior funds, Arctaris had replicated this blended-financing investment model across prior funds. Arctaris typically commits 80 percent of the capital and seeks partners to invest the remaining 20 percent.[65]

---

60. *Kresge Foundation Commits $22M to Back Arctaris, Community Capital Management Opportunity Zone Funds*, Cision PR Web (Mar. 18, 2019), https://www.prnewswire.com/news-releases/kresge-foundation-commits-22m-to-back-arctaris-community-capital-management-opportunity-zone-funds-300813622.html.
61. *Kresge Commits $22 Million to Boost Opportunity Zone Transparency*, Philanthropy News Digest (Mar. 20, 2019), https://philanthropynewsdigest.org/news/kresge-commits-22-million-to-boost-opportunity-zone-transparency.
62. Cody Evans & Agnes Dasewicz, *How Foundations Can Help Opportunity Zone Communities Succeed*, Stanford Social Innovation Review (Feb. 7, 2019), https://ssir.org/articles/entry/how_foundations_can_help_opportunity_zone_communities_succeed.
63. *Id.*
64. Arctaris Impact Investors, *Arctaris Opportunity Zone Fund*, Wisconsin Economic Development Association, Arctaris, http://www.weda.org/wp-content/uploads/2020/02/Ben-Arctaris-Fund-1.pdf (last visited Apr. 2, 2021).
65. *Arctaris Commits $40 Million to Erie Opportunity Zones*, Impact Alpha (July 1, 2020), https://impactalpha.com/acrtaris-commits-40-million-to-erie-opportunity-zones//.

The "Finance Authority of Maine" (FAME) was the first state entity to agree to provide a guaranty specifically for QOZ investments. FAME committed up to $10 million in guarantees to Arctaris under its commercial loan insurance program to support Opportunity Zone investments in Maine. FAME's funds would anchor $50 million of matching investments from Arctaris into economic and community development projects in Maine, including growth-oriented manufacturing businesses, high-speed internet via broadband fiber, and solar power infrastructure.[66]

Arctaris also successfully applied this model in Erie, Pennsylvania, launching a $40 million Opportunity Zone initiative that invests in projects to revitalize the downtown corridor in Erie, including mixed-use real estate projects. The initiative is being supported by Erie Insurance, which committed $50 million to the Arctaris Opportunity Zone Fund in June 2020. The Erie Community Foundation committed $5 million as a PRI to Arctaris to expand mission-related projects in the community.[67]

There are also several local and state initiatives that have launched to complement and foster investments in Opportunity Zones. A report by Council on Development Agencies indicated that 55 percent of respondents to their survey on Opportunity Zones indicated that their states had dedicated staff working on Opportunity Zones.[68]

Climate Change: An Integrated Approach

As Opportunity Zone legislation matures, ideally more clean energy projects will emerge. Clean energy, solar and wind energy, projects could be a valuable use case for Opportunity Zones. For example, North Sky Capital, a climate change leader, illustrates an integrated approach to OZ. It launched a $100 million Opportunity Zone fund focused on investing in sustainable infrastructure projects. North Sky is a twenty-year old private markets firm and a recognized thought leader in impact investing. Previously, North Sky had raised approximately $1.5 billion of commitments across its various strategies, including roughly $1 billion across nine impact funds to focus on investing in the development, construction, and/or operations of North America's sustainable infrastructure projects. North Sky's first Opportunity Zone project was a renewable natural gas facility at the "Victor Valley Wastewater Reclamation Authority" (VVWRA), located in San Bernardino County, California.[69]

The project utilized Anaergia's Omnivore high solids anaerobic digestion retrofit to triple capacity and increase redundancy of the existing digester infrastructure. Sludge and food waste will be digested to generate biogas that will be conditioned and upgraded into pipeline quality natural gas utilizing systems designed and supplied by Anaergia affiliates.

---

66. Finance Authority of Maine Agrees to Partner with Arctaris Impact to Help Attract Opportunity Zone Capital to Local Investments, BUSINESSWIRE (July 10, 2019), https://www.businesswire.com/news/home/20190710005254/en/Finance-Authority-of-Maine-Agrees-to-Partner-With-Arctaris-Impact-to-Help-Attract-Opportunity-Zone-Capital-to-Local-Investments.

67. *Arctaris Commits $40 Million to Erie Opportunity Zones*, IMPACT ALPHA (July 1, 2020), https://impactalpha.com/acrtaris-commits-40-million-to-erie-opportunity-zones//.

68. Rittner et al., CDFA OPPORTUNITY ZONES REPORT: STATE OF THE STATES (2018), https://www.cdfa.net/cdfa/cdfaweb.nsf/ordredirect.html?open&id=201808_OZSofS.html.

69. *North Sky Capital Invests in California Renewable Natural Gas Project Located in an Opportunity Zone*, NORTH SKY CAPITAL (Nov. 10, 2020), https://northskycapital.com/north-sky-capital-invests-in-california-renewable-natural-gas-project-located-in-an-opportunity-zone//.

In addition, Anaergia will operate the gas upgrading facility.[70] Not only does the project beneficially reduce more than 6,000 metric tons of methane (1.5 million CO_2 tons equivalent) per year, which otherwise would have been flared or released into the atmosphere. The energy generated was estimated to displace more than two million gallons of diesel fuel per year and create approximately thirty prevailing wage jobs via construction and related work.[71]

The Biden Administration has been clear in its prioritization of climate change and almost certainly will create new programs to support climate infrastructure including solar and wind energy producers and projects that could qualify as a QOZ business.

Conclusion

Although not all Opportunity Zone investments will be community investments, mission-driven investors in the United States now have another new impact investing tool in their toolkit to create better social and environmental outcomes for communities that have long been underserved by traditional capital markets. This chapter serves as a simple, baseline source of information to help interested attorneys and their clients, particularly new entrants to impact first community investing, better understand Opportunity Zones as a tool for serving low-income communities that also benefits taxpayers.

Opportunity Zone legislation has catalyzed conversations about investment in general and actual investment activity in low-income communities that has been overlooked and underestimated for decades. These initiatives have unlocked private capital that had not otherwise been interested in these distressed communities while encouraging longer term investments in these communities. One of the leaders in spearheading the Opportunity Zone Legislation, Steve Glickman,[72] noted, "As I boil down the philosophical difference between this program and others—it is the fundamental idea that it is more important to create something big and long-lasting that could turn places around at the expense of including investments that may not require the incentive. The problem is so big that it cannot be solved with individual projects."

Investors have and are continuing to seek to leverage this tax incentive to optimize the benefit of the capital gains deferment which is time bound. However, there is an ongoing need to educate attorneys, real estate developers, entrepreneurs, investors, and other community stakeholders. Legal advisors can encourage impact capital to flow into Opportunity Zones by helping their clients mitigate their legal risk. With an improved understanding of the Opportunity Zone rules, capital allocators, investors, and fund managers could do more than invest tax-advantaged capital into quick-turn real estate projects, most of which would have been completed even without this legislation.

70. https://northskycapital.com/north-sky-capital-invests-in-california-renewable-natural-gas-project-located-in-an-opportunity-zone/, *Id.*

71. https://northskycapital.com/north-sky-capital-invests-in-california-renewable-natural-gas-project-located-in-an-opportunity-zone/, *Id.*

72. Steve Glickman is co-founder and former CEO of the Economic Innovation Group (EIG), a bipartisan research and policy organization in Washington, DC, focused on addressing economic inequality through the creation of a new marketplace for private equity investments in distressed communities.

Chapter 4
Social Impact Bonds: Overview and Lessons Learned

Navjeet Bal and Leslie Cornell (with case study by Hilary Jackler)

Introduction

"Social Impact Bonds" (SIBs) are an innovative financing tool designed to finance the expansion of data-driven social services. SIBs bring together governments, social service providers, and impact investors to fund social services, which improve people's lives by either seeking to avert the consequences of a social problem and/or provide better opportunities for vulnerable people to succeed. Working capital to scale up services is provided by impact investors, who are then repaid by governments if and when agreed-upon outcomes are achieved. Intermediary organizations play an important role in bringing together governments, impact investors, and social service providers; structuring the terms of the project and the financing; and holding the contractual and funding relationships among the parties.

As one example of a SIB, Social Finance partnered with the Commonwealth of Massachusetts and "Jewish Vocational Services" (JVS) to structure and fund a SIB focused on providing English language learning and occupational skills training to 2,000 recent refugees and immigrants in Greater Boston. JVS, which has been in existence since 1938, was interested in scaling up its services to an even larger population. The Commonwealth was interested in paying for outcomes—improved wages—for the service population. Social

Finance, Inc., as the intermediary for the project, partnered with the Bank of America Merrill Lynch to raise $12.4 million in a private placement under an equity structure. The Commonwealth agreed to make up to $15 million in outcomes payments tied to program engagement, increased earnings outcomes, and increased access to and persistence in secondary education, measured across four different program tracks offered by JVS.[1]

SIB financings are built on performance-based contracts in which government, as an outcomes payor, contracts with an intermediary organization to deliver a specific set of social services for a specified service population. The services are intended to deliver a particular set of measurable outcomes (such as reduced rates of recidivism or improved readiness for kindergarten), which provide a benefit to the larger community. In return, government makes a payment upon achievement of the agreed-upon outcomes, reflecting such benefits. The intermediary partners with one or more social service providers to deliver services designed to achieve the desired outcome. Private impact investors, such as institutional investors, community development financing institutions, high net worth individuals, or foundations, provide the up-front operating capital for the expansion of the targeted social services. A core element of a SIB is the concept of risk transfer. In a SIB, a government transfers the risk that it will pay for social services that are not effective to the private impact investors who bear the financial risk instead. In a completed SIB, the government payor repays investors to the extent that the targeted social outcomes are achieved. These outcome-based payments are interchangeably referred to as success payments, performance payments, or (as is used in this chapter) Outcome payments. Each SIB is structured around at least one well-defined social outcome in a particular intervention area.

A SIB is the most commonly understood "Pay for Success" (PFS) tool. The term "Pay for Success" refers to a contracting model for implementing and paying for social services based on the achievement of outcomes. Other examples of PFS include performance-based contracting or outcomes rate cards in which governments directly procure for and pay for achievement of outcomes and not just the delivery of services. SIBs fall comfortably under the umbrella of PFS and are often referred to as PFS financings because of the role of the private sector in providing the risk capital for expansion of a given social service.

PFS has expanded since the first project was launched in the United States in 2012 and many potential PFS projects are in preliminary stages across the nation. There is strong bipartisan support for SIBs and PFS projects generally at both the federal and state levels. Permission to use performance-based contracting has been built into the Federal Workforce Innovation and Opportunity Act and the Every Student Succeeds Act.[2] Federal support has also been provided for both PFS feasibility and transaction structuring through the Social Innovation Fund under the "Corporation for National and Community Service" (CNCS).[3]

Most recently, the "Social Impact Partnerships to Pay for Results Act" (SIPPRA), which became law in February 2018, appropriates $100 million to the U.S. Department of the

---

1. Social Finance, Inc., Massachusetts Pathways to Economic Advancement Project. (n.d.). Retrieved June 9, 2020, from https://socialfinance.org/focus-areas/workforce/massachusetts-pathways-economic-advancement-project/.
2. Workforce Innovation and Opportunity Act, §§ 29-3101-3361 (2014); Every Student Succeeds Act, §§ 20-28-70 (2015).
3. Corporation for National and Community Service—Social Innovation Fund. (n.d.). Retrieved Aug. 23, 2022, from https://americorps.gov/funding-opportunity/social-innovation-fund.

Treasury to support the launch of state and local PFS initiatives. In its first round of applications, SIPPRA encouraged state and local governments to structure local PFS projects, including SIBs, leveraging substantial federal resources. The SIPPRA funding can be used for feasibility studies, evaluations, or Outcome payments across a range of social issue areas, including child welfare, family stability, homelessness, education, health, employment, recidivism, and veterans.[4] Funding under SIPPRA is expected to be awarded in 2020.

The Social Impact Bond Model

Roles in Transaction and the Contracting Relationship

Outcomes Payors

The entity that agrees to make payments if the specified outcomes ("Outcomes") are met is referred to as the "Outcomes Payor." Typically, this is the entity, usually government, that stands to benefit through cost savings or a community benefit from the achievement of a particular outcome.

State and local governments spend enormous sums of money every year addressing social issues, but most current social spending inhibits innovation and does not focus on effective Outcomes. Tight budgets restrict the implementation of new, potentially effective programs and the scaling of proven interventions. Furthermore, the budget process tends to favor those programs that were previously funded. SIBs were conceived as a way to counteract challenges faced by government entities (low-risk tolerance and limited funding) and shift the risk of innovation and scaling from taxpayers to private investors.

It should be noted that other private or public interests can assume the Outcomes Payor role and function if they are the source of backend Outcome payments. For example, health care providers and insurance providers could serve as Outcomes Payors as they also are incentivized to provide more effective services to a particular "Service Population" up-front in an effort to reduce the need for more expensive services down the road. Similarly, private employers which stand to gain from a workforce development intervention can also serve as Outcomes Payors.

The success of a SIB is dependent on the commitment and engagement of the interested Outcomes Payor. The Outcomes Payor is one of the earliest participants in the transaction. Initial responsibilities of the Outcomes Payor include identifying priority areas for a PFS intervention, determining desired social and fiscal performance metrics and committing financial and political resources to the process. In the model case, the Outcomes Payor only contracts with the Intermediary. The Intermediary then contracts with the Service Provider, Funders, and an independent Evaluator. The Outcomes Payor is ultimately responsible financially for making any applicable Outcome payments to the Intermediary, which then repays Funders (plus any returns).

Intermediary

In a SIB, an intermediary organization (the "Intermediary") acts as a project coordinator and manager and is the central party which holds the contractual and funding

4. Social Impact Partnerships to Pay for Results Act: S. 963, 115 Cong. (enacted).

relationships with each of the other participants. Intermediaries are most often involved in developing a SIB from its inception, starting with a feasibility study, which leads to the SIB project design and developing the governing agreements. Certain Intermediaries also raise the necessary private impact capital for the SIB and then oversee the governance of the SIB through to its completion.[5] Generally speaking, the Intermediary is the PFS specialist in the transaction.

The Intermediary will typically be a party to all primary contracts in the SIB. The Intermediary works with the Outcomes Payor to understand its goals by identifying the problem it is trying to solve, the optimal evidence-based services and providers, the Outcomes to be achieved, how they will be measured, and the outcome price the Outcomes Payor is willing to pay. The Intermediary and the Outcomes Payor then enter into a PFS Contract (see Governing Documents—PFS Contract below) that lays out the rights and responsibilities of the parties and describes the target Service Population, the services to be provided, the evaluation methodology, the Outcomes and Outcome prices, and the governance process. The Intermediary then enters into a Service Agreement (see Governing Documents—Service Agreement below) with the Service Provider, a contract with the independent Evaluator (see Governing Documents—Evaluation Agreement below), and financing agreements with the Funders (see Governing Documents—Funding Agreement below).

The role of the Intermediary is new, and several new and existing organizations have developed the capacities to work with Outcomes Payors to structure SIBs. Examples of Intermediary organizations include: Social Finance US, which is part of a global network of nonprofit Intermediary organizations dedicated to developing SIBs and development impact bonds; Enterprise Community Partners, which leverages its experience in affordable housing to implement SIBs addressing the needs of the chronically homeless; and Third Sector Capital Partners and Corporation for Supportive Housing, each of which focuses primarily on working with governments and service providers to develop outcomes-based projects.

Funders

SIBs are designed to apply the mechanics of traditional capital markets to the funding of the expansion of social services. A SIB allows impact investors (or "Funders") to receive both a financial return and a social return on their investment. Therefore, SIBs offer the potential to promote a "double bottom line," that is, provide effective solutions for social problems and financially reward risk-bearing investors for their support of successful social services. To date, such investments have been done as both debt structures, with senior and subordinate lenders, and equity structures with preferred and common investors.[6]

Funding for SIBs thus far has come from private institutional investors, community development finance institutions, high net worth individuals, and philanthropic foundations. Most projects, either debt or equity, have a blended capital stack with senior, subordinate,

5. Social Finance, Inc.—Social Investment. (n.d.). Retrieved June 9, 2020, from http://socialfinance.org/what-we-do-2/social-investment/.

6. A. C. Curran (2017, Apr.). *Inroads to Innovation: State Adoption of Pay for Success Legislation* [PDF]. Chicago: Chapman and Cutler LLP.

and in some cases, pure philanthropic grants or guarantees providing funding. Within the growing impact investment sector, SIBs offer an investment opportunity where the return on investment is specifically tied to measurable impact.

Service Providers

The "Service Provider" is an independent organization that is responsible for implementing the "intervention" services ("Intervention") for the benefit of the Service Population. Typically, the Service Provider is an established nonprofit organization and, in nearly all U.S. SIBs, these organizations have proven on some scale to have achieved successful Outcomes within their particular area of focus. SIBs funnel funding to the Service Provider in order to finance the expansion of the offered services. In contracting for the Intervention, SIBs allow for single providers or the coordination of multiple organizations with different skills or areas of focus. The Service Provider will typically enter into a Service Agreement (see Governing Documents—Service Agreement below) with the Intermediary but will not be a party to any other governing agreement.

Evaluator

Program evaluation or validation is a key component of a SIB, as it allows projects to assess the effectiveness of their Intervention and measure the extent to which performance benchmarks are achieved in order to determine the level of repayment to Funders. In order for a SIB to work, benchmarks and the appropriate evaluation methodology must be carefully defined before any services are provided. Having an independent "Evaluator" is central to providing both the Outcomes Payor and the Funders with comfort that Outcomes are being met, and that Outcome payments have been earned, consistent with the methodology laid out in the PFS Contract (see Governing Documents—PFS Contract below).

Constituent/Service Population

Constituents are the individuals who receive Intervention services pursuant to the project (i.e., the Service Population) and are central to the mission of a PFS transaction. They are the people who will directly benefit from a successfully implemented SIB through the funding and scaling of social interventions. These individuals almost always have an existing relationship with an Outcomes Payor, primarily through remedial programs already funded through taxpayer dollars.

Governing Documents

There are numerous challenges in implementing a SIB that will provide financial and societal benefits. For example, in choosing a Service Population, there must be a clearly defined group receiving social services and an effective evaluation strategy to evaluate the progress this group makes over the course of the delivery of the Intervention. There must also be safeguards in place to ensure the Service Provider does not work with only the easiest cases to achieve the Outcomes. These types of challenges mean that the agreements executed by the parties are critically important to the success or failure of a SIB project.

There is no prescribed set of documents needed in a SIB financing. There is no regulatory authority, and there are few limitations outside general contract law. The form of these transactions can be, and already has, shifted significantly across projects, although form documents are beginning to emerge. However, a true SIB financing will likely encompass the concepts underlying each of the following documents in some combination.

Pay for Success Contract

The primary governing agreement is the contract between the Outcomes Payor and the Intermediary (the "PFS Contract"). The PFS Contract includes all of the operational and governance terms associated with the project. The main part of the PFS Contract sets forth the obligations of the Outcomes Payor and the Intermediary, as well as termination provisions. The Outcomes Payor is typically obligated to make Outcome payments upon achievement of Outcomes, and to set forth the funding mechanism to make such payments. The Intermediary is responsible for procuring the Service Provider to provide the services and deliver the Outcomes. The Intermediary is also typically responsible for procuring the independent Evaluator. The parties may set forth data sharing and confidentiality provision in the PFS Contract or in a separate agreement. The PFS Contract also sets forth the term of the project, as well as early termination provisions. The early termination provisions allocate the risk of paying for the social services delivered to the date of termination between the Outcomes Payor and the Funders, depending on the reason for early termination.

The PFS Contract also sets forth (1) the operational parameters of the project, including the services to be delivered, the Service Population, and target geographies; (2) the Outcomes to be achieved and the evaluation methodology to be applied; (3) the Outcome prices applicable to each of the Outcomes; and (4) the governance process for the project.

Other contracts such as the Service Agreement and the Evaluator Agreement may reference the applicable schedules to the PFS Agreement.

Funding Agreement

The Funding Agreement between the Funders and the Intermediary is structured similarly to traditional financing agreements and may take the form of either a credit facility for a debt instrument or an equity investment in a limited liability company or corporation. It includes covenants of all executing parties as to the security of the financing and repayment terms. In addition, the Funding Agreement prescribes the terms of the funding (e.g., grant, loan, investment) and will detail the benchmarks for repayment and investment returns. In a debt financing, the Funders may also enter into a subordination agreement, laying out the respective rights of the senior and subordinate lenders. Funding Agreements, as primarily "impact first" investments, do have significant differences from traditional financing agreements, as discussed below under "Unique Issues in SIBs—Credit Documents/Fiduciary Obligations."

Service Agreement

The Service Agreement, an agreement between the Service Provider and the Intermediary, will lay out the planned Interventions to be provided and how such Interventions will be funded by the Intermediary. Contracts with the Service Provider or providers can be traditional fee-for-service, pay-for-performance, or some combination.

Evaluation Agreement

As discussed above, evaluation is necessary for a SIB to work as conceived. An evaluation agreement between the Intermediary and a third-party evaluator will describe the duties and responsibilities of an independent Evaluator, including prescribing how and when data will be collected.

Veterans Coordinated Approach to Recovery and Employment Project

To further illustrate the mechanics of a SIB in a practical example, the below section describes an actual SIB, including the parties, the legal structure, and the Intervention.

In July 2018, Social Finance, Inc., partnered with the U.S. Department of Veterans Affairs (the "VA"), the Commonwealth of Massachusetts, acting through its Executive Office for Administration and Finance, the Neighborhood Jobs Trust of the City of Boston together with the Economic Development and Industrial Corporation of Boston, and the City of New York, acting through its Department of Veterans' Services, to launch the Veterans Coordinated Approach to Recovery and Employment Project ("Veterans CARE Project"), a SIB that supports unemployed or underemployed Veterans with "posttraumatic stress disorder" (PTSD) in attaining competitive, compatible employment. The Veterans CARE Project was the first PFS project in the United States to focus on improving employment and health Outcomes for veterans, the first SIB to involve a federal agency as the lead government payor, and the first multi-state SIB.

The Veterans CARE Project was designed to serve 480 veterans over three years in New York City, Boston, Brockton, Massachusetts, and Central and Western Massachusetts. Under this project, the "Tuscaloosa VA Medical Center" (TVAMC) oversees the delivery of "Individual Placement and Support" (IPS), an evidence-based approach to supported employment, to program participants at local VA medical centers. The Outcomes Payors repay private lenders if the project successfully achieves positive Outcomes for participants. The Veterans CARE Project measures four Outcomes: (1) earnings, (2) sustained competitive employment, (3) fidelity to the IPS model, and (4) job satisfaction.

Outcome Payors: (1) Commonwealth of Massachusetts, acting through its Executive Office for Administration and Finance; (2) the Neighborhood Jobs Trust of the City of Boston together with the Economic Development and Industrial Corporation of Boston; (3) the City of New York, acting through its Department of Veterans' Services; and (4) U.S. Department of Veterans Affairs (collectively, the "Veterans CARE Payor Group").

Intermediary: Social Finance, Inc.

Independent Evaluator: Westat, Inc.

Service Provider: "Tuscaloosa Research and Education Advancement Corporation" (TREAC) is a nonprofit corporation that conducts research and education activities in support of TVAMC.

Public Sector Issue: Veterans with PTSD face significant barriers to employment. PTSD interferes with a person's ability to thrive in the workforce and has been found to negatively impact sustained employment. Moreover, a negative cycle exists between unemployment and PTSD; persistent unemployment is often linked to negative health conditions, including depression, which can exacerbate PTSD symptoms. Up to 20 percent of veterans from recent tours of duty have PTSD, and a 2015 analysis found that veterans' labor force participation declined over the previous thirty-five years in close correlation with growth in service-connected disability.[7,8]

Intervention: IPS is a model of supported employment for people with serious mental illness. IPS-supported employment helps people living with behavioral health conditions work at regular jobs of their choosing. This highly personalized approach to supported employment emphasizes rapid job search, matching an individual's needs and preferences, and integrated mental health care. Prior to the implementation of the Veterans CARE Project, numerous studies had already shown significant IPS effectiveness. In twenty-five randomized controlled trials (including two studies focused on unemployed Veterans with PTSD), IPS showed an average competitive employment rate of 56 percent compared to 23 percent of controls. A meta-analysis of seventeen randomized controlled trials found that people receiving IPS services were 2.4 times more likely to be employed than controls.[9] Participants in IPS attain employment faster, hold their jobs for longer, and work more hours. In four "randomized controlled trials" (RCT), over an eighteen-month period, approximately three times as many people receiving IPS services achieved employment and worked more hours, and people receiving IPS services worked overall four times as many hours compared to controls.[10] Furthermore, evidence from the RCT suggested that IPS is more effective than alternative vocational approaches regardless of a variety of client background factors (e.g., ethnicity, gender, socioeconomic status).

There are eight distinct principles associated with the IPS model: a focus on competitive employment, eligibility based on client choice, integration of rehabilitation and mental health services, attention to worker preferences, personalized benefits counseling, rapid job search, systematic job development, and time-unlimited, individualized support.

Population—Up to 480 Veterans with Service-Connected PTSD: Veterans served via four VA Medical Centers in Massachusetts and New York.

Outcomes Measured: The project measures four Outcomes: (1) earnings, (2) sustained competitive employment, (3) fidelity to the IPS model, and (4) job satisfaction.

Funding and Payments: Social Finance, Inc., raised $5.1 million from five impact investors to fund service delivery, including BNP Paribas, The Northern Trust Company, The Dakota Foundation, Deutsche Bank Americas Foundation, and The Robin Hood Foundation. The returns these lenders will receive from the Veterans CARE Project are dependent upon the achievement of agreed-upon outcome metrics. There are four distinct payment points at which Outcomes are measured and Outcome payments are made. To the extent that outcomes are met and validated by the independent evaluator, the Veterans CARE Payor Group could collectively make up to $6 million in Outcomes Payments. If the highest level of Outcomes is not met, returns to these lenders will be reduced.

---

7. Institute of Medicine (US) Committee on the Initial Assessment of Readjustment Needs of Military Personnel, Veterans, and Their Families. Washington (DC): National Academies Press (US); 2010.
8. C. Coile, M. Duggan, & A. Guo. Veterans' labor force participation: What role does the VA's disability compensation program play? Am Econ Rev. 2015; 105(5):131–136.
9. Evidence for IPS. (n.d.). Retrieved June 9, 2020, from https://ipsworks.org/index.php/evidence-for-ips.
10. Evidence for IPS. (n.d.). Retrieved June 9, 2020, from https://ipsworks.org/index.php/evidence-for-ips.

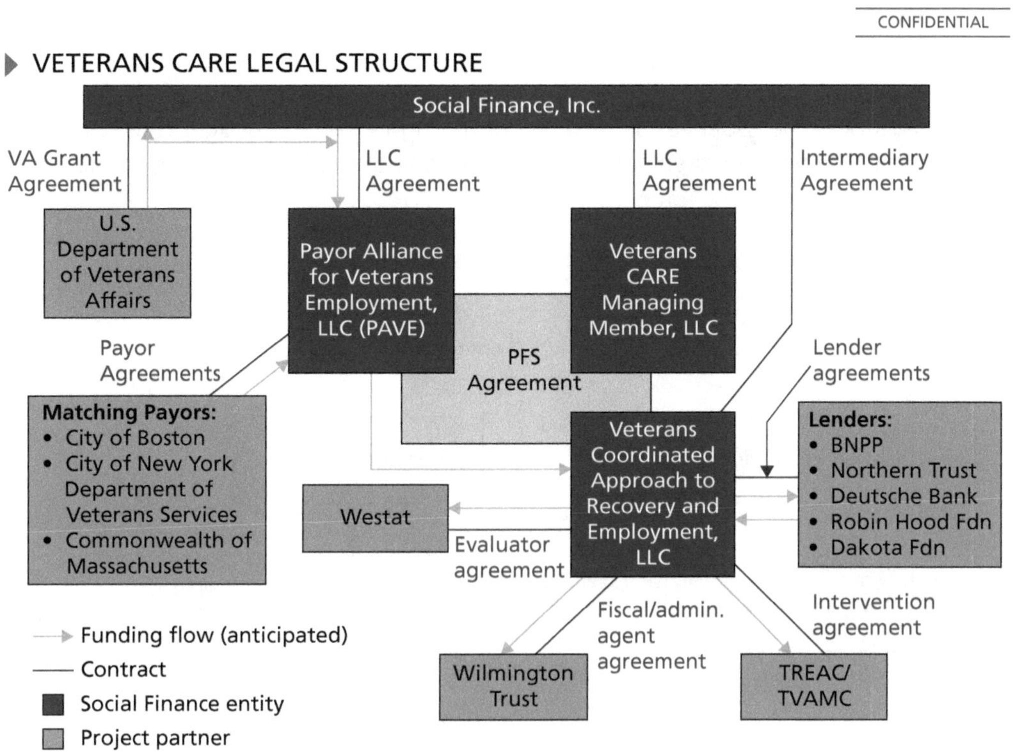

Legal Issues Related to PFS Transactions

Contracting Structures

Debt Mechanics

A SIB debt financing works in a similar manner to other debt transactions. The Intermediary borrows capital from lenders and issues a note promising repayment with defined interest rates upon the achievement of specific Outcomes. No ownership interest is granted. The Intermediary contracts separately with the Outcomes Payor, the Service Provider, and the Evaluator.

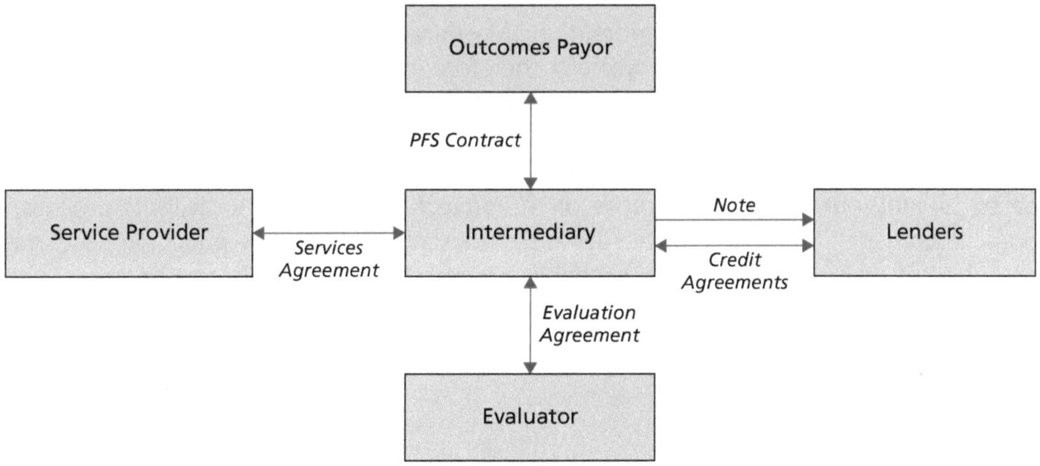

Equity Mechanics

A PFS equity financing works in a similar manner to other equity transactions. An ownership interest in the Intermediary is transferred to the investors via an issuance of common or preferred stock. The issuance can be direct or through a placement agent. As with a debt financing, the Intermediary then contracts separately with the Outcomes Payor, the Service Provider, and the Evaluator.

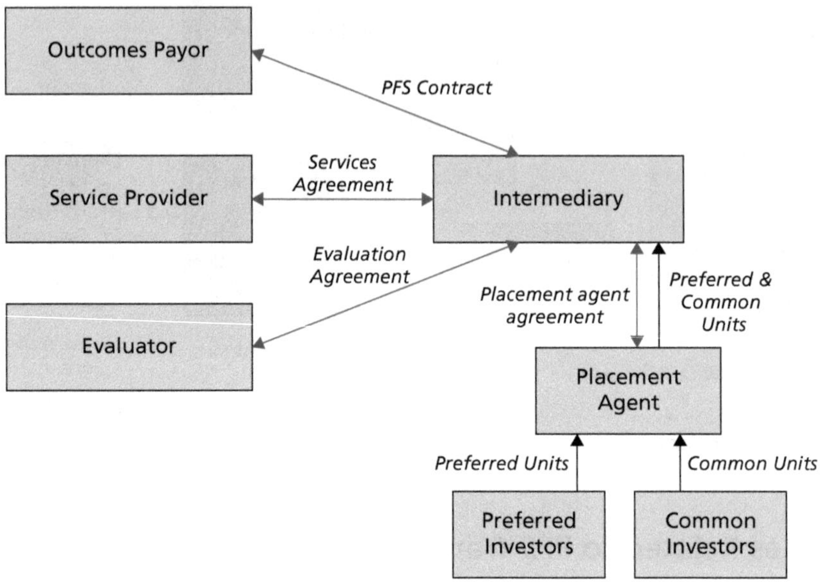

Unique Issues in SIBs

Credit Documents/Fiduciary Obligations

As noted above, SIBs may be structured as either debt or equity transactions, with provisions that are similar to commercial transactions. However, there are some important ways in which SIBs differ from more commercial transactions. As described above, SIBs are a financing mechanism to raise expansion capital for the delivery of social services to a vulnerable population. Investors are taking on the risk that the services may not achieve the targeted Outcomes, and, therefore, that they may not receive a return of all or a portion of their investment. Investors typically, therefore, cannot hold the Outcomes Payor or Intermediary in default for failure to make a payment, if that failure is due to the project not achieving the targeted Outcomes.

Furthermore, the Intermediary which issues the debt or equity interests is typically obligated to carry out the public purpose of the project, which is set forth in its organizational documents. In the Veterans CARE Project described above, the public purpose was described as "securing employment rehabilitation and support services to Veterans with service-connected Post-Traumatic Stress Disorder (PTSD) at certain Veterans' Administration Medical Centers across the United States." Therefore, the usual fiduciary obligations owed to lenders or investors are subject to the Intermediary's obligation to further the public purpose of the SIB project. This is important as the Intermediary must be able to act in the best interests of the public purpose of the project; balance the needs and interests of all of its contracting partners, including government, service providers, and funders; and hold harmless the Service Population.

Given that SIBs are intended to provide services to a vulnerable population, any termination provisions must provide for a "wind-down" period to allow for the orderly transition of the individuals receiving services to other service providers or to other funding streams. Investor funds continue to be applied to pay for services during such "wind-down" period.

PFS Contract/Early Termination Provisions and Risk Transfer

The primary risk of a SIB is that even an evidence-based intervention may not always achieve desired Outcomes. In addition, the maximum amount available to be paid as Outcome payments will typically only be paid upon achievement of maximum outcome levels. Funders, then, are facing a substantial risk when looking at a SIB investment because there is, in some cases, a potential for a zero return of capital. In order to mitigate this risk and to strike an effective balance of risk transfer between the Outcomes Payor and the Funder, PFS Contracts will generally include nonstandard early termination clauses. As an additional complicating factor, SIBs have an underlying Service Population that has to be considered. If an early termination occurs, there must be a responsible wind-down of services for this population such that no harmful effects occur.

Early termination clauses are both an integral and substantially negotiated part of designing an effective SIB. In the event that a project's early results indicate it has been unsuccessful, early termination allows investors to mitigate losses. A PFS Contract can outline many reasons for early exit, such as (1) an appropriations failure by an Outcome Payor, (2) termination of ancillary agreements such as the Service Agreement or the Evaluation Agreement, and (3) project-specific termination events related to outcome targets like under-enrollment of project participants, lack of Intervention resources, or changes in government funding flows which would impact project budgets. Early termination clauses should also include terms for the responsibilities of each party in the event of an early termination, such as project wind-down costs, early termination fees, and whether evidence is needed to justify termination.

Underlying Service Population

The underlying purpose of a SIB, the Service Population and the delivery of an Intervention to that population, is easy to lose sight of in the negotiation of all the contract terms and project structuring. Keeping the Service Population as a central focus is critical when building these transactions, including early termination provisions which should provide for either an effective wind-down of services for individual program participants or the transfer of program participants to a similar service or intervention. In addition, adequate protection such as data privacy considerations, informed consent, and review by an Independent Review Board of any proposed evaluation study are central to structuring the delivery of services and the evaluation methodology in SIBs.

Evaluation Methodology

Evaluation is a critical component of a model SIB; however, reverting complex evaluation methodologies to contract language is a difficult undertaking. While it is crucial that project partners agree on the exact methodology for evaluation and describe it accurately in the PFS Contract, the governance committees must have the authority to make adjustments, clarifications, or technical fixes throughout the project.

Data Sharing

A SIB relies on the gathering and evaluation of data related to determined social Outcomes. Oftentimes, SIBs rely on administrative data held by government agencies such as wage data, criminal justice data, health data, or educational data. Getting access to this information for the individuals involved in a particular project is subject to applicable state and federal data privacy laws such as the "Health Insurance Portability and Accountability Act" (HIPAA) or the "Family Educational Rights and Privacy Act" (FERPA). A data sharing agreement will specify the data to be analyzed and provide that such information has to be shared by the applicable government agency with the independent Evaluator. The Evaluator is responsible for analyzing the information and providing reports to the other project partners which present the data in an aggregated fashion, without any personally identifiable information included to protect the privacy of the individuals whose Outcomes are being measured.

Active Performance Management, Governance, and Learning Agenda

Another unique aspect of SIBs is the governance structure built into the PFS Contract which allows for review of data and project operational information on an ongoing basis and, more importantly, allows for course corrections in the operational aspects of the project. Typical service delivery contracts are fairly rigid and do not allow the government partner and service provider to flex project parameters easily. In a SIB where the focus is on *outcomes*, the "management committee" established pursuant to the governance structure and comprised of representatives from the Outcomes Payor, the Service Provider, and the Intermediary empowered to make adjustments to the delivery of services with the goal of optimizing Outcomes. For example, in the Veterans CARE Project described above, the management committee reviews enrollment data on an ongoing basis, identifies and addresses any potential challenges, and manages the project change process to implement changes with the appropriate level of oversight.[11]

The Intermediary plays an important role in the governance structure, providing "active performance management" of the project on an ongoing basis—keeping track of operational and budget aspects of the project to optimize achievement of the specified Outcomes.

While each project has specified Outcomes for which the Outcomes Payor will make payment, some projects may have a "learning agenda" that measures other ancillary outcomes for the Service Population. These learning outcomes do not result in additional payment, but they do provide helpful information to the Service Provider and the Outcomes Payor about the efficacy of the services in achieving a wider range of outcomes.

---

11. Original contract on file with authors.

Description of Legal Roles

Counsel to each of the parties in a SIB have many and varied considerations. As discussed above, unique aspects to a SIB from other financings and each of these components may affect the parties in a different way. Depending on which SIB party a counsel represents, there are certain fundamental protections that the legal review should monitor and negotiate. The following addresses each type of counsel in a SIB and some of the primary considerations such as counsel will encounter in a traditional SIB, plus some sample contract language that can be useful in demonstrating the particular considerations.

Government/Outcomes Payor Counsel

Counsel to an Outcomes Payor can include either or both in-house lawyers and external counsel, but, in any case, this can be one of the most challenging legal roles in a SIB transaction. In particular, government payors are often highly regulated with regard to contracting and the PFS Contract is typically unlike any contract a governmental entity is accustomed to seeing, reviewing, and approving. SIB project partners may need to navigate complex procurement rules in order to enter into a SIB financing with a governmental entity.

> **Authorization:** Outcomes Payors must have statutory authority and/or authority under its organizational documents to enter a project/PFS Contract. Some government entities have concluded that entering into a PFS Contract is authorized by their general authority to enter into contracts. Other government payors seek specific legislative or other authorization to enter into PFS Contracts. It should be noted that where an Intermediary is the entity raising the private capital and entering into the Funding Agreements with the Funders, the government does not need to seek authority to issue debt.
>
> When a government entity seeks specific authority, it can be granted through legislation passed through the applicable government body, a resolution or ordinance of the government body, or a resolution or written direction from a board of directors. To date, several states have adopted legislation that limits the implementation of the PFS structure to targeted Outcomes, services, or populations. In other cases, states have adopted legislation that can be broadly applied across state social services to implement a range of PFS Contracts.[12]
>
> *Sample Language [Resolution]: "[Outcomes Payor] is authorized and empowered to execute and deliver from time to time, in the name of and on behalf of such [Outcomes Payor], such contracts, agreements, instruments, certificates, notices or other documents as necessary or desirable for the conduct of its business, including but not limited to any pay for success contracts and related agreements and documents, fee and services agreements, and such other agreements, instruments, certificates, notices or other documents as may be required in connection therewith, or any amendment, restatement, modification or supplement thereto for a particular project . . ."*

---

12. Nonprofit Finance Fund (n.d.). Pay For Success Activity Map. Retrieved Aug. 24, 2022, from https://nff.org/pay-success-projects.

Sample Language [Legislation]: "Notwithstanding any general or special law to the contrary, the [Designated Contracting Agency or Party] may enter into pay for success contracts. Each contract shall include: (1) a requirement that a portion of the payment be conditioned on the achievement of specific outcomes based on defined performance targets; (2) an objective process by which an independent evaluator or validator will determine whether the performance targets have been achieved; (3) a calculation of the amount and timing of payments that would be earned during each year of the agreement if performance targets are achieved as determined by the independent evaluator or validator; and (4) a sinking fund requirement under which the [Designated Contracting Agency or Party] shall request an appropriation for each fiscal year that the contract is in effect, in an amount equal to the expected payments that the [Outcomes Payor] would ultimately be obligated to pay in the future based upon service provided during that fiscal year, if performance targets were achieved."[13]

Appropriations/Funding Risk: The term "appropriations risk" refers to the fact that, in most governmental jurisdictions, the governing body must affirmatively approve any government spending by setting aside (or appropriating) such money under an appropriations bill. Appropriations laws usually make funds available for only a one- or two-year period; however, the term of a PFS Contract can span several years before any Outcome payments may be due. Furthermore, one legislature typically cannot bind a future legislature to spend money later. Therefore, there is a risk (to investors) that even though a contract has been signed by a government entity, the legislative body of that entity will not appropriate funding for the payment of obligations due under that PFS Contract in the year in which Outcome payments would be due. As a result, in some governmental jurisdictions, regulatory changes or special approval may be needed to allow for multiyear contingency-based contracting. One way to circumvent the multiyear appropriations issue is to require, in the PFS Contract, a government payor to pre-fund all possible Outcome payments to a third-party held sinking fund. Funds can be returned to such governmental entity at the end of the contract term if the full amount was not needed to make Outcome payments.

Sample Language [PFS Contract]: "The [Outcomes Payor], acting through the [Designated Contracting Agency or Party], will annually request from [Government Entity] a request for appropriation, beginning in fiscal year [20__] and ending in fiscal year [20__], in the amount, together with amounts previously appropriated, that is necessary to make all Outcome Payments required to be paid under this PFS Contract. Any amounts so appropriated or received [shall be held in trust by [Outcomes Payor] until applied to make Outcome payments in accordance with this PFS Contract]/[transferred to third party trust account upon receipt to be held in trust to make Outcome payments]. Funds so appropriated are not eligible to return to the

13. *See, generally*, MASS. GEN. LAWS ch. 10, § 35VV (2012).

[Government Entity's] general fund until completion of the Project on _________, 20___ or termination of the project."

Sample Language [Legislation]: The [Designated Contracting Agency or Party] may provide that payments in future years under any such contracts shall constitute a general obligation of the [Outcomes Payor] for which the full faith and credit of the [Outcomes Payor] shall be pledged for the benefit of the providers of the contracted government services, but the total amount of payments under such contracts secured by a pledge of the full faith and credit of the [Outcomes Payor] shall not exceed, in the aggregate, $xx,000,000.[14]

Termination: As discussed above, termination of the PFS Contract and the project is a substantive negotiation point for all counsel as there are multiple issues that arise with respect to termination that are not present in more commercial financings (see "Intermediary Counsel—Termination" and "Funder Counsel—Termination" below). For an Outcomes Payor counsel, those issues include (1) ability to terminate in the event of a funding or appropriations failure, (2) obligations to make Outcome payments if a Funder defaults, and (3) continued Intervention treatment and payment for a Service Population during and after project termination (see also "Intermediary Counsel—Termination").

Sample Language: The execution or continuation of this PFS Contract is dependent upon the availability of funding. The [Outcome Payor's] deposit and payment obligations are payable only and solely from funds appropriated and available for this PFS Contract. The absence of appropriated or other lawfully available funds shall terminate this PFS Contract.

This PFS Agreement may be terminated by [Outcomes Payor], by written notice to the other parties hereto, if a Funder capital shortfall is not cured within 60 days of such written notice.

Risk Transfer: In a SIB, all or a portion of the risk that the services delivered by the Service Provider will not achieve the specified Outcomes is borne by the private Funders. Under a typical service contract, an Outcomes Payor contracts for certain services to be delivered to a certain population in order to ameliorate a social or public problem or cost. The primary risk to the Outcomes Payor in that case is that limited financial resources have been expended but the Service Population is not effectively served and, therefore, the preexisting issue is not addressed. In a well-structured SIB transaction, all or a portion of the financial component of this risk is transferred from the Outcomes Payor to the Funders. Both parties then share some of the risk involved in trying to solve the underlying issue.

---

14. *See, generally*, MASS. GEN. LAWS ch. 10, § 35VV (2012). ("The secretary may provide that payments in future years under any such contracts shall constitute a general obligation of the commonwealth for which the full faith and credit of the commonwealth shall be pledged for the benefit of the providers of the contracted government services, but the total amount of payments under such contracts secured by a pledge of the full faith and credit of the commonwealth shall not exceed, in the aggregate, $50,000,000.")

The range of financial risk can shift between the Outcomes Payor and the Funder. Especially in early SIBs, Funders took on all of the financial risk associated with a project—if stated project Outcomes were not met, Funders did not receive any payments. Additional models have developed in which the financial risk may be shared between the Outcomes Payor and the Funder. In such projects, the Funder is guaranteed some return of capital and only a portion of the overall possible Outcomes Payments are "contingent" on the realized success of the project.

This "contingency" amount can depend on many factors, including the ability to attract Funders to the project and historical or empirical evidence of the effectiveness of the Intervention. When structuring a SIB transaction, Outcomes Payor counsel must make sure there is a satisfactory risk transfer to the Funder that makes the other obstacles of structuring worthwhile.

Procurement/Contracting Process: In most instances, governments have employed competitive bidding processes for selecting projects, service providers, or both. Once a program is launched, some Outcomes Payors will take an active role in monitoring the progress of the service provider, while in other cases the monitoring is left entirely to the Intermediary.

Intermediary Counsel

The Intermediary is the "quarterback" of the SIB because it is instrumental in advising the structuring and execution of the SIB project. An Intermediary will enter into contracts with all other parties to a SIB transaction, and Intermediary counsel will likely have additional project management responsibilities in order to keep the financing moving forward. Again, Intermediary counsel can be in-house, external, or both. Most of the primary project agreements will be drafted by Intermediary counsel, including the Service Agreement, the Evaluation Agreement, the Funding Agreements, and the central project contract, the PFS Contract.

Valid Organization and Authority: Intermediary counsel must ensure that the Intermediary has valid, binding authority to enter into the various contractual arrangements. Depending on the organization of the Intermediary entity, this could require statutory authority or approval of a governing body. It is recommended in most cases to isolate the responsibilities of the Intermediary for a particular SIB transaction through the creation of one or more special purpose vehicles which can act on behalf of the Intermediary but provide some protection to the Intermediary by removing it from contractual obligations. If a special purpose vehicle is used, Intermediary counsel will establish such entity by creating an appropriate corporate structure, drafting organizational documents, and registering such entity with the appropriate governmental bodies in a given jurisdiction.

Sample Language [PFS Contract]: [Intermediary] is a [corporate entity] validly existing and in good standing under the laws of the State of [Jurisdiction of Organization], is qualified to conduct business in the [State of Jurisdiction and State of Project], and has full corporate power and authority to conduct its business as presently conducted and to enter into and perform under this PFS Contract.

The execution, delivery and performance by [Intermediary] of this PFS Contract and the performance by [Intermediary] under this PFS Contract have been duly authorized by all necessary corporate action. This PFS Contract has been duly executed and delivered by [Intermediary] and, assuming the due authorization, execution and delivery by [Outcomes Payor], and subject to the effect of applicable Laws (e.g., bankruptcy, insolvency, reorganization, moratorium and similar Laws relating to the rights of creditors generally), constitutes a legal, valid, and binding obligation of [Intermediary], enforceable against [Intermediary] in accordance with its terms. The execution and performance of this PFS Contract by [Intermediary] will not violate any provision of Law and will not conflict with or result in any breach of any of the terms, conditions or provisions of, or constitute a default under or require a consent or waiver under, [Intermediary]'s organizational documents or any decree, judgment, order applicable to [Intermediary].

Sample Language [Board Resolution]: Each of the Authorized Officers of [Intermediary] be, and each of them hereby is, acting alone or together, authorized and empowered to execute and deliver from time to time, in the name of and on behalf of [Intermediary] such contracts, agreements, instruments, certificates, notices or other documents as necessary or desirable for the conduct of its business, including but not limited to pay for success contracts and related agreements and documents, fee and services agreements, credit or loan agreements, security or pledge agreements, subordination and intercreditor agreements and such other agreements, instruments, certificates, notices or other documents as may be required in connection therewith, each of which will be in such form and substance as may be acceptable to any Authorized Officer, which acceptance by such Authorized Officer shall be conclusively evidenced by such Authorized Officer's execution thereof, and such execution to be conclusive evidence that the same shall have been authorized and approved by [Intermediary] in every respect.

No Financial Obligation: An Intermediary is an independent party to the SIB transaction in that it does not share in the risk of the financing. The prominence of the Intermediary in the structuring of the SIB and its positioning in the middle of the contracting is such that parties may wish to obligate the Intermediary in order to secure their own interests. Intermediary counsel should review agreements with the mindset that Intermediary is a conduit entity that should be shielded from any outcomes-based or project-related financial obligations. In some instances, the Intermediary will accept some of the financial risk by taking a deferred fee approach when structuring the capital.

Sample Language: Notwithstanding anything herein to the contrary, the [Intermediary] shall in no event be liable in any way for amounts outstanding with respect to the [Funding, including Outcome payments, expenses, principal or interest] or any other amount or obligation that may arise under the [Project Agreement].

Monitors Project Fidelity in Written Contracts: In terms of the project management role, one of the critically important responsibilities of Intermediary counsel is to ensure that the project as structured, negotiated, and approved by all contract parties is accurately and consistently represented across the various agreements. A helpful method for applying project terms to multiple agreements is to memorialize these terms in schedules or appendices that can be incorporated into multiple contracts. Terms that can benefit from this treatment include Intervention design and implementation, evaluation methodology, outcome payment calculations, and governance structures.

Caution! It can be tempting to ensure accuracy by memorializing extremely detailed descriptions of the project terms in the contracts. However, SIB transactions are based on delivery of services to a varied population under changing circumstances and are developed with the philosophy that services could be better delivered via evolving and adaptable implementation. When project terms as anticipated are cemented in contract language, the description can hinder the on-the-ground adaptability and flexibility of project partners to react to real-time evidence to correct course and ensure better Outcomes.

Termination: One of the most significant considerations when drafting a termination provision for a SIB transaction is that the underlying Service Population has started to receive Intervention treatment and may be relying on continuation of services. If Funder capital and services are suddenly cut off, the population that was meant to be served by the SIB can be harmed. All of the parties have a mutual responsibility to consider the underlying Service Population and a responsible wind-down of services in the event of a termination. The Intermediary and its counsel should carefully draft the termination section of the PFS Contract with this consideration in mind. The governance structure can be a useful mechanism to address issues that are difficult to predict ahead of time.

Furthermore, the financial risk of an early termination of the project must be allocated between the Funders and the Outcomes Payor. When a project winds down early, there may not be sufficient Outcome payments that can be calculated and invoiced to the Outcomes Payor in order to return capital to Funders for costs of services that have already been delivered. If the project is ended, Funders will lose the ability to recoup those costs through future Outcome payments. Either the Outcomes Payor must pay for costs of services delivered notwithstanding the calculation or achievement of Outcomes, or the Funders must accept the risk of loss in an early termination. One useful approach is to allocate the risk in part based upon the reason for early termination, where Funders bear more risk in a Funder-prompted early termination and Outcomes Payors bear more risk in an Outcomes Payor-prompted early termination.

Sample Language:

Effect of Termination: Upon issuance of a notice of termination by [Intermediary], no additional participants will be enrolled in the services, provided that any participants will continue to receive the services for a period of time to be determined by the [Management Committee] to ensure the orderly transfer of such participants to alternate services.

Wind-Up. Upon a notification of termination by one or more of the parties, [Intermediary] will prepare a project termination budget (the "Project Termination Budget") consisting of the following costs which shall shall be at the standard, uninflated rates of such provider:

any extraordinary costs for the [Service Provider] incurred as a result of the termination event and required for wind-up of Intervention services, such as severance, occupancy, etc.;

any extraordinary costs incurred as a result of the termination event and required for wind-up of services by the Evaluator, including but not limited to costs to expedite measurement of outcomes; and

any extraordinary costs incurred by [Intermediary] as a result of the termination event and required for wind-up of services, including fees to [Intermediary] to oversee wind-up activities.

Following receipt of a notice of termination from one of the parties, [Outcomes Payor] will pay to [Intermediary] the amounts set forth below:

(A) *Payments based on Outcomes and Early Outcomes, if achieved, which will consist of the following:*

    (1) *Outcome payments for participants for whom Outcomes have been fully achieved and calculated in accordance with this PFS Contract, but not yet made, if any; and*
    (2) *Early Outcome payments for participants for whom some portion of services have been delivered and early Outcomes can be calculated as of the effective date of termination of this PFS Contract;*

(B) *In the case of a termination event that is prompted by the Outcomes Payor, Payments based on costs of services rendered for participants for whom Intervention services have been delivered, but Outcome payments and early Outcome payments do not cover the full amount of Funder capital deposited with the Intermediary (with no financial return on such capital to Funders) that has been expended for purposes of the project and is not otherwise available to be retrieved and returned to the Funders (the "Remaining Project Costs"), up to the date of termination; and*

(C) *In the case of a termination event that is prompted by the Outcomes Payor, the full amount of the Project Termination Budget [and an additional payment in an amount equal to the remaining unpaid principal and interest at the rates set forth in the Funding Agreements, together with an amount equal to [2%] of the outstanding principal amount of the loan received by [Intermediary] from the Funders].*

Funder Counsel

As Funder counsel, the overarching concern is arguably to secure and protect the Funder's investment as much as possible and to maximize the possible Outcome payment. However, it is worth noting that in this phase of the SIB life span, SIBs are still primarily an instrument of an "impact first" investor (as opposed to a "finance first" investor primarily interested in capital gains). As such, Funder counsel should dually consider the best interest of the project and the underlying Service Population as well as the financial interests of the Funder when negotiating contract terms. The Funding Agreements, the primary contracting documents to be negotiated by Funder counsel, will vary significantly depending if the project is structured as a debt or equity investment. However, the same principal contract terms will apply in either case.

Securing Outcome Payments: In all cases, a SIB is a risky investment for an investor because payment is contingent on Outcomes. However, risk of Outcomes notwithstanding, Funder counsel should consider the security of such Outcome payments and the obligation of the Outcomes Payor to make those payments under the contract if and when Outcomes are achieved. Outcome payments can be "secured" in a number of ways, including (1) in the case of a government entity, a waiver of sovereign immunity or a pledge of the full faith and credit of such jurisdiction or (2) the deposit of funds for Outcome payments into a trust account or a third-party controlled escrow account in which lenders or investors can perfect a first priority lien.

Sample Language: To secure the prompt payment and performance of any and all obligations, [Intermediary as borrower] hereby pledges, assigns and grants to the [Funder], a first priority security interest in, and lien on, the deposit account held at the [Fiscal Agent] in the name of [Intermediary as borrower] bearing account number [_______] (and including any subaccounts thereof), and the investment property, securities entitlements and money held therein.

Governance: Funder counsel will want to watch and negotiate the Funder's rights to monitor the project. Depending on the motivation of the Funder, there can be substantial variation in the level of involvement a particular Funder may wish to have with respect to a given SIB project; therefore, Funder counsel must discuss with their client the level of involvement and oversight that should be sought. Monitoring can range from the receipt of status/progress reports to a nonvoting, observer seat on the executive committee which oversees the project. The level of oversight sought should correspond not only to the motivation of the Funder but the expertise of the Funder with regard to the Intervention or the Service Population.

Sample Monitoring Terms:

(1) A quarterly statement from the Fiscal Agent with respect to the pledged deposit control account listing withdrawals, deposits, current balance, and accrued interest.

(2) A semi-annual program report prepared by the Intermediary setting forth project benchmarks such as enrollment and demographic data and a certification by the Intermediary that the project continues to be operated substantially in compliance with the Project Agreements.

(3) A nonvoting, observer seat on an executive committee tasked with general oversight of the project.

Modification/Termination Rights: As discussed, Funders face a substantial risk when looking at a SIB investment because there is, in some cases, a potential for a zero return of capital. In order to mitigate this risk, Funder counsel should carefully review termination language and may wish to limit the ability of the parties to structurally change the project without the input or oversight of the Funder.

Sample Language: [Intermediary] agrees that it shall not (i) make, consent to or otherwise permit to be made any amendments to or modifications of any Project Agreements (other than clarifications or amendments to correct obvious or technical errors) without the consent of [Funder], (ii) terminate, consent to the termination of or otherwise permit the termination of any Project Agreement without the consent of [Funder] [or (iii) otherwise amend, modify or terminate any of the Project Agreements in violation of the terms of the Funding Agreements.]

Intercreditor Rights: Often, there will be more than one Funder associated with a SIB. Funder roles can include senior or junior debt, common or preferred stockholders, or even philanthropic recoverable or nonrecoverable grants. Funder counsel will negotiate the terms of any relevant intercreditor, subordination, or grant agreement as necessary.

Service Provider/Evaluator Counsel

Issues that the counsel to the Service Provider or Evaluator should consider do not differ substantially from any other contracting these entities may do. Counsel should carefully review the services to ensure that implementation or evaluation methodology lines up with the activities and plans of the client, but in most cases, no portion of the payment terms should be contingent on Outcomes.

Conclusion

SIBs have emerged in the last few years as a financing mechanism to bring private impact investment capital to fund the expansion of data-driven social interventions, with repayment coming from government in recognition of improved life Outcomes for the Service Population, as well as an improved community benefit. As a financing mechanism, SIBs aim to replicate the structure of traditional debt or equity financings in order to minimize the barriers to raising private impact investment capital within the unique structure of a SIB. In terms of an allocation of risk between the private impact investment capital and government, SIBs most closely resemble a "P3" arrangement (public–private partnership) where some or all of the risk of service delivery is borne by the providers of private capital. The governance structure of SIBs resembles the governance structure of P3 contracts which similarly provide for more flexibility in the relationship between the Service Provider and Outcomes Payor.

Based on these precedents, form agreements for PFS Contracts, Funding Agreements, Service Agreements, and Evaluator Agreements are being developed. As the SIB market continues to evolve, these form agreements will foster growth in a manner that recognizes the interests of all of the parties, while keeping a focus on ensuring the delivery of services to a vulnerable population.[15]

The growth in impact investments has also given rise to an ongoing debate about how best to measure impact and how best to ensure that an investment is returning both a financial return and a social return. SIBs occupy a unique place in this conversation as the financial return on a SIB is directly tied to a measurable social impact.

Checklist of Questions or Issues

- ✓ Is this transaction a SIB?
- ✓ Private investor/lender capital used to finance the delivery of social or public services?
- ✓ All or a portion of repayment is dependent on Outcomes?
- ✓ An Intermediary entity exists at the center of the contracting structure?

Considerations for Counsel

Services and Service Population

- ✓ What population is being served?
- ✓ Is this the most effective way to serve this population?
- ✓ Is there a close relationship between the Intervention's expected results and the benefit to the agency or department making Outcome payments?
- ✓ Is the risk transfer sufficient to make the additional costs associated with a SIB a satisfactory option?

Data Sharing

- ✓ Is data available to evaluate this population and this Intervention?
  - ✓ Which agency holds the data?
  - ✓ What are the restrictions and options for sharing these data with the Evaluator?
- ✓ Review applicable state and federal data privacy laws.

Authorization/Appropriations Risk

- ✓ Does the government/Outcomes Payor have the requisite authority to enter into the PFS Contract?
- ✓ How can the appropriation risk be mitigated—through a general obligation pledge or setting aside funding up-front or an annual basis to be held until needed to make Outcome payments?

Early Termination Provisions

- ✓ Provide for orderly wind-down of services.

---

15. *See generally*, Nonprofit Finance Fund (n.d.). Pay For Success Resources. Last visited on Aug. 25, 2022, https://nff.org/invest-in-results.

- ✓ Identify the various reasons for an early termination, including a failure to make appropriations, failure to make payment, under-enrollment in the project, failure of the Funders to meet their capital calls, default under a Service Agreement or Evaluator Agreement.
- ✓ Provide for payment of Outcome payments and early Outcome payments as well as a return of capital in those instances where the Outcomes Payor is at fault.

Case Study

Overview of the Cuyahoga Partnering for Family Success Program and Key Legal Issues in Pay for Success Projects

Written by Hilary Jackler

The Cuyahoga Partnering for Family Success Program

In 2014, the first county-level pay for success project launched in the United States and continued until 2019. The parties involved were Cuyahoga County (the governmental entity), FrontLine Service, Inc. ("FrontLine"; the service provider), Enterprise Community Partners, Inc. (which established Cuyahoga PFS, LLC (the "SPV" or social purpose vehicle) to act as the project manager and fiscal agent), Case Western Reserve University ("Case Western"; the independent evaluator), and The Reinvestment Fund, The George Gund Foundation, The Cleveland Foundation, Sisters of Charity Foundation of Cleveland, and Nonprofit Finance Fund (collectively, the "Funders").

The project was designed to provide services to individuals with children who are currently homeless and have been determined by the Department of Children and Family Services within the Cuyahoga County Office of Health and Human Services to have children placed in foster care. The PFS contract contemplated that over a twelve- to fifteen-month period, FrontLine would assist clients to address their basic needs, obtain housing placement, trauma therapy, and family reunification services. FrontLine would link each client to housing and deliver an evidence-based homelessness transition therapy known as "Critical Time Intervention" with a goal of shortening the period of homelessness for child-welfare-involved families, assisting families to seek and secure affordable and stable housing, adding practical assistance during critical transition periods, providing trauma intervention, and enhancing family preservation services.

Cuyahoga County agreed to make certain "success payments" if the interventions resulted in a reduction in the number of foster care days when comparing the combined number of out-of-home placement days for children in the treatment group versus the out-of-home placement days for children in a control group. The success payment is equal to $75 per reduced foster care day, which represented the current combined average cost of foster care and related placement services, up to a cap of $5,000,000.

The primary agreements executed to implement this project were as follows:

(1) *PFS Contract:* A PFS Contract was executed among Cuyahoga County, FrontLine, and the SPV. The PFS Contract described the overall project parameters and

identified the roles, responsibilities, risks, and rights of the governmental entity, service provider, and intermediary.

(2) *Loan Agreements and Grant Agreements:* The SPV executed a loan agreement or a grant agreement, as applicable, with each of the Funders setting forth the terms of payment by the Funder to the SPV and the payment of any success payments from the SPV to the Funder.

(3) *Independent Evaluator Agreement:* The SPV and Case Western entered into an Independent Evaluator Agreement identifying the evaluation services to be provided by Case Western.

A graphical summary of the transaction is as follows:

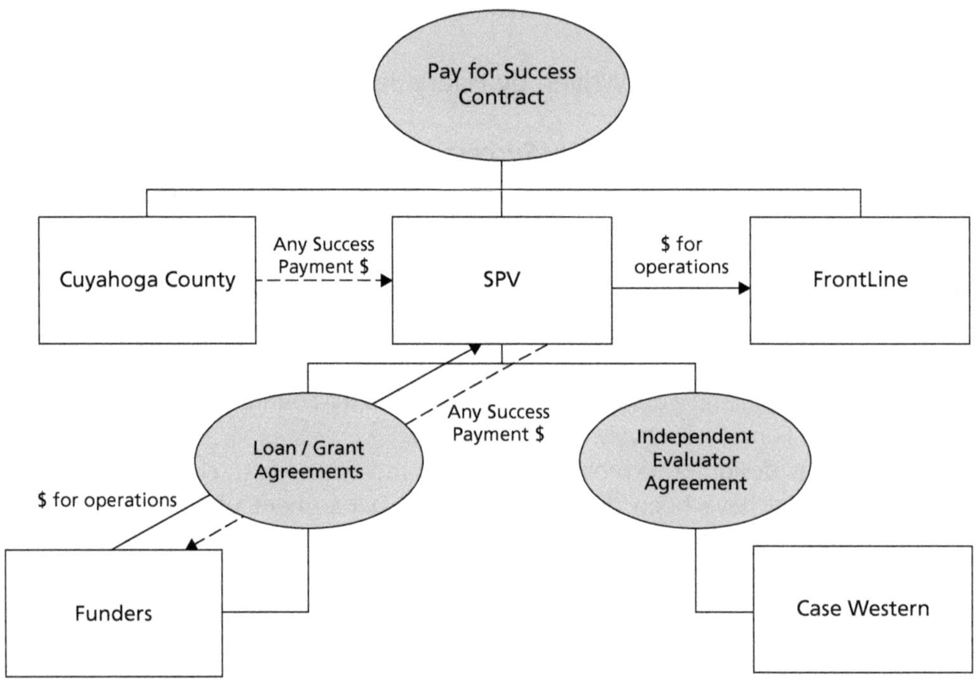

Key Legal Issues in Pay for Success Transactions

Regardless of the entity represented, in approaching a PFS project, attorneys will need to focus on the following topics:

(1) *Legal Framework Development:* In order to determine what legal agreements are required, attorneys will want to understand the roles and responsibilities of each of the parties, how the project will operate, and the goals of all parties. Even though every party may not be a party to each agreement, attorneys may wish to monitor the contents of all agreements to determine whether any rights or obligations could impact their clients.

(2) *Understanding the Legal Authority of Each Participant:* Attorneys will want to ensure that each party has the legal authority to enter into the agreement(s) and perform their responsibilities. This is particularly important with respect to the

governmental entity for which specific authorizing legislation and/or appropriations may be required.

(3) *Clearly Defining the Metrics of Success:* It is important for the parties to define clearly and specifically the metrics of success. These metrics will be used not only to determine financial obligations but also to drive the project toward a certain end goal.

(4) *Termination Rights and Processes:* While it is likely that all parties are entering into the project with the best of intentions, it is nonetheless important for attorneys to help their clients consider what could go wrong and/or what could lead a party to want to terminate prior to the expiration of the agreement(s). Termination rights need to be defined clearly, and the impact of the termination needs to be identified for each scenario.

(5) *Mitigate Risks:* Attorneys will constantly be assisting their clients to identify risks with respect to their participation in the project and mitigate those risks to the extent practicable.

Attorneys will also want to focus on particular additional areas given their client's role in the project, such as those listed in the following table.

Additional Areas of Focus Areas Depending upon Attorney Role	
Client	**Attorney Areas of Focus**
Governmental Entity	• Ensuring procurement processes are followed • Identifying existing legal authority and/or advising on new authorities required to enter into the transaction • Complying with appropriations laws with respect to any success payments • Ensuring any standard governmental requirements are incorporated into any contracts • No or specified liability in the event that "success" is not achieved
Service Provider	• Ensuring all responsibilities relating to services are clearly defined—both for the service provider and any other entities for which action is required in order for the service provider to perform • Processes for payments for services • No or specified liability in the event that "success" is not achieved, and success payments are not paid
SPV	• Defining the SPV's responsibility to each party and each party's responsibilities to the SPV to ensure the overall transaction will work • SPV's rights to receive funds to support the project and for its own operations • SPV's obligations to pay funds to other parties (including no or specified liability if success payments are not paid)
Lender/Grantor	• Timing, terms, and conditions with respect to provision of funds to the SPV and receipt of any success payments • Definition of role (if any) during project operation (i.e., certain approval rights, notices, etc.)
Evaluator	• Defining the evaluator's services and any inputs required from other parties in order for the evaluator to perform • Payments for services

Practice Tips for Pay for Success Transactions

Parties entering into a pay for success transaction are driven to achieve a specific success that hopefully—but may not—be attainable. Pay for success projects are typically designed to deviate from, with a goal of improving upon, the status quo. However, despite each party conducting extensive due diligence up-front and even performing exactly as the contracts provide, there is a risk that the project does not meet the metric of "success" set forth in the pay for success contract. The funders contractually agree to bear the financial risk by outlaying money that may never be recovered, but each party also has reputational and operational risks.

With this unique backdrop, attorneys will want to consider the following in their drafting of transaction agreements:

(1) Acknowledge the unique construct of pay for success transactions—in particular, the reputational risk of all parties in characterizing "success" (and that being "unsuccessful" does not necessarily equate to the project being a failure or a party not performing exactly as required) and the uncertainty of achieving "success."

(2) Consider what each party needs to be doing to achieve "success." While there may be multiple transaction documents, they all need to fit together in a way that drives "success" within the desired time frame.

(3) Carefully determine what the appropriate success metrics for the project will be, recognizing that the metric will be what motivates behavior by all parties. Define it clearly so there is no ambiguity with respect to payment obligations or calculation of success.

(4) Develop a transaction structure that will allow for collaboration, the early identification of areas of concern, a framework for expeditiously solving any problems or disputes, and enough flexibility to address those items unknown to the parties at execution.

(5) If the parties are aware of certain contingencies up-front, identify within the contract what happens if the contingencies are or are not satisfied. Similarly, try to pinpoint the specific scenarios that would make your client and others consider terminating the project early and address what each party's rights and responsibilities are in each such event.

Chapter 5
Green Capitalism: The Case of the Environmental Impact Bond

Etienne C. Toussaint

Introduction

Perhaps the residents in attendance at the community meeting should have seen it coming. It was April 2014, and the financially struggling local government of Flint, Michigan, was desperately trying to keep the city afloat. A palpable tension flooded the room as government officials attempted to explain the city's recent switch from water purchased from the City of Detroit to water pumped from the local Flint River.[1] Community anxiety and collective distrust swelled. By October of that same year, the automotive company General Motors would elect to take its local auto plant off Flint River water because of corrosion to its engine parts. In January 2015, filtered water coolers would be installed in the state's government office buildings to ensure the health and safety of employees and visitors. Danger signs would continue to emerge, but for most Flint residents sitting in that April meeting, there were few options to avoid what would eventually be confirmed as the sad truth—Flint's drinking water had been contaminated by disease-causing bacteria, carcinogens, and lead.[2]

---

1. Dustin Stephens, *The Flint Water Crisis: A Loss of Trust*, CBS News (June 17, 2018), https://www.cbsnews.com/news/the-flint-water-crisis-a-loss-of-trust/.
2. Melissa Denchak, *Flint Water Crisis: Everything You Need to Know*, NRDC (Nov. 8, 2018), https://www.nrdc.org/stories/flint-water-crisis-everything-you-need-know.

The water crisis in Flint became national news when it was discovered that countless residents, including children, were getting sick from the contaminated water flowing through the city's outdated pipes. But Flint, Michigan, is not the only city in America facing infrastructure challenges that threaten the public health of its residents and the environmental stability of its waterways. With over 750 cities across the country operating outdated sewer systems that couple water collection with waste disposal, including our nation's capital, it is becoming increasingly clear that America has a serious water problem.[3] As stormwater continues to be funneled into the same pipes that handle raw sewage, and as levels of stormwater runoff rise year after year due to the compounding effects of climate change,[4] Washington, D.C., and other cities around the country are now seeking cost-effective solutions to save America's precious waterways, protect the public health of its citizens, and conserve the ecosystem.[5]

Even more, diminished water quality, severe flooding, and related environmental challenges stemming from climate change have been disproportionately borne by low-income and other marginalized communities.[6] As a result, environmental justice advocates have demanded progressive public policies and law reforms to shore up crumbling infrastructure in urban centers and rebuild outdated waterways in rural peripheries. Yet, local governments have failed time and time again to meet federal and state environmental regulations.[7] Further, they have struggled to comply with ambitious consent decrees issued by federal agencies,[8] in many cases due to fiscal austerity or outright political intransigence.[9]

---

3. Laurie Mazur, *Why Environmental Impact Bonds Are Catching On*, Governing: The States and Localities (May 25, 2018), http://www.governing.com/gov-institute/voices/col-environmental-impact-bonds-washington-dc-baltimore-atlanta.html.

4. *See* U.S. Glob. Change Rsch. Program, Climate Change Impacts in the United States 7–13 (2014), http://s3.amazonaws.com/nca2014/low/NCA3_Climate_Change_Impacts_in_the_United%20States_LowRes.pdf?dodownlo=1.

5. Since the 1940s, Washington, D.C., has seen a steady rise in regional temperatures. This climate change has dramatically shifted rainfall patterns, increasing the intensity of droughts and floods beyond the capacity of a stormwater system built in the early 1900s. Average annual precipitation in the D.C. metropolitan area has increased five to ten percent since the original water system was built, increasing the strain on the system and causing floods. For example, in June 2006, a severe rainstorm flooded several federal buildings and museums around Federal Triangle, causing $10 million in damage across the region. *See* U.S. Env't Prot. Agency, EPA 430-F-16-064, What Climate Change Means for the District of Columbia (2016), https://19january2017snapshot.epa.gov/sites/production/files/2016-11/documents/climate-change-dc.pdf; Dist. Dep't of Transp., Climate Change Adaptation Plan, https://ddot.dc.gov/sites/default/files/dc/sites/ddot/publication/attachments/ddot_climate_adaptation_plan.pdf.

6. Stephane Hallegatte et al., Shock Waves: Managing the Impacts of Climate Change on Poverty 3–12 (2016), https://openknowledge.worldbank.org/handle/10986/22787.

7. Sam Ross-Brown, *Beyond Flint: How Local Governments Ignore Federal Water Standards*, Am. Prospect (Feb. 24, 2016), https://prospect.org/article/beyond-flint-how-local-governments-ignore-federal-water-standards.

8. Eric Letsinger, *Sharing the Risks and Rewards: Could the "Pay for Success" Model of Environmental Impact Bonds Be the Future of Water Infrastructure Financing?*, Water Fin. & Mgmt. (June 18, 2018), https://waterfm.com/sharing-risks-rewards/?isid=Mzg4MDE2Mw ("Last June, the American Society of Civil Engineers (ASCE) gave the country's infrastructure an overall rating of "D+," estimating an additional $206 billion per year above current projected spending that is needed to improve our water, waste management, energy, and transport systems and restore their basic function. If that gap is not filled, the ASCE predicts that poor infrastructure will cost the country $3.9 trillion in lost GDP, $7 trillion in lost business sales, and 2.5 million lost jobs by 2025.").

9. *See America's Proposed Budget Cuts Will Be Bad for the Environment*, Economist (Mar. 23, 2017), https://www.economist.com/international/2017/03/23/americas-proposed-budget-cuts-will-be-bad-for-the-environment (discussing the impact of the Trump Administration's proposed budget cuts to climate change mitigation policies and programs).

Some scholars argue that the deteriorating infrastructure and contaminated water supplies in poverty-stricken communities like Flint, Michigan, are part and parcel of a neoliberal politics of abandonment that overwhelms low-income and racially segregated communities nationwide. This system of "racial capitalism," to echo the phrase popularized by political theorist Cedric Robinson, exploits racial biases and prejudices that define zones of underdevelopment to justify the future economic gain of real estate developers and speculators.[10] Notwithstanding concerns that a reliance on private capital to advance community development often perpetuates urban decay and blocks progressive visions of economic development, such as the community ownership and control of property, environmental advocates and lawmakers have increasingly turned to private capital for help.

In some respects, the whims of politics have stymied existing environmental interventions that bring well-proven methodologies and data-driven tools. Although the benefits of watershed management and environmental conservation, for example, have been known for some time, the political decision-making process has often dictated their adoption.[11] In the 1990s, when New York City was faced with the prospect of financing and constructing a new $6 billion water-treatment facility to meet Clean Water Act (CWA) requirements, posing an additional $250 million in annual maintenance expenses, local government politics facilitated another option.[12] Instead of embarking upon the costly construction of a new facility, New York City opted to make an immediate and one-time "forward-looking" investment of $1.5 billion toward the conservation and management of its existing reservoir system.[13] Although the investment boded financial and operational risks, it paid off handsomely, saving New York City billions of dollars over the next twenty years and conserving over 25,000 acres of land.[14] Unfortunately, many local governments do not believe that they can integrate long-run costs and benefits into their day-to-day decision making.[15] As a result, political leaders increasingly rely upon public–private partnerships to mobilize private capital toward resolving "negative externalities"—the unintended social and economic consequences of existing market mechanisms.[16] Many cities have already explored

---

10. *See* Laura Pulido, *Flint, Environmental Racism, and Racial Capitalism*, 27 Capitalism Nature Socialism 1, 1–16 (2016) ("The devaluation of Black (and other nonwhite) bodies has been a central feature of global capitalism for centuries and creates a landscape of differential value which can be harnessed in diverse ways to facilitate the accumulation of more power and profit than would otherwise be possible."); *see also, generally*, Cedric Robinson, Black Marxism 2 (Univ. of N.C. Press, 2000) (1983) (advancing the concept of racial capitalism to explain how "the development, organization, and expansion of capitalist society pursued essentially racial directions").
11. *Cities Define Key Obstacles to Achieving Climate Goals & Solutions to Overcome Them*, United Nations: Sustainable Dev. Goals (2016), https://www.un.org/sustainabledevelopment/blog/2016/05/cities-define-key-obstacles-to-achieving-climate-goals-solutions-to-overcome-them/.
12. Andrew C. Revkin, *Billion-Dollar Plan to Clean New York City Water at Its Source*, N.Y. Times, Aug. 31, 1997, https://www.nytimes.com/1997/08/31/nyregion/billion-dollar-plan-to-clean-new-york-city-water-at-its-source.html.
13. Eve Boyce & Marcy Lyman, *Conservation Partnerships with Water Utilities*, Conservation Fin. Network (Apr. 24, 2018), https://www.conservationfinancenetwork.org/2018/04/24/conservation-partnerships-with-water-utilities.
14. *Id.*
15. *See* Michael P. Vandenbergh & Jonathan M. Gilligan, *Beyond Gridlock: The Private Governance Response to Climate Change*, 40 Colum. J. Envtl. L. 217, 224 (2015).
16. *See* Richard C. Schragger, *Is a Progressive City Possible? Reviving Urban Liberalism for the Twenty-First Century*, 7 Harv. L. & Pol'y Rev. 231 (2013); David Hall, *Greening the Future: A Case for Environmental Impact Bonds*, 2 Pol'y Q. 13, 41 (2017) (explaining that negative externalities occur when "an activity or transaction by some party causes an unintended loss or gain in welfare to another party, and no compensation for the change in welfare occurs").

social finance innovations toward this end,[17] from the development of microfinance institutions to the promotion of social enterprise lending schemes. In each case, they offer aid to citizens who have been harmed by the pro-growth ideology that dominates urban politics.[18]

An emerging social finance tool, the "environmental impact bond" (EIB), has unveiled a new world of opportunities for cities like Flint, Michigan, to experiment with privately financed approaches to mitigating climate change.[19] In the case of Washington, D.C., the EIB has facilitated the development of large-scale green infrastructure that promises to stem the tide of stormwater runoff. Unlike traditional bonds, which are generally fixed-income instruments that yield variable or fixed interest payments to lenders, the EIB is a "pay-for-performance" contract that monetizes the future cost savings of targeted environmental interventions and passes those savings to private lenders.[20] Accordingly, these performance-based contractual arrangements establish public–private partnerships that help finance public programs with investments from impact investors.[21] Unlike the fixed-income bond, EIBs link investor returns to project performance with an ultimate goal of reducing the financial, execution, and regulatory risks of public infrastructure development.

To be sure, leveraging private capital through public–private partnerships to conserve and improve natural resources is not a new idea. In fact, although the EIB is a nontraditional credit instrument, many are structured as debt securities that are negotiable in the secondary market. As a result, EIBs might be more appropriately categorized under the broader class of debt securities called "green bonds," which are fixed-income instruments earmarked for climate and environmental projects.[22] As Professor Stephen Park explains, green bonds include "any type of bond instrument where the proceeds will be exclusively applied to finance or refinance in part or in full new . . . [and] existing eligible green projects."[23]

The first green bond was issued by the International Bank for Reconstruction and Development in 2008, with a value of Swedish Kroner (SEK) 2.7 billion and a maturity of six years.[24] Since that time, the World Bank has raised over $11 billion in investments for green bonds to finance environmental projects addressing climate change and related

---

17. *See* Sarah Dadush, *Regulating Social Finance: Can Social Stock Exchanges Meet the Challenge?*, 37 U. Pa. J. Int'l L. 139 (2015) (defining social finance as a mainstream source of funding of goods for the poor across the world, driven by social and commercial imperatives).

18. Framework Convention on Climate Change, *Adoption of the Paris Agreement*, U.N. Doc. FCCC/CP/2015/L.9/Rev.1 (Dec. 12, 2015); *see* Gerald F. Davis & Suntae Kim, *Financialization of the Economy*, 41 Ann. Rev. Soc. 203, 213–14 (2015); *See* Antony Bugg-Levine et al., *A New Approach to Funding Social Enterprises*, Harv. Bus. Rev. (Jan.–Feb. 2012), https://hbr.org/2012/01/a-new-approach-to-funding-social-enterprises (discussing various social finance initiatives and explaining how they return a profit for investors).

19. Susan R. Jones, *Is Social Innovation Financing through Social Impact Bonds the Last Hope for Community Economic Development Programs during the Trump Administration?*, 26 J. of Affordable Hous. & Cmty. Dev. L. 351, 384 (defining an EIB as "a pay-for-performance contract that addresses an environmental issue.").

20. *Id.*

21. *See, generally,* Cristina Balboa, *Accountability of Environmental Impact Bonds: The Future of Global Environmental Governance?*, 16 Glob. Env't Pol'y 2 (2016).

22. Echo Kaixi Wang, *Financing Green: Reforming Green Bond Regulation in the United States*, 12 Brook. J. of Corp., Fin. & Com. L. 2, 467, 468 (2018).

23. *See* Stephen Park, *Investors as Regulators: Green Bonds and the Governance Challenges of the Sustainable Finance Revolution*, 54 Stan. J. of Int'l L. 1, 12 (2018).

24. International Finance Corporation: World Bank Group, Next Season's Green Bond Harvest: Innovations in Green Credit Markets (June 2014), https://openknowledge.worldbank.org/handle/10986/26055 [hereinafter Next Season's Green Bond Harvest].

environmental challenges across the globe.[25] Until recently, due to the risks associated with environmental projects addressing climate change, financing for green investments comprised a conservative mixture of private equity and venture capital, coupled with significant contributions of government funding.[26] Technological advancements, alongside the World Bank's issuance of the *Strategic Framework for Development and Climate Change*, have encouraged the development and support of market-based financing mechanisms. Such advancements have also paved the way for innovative public equity and debt financing models.

Despite this momentum, the adoption of green bonds has been slow for several reasons. First, green infrastructure financing has customarily been raised through traditional municipal bonds, an expensive option for many local governments.[27] Due to the small transaction size of many environmental projects, coupled with the low credit rating of many green portfolios compared to non-green options, attracting institutional investors into the green bond market has been difficult.[28] Second, green bond regulation in the United States is lacking, presenting both execution and regulatory risks that have triggered political divides on the appropriate public policies to resolve them. Although several investment banks have adopted the *Green Bond Principles*—a collaborative policy project that aims to standardize financing practices in the green bond market to ease the concerns of issuers, underwriters, and investors—the principles are voluntary and, thus, lack the force of law. Third, the misappropriation of green bond proceeds has been a deterrent to green bond market growth. Such misappropriation is called "greenwashing" when companies falsely claim an environmental mission for branding purposes (e.g., an oil company claiming to reduce greenhouse gas emissions when their actions prove otherwise) to attract new customers and boost profits.[29]

Most of the green bonds that have been issued in the United States have fallen under the general category of "use-of-proceeds" bonds, or asset-linked bonds, which are standard recourse-to-the-issuer debt obligations.[30] Use-of-proceeds bonds are not dependent on revenues from funded projects, but instead rely primarily upon the credit rating of the issuer (traditionally, triple-A rated multilateral development banks) and are backed by the issuer's entire balance sheet.[31] As a result, they are less risky for institutional investors because their

---

25. *Green Bonds*, World Bank (Aug. 29, 2022), http://treasury.worldbank.org/en/about/unit/treasury/ibrd/ibrd-green-bonds; *see* Park, *supra* note 23, at 8 ("A green bond is a debt security issued by a government entity, a multilateral institution, or a corporation in order to raise capital from investors for a project that contributes to a low-carbon, climate-resilient economy.").

26. Next Season's Green Bond Harvest, *supra* note 24, at 3.

27. Traditional environmental bonds are expected to be repaid at maturation, placing the financial risk solely on the bond issuer. *See, generally*, Balboa, *supra* note 21.

28. However, the introduction of Corporate Green Bonds has helped to grow the market. *See* Next Season's Green Bond Harvest, *supra* note 24, at 4 ("Corporate Green bonds bring competitive risk-adjusted returned to suit varying risk preferences as they offer investors green exposure without increasing their risk appetite as the bonds carry exactly the same credit profile, and pay the same yield, as the issuer's conventional bonds.").

29. Greenwashing occurs when firms do not implement all the standards included under private governance regimes, while still seeking to free ride from the reputational benefits of the regime. *See* Aseem Prakash & Matthew Potoski, *Collective Action through Voluntary Environmental Programs: A Club Theory Perspective*, 35 Pol'y Stud. J. 773, 779 (2007).

30. Generally, recourse debt grants the lender certain rights to assets beyond the collateral to recover full payment of the borrower's obligations in the event of default.

31. Next Season's Green Bond Harvest, *supra* note 24, at 8.

prices are flat and their credit profile is pari passu to vanilla bonds. More recently, green bonds have been structured as "project bonds," which are used to fund projects that are secured by the assets for which construction is being funded.[32] Additionally, green bonds have been structured as "securitized bonds," whereby the bond is composed of several projects pooled together into a tradable security (e.g., solar leases or green mortgages).[33] The EIB seeks to overcome some of the hurdles of the traditional green bond market by targeting socially conscious impact investors who are willing to bear the brunt of the financial risks associated with environmental projects.[34] This risk-sharing arrangement, which mimics the "social impact bond" (SIB) model of financing, sets the EIB apart from conventional green bonds.

As a result, Washington, D.C.'s effort to fund green infrastructure in the nation's capital with an EIB has been hailed as a solution to America's water crisis. The first of its kind, the Washington, D.C. EIB promises to not only reduce stormwater runoff,[35] but also augment access to green space, reduce heat in dense urban neighborhoods, improve air quality, raise property values, and generate new jobs in landscape maintenance.[36] Private investors stand to gain from their impact investments,[37] while community members stand to gain from a strengthened economy and rehabilitated environment. To deter greenwashing, principles of corporate social responsibility are built into the fabric of every EIB deal through the monitoring of project performance, which furnishes stakeholders with greater assurance that their investments will not be misappropriated by the whims of corporate management.[38] The pay-for-success strategy driving the EIB appears to be a win–win–win.

Still, the EIB model may ultimately suffer from either slow adoption or, alternatively, hasty implementation that can trigger collateral consequences due to a lack of oversight and regulation. Further, it remains uncertain whether the EIB's risk-sharing design equitably spreads the costs and benefits of environmental projects among their many stakeholders, especially the often forgotten community residents who typically play a minimal role in deal development and project implementation.[39] As more cities begin to explore the EIB, they must consider not only *how* such public–private partnerships can be implemented in an

---

32. *Id.* at 5.
33. *Id.*
34. Letsinger, *supra* note 8 ("According to the Forum for Sustainable Investment, managed U.S. assets committed to impact investing grew from $640 billion in 1995 to $6.57 trillion in 2014.").
35. Stormwater runoff occurs when rainwater that falls on roads, parking lots, rooftops, and other paved surfaces does not soak into the ground. Instead, the water flows across the ground and may cause flooding in local streams, lakes, wetlands, or urban areas. *See What Is Stormwater Runoff and Why Do We Need to Reduce It?*, CTR. FOR WATERSHED PROT. (Sept. 11, 2017), https://www.cwp.org/reducing-stormwater-runoff/.
36. Mazur, *supra* note 3.
37. Alongside promoting social good, investors benefit by enhancing their reputation for corporate social responsibility. *See* Park, *supra* note 23, at 11 ("[B]y purchasing green bonds, investors signal to other market participants their pledge to sustainability"); *see also* Adam Harmes, *The Limits of Carbon Disclosure: Theorizing the Business Case for Investor Environmentalism*, 11 GLOB. ENV'T POL. 98, 105 (2011).
38. Park, *supra* note 23, at 13.
39. *But see First Publicly-Issued EIB awarded to City of Atlanta Department of Watershed Management*, WATERWORLD (Feb. 26, 2019), https://www.waterworld.com/drinking-water/potable-water-quality/article/16218885/first-publiclyissued-eib-awarded-to-city-of-atlanta-department-of-watershed-management (discussing the first environmental impact bond offered on the public market, led by Quantified Ventures, the impact investment firm, and Neighborly, the mission-oriented broker dealer).

economically efficient and environmentally friendly way, but also *whether* the EIB can foster true accountability, inclusivity, and long-term prosperity for all.[40]

The D.C. Environmental Impact Bond

The Washington, D.C. EIB offers a promising vehicle to steer private capital toward addressing environmental challenges across the United States, including those triggered by urbanization. This section describes how environmental advocates steered Washington, D.C. toward (1) crafting public policy to address its ongoing water crisis, (2) pioneering a "greening" of its "combined sewer overflow" (CSO) mitigation strategy, and (3) leveraging the social impact bond (SIB) framework to model the country's first EIB.

Averting an Environmental Crisis

During periods of heavy to severe rainfall, approximately two billion gallons of CSOs—a combination of untreated wastewater, untreated industrial waste, and stormwater—exceed the capacity of Washington, D.C.'s sewer system and overflow into the Anacostia River, the Potomac River, and the Rock Creek tributaries.[41] This system strain has negatively impacted the quality of water collected from rivers, creeks, and tributaries in the region by increasing the volume of nitrogen and phosphorous in the water, disrupting the delicate balance of chemicals necessary to sustain healthy fish and wildlife.[42] As one of the country's regions most affected by climate change and aging infrastructure, Washington, D.C. has struggled to comply with federal regulation on CSOs for over two decades.[43]

The narrative begins in 1989 when the Environmental Protection Agency (EPA) recognized an urgent need for CSO mitigation across the country and, accordingly, issued a formal CSO Control Policy for the United States. The EPA's guidelines established a nationwide approach to water contamination through site-specific permitting requirements under the National Pollutant Discharge Elimination System (NPDES).[44] A revised version of the EPA's CSO Control Policy was issued in 1994, requiring all holders of NPDES permits to develop a Long-Term Control Plan (LTC Plan). However, compliance with the EPA's policy was sluggish. In 1996, Washington, D.C. established the District of Columbia Water and Sewer Authority (DC Water) as an independent public–private agency charged with managing water and sewage services for the capital region, a demographic community that has since

---

40. *See, generally*, Balboa, *supra* note 21.

41. John Lisle, *DC Water Awarded Grant from Harvard University to Develop Innovative Green Infrastructure Financing Model*, DC Water (Mar. 12, 2015), https://www.dcwater.com/whats-going-on/news/dc-water-awarded-grant-harvard-university-develop-innovative-green.

42. Stormwater is currently the only major source of nitrogen pollution that is still increasing in the Chesapeake Bay watershed. *See Environmental Impact Bonds*, Chesapeake Bay Found., http://www.cbf.org/how-we-save-the-bay/programs-initiatives/environmental-impact-bonds.html; U.S. Env't Prot. Agency, Keeping Raw Sewage & Contaminated Stormwater Out of the Public's Water (2011), https://www3.epa.gov/region02/water/sewer-report-3-2011.pdf.

43. Brett Christophers, *Risk Capital: Urban Political Ecology and Entanglements of Financial and Environmental Risk in Washington, D.C.*, 1 Env't & Plan. E: Nature & Space 144, 146 (2018).

44. National Pollutant Discharge Elimination System, 64 Fed. Reg. 68,722 (Dec. 8, 1999) (to be codified at 40 C.F.R. pts. 9, 122, 123 & 124) (permitting license holders to discharge certain pollutants into receiving waters).

grown to more than 670,000 residents and over 17.5 million annual visitors.[45] Yet, movement in Washington, D.C. on CSO mitigation meandered due to political gridlock. It would take ardent environmental advocacy to finally move DC Water to action on D.C.'s water contamination problem.

The codification of the EPA's 1994 CSO Control Policy into the CWA during the year 2000 finally provided a mechanism for federal enforcement.[46] That same year, several environmental advocacy organizations (officially joined by the EPA in 2002) filed suit against DC Water for violation of the CWA by failing to comply with the EPA's CSO standards in its management of pollutant discharge into the regional sewershed.[47] In 2004, DC Water finally launched its LTC Plan in response to the EPA's requirements under the 1994 CSO Control Policy.[48] And, in 2005, DC Water entered into a Consent Decree with the United States Department of Justice (DOJ), the EPA, and the District of Columbia that required the agency to seek strategies and solutions to further mitigate CSOs and to comply with established environmental guidelines.[49]

The resulting plan—named the Clean Rivers Project[50]—called for a $2.6 billion deepwater tunnel system that would capture and mitigate ongoing CSOs by 96 percent overall.[51] The Clean Rivers Project's design relies primarily upon a "gray infrastructure" solution,[52] which entails the construction of human-engineered pipes, pumps, tanks, and tunnels that, in D.C.'s case, would take at least twenty years to fully develop.[53] The initial project design also included a paltry guaranteed investment of $1.7 million—less than 1 percent of the project budget—to develop green infrastructure in the district, which some critics have argued was simply "window dressing" to appease environmental advocacy groups.[54]

Greening the Clean Rivers Project

By the midway point of the Clean Rivers Project's implementation, notwithstanding notable progress, DC Water had incurred substantial costs. By September 2014, DC Water was carrying $2.5 billion of long-term debt (up from $785 million ten years prior), with annual interest expenses increasing toward $70 million (almost a $50 million increase in one decade).[55] This galumphing cost increase was largely funneled into the fees and service

---

45. Letsinger, *supra* note 8.
46. *See* U.S. Env't Prot. Agency, EPA 333-R-01-003, Report to Congress: Implementation and Enforcement of the Combined Sewer Overflow Control Policy (Dec. 2001), https://www.epa.gov/sites/production/files/2015-10/documents/csortcexecsum.pdf.
47. *See* Taylor v. D.C. Water & Sewer Auth., 205 F.R.D. 43 (D.C. 2002), where Anacostia Watershed Society, Kingman Park Civic Association, American Canoe Association, Friends of the Earth, and Sierra Club all joined to file suit against DC Water.
48. Christophers, *supra* note 43.
49. Final Consent Decree, Anacostia Watershed Soc'y et al. v. D.C. Water and Sewer Auth. Et al., Civ. No. 1:CV00183TFH (D.D.C. Dec. 16, 2004), https://www.epa.gov/sites/default/files/documents/dcwasa-cd.pdf; Jennifer North & Gloria Gong, Harv. Kennedy Sch. Gov't Performance Lab, DC Water Environmental Impact Bond (2017), https://govlab.hks.harvard.edu/files/siblab/files/dc_water_eib_project.pdf.
50. *Clean Rivers Project*, DC Water (2018), https://www.dcwater.com/clean-rivers-project.
51. Christophers, *supra* note 43.
52. *See* Leda Zimmerman, *Greening Gray Infrastructure*, MIT: Spectrum (Winter 2014), https://spectrum.mit.edu/winter-2014/greening-gray-infrastructure/.
53. Mazur, *supra* note 3.
54. Christophers, *supra* note 43.
55. *Id.*

charges imposed on retail and wholesale users of water and sewage services across the District. In other words, the costs of upgrading the infrastructure was being externalized to the end consumer. Water and sewer rates increased significantly faster than inflation, with the average monthly DC Water bill rising from $33.65 in 2004 to $74.05 in 2014, a percentage increase well above 100 percent.[56] Facing the pressure of a ratepayer-backed debt-financed system, coupled with calls from environmental advocates for green infrastructure to be incorporated into ongoing urbanization,[57] DC Water began to consider alternate options for CSO cleanup.

Dating back to 2009, green infrastructure had already been identified by environmental advocates and political leaders within the District as a more sustainable, efficient, and cost-effective solution than the ongoing gray infrastructure model.[58] But its inclusion required a willingness to test technical innovations that had not previously been implemented in D.C. In January 2014, DC Water published a formal proposal to modify its 2005 Consent Decree to incorporate green infrastructure demonstration projects, such as green roofs, rain gardens, and permeable paving.[59] After significant revision following a three-month public comment period,[60] in May 2015, DC Water re-negotiated its 2005 Consent Decree with the DOJ and EPA to officially include green infrastructure in the CSO cleanup plan. Under the revised plan, which became effective in January 2016, at least $90 million would be allocated toward the development of eight sequential green infrastructure pilot projects, with five projects located in the Rock Creek sewershed, and three projects located in the Potomac.[61]

DC Water also took steps to implement a "greening" of the financial facets of the Clean Rivers Project. In 2014, it issued its first green bond with a face value of $350 million. Since 2014, at least $225 million of green bonds have been issued to help pay for the revised Clean Rivers Project ($100 million in 2015, $25 million in 2016, and $100 million in 2017).[62] The $25 million green bond issued in 2016 has arguably gained the greatest attention because of its use of the innovative pay-for-success financing framework to fund green infrastructure projects under the revised project. In so doing, in October 2016, DC Water announced that the nation's first EIB would be established in Washington, D.C., leveraging the SIB financing model in the environmental context.

Leveraging the SIB Model

With a total private investment of $25 million, which at the time was one of the largest environmental pay-for-success projects in the world, the Washington, D.C. EIB promised to

56. *Id.*
57. *Id.*
58. North & Gong, *supra* note 49.
59. Press Release, Strategy to Reduce District of Columbia's Sewer Overflows Will Include Green Infrastructure, Dept. of Just. (May 20, 2015), https://www.justice.gov/opa/pr/strategy-reduce-district-columbia-s-sewer-overflows-will-include-green-infrastructure.
60. Mike DeBonis, *"Green" Modifications Proposed to D.C. Clean-Water Plan; Environmentalists Are Skeptical*, Washington Post (Jan. 23, 2014), https://www.washingtonpost.com/local/dc-politics/green-modifications-proposed-to-dc-clean-water-plan-environmentalists-are-skeptical/2014/01/23/e4c43068-8459-11e3-bbe5-6a2a3141e3a9_story.html?noredirect=on&utm_term=.edc5a879ee51.
61. Christophers, *supra* note 43.
62. *Id.*

address CSO problems in the District by providing upfront capital for green infrastructure development. Brokered by impact investing firm Quantified Ventures, and funded by institutional investors Goldman Sachs ($23 million of the investment) and the Calvert Foundation ($2 million of the investment), the Washington, D.C. EIB financed the development of (at minimum) twenty equivalent impervious acres of green infrastructure in the Rock Creek sewershed to manage stormwater runoff of up to a volume equivalent to 1.2" of rain.[63] The green infrastructure would include bioretention facilities (also called bioswales or rain gardens), permeable pavements, green roofs, and rain barrels to mimic the absorption and filtering processes found in nature that decrease surges of stormwater and reduce CSOs.[64]

The terms of the Washington, D.C. EIB incorporated key elements of the SIB model, which was first introduced in the United States in 2012. A performance-based contracting strategy, the SIB, facilitates public–private partnerships that finance prevention-focused and forward-looking social projects based upon quantifiable and measurable outcomes.[65] These projects reduce government expenditures while addressing costly social problems, such as prison recidivism, homelessness, and early childhood education.[66] Much like a traditional SIB, private investors under the EIB framework assume up to 100 percent of the financial risks of environmental projects by agreeing to a return on their impact investments only when the program has achieved predetermined performance metrics.[67] Under the pay-for-success structure adopted by the Washington, D.C. EIB, the parties agreed to a balanced risk-sharing arrangement. Specifically, the impact investors agreed to bear *most* of the financial risks if the project underperformed, while DC Water agreed to repay the investors their loan and a modest return on their investment if performance metrics exceeded expectations.[68]

Although both the SIB and the EIB focus on program outcomes, EIBs target environmental outcomes that are backed by proven scientific models. Thus, EIBs are perceived as a more reliable source of revenue streams. Further, unlike the social programs that comprise many SIBs where human behaviors prove difficult to quantify and assess, established metrics and

---

63. *Private Placement Agreement: $25,000,000 District of Columbia Water and Sewer Authority Public Utility Subordinate Lien Multimodal Revenue Bonds, Series 2016B (Environmental Impact Bonds)* 3, DAC Bond, https://www.dacbond.com/dacContent/doc.jsp?id=0900bbc7801b7696 [hereinafter *Private Placement Agreement*]; North & Gong, *supra* note 49, at 7. ("One equivalent impervious acre of green infrastructure does not mean that the green infrastructure installed is one acre in size but instead indicates that the green infrastructure installed is designed to manage the equivalent of one acre of storm water as converted from cubic feet.")

64. *See, generally*, U.S. Env't Prot. Agency, EPA 832-R-15-016, Tools, Strategies and Lessons Learned from EPA Green Infrastructure Technical Assistance Projects (Dec. 2015), https://www.epa.gov/sites/production/files/2016-01/documents/gi_tech_asst_summary_508final010515_3.pdf.

65. *See, generally*, Etienne Toussaint, *The New Gospel of Wealth: On Social Impact Bonds and the Privatization of Public Good*, *56* Houston L. Rev. 1 (2018) [hereinafter *New Gospel of Wealth*]; *see also* V. Kasturi Rangan & Lisa A. Chase, *The Payoff of Pay-for-Success*, Stan. Soc. Innovation Rev. (Fall 2015), http://ssir.org/up_for_debate/article/the_payoff_of_pay_for_success.

66. Jones, *supra* note 19, at 353.

67. However, there is diversity among SIBs, with some models allowing for investor returns prior to full program evaluation. *See* Gary Painter et al., *Social Impact Bonds: More than One Approach*, Stan. Soc. Innovation Rev. (2018), https://ssir.org/articles/entry/social_impact_bonds_more_than_one_approach.

68. U.S. Env't Prot. Agency: Water Infrastructure & Resiliency Fin. Ctr., DC Water's Environmental Impact Bond: A First of Its Kind (Apr. 2017), https://www.epa.gov/sites/production/files/2017-04/documents/dc_waters_environmental_impact_bond_a_first_of_its_kind_final2.pdf [hereinafter DC Water's Environmental Impact Bond].

data-driven remediation strategies already exist for most environmental markets.[69] To be sure, climate change presents new challenges and unidentified risks for existing environmental models. Still, in the case of "untested" environmental projects, by placing financial risks in the hands of the private sector, the EIB provides a mechanism for governments to explore innovations in environmental conservation by leveraging the goodwill of private investors as a shield against project underperformance and a sword against political roadblocks. However, the devil is in the details. The primary tools and strategies used to implement the Washington, D.C. EIB offer lessons and warnings for the future.

Tools and Strategies

The Washington, D.C. EIB was designed with a five-year timeline, including one year of pre-construction monitoring, followed by two years of construction, one year of post-construction monitoring, and a six- to nine-month period of evaluation and data synthesis. The project incorporates the SIB model of financing and seeks to mitigate execution, financial, and regulatory risks for the various stakeholders by tying investor returns to project performance. The following sections describe (1) the underlying SIB model that shaped the design of the Washington, D.C. EIB; (2) how DC Water leveraged the SIB model to structure the nation's first EIB, characterized by (a) a three-tiered repayment scheme and (b) predetermined performance metrics; (3) how the Washington, D.C. EIB plans to monitor and measure ongoing project performance; and (4) the role of lawyers in structuring the complex multi-stakeholder deal.

The Pay-for-Success Model

Pay-for-success financing models, commonly known as social impact bonds, or SIBs, have increased in popularity within the United States and around the globe.[70] Nevertheless, the SIB is relatively new and unfamiliar to most policymakers. It was first launched in Peterborough, England, in 2010[71] and was subsequently implemented in the United States for the first time in New York City in 2012.[72] Since then, there have been well over one hundred SIB projects introduced in cities around the world.[73] By facilitating strategic partnerships between stakeholders in the private sector, philanthropic sector, and government sector, the SIB facilitates forward-looking and preventative social programs that tackle a wide range of social challenges, from criminal justice to homelessness to public health.[74]

69. Cathy Clark & David Nicola, *Bringing Social Impact Bonds to the Environment*, Stan. Soc. Innovation Rev. (2013), https://ssir.org/articles/entry/bringing_social_impact_bonds_to_the_environment.

70. Keith Johnson, *Trends in Social Financing: Pay for Success*, Mission Capital (2018), https://www.missioncapital.org/insights-and-ideas/blog/trends-in-social-financing-pay-for-success/.

71. *See New Gospel of Wealth*, *supra* note 65, at 190.

72. *Id.* at 194.

73. *See* Emily Gustafsson-Wright & Izzy Boggild-Jones, *Paying for Social Outcomes: A Review of the Global Impact Bond Market in 2017*, Brookings (Jan. 17, 2018), https://www.brookings.edu/blog/education-plus-development/2018/01/17/paying-for-social-outcomes-a-review-of-the-global-impact-bond-market-in-2017/ ("2017 was an exciting year for social and development impact bonds around the globe, with 32 new contracts signed. This brings the total up to 108 contracted impact bonds globally, along with many more in design").

74. *See* Etienne Toussaint, *Incarceration to Incorporation: Economic Empowerment for Returning Citizens through Social Impact Bonds*, 25 ABA J. of Affordable Hous. & Cmty. Dev. L. 61 (2016); Jones, *supra* note 19, at 358.

Leveraging the expertise of nonprofit service providers, the rigorous measurement and evaluation methods of private consulting firms, and the financial savvy of mission-driven impact investors, the SIB also helps to expand the pool of investment capital for important, yet often underfunded, social services.[75] Even more, it reduces the risks typically associated with implementing innovative social programs because impact investors agree to be repaid only if the SIB program meets predetermined performance benchmarks.[76] If the social program fails, the impact investment effectively becomes a philanthropic grant.

Still, SIBs are not without their challenges. Indeed, SIBs have faced criticism from scholars and practitioners for their transactional complexity, which can hinder implementation for under-resourced governments; for their execution risks, which vary based upon the resources of service providers and other stakeholders involved in program development; and for their political risks, which can hinder long-term governmental support and private sector buy-in.[77] Further, some scholars have argued that the growth of SIBs as a vehicle for public service delivery may divert funding away from the philanthropic and nonprofit sector, forcing the public sector to wrestle with the challenges of funding drain and mission drift.[78] Lastly, the SIB poses moral and ethical concerns for democratic governments, threatening to undermine the role of government in the protection and advancement of the public good by reducing public service to a monetary cost–benefit analysis. Ongoing education on the SIB model—such as the training resources provided by the Nonprofit Finance Fund, a nonprofit organization that administers the Pay for Success Learning Hub[79]—will likely remain a necessary part of the SIB's future growth and development.

The D.C. EIB Investment Strategy

The Washington, D.C. EIB is the first pay-for-success contract to utilize a thirty-year tax-exempt municipal bond structure. With a stated maturity date of October 1, 2046, the bond includes a mandatory tender at the fifth year of project implementation on April 1, 2021. As a mandatory tender bond, it not only features a traditionally long maturity period but also integrates a shorter term (defined as six months to five years) maturity tender date when the interest rate will be adjusted, and the bondholder will surrender the security to the issuer (or its agent) for purchase. In the case of the Washington, D.C. EIB, the bond will be put back to the bondholder, who will roll the bond into the next tender period. The private placement was funded by two institutional investors, the Goldman Sachs Urban Investment Group and Calvert Impact Capital, both with a demonstrated interest in using impact investments to address climate change. The impact investment of $25 million came with a 3.43 percent interest coupon, payable semiannually for the first five years of the bond.

75. *See New Gospel of Wealth*, *supra* note 65.

76. *Id.* at 158.

77. *Id.* at 206–17.

78. *See* Jones, *supra* note 19, at 361.

79. The Pay for Success Learning Hub has been called the leading national repository for information on the pay-for-success financing framework. *See id.* at 378 (explaining that NFF has facilitated "more than 200 PFS trainings, presentations, webinars, workshops, and convenings across the country for service providers, governments, and investors."); *see also Ten Notable Resources for Pay for Success*, INTERSECTOR PROJECT http://intersector.com/lists/pay-for-success/.

Under the terms of a "Private Placement Agreement" (PPA),[80] Washington, D.C.'s payment obligations were made subordinate to DC Water's outstanding senior obligations on its publicly issued bonds. After the five-year mandatory tender, the PPA calls for a multi-million-dollar contingent payment to the institutional investors by DC Water or, alternatively, a similar payment to DC Water by the institutional investors.[81] Whether payment flows from the private sector to the public, or from the public sector to the private, is contingent on the success of the EIB in reducing stormwater runoff in the region.

Specifically, under the PPA, there is a three-tiered repayment scheme based upon the success of the project in meeting predetermined performance metrics. If stormwater runoff in the target area is reduced by a value greater than 41.3 percent, qualifying as a "better-than-expected" result, then the impact investors will receive a one-time additional outcome payment of $3.3 million from DC Water, in addition to their basic principal investment and the 3.43 percent interest coupon payable on the EIB.[82] DC Water's ability to pay relies upon revenues from its customers. Accordingly, the payment to impact investors is limited to the available net revenues of DC Water after all payments on outstanding senior and subordinated debt obligations have been made. Alternatively, if stormwater runoff is reduced by a value between 18.6 and 41.3 percent of the baseline value, which is the expected percentage reduction based on leading environmental models, then the impact investors will receive no additional payment other than their basic principal investment and the 3.43 percent interest coupon payable on the EIB.[83] Lastly, if stormwater runoff is reduced by less than 18.6 percent of the baseline value, qualifying as a "worse-than-expected" result, then the impact investors will make a one-time risk share payment to DC Water of $3.3 million.[84] Rather than the impact investors actually transferring additional funds under the worse-than-expected scenario, DC Water will subtract that amount from the principal and interest that it would have otherwise been obligated to pay the investors under the PPA, effectively turning the capital investment into a nonrefundable grant.

Measuring Project Performance

Under the PPA, program evaluation for the Washington, D.C. EIB will be conducted by a three-phase process. First, prior to construction, DC Water will monitor the existing stormwater runoff and measure rainfall data *without* the green infrastructure to determine baseline performance levels. Second, DC Water will establish appropriate outcome ranges based on projected reductions in stormwater runoff per acre, which will be confirmed by independent engineering firms. Finally, after construction has been completed, DC Water will monitor stormwater runoff *with* the newly constructed green infrastructure to calculate its effectiveness compared to the projected reductions. Under the PPA, DC Water must monitor project performance for twelve months following construction.[85]

80. *Private Placement Agreement*, *supra* note 63.
81. DC Water's Environmental Impact Bond, *supra* note 68.
82. *Private Placement Agreement*, *supra* note 63, at 12.
83. *Id.*
84. *Id.*
85. *Id.* at 9–10.

Following the measurement process, DC Water must deliver a final report to relevant stakeholders within 180 days of the conclusion of the monitoring period to verify the effectiveness of the green infrastructure program.[86] As part of the evaluation process, an independent third-party validator must confirm the findings of DC Water's final report in a separate opinion letter, which is due within forty-five days of the report's delivery.[87] The performance outcome assessment ultimately determines whether the impact investors will be required to make a risk-share payment, receive an outcome payment, or simply tender the bonds for a return of the principle investment and interest coupon payable by DC Water.

On May 27, 2021, DC Water announced the success of its initial EIB-funded green infrastructure projects in Rock Creek, which boasted a reduction of stormwater runoff by nearly 20 percent. In its final report on Rock Creek Project 1, DC Water noted, "significant information has been learned in terms of design, construction, and monitoring approaches that have added to DC Water's body of knowledge and expertise related to GI [green infrastructure]. Collectively, the information gained through the performance monitoring and the resulting optimization allowed DC Water to be responsive, make corrections, and ensure a future for green infrastructure at DC Water."

The Lawyer's Role

There are several stakeholders that participate in the development and life cycle of an EIB. In addition to the government entity and the impact investors who form the basis of the public–private partnership, the EIB framework also relies upon social service providers, a financial advisor, a technical advisor, and a pay-for-success transaction coordinator.[88] Additionally, lawyers play a foundational, yet often unspoken role in negotiating and structuring EIB deals. The SIB financing model that drives the design of the EIB requires a complex arrangement of multi-party contracts that dictate the financial and legal rights, duties, and obligations of each stakeholder, demanding expertise across a broad range of legal fields, from structured finance to tax law to fund formation. As a result, each party is typically independently represented by counsel who seek to advance their client's best interests while supporting the project's underlying mission.

As the demand for pay-for-success financing increases, so too will the demand for knowledgeable and skilled attorneys who can construct the financial and legal frameworks necessary to develop impact investment funds and SIB payment schemes. Due to the novelty of the SIB model, a significant portion of the legal work and training devoted to pay-for-success contracting has come in the form of pro bono counsel, frequently from law firms that can internalize the high transaction costs.[89] Indeed, in the case of the Washington, D.C. EIB, the global law firm Orrick, Herrington & Sutcliffe LLP served as counsel for the investors, and global law firm Squire Patton Boggs LLP served as the bond counsel for Washington, D.C.

---

86. *Id.*

87. *Id.*

88. In the Washington, D.C. EIB, Public Financial Management, Inc. serves as the financial advisor, the Harvard Kennedy School Government Performance Lab serves as the technical advisor, and Quantified Ventures serves as the transaction coordinator. Press Release, Goldman Sachs, Fact Sheet: DC Water Environmental Impact Bond https://www.goldmansachs.com/media-relations/press-releases/current/dc-water-environmental-impact-bond-fact-sheet.pdf [hereinafter Fact Sheet DC].

89. Jones, *supra* note 19, at 382.

Various nonprofit organizations have taken steps to expand the pool of attorneys available to structure social finance deals. For example, TrustLaw, the pro bono legal program pioneered by the Thompson Reuters Foundation, sponsors a "Social Enterprise and Impact Investing Training Program" to help increase awareness of the need for such legal services.[90] Additionally, in 2015, the Global Impact Investing Network (GIIN) launched the Legal Practitioners Track—"an action-oriented practitioners network that fosters a community of practice among legal experts in the field and provides a platform for legal innovation and thought leadership."[91] Furthermore, the Grunin Center for Law and Social Entrepreneurship at New York University Law School maintains the Impact Investing Legal Working Group, which converges lawyers, impact investors, nonprofit organizations, and academics to study changes in the field.[92] As new pay-for-success deals are negotiated, and as lawyers increasingly recognize a need for their legal skills in public finance, project finance, real estate law, fund formation, and tax law to structure SIB deals, more law firms will launch new SIB/EIB practice groups.[93]

Lawyers will also continue to explore new financing strategies that can be used alongside the pay-for-success model. Some strategies will emerge from the green bond market itself. For example, some green projects have used the project bond model of financing, which uses the assets of the green project (e.g., physical infrastructure and energy production revenues) as security for the green bonds. In such cases, since environmental projects bring construction and delivery risks that often hinder premium credit ratings, impact investors may require that project bonds meet the Green Bond Principles or, alternatively, that they are backed by a bond guarantee. Another financing strategy that may grow in appeal is the "asset-backed bond" (ABB) model, where financing is based on the risk of asset pools rather than the risks associated with individual projects or the credit risk of a project sponsor. Credit enhancements or bond guarantees can facilitate the securitization of green assets, which ultimately reduces the borrowing costs for climate-related projects.[94] For example, in 2013, Hannon Armstrong Sustainable Infrastructure issued a $100 million ABB backed by the cash flow of over one hundred energy-efficient projects at twenty properties around the United States.[95] Developing the legal framework for these various financing strategies is important to building an ecosystem to support the pay-for-success model.

Key Legal Questions

The financial and nonfinancial costs associated with the Washington, D.C. EIB are distributed among various parties in the transaction. Some of these costs are unique to green infrastructure projects and distinct from the categories of risk generally associated with

90. Thomson Reuters Found., TrustLaw, https://www.trust.org/documents/trustlaw/trustlaw-brochure-en.pdf?v5.
91. *See The GIIN–ISLP Host Inaugural Legal Practitioners Track European Convening*, Int'l Senior Laws. Project (June 3, 2017), https://islp.org/giin-islp-hosts-inaugural-legal-practitioners-track-european-convening/.
92. *See Grunin Center for Law and Social Entrepreneurship*, NYU School of Law, https://www.law.nyu.edu /centers/grunin-social-entrepreneurship.
93. *See, e.g.*, *Impact Finance & Investment*, Orrick, https://www.orrick.com/Practices/Impact-Finance (describing Orrick as "the first global law firm to establish an Impact Finance and Investment practice, leading the sector as we support investors and entrepreneurs who aim to make social and environmental impacts alongside financial returns").
94. Next Season's Green Bond Harvest, *supra* note 24, at 10.
95. *Id.*

social service delivery, while other costs are common to projects that utilize the pay-for-success financing model. This section discusses (1) the financial risks, (2) the execution risks, and (3) the regulatory risks associated with the EIB.

Financial Risks

One of the most celebrated features of the pay-for-success model is the perceived transfer of financial risk from the government to the private sector. In the case of the Washington, D.C. EIB, the impact investors are required to make a risk share payment of $3.3 million to DC Water if the project underperforms, forfeiting the return of their capital investment. In theory, this balancing of risk share payments enables the government to recapture the costs associated with performance deficiencies, encouraging innovation in social service delivery, and mitigating the imposition of negative externalities on community members (e.g., via increases in taxes or utility service fees). However, every pay-for-success deal is unique and merits scrutiny. Two important financial risks emerge in the case of the EIB: (1) the risk of unexpected market conditions that threaten to increase the interest rate; and (2) the counterparty risks that stem from changes in project costs and benefits over time.

Notably, DC Water assumed part of the financing risk in the Washington, D.C. EIB by agreeing to an interest rate reset in year five of project implementation on the mandatory tender date.[96] As a result, the deal structure subjected DC Water to uncertain market conditions that could have led to greater costs if interest rates had risen significantly. This deal term adds fuel to the argument of critics who believe pay-for-success projects impose hidden transaction costs that call into question their long-term viability. Even more, such hidden costs may ultimately be borne by community residents in the form of increased fees for utility services. Thus, it is the community who may pay the greatest cost in such cases. In response, impact investment firms like Quantified Ventures have taken steps to reduce the administrative expenses associated with the precontract or "set-up" phase of EIBs, leveraging program-related investments to support capacity-building initiatives.[97] By reducing the cost of contract creation and project administration, capacity-building measures may make the EIB a more affordable option for local governments. Still, other safeguards may be needed to contain cost increases.

The Washington, D.C. EIB incorporated several safeguards into the PPA to protect DC Water from the risk of project failure. Specifically, the PPA established a prior legal claim to project revenues for DC Water, avoiding the unwelcome scenario of D.C. government being legally obligated to pay their impact investors a return on investment upon the achievement of better-than-expected outcomes, yet rendered unable to pay outstanding senior obligations on publicly issued bonds due to unexpected project costs.[98] Thus, it appears that DC Water has the upper hand with respect to financial risks.

---

96. *See Fact Sheet DC*, *supra* note 88.

97. John Stroud, *Why Social Impact Bonds Make Sense for Municipalities*, VALUE WALK (June 27, 2018), https://www.valuewalk.com/2018/06/social-impact-bonds-municipalities/.

98. Alisa Valderrama, *Pay for Performance Meets Green Infrastructure*, NRDC (Oct. 21, 2016), https://www.nrdc.org/experts/alisa-valderrama/pay-performance-meets-green-infrastructure ("A financing structure where repayment is dependent in part on project performance is appealing because it reduces the financial risk that a city or utility would otherwise need to assume in installing green infrastructure to meet its water quality goals.").

Further, the institutional investors bear the counterparty risk associated with the EIB—the likelihood that one or more parties will default on their contractual obligations due to changes in costs and benefits over time. Since the outcome payments are offset against the principal investment and interest due to the impact investors on the mandatory tender date, and since they are subordinate to the outstanding senior obligations of DC Water (i.e., the contingent payment will only be payable after other payments referenced under the PPA have been made), D.C. government is effectively guaranteed payment of the risk share. DC Water and the nonprofit service providers appear able to hedge the risk of human error (e.g., poorly constructed green infrastructure) and political uncertainty that threatens project completion (e.g., a change in political support) with the guaranteed capital contribution of the impact investors. As a result, the Washington, D.C. EIB has been hailed by the EPA's Water Infrastructure and Resiliency Finance Center as a model for utilities throughout America.[99]

Yet, scholars have argued that the costs (both visible and invisible) of the Washington, D.C. EIB are not much different than the costs associated with traditional bonds, especially considering D.C.'s usage of a private placement, which often comes with rates that are twenty to one hundred basis points higher than comparable public offerings.[100] For example, the PPA calls for the impact investors to be reimbursed for up to $200,000 for expenses incurred in connection with their purchase of the bonds.[101] Furthermore, despite praising the deal for its inventiveness, the EPA's Water Infrastructure and Resiliency Finance Center noted that the interest rate DC Water agreed to pay Goldman Sachs and the Calvert Foundation may actually exceed market rates when compared to similarly rated five-year municipal bonds.[102] Ultimately, DC Water remains wholly responsible for the risks associated with construction (i.e., delays or cost overruns), changes in applicable laws or regulations, the operation and maintenance of the transaction, and the financial risk of the interest rate reset on the mandatory tender date. Moreover, none of these costs consider the historic financial and nonfinancial costs accrued during the explorations of the EIB altogether.

Execution Risks

DC Water bears primary responsibility for the design, construction, implementation, and maintenance of the green infrastructure that will be incorporated into the Clean Rivers Project. Although both Goldman Sachs and the Calvert Foundation will provide experts to review the project plan, neither investor bears primary responsibility for project cost overruns or unexpected challenges that arise during project development. Whether such challenges occur during implementation typically hinges on the reliability of the technical intervention. Simply put, is the environmental project a "proven" intervention that is well supported by environmental scientists? Since unproven interventions pose greater risks to stakeholders, it remains uncertain whether the EIB framework will spur true innovation in environmental conservation and protection. Perhaps it makes sense, in the case of the Washington, D.C. EIB, why the green infrastructure selected was already a proven

---

99. *Id.*
100. *See* Christophers, *supra* note 43.
101. *Private Placement Agreement*, *supra* note 63, at 14.
102. *Id.*

technology for CSO reduction.[103] Yet, this pragmatic reality begs the question—why not simply use public funds to directly implement green infrastructure solutions?

Although the additional investment capital from impact investors opens the door for new environmental projects that otherwise might go unfunded in the short term, scholars have noted that there are inherent tensions and controversial incentives embedded in the unregulated EIB model, principally because its public benefit is tied to the financial profit of private investors.[104] Indeed, EIB programs are selected not merely for their desired policy outcomes, but also because they incorporate quantifiable performance metrics that are linked to governmental cost savings that are likely to yield investor profits.[105] Thus, it remains uncertain whether EIBs will ever pursue audacious environmental goals that are difficult to measure, or whether impact investors will ever support truly innovate projects that bring no guarantee of measurable profits.[106] Some scholars contend that the true hedge afforded by the EIB is not the risk of innovation but rather the *performance* risk of government stakeholders amid the unpredictability of partisan politics.[107]

In practice, the EIB must balance government accountability to the public with private sector accountability to shareholders. Impact investors are likely to be wary of backing unproven EIB projects because of the risk of experiencing the "cliff effect"—small changes in expected program outcomes that result in contract failure with no success payments.[108] Even though these risks can be mitigated through clever contract drafting that creates tiered outcome payment schemes, some impact investors may nevertheless seek projects with conservative performance standards to mitigate the execution risks that stand between their capital investment and their financial return. Such a trend could dampen government efforts to boldly confront the environmental challenges facing our nation's cities, posing a roadblock to the long-term success of environmental justice initiatives.

Regulatory Risks

DC Water also bears the primary regulatory risks of its green infrastructure project. The impact investors are only expected to comply with standard private placement rules. Thus, any changes in law, regulation, or policy that impact the environmental project are the primary responsibility of local government actors. These regulatory risks operate during the entire life cycle of the project, which remains the responsibility of DC Water as it manages the operation and maintenance of the green infrastructure. In other words, DC Water must

103. *Id.*
104. Mark Rosenman, *How Social Impact Bonds Put Private Profit Ahead of Public Good*, PBS (Feb. 19, 2014), https://www.pbs.org/newshour/nation/social-impact-bonds-put-private-profit-ahead-public-good.
105. *See* Mildred E. Warner, *Private Finance for Public Goods: Social Impact Bonds*, 16 J. of Econ. Pol'y Reform 4303–319 (2013).
106. *See, generally*, Balboa, *supra* note 21; *see also* Park, *supra* note 23, at 9 (explaining, "value-seeking" mainstream investors seek maximum returns, as opposed to "values-based" investors driven by moral or religious beliefs").
107. This risk is present in the Washington, D.C. EIB. *See* Christophers, *supra* note 43, at 158–59 ("Not only was the modified Consent Decree vague about where exactly green infrastructure would be installed and whether the necessary land was available . . . The Decree was, in this regard, also riddled with inconsistencies . . . cause for concern and indicate that DC Water does not actually know whether adequate opportunities for green infrastructure practices exist on publicly-owned land.").
108. *See* Balboa, *supra* note 21, at 37.

constantly monitor whether technical changes in implementation or operation will trigger regulatory oversight or introduce new legal concerns.

A key question emerges when considering the life cycle of the EIB—who defines *success* for each EIB? The potential for unethical behavior in the establishment of performance metrics without neutral oversight poses regulatory risks akin to the greenwashing that manifested in earlier forms of green investments. Even where EIB programs are deemed successful based upon a fair assessment of predefined performance metrics that are governed by industry-approved standards, one might question whether such proclamations induce a kind of success myopia—an overstated perception of progress that blinds governments and environmental advocates alike to the broader social, political, and environmental justice concerns that plague low-income communities.[109] For example, in Washington, D.C., it will be important to monitor and assess who obtains new green industry jobs and who benefits from increases in property values. At best, these questions highlight the need for an overarching regulatory framework that integrates the concerns of marginalized communities, a challenge facing pay-for-success schemes more generally.

Due to a lack of traditional, "hard" law-based regulations in the social finance realm, even after incorporating the broader universe of corporate social responsibility guidelines, green investments are typically only governed by quasi-regulatory tools and market-based governance regimes. These quasi-regulatory systems are facilitated by third-party assurance providers, consulting organizations, and ratings and ranking schemes administered by industry watchdogs.[110] The current green bond market follows this trend. Regulation of the green bond market is decentralized and primarily shaped by the very institutional investors that use its financial instruments.[111] The green bond market has sought to overcome concerns of irresponsible governance by emphasizing transparency in the use of investment funds and, in some cases, requiring third-party certification. For example, the World Bank reports on the sustainability and impact of green bonds for each project it authorizes.[112] Still, it remains unclear whether a quasi-regulatory scheme will be enough to curtail unethical behavior and promote best practices.

These unanswered questions will likely become more pressing as the EIB grows in popularity. Currently, there is little incentive for EIBs to address the underlying sociopolitical dimensions of environmental challenges like water quality. For example, the drivers of racial discrimination that animate environmental injustice in many low-income Black communities are difficult to capture with quantitative performance metrics. While we can clean the air and purify the water, how do we combat the historic social and economic implications of air pollution and unclean water on the lives of low-income Black people? These challenges suggest that some of the harms of environmental injustice may linger even after EIBs have been deemed a success.

---

109. Luke Cole & Sheila Foster, From the Ground Up: Environmental Racism and the Rise of the Environmental Justice Movement in Critical America (NYU Press, 2000).

110. *See* Park, *supra* note 23.

111. See Benjamin J. Richardson, *Keeping Ethical Investment Ethical: Regulatory Issues for Investing for Sustainability*, 87 J. Bus. Ethics 555, 559 (2009).

112. *See, e.g.*, World Bank Treasury, Green Bond Impact Report 11–23 (June 2016), https://thedocs.worldbank.org/en/doc/896401507751975254-0340022017/original/reportimpactgreenbond2016.pdf.

Even more, investors with diversified portfolios may remain blind to the irony of investing in EIBs alongside corporate activities that are linked to the negative externalities they seek to address.[113] Consider, for example, an investment bank that provides financing for a climate change project as part of its green portfolio, while providing financing for the construction of a coal power plant as part of business as usual. Even where corporate shareholders voice concern for questionable board actions, it remains uncertain whether shareholder activism can change harmful corporate behaviors that conflict with the underlying goals of EIBs.[114] Ultimately, many critics wonder whether the EIB will simply become another market-based tool for wealthy investors to profit from the environmental poverty of marginalized communities.

Lessons and Critiques

There are several lessons that emerge from the implementation of the Washington, D.C. EIB. First, one of the goals of the D.C. project is to contribute to research on the effectiveness of green infrastructure in CSO mitigation and related environmental measures.[115] Several cities have already integrated green infrastructure into their water systems, including New York City, San Francisco, and Portland. In New York City, beginning in 2012, the Department of Environmental Protection's Office of Green Infrastructure built and monitored demonstration projects totaling sixty-three acres in the Newtown Creek, Hutchinson River, and Jamaica Bay neighborhoods with an overall cost of approximately $5.3 billion.[116] From 2009 to 2015, the San Francisco Public Utilities Commission spearheaded eight Early Implementation Stormwater Management Projects in partnership with the San Francisco Estuary Institute, a multibillion dollar project to modernize the city's outdated sewer system.[117] In 2008, the city of Portland, Oregon, launched "Grey to Green," a five-year environmental services initiative to promote green infrastructure as part of the Portland Watershed Management Plan.[118] The success of the Washington, D.C. EIB will further demonstrate the benefits of large-scale green infrastructure and may signal a shift in the way cities address climate change moving forward. Indeed, in June 2021, the city of Buffalo in New York closed on a $54 million EIB, the country's largest as of that date. According to Mayor Byron W. Brown, it will be "the first in the nation to use an EIB to provide

113. *See* Balboa, *supra* note 21, at 39.
114. See Klaus-Michael Menz, *Corporate Social Responsibility: Is It Rewarded by the Corporate Bond Market? A Critical Note*, 96 J. Bus. Ethics 117, 120–21 (2010).
115. *University of New Hampshire Stormwater Center*, Univ. of New Hampshire, https://www.unh.edu/unhsc/.
116. Renee Cho, *Building NYC's Resilience to Climate Change with Green Infrastructure*, Colum. Climate Sch.: State of the Planet (Jan. 13, 2012), https://news.climate.columbia.edu/2012/01/13/building-nyc%E2%80%99s-resilience-to-climate-change-with-green-infrastructure/; Michael R. Bloomberg & Cas Holloway, City of New York, NYC Green Infrastructure Plan: A Sustainable Strategy for Clean Waterways (2010), http://www.nyc.gov/html/dep/pdf/green_infrastructure/NYCGreenInfrastructurePlan_ExecutiveSummary.pdf.
117. *San Francisco Green Infrastructure Project Recognized by EPA*, WaterWorld (Nov. 16, 2018), https://www.waterworld.com/wastewater/article/16225337/san-francisco-green-infrastructure-project-recognized-by-epa.
118. *Grey to Green Accomplishments*, City of Portland, Oregon: Env't Servs., https://www.portlandoregon.gov/bes/article/321331; *Portland's Green Infrastructure*, City of Portland, Oregon (Jan. 15, 2015), https://www.portlandoregon.gov/fish/article/515504.

property owners the ability to fund green infrastructure projects."[119] Notwithstanding such progress, questions remain regarding how EIB infrastructure development will impact the cost of water and sewage services for end users. Will governmental cost savings be passed along to the end user in the short term, or will they facilitate other community development initiatives? Will end users be shielded from the spillover effects of unexpected cost increases, or will they see their rates vacillate? Without a regulatory framework to balance the needs of citizens against the ambitions of impact investors, many of these questions will go unanswered.

Second, by structuring its financing through a privately placed municipal bond, the Washington, D.C. EIB provides another option for future pay-for-success projects, including those outside of the environmental realm. Most pay-for-success deals in the United States (to date) have been structured though an operating loan. Due to the familiarity of bond financing to many local governments, a pay-for-success deal structured as a municipal bond may help to reduce transaction costs. The parties in the Washington, D.C. EIB were able to utilize familiar contracts and financing documents, while also leveraging DC Water's existing bond issuance process to save valuable time and resources. Nevertheless, the project required almost two years to structure and finalize because of the complexities of the EIB model, which included determining how the project could qualify for tax-exempt status while meeting United States Treasury regulations for municipal bonds with contingent payments.[120] While future EIBs may benefit from faster deal timelines by rinsing and repeating the municipal bond structure, the complexities of the EIB will continue to require customization and careful guidance from skilled legal counsel, making the EIB an expensive tool for governments without adequate resources or access to robust pro bono legal representation.

Third, the EIB is likely to spark the interest of jurisdictions that are wary of using the pay-for-success model for human social services but want to, nonetheless, participate in the social finance movement. With human social services, even if the evidence base for success is strong, and even if the social program is implemented according to the plan, there remains a risk that the target population will be impacted in unexpected ways that thwart programmatic goals. In some cases, the social program may result in failure simply due to unanticipated human errors or unexpected diversions in human responses to well-meaning and data-driven interventions. Conversely, with environmental projects, such as green infrastructure, there is less risk of interference from human behavior (other than during project construction and maintenance phases), and there is greater predictability in project outcomes and cost savings to the public.[121] Provided that an EIB project has been designed, constructed, and installed according to best engineering practices, it is likely to yield the results expected by data-driven models. Further, where EIBs come with implementation

119. *See* WFM Staff, *City of Buffalo to Launch Nation's Largest Environmental Impact Bond*, Water Fin. & Mgmt. (Mar. 2, 2020), https://waterfm.com/buffalo-launch-environmental-impact-bond/; *Buffalo Sewer Authority Issues $54M Environmental Impact Bond*, WaterWorld (June 28, 2021), https://www.waterworld.com/drinking-water/infrastructure-funding/press-release/14205898/buffalo-sewer-authority-issues-54m-eib.

120. *See* North & Gong, *supra* note 49.

121. *See* Balboa *supra* note 21, at 34–35 ("For water quality, as an example, a reasonable investment in watershed forest conservation could preempt a larger downstream investment in infrastructure to provide clean drinking water.").

risks, they can be transferred to impact investors who often have the resources necessary to secure the best experts in the fields of environmental conservation and remediation. Incentive structures can be baked into project development and construction contracts to incentivize experts to surpass project success metrics.

Still, there are important critiques to keep in mind as local governments with diverse political leanings wrestle with the normative assumptions embedded in the EIB's design and the implications for environmental governance.[122] The EIB model suggests that the value of environmental remediation and public infrastructure development can be reduced to a financial cost–benefit analysis. Further, it suggests that environmental governance can be outsourced to the private sector when public resources are unavailable. Some argue that private governance is useful where public governance is weakly enforced or nonexistent, providing avenues for flexibility, adaptability, and collaboration.[123] Others hold fast to the notion that public services intended to benefit the public good must not only be inspired by an ethical and moral commitment to public interest but must also be regulated by an independent public entity to ensure democratic accountability[124] amid the ongoing threat of regulatory arbitrage.[125] Some scholars even maintain that, under human rights law, there exists both legal and moral duties for governments to directly address the impacts of climate change by steering public funds toward established remedial programs, notwithstanding contested cost considerations.[126] With a lack of accountability to the public under emerging EIB models, some firms may attempt to exploit private governance and engage in greenwashing to enhance their reputation, a practice that has proven disruptive to prior environmental efforts. These collateral consequences can have long-term impacts on marginalized communities that often suffer the most from environmental degradation.

As scholars, lawmakers, and environmental advocates consider strategies to enhance the EIB model, establishing a hybrid public–private governance regime must be a priority item on the agenda.[127] Specifically, governments should explore how public oversight can complement existing due diligence reporting requirements and quality assurance standards that are already embedded into the design of pay-for-success contracts. Governments must also wrestle with the potential for contradictory outcomes of public oversight, including increases in public costs and shifts in stakeholder interests that could stifle the very

---

122. *See New Gospel of Wealth*, *supra* note 65, at 180–89 (discussing the ethical implications of social impact bonds for local governance).

123. *See* Eric W. Orts, *Reflexive Environmental Law*, 89 NW. U. L. REV. 1227, 1238–39 (1995) (noting that traditional "command-and-control regulation" may be too static in certain instances); Lesley K. McAllister, *Regulation by Third Party Verification*, 53 B.C. L. REV. 1, 15 (2012) ("[T]he interaction with third-party verifiers may be perceived by regulated entities less as a judgment day and more as an opportunity to learn and improve.").

124. *See* Park, *supra* note 23, at 31 ("Private governance regimes themselves may be vulnerable to interest group pressures while lacking the public accountability mechanisms to identify, mitigate, and disclose them"; *see also* Dana Brakman Reiser & Claire R. Kelly, *Linking NGO Accountability and the Legitimacy of Global Governance*, 36 BROOK. J. INT'L L. 1011, 1025–26 (2011) (highlighting the weakness of internal accountability mechanisms for many NGOs)).

125. *See* Park, *supra* note 23, at 31 ("The existence of multiple private governance regimes, coupled with nonexclusive jurisdiction between them, allows a firm to select a regulatory framework that is most conducive to its interests.").

126. *See* John H. Knox, *Climate Change and Human Rights Law*, 50 VA. J. INT'L L. 163, 165–67 (2009).

127. *See* Michael P. Vandenbergh, *Private Environmental Governance*, 99 CORNELL L. REV. 129, 177 (2013) (discussing the need to assess private environmental governance regimes and the potential for public–private hybridity).

innovations that the EIB seeks to inspire.[128] Thus, it is critical that community stakeholders be granted a seat at the table during project design phases to ensure that program development benefits all parties.

Future Opportunities

Alongside providing a funding platform for environmental conservation and remediation, the EIB model will impact community economic development in a few complimentary ways. First, investments in green infrastructure can open the door for new employment opportunities, a critical issue for low-income communities suffering from failing infrastructure and contaminated water supplies. After green infrastructure has been constructed, it must be regularly maintained—permeable pavements must be cleaned to prevent silt and debris from clogging the system, rain gardens and bioretention cells must be cleared of debris to maintain the growth of plants and shrubs, and so on.[129] Local residents can be trained to take advantage of new green jobs. New cooperatively owned small businesses can be launched by community members to provide ongoing maintenance services. EIB programs that embed policies for local employment and small business development will ensure that as green infrastructure systems help reduce stormwater runoff and reduce CSOs, important environmental and economic justice concerns are also addressed.

The Washington, D.C. EIB provides a noteworthy example. It includes the innovative National Green Infrastructure Certification Program, a partnership with the Water Environment Federation. The certification program is designed to educate, train, and ultimately certify District residents to build, inspect, and maintain green infrastructure facilities like rain gardens, roof gardens, and permeable pavements.[130] Still, while the initiative offers great hope for equitable development that economically empowers D.C. residents, the early phases of the program have had a relatively small impact. As of July 2017, only fifty-four D.C. residents had been trained through the program (although news sources provide conflicting statistics, and more recent data suggest positive trends).[131] As of March 2018, news sources indicate that as few as twenty residents had found new jobs through the program.[132] As more District residents are trained in the future, the program will hopefully yield a positive visible impact in low-income neighborhoods across the District.

---

128. *See, e.g.*, Marc Jones, *Don't Strangle Green Bond Market, EBRD Urges Regulators*, Reuters (July 6, 2016), https://in.reuters.com/article/markets-greenbonds-ebrd-idINKCN0ZL2JL (quoting Andras Simor, Vice President of the EBRD, stating, "[w]e feel that this market needs nurturing. This market needs to grow and if you put regulation on top of it then you actually might harm it rather than develop it").

129. *See* North & Gong, *supra* note 49.

130. Allyson Chiu, *A Program that Builds Green Infrastructure in the D.C. Area Sustains the Environment, Local Workforce*, Washington Post (Mar. 13, 2018), https://www.washingtonpost.com/local/a-program-that-builds-green-infrastructure-in-the-dc-region-sustains-the-environment-local-workforce/2018/03/12/15ad966e-1bc4-11e8-ae5a-16e60e4605f3_story.html?noredirect=on&utm_term=.8205775d575b.

131. *DC Water Green Infrastructure Training Program Creating New Job Opportunities for District Residents*, DC Water (July 14, 2017), https://www.dcwater.com/whats-going-on/news/dc-water-green-infrastructure-training-program-creating-new-job-opportunities; *but see* Chiu, *supra* note 130.

132. Jackie Snow, *This DC Program Prepares Area Youth for a Green Workforce*, Smart Cities Dive (June 29, 2017), https://www.smartcitiesdive.com/news/this-dc-program-prepares-area-youth-for-a-green-workforce/446071/; WFM Staff, *More than 200 Now Certified in Green Infrastructure*, Water Fin. & Mgmt. (Jan. 12, 2018), https://waterfm.com/200-plus-now-certified-green-infrastructure/ (explaining many have been certified in green fields because of these types of projects).

Second, the EIB model can inspire development of related community-building initiatives. Local governments interested in the EIB model should quantify the collateral costs and benefits of green infrastructure to the communities where they will be housed. A community "asset mapping" approach can help inventory the tangible and intangible forms of capital, capacity, and values—from people to cultural, physical, and nonphysical structures; formal and informal institutions; large and small businesses; and institutional and grassroots nonprofit organizations—that already exist in target communities.[133] By working collaboratively with community-based and mission-driven institutions, government stakeholders can draw upon participatory governance models to engage community members during the green infrastructure development process.[134] A community-*building* approach that recognizes the intersectional nature of infrastructure development (i.e., the implications for employment, transportation, health, education, criminal justice, etc.) may motivate a larger number of stakeholders to support project expansion and may facilitate greater community buy-in.[135] Moreover, such an approach carves out space for the EIB to integrate a diverse collective of social justice advocates into the conversation, including movement lawyers, community organizers, and academics who are committed to community economic empowerment.[136]

If the EIB becomes the "new normal" for financing environmental conservation and remediation projects, a key question remains. Who will provide the environmental interventions that do not fit the economic cost-savings calculus of the EIB model, such as air pollution in low-income Black communities that have yielded detrimental health outcomes? This issue has surfaced in recent history, most notably during the COVID-19 pandemic that emerged in 2020.[137] Who will pay for success in those communities? Until governments engage the true costs and benefits of EIB programs—which must transcend data-driven performance metrics and engage the complex social and political realities that plague low-income communities—then, notwithstanding short-term improvements in environmental quality, the pay-for-success model may nevertheless increase the wealth gap and the marginalization of low-income neighborhoods for the foreseeable future.[138]

---

133. Kyla Fisher et al., *Applying Asset-Based Community Development as a Strategy for CSR: A Canadian Perspective on a Win-Win for Stakeholders and SMEs*, 18 Bus. Ethics: A Eur. Rev. 66, 66–82 (2009); Christopher M. Raymond et al., *Mapping Community Values for Natural Capital and Ecosystem Services*, 68 Ecological Econs. 1301, 1301–15 (2009); Alison Mathie & Gord Cunningham, *From Clients to Citizens: Asset-Based Community Development as a Strategy for Community-Driven Development*, 13 Dev. in Prac. 474 (2003).
134. See, e.g., Vijayendra Rao & Ana M. Ibanez, *The Social Impact of Social Funds in Jamaica: A Mixed-Methods Analysis of Participation, Targeting, and Collective Action in Community-Driven Development* 1–15 (World Bank, Working Paper No. 2970, 2003); Participatory Budgeting in New York City, 2012–2013 Rulebook (2012), https://www.participatorybudgeting.org/wp-content/uploads/2012/07/Rulebook.pdf; Mike Menser & Ron Hayduk, *Participatory Budgeting: Governing at the Grassroots*, PSC CUNY (Feb. 24, 2014), https://www.psc-cuny.org/clarion/february-2014/participatory-budgeting-governing-grassroots (describing participatory budgeting as "a democratic process in which community members directly decide how to spend some part of a public budget").
135. Troy Gloverm, *Building Relationships, Accessing Resources: Mobilizing Social Capital in Community Garden Contexts*, 37 J. of Leisure Rsch. 450, 450–74 (2017).
136. Scott L. Cummings, *A Critical Reflection on Law and Organizing*, 48 UCLA L. Rev. 443, 443–517 (2001).
137. *See* Phil McKenna, *EPA Finds Black Americans Face More Health-Threatening Air Pollution*, Inside Climate News (Mar. 2, 2018), https://insideclimatenews.org/news/01032018/air-pollution-data-african-american-race-health-epa-research.
138. *See* Park, *supra* note 23, at 34 ("At the heart of legitimacy debates in the green bond market is a governance question: what is the optimal process for assessing the environmental impact of a green bond? Unless consensus is found on the answer to this question, green bonds may be relegated to permanent niche status.").

Conclusion

The Washington, D.C. EIB is the first of its kind in the United States, but it certainly will not be the last. Other cities such as Baltimore, Atlanta, and Albany are already beginning to follow suit, establishing the groundwork for new EIB projects nationwide. In partnership with the Chesapeake Bay Foundation and the Kresge Foundation, Baltimore plans to issue up to $6.2 million in EIBs to finance stormwater management in three dozen neighborhoods.[139] Furthermore, Atlanta recently became the first publicly offered EIB, allowing residents to participate for the first time in pay-for-success contracting in their own flood-prone neighborhoods to finance approximately $14 million worth of green infrastructure projects.[140] Structured by Quantified Ventures and Neighborly, a mission-oriented broker dealer, the Atlanta EIB gives the City of Atlanta Department of Watershed Management funding for green infrastructure to reduce stormwater runoff in the Proctor Creek watershed. The publicly offered EIB will undoubtedly be an attractive strategy for those seeking to leverage the investment capital of pay-for-success while facilitating economic empowerment for residents who are typically left without a seat at the deal table. As Eric Letsinger, CEO of Quantified Ventures, stated, "The Atlanta Environmental Impact Bond provides other municipalities with a blueprint for an efficient and accessible financing option for important green infrastructure projects that, thanks to the innovative publicly-traded structure, is more easily replicable."[141]

The EIB comes with trade-offs for the government, varying from deal to deal based on negotiated terms. In the case of the Washington D.C. EIB, DC Water accepted interest rate uncertainty by agreeing to a mandatory tender at year five of the bond and a remarketing of the bond interest rate, both of which were perhaps necessary to attract impact investments from Goldman Sachs and the Calvert Foundation. Further, while the use of a one-term bond was designed to maximize investor appeal, D.C. likely sacrificed the benefits of level debt service.[142] Even more, there were undoubtedly political concessions made in the Washington, D.C. EIB. Not everyone has embraced the EIB model, with some arguing that there are cheaper ways to address environmental challenges.[143]

---

139. Press Release, Chesapeake Bay Found., CBF, Quantified Ventures to Help Baltimore City Try a New Idea: "Pay For Success" Environmental Projects (Mar. 26, 2018), https://www.cbf.org/news-media/newsroom/2018/maryland/cbf-quantified-ventures-to-help-baltimore-city-try-a-new-idea-pay-for-success-environmental-projects.html; Baltimore City Dep't of Pub. Works, Annual Report: Fiscal Year 2018, https://publicworks.baltimorecity.gov/sites/default/files/Annual%20Report%202018.pdf.

140. Mazur, *supra* note 3; Tate Williams, *A New Way to Finance Green City Projects, with a Boost from Foundations*, Inside Philanthropy (Apr. 2, 2018), https://www.insidephilanthropy.com/home/2018/4/2/a-new-way-to-finance-green-city-projects-with-a-boost-from-foundations.

141. *See* WFM Staff, *Atlanta DWM Completes First Publicly Issued Environmental Impact Bond*, Water Fin. & Mgmt. (Mar. 4, 2019), https://waterfm.com/atlanta-dwm-completes-first-publicly-issued-environmental-impact-bond/.

142. Level debt service provides a schedule whereby the combined principal and interest payments remain relatively constant during the life cycle of the bond. *Level Debt Service*, Mun. Secs. Rulemaking Bd., http://www.msrb.org/glossary/definition/level-debt-service.aspx.

143. Michelle Froese, *Three Challenges that May Affect Green Bond Issuance*, Windpower Eng'g & Dev. (Mar. 13, 2019), https://www.windpowerengineering.com/three-challenges-that-may-affect-green-bond-issuance/ (explaining three key challenges faced with Green Bonds: Muddy waters or what qualifies as a Green Bond; Standard Setting, as there is a current lack of a regulatory involved scheme for Green Bonds; and a purpose it is unclear if a "Green Bond" is necessary for this purpose or if a regular bond would be sufficient without so much uncertainty and ambiguity); Wang, *supra* note 22.

Despite these shortcomings, in return for taking a risk with the EIB, DC Water obtained financing tied to the performance of green infrastructure assets that are under development. The EIB framework enabled DC Water to manage the risks commonly associated with developing green infrastructure, while establishing a replicable and scalable approach to environmental mitigation in the Washington D.C. region. Furthermore, the EIB has enabled DC Water to begin expanding local hiring through its workforce development program in partnership with the Water Environment Federation, which has an established goal of filling 51 percent of the newly created jobs under the Washington, D.C. EIB with certified D.C. residents.[144] Washington, D.C. has already received commendation for embracing this innovative financing platform. In May 2017, the Government Finance Officers Association awarded the 2017 Award for Excellence in Capital Financing and Debt Administration in Government Finance to DC Water for its green infrastructure project utilizing the EIB model.[145] The project also won Bond Buyer's 2016 Deal of the Year award for Non-Traditional Financing. For now, it seems that the EIB is working in D.C. Hopefully, more cities will follow suit.

---

144. *DC Water, District of Columbia Reach Agreement with DOJ and EPA to Implement Green Infrastructure Program*, DC WATER (May 20, 2015), https://www.dcwater.com/whats-going-on/news/dc-water-district-columbia-reach-agreement-doj-and-epa-implement-green.

145. The Government Finance Officers Association (GFOA) mission is to advance excellence in state and local government financial management. *About GFOA*, GOV'T FIN. OFFICERS ASS'N, http://www.gfoa.org/about-gfoa; *DC Water Wins Prestigious Finance Award*, DC WATER (May 30, 2017), https://dcwater.com/whats-going-on/news/dc-water-wins-prestigious-finance-award-0.

Chapter 6
State and Local Policies for Social Impact Investing

John Duda

Social impact investing—the direction of capital toward projects that will meet the needs of underserved communities and the public as a whole—can and should be a public priority.[1]

Understanding how policy has structured and can restructure the impact investing landscape is critical for legal practitioners as they advise their clients on how to create and utilize investment approaches for greater social and economic good. These clients need to know where in the investment landscape their efforts are situated, and what possibilities for more impact exist as their clients navigate this landscape. Practitioners can also help their clients as advocates for changing the policies undergirding the investment landscape so that more capital can more easily find its way toward more socially beneficial outcomes. This chapter highlights examples from a range of state and local policies that lay the framework for better investments, spur investment, or create new investments through the strategic allocation of public resources.

Public policy for social impact investing covers a diverse set of activities and institutional designs. The chapter begins with an analysis of how public jurisdictions both shape *and* participate in the investment landscape, operating themselves as investors with significant financial capital. Zooming out, it then highlights the need to defining "impact" in a way

1. A useful resource cataloging policies for state and local impact investment can be found in Matt Eldridge et al., *State and Local Governments and Impact Investing: A Guidebook for Strategic Engagement*, Urban Institute, 2019, https://www.urban.org/sites/default/files/publication/99845/state_and_local_govt_and_impact_investing_0.pdf.

which maximally captures the kinds of transformative—rather than merely palliative—effects on investment outcomes.

From there, it moves onto an exploration of some of the representative leading edges of both public policy shaping the impact investment landscape and public policy mobilizing public financial resources for social impact through strategic investment. Examining the role of the public sector as an impact investor, it highlights strategies around connecting public divestment from investments with harmful impacts to reinvestment in socially beneficial ones and underscores the need for public participation in public investment decisions. It also explores the potential of public banking as a key emerging strategy for public investment of operating funds at the state and local levels.

Turning toward catalytic policies that reshape the investment landscape, it shows how local jurisdictions can work to remove regulatory barriers to broad-based impact investment while also supporting the growth of a pipeline of transformative enterprises, aligned with a democratic and equitable economy, that can absorb impact investment capital. Finally, it traces how states and cities can supplement regulations and incentives designed to constrain the flow of traditional sources of private capital with strategies that promote the formation of alternative institutions that more naturally produce the kind of impact outcomes needed to address pervasive economic inequities.

Practitioners in the field of investment for social and economic equity must understand the policy and political context to effectively use and advise on the tools that are most effective in directly addressing racial and economic inequities. Learning from the leading edge of innovative practice and advocacy helps practitioners understand that "impact investment" does not always have to be understood as something done *by* wealthy investors who have resources *to* communities which lack them. In many of the cases outlined below, the practice of impact investment is one in which *existing* public and community assets are identified, aggregated, and deployed to serve public and community ends. Finally, by paying attention to the most powerful examples of grassroots innovation can help practitioners understand that "impact" is a matter of both content—the returns and benefits that accrue to a community, its residents, and businesses—and form—the creation of democratic institutions capable of building and holding community financial power.

Public Policy: Shaping *and* Participating in the Investment Landscape

The market does not allocate capital in a vacuum—the tracks laid by public policy establish which asset classes, which industrial priorities, and which geographies will most easily connect to investment resources. The impact here can be dramatic—consider New Deal–era federal housing policy. In order to help jumpstart the Depression-era economy, policymakers created a new public framework for insuring housing loans, while standardizing and popularizing a new long-term (thirty-year) model for these mortgages and developing a secondary market that allowed mortgage originators to sell loans to investors, freeing up credit. The resulting capital flows reshaped America—simultaneously rescuing the construction industry, elevating homeownership into the middle class's primary wealth-building opportunity, *and* reifying and institutionalizing brutally exclusive racial discrimination in housing. We can and should recognize the extent to which policy interventions program the rules of our system of capital allocation. Moreover, learning from past mistakes like those made during the New Deal, we should demand that these rules are designed to deliver equity, not exclusion. Impact investing is not just about activating individual or institutional investors to do good with their money, it is about establishing the context in which these investments are made and whose definition of "good" is built into these contexts.

Furthermore, we should recognize that government itself has the capability to be a large investor. For instance, the country of Norway has diverted profits from oil revenues into a massive sovereign wealth fund, investing these profits in a range of asset classes worldwide. The fund now holds over $1 trillion—more than $200,000 for every resident of the country—and the significant returns on its investments can be spent to fund public goods.[2] When the public itself is an investor, policy interventions can directly determine the flow of capital to and from sectors, regions, and specific industries. The large-scale and long-term perspective of public capital offers policymakers significant opportunities to create socially beneficial impact through strategic investment, opportunities which may not exist for smaller private investors.

While the two dramatic examples above are at the national level, state and local governments also have tremendous—and largely untapped—resources that can (1) catalyze third-party investment capital to projects with social impact and (2) directly supply public investment capital to projects with social impact.[3] These state and local strategies are especially important in the face of decades of retreat of federal government support for local jurisdictions, with resulting subnational budgets increasingly balanced on the backs of the poor. Pools of public and private capital simply cannot be ignored and must be shepherded intentionally to where they will have the most impact rather than assuming market preferences, and return maximization will result in broad prosperity. This imperative—to use every weapon, however imperfect, in the fight against austerity politics—is more important than ever in the wake of the COVID-19 pandemic, where, at the time this chapter was being finalized, it seems likely that a wholesale rescue and reconstruction of the local economic fabric across multiple sectors will be urgently needed. Provocatively, the multiple rounds of emergency aid deployed by the federal government and the Federal Reserve have shown the extent to which the landscape of capital provision is less a function of outcome-optimizing market dynamics and more a matter of explicitly political choices. In 2007–2008, a similar breach in economic "common sense" rebounded largely to the benefit of extractive corporations and concentrated wealth. For instance, from 2007 to 2016, the median net worth of the richest fifth of Americans increased by 13 percent, while every part of the bottom four-fifths saw their net worth fall by at least 20 percent.[4] Whether policy advocates for a more inclusive and equitable economic system can take advantage of the current opening remains to be seen.

2. *Norway Wealth Fund Grows to Record 10 Trillion Crowns*, Reuters, Oct. 25, 2019, https://www.reuters.com/article/us-norway-swf-record/norway-wealth-fund-grows-to-record-10-trillion-crowns-idUSKBN1X41AO.

3. The discussion below is organized around the distinction between "public investment policies" and "catalytic policies," although as will be seen, while helpful analytically, in practice the line between the two kinds of efforts tends to blur together—in particular, sometimes public impact investments are made precisely because they play a catalytic role.

4. Juliana Menasce Horowitz et al., *Most Americans Say There Is Too Much Economic Inequality in the U.S., but Fewer than Half Call It a Top Priority*, Pew Research Center, Jan. 2020, https://www.pewresearch.org/social-trends/2020/01/09/trends-in-income-and-wealth-inequality/.

Defining Impact

It is imperative to advance both public and private impact investment, but as long as the American economic system is structured to value returns of capital over the needs of communities, the definition of "impact" must be explored and challenged in a clearheaded and rigorous way. What is an equitable and transformative investment versus an investment that does "some" good while reinforcing systems of extraction, disinvestment, and structural bias? What are the acceptable trade-offs between financial return and social benefit? Does a given investment meet a community need on its own terms, or does capital structure control?

Being clear and ambitious about the meaning of "impact" is particularly important when we are talking about policymakers making public investments. We can and should hold policymaker's choices to a higher standard than private investment market choices. A public impact investment could be designed to not realize a return if it was achieving a public good—and this would not be a philanthropic exception to the rule, but part and parcel of government's normal use of its resources to secure public goods. Mobilizing private capital to solve social problems implies, generally, that profit will accrue to the investors being mobilized. No such assumption needs to be made when the government itself is making investments.[5] At the same time, questions of who benefits from a public investment, or a public policy incentivizing investment, and who gets to participate in making that decision become of paramount importance.

Public investment should be viewed through the lens of a "democratic economy" framework. In particular, rather than treating public interventions in the economy as accommodations of or adjustments to our current, extractive, and inequitable economic system, we should treat them as the kernel of a new economic system.[6] This new system would be centered around inclusion and reparative justice, grounded in community participation and control, built around broad forms of collective and community ownership, and generally oriented toward nonextractive and circular modes of value creation, both economically and ecologically. It would neither accelerate the unequal concentration of wealth nor facilitate the further development of corporations designed to maximize profit for private shareholders. Lawyers can play a key role in designing the institutions of this kind of new economic system, and in shaping and helping clients work within the kinds of regulations and policies that will institutionalize the new set of norms this system demands.

Benchmarking potential public investments or investment-enabling policies against a vision of systemic economic change helps narrow down the universe of possible impact investments considerably—public capital and public power over the rules of capital is a precious resource, and it should be deployed as catalytically as possible. For instance, a state looking to invest public funds in local economic development in historically underserved communities might focus on projects with some degree of worker or community ownership, instead of funding business in general, where a range of extractive ownership models

5. That is not to say that financial discipline, prudence, and due diligence should not play a role in public investment strategies—if we are interested in effective and strategic use of limited public resources of course they should!

6. See Ted Howard & Marjorie Kelly, The Making of a Democratic Economy (Berrett-Koehler 2019).

means that increased economic activity does not necessarily translate to broad-based or equitable prosperity.

Meanwhile, the larger pool of private capital, more constrained by the imperative for financial returns, can be induced to deploy across a wider spectrum of "impact" investments—from the simply "less bad" to the truly transformative. Indeed, part of the problem that public investment can help solve is that there is more capital available that can be absorbed by investments of the latter type—the democratic economy is still far from dominant, and without a conscious and intentional effort to transfer resources into new economic institutions and the support structures and ecosystems they need to thrive, we will not be laying the tracks toward a new system the rest of the economy can follow.

In practice, this means moving resources out of the extractive economy into communities which have been historically denied these resources, in ways designed to ensure these resources stay owned at the institutional level by those communities and their members. This involves forms of ownership designed to sustain and extend broadly held wealth and meaningful community control, such as cooperatives or community land trusts. Without initial investments—including at-risk equity investments, forgivable and below-market loans, or even outright grants—in these enterprises and the ecosystem institutions designed to support them, investment activity will not be able to generate meaningful, durable, and equitable economic alternatives.

Strategies and Examples: The Public as Investor

State and local governments are already engaged in large-scale investments. Public pension and retirement funds are an illustrative pool of public resources in this regard—meeting the future needs of current public employees creates quite massive pools of investment dollars under direct public control. For instance, California's public retirement fund CALPERS (California Public Employees' Retirement System) alone manages a $372 billion portfolio on behalf of 2 million members.[7] Taken together as a whole, state and local funds manage nearly *four trillion dollars*.[8]

Divestment versus Reinvestment

Recent energy around the socially responsible business narrative has translated to new policies helping align some of these trillions of dollars with social value. Screening policies have been introduced, for instance, to help state and local funds divest from industries doing direct harm to the public, like fossil fuel companies and private prisons.[9] The requirements

7. *Priorities for the Future*, CALPERS, https://www.calpers.ca.gov/docs/forms-publications/priorities-for-the-future-2019.pdf (last visited Aug. 29, 2022).

8. *State Pension Funds Reduce Assumed Rates of Return*, Pew Trusts, https://www.pewtrusts.org/en/research-and-analysis/issue-briefs/2019/12/state-pension-funds-reduce-assumed-rates-of-return (last visited Mar. 2, 2020).

9. Oscar Perry Abello, *NYC Pension Funds Made a $48 Million Statement about Private Prisons*, Next City (June 12, 2017), https://nextcity.org/daily/entry/nyc-public-pension-funds-divest-private-prisons; Rachel Dovey and Anna Petrini, *Philadelphia Will Stop Investing in Private Prisons*, Next City (Oct. 30, 2017), https://nextcity.org/daily/entry/philadelphia-stop-investing-private-prisons; *Policies Drive Public Pension Divestments*, National Conference of State Legislatures (July 2019), https://www.ncsl.org/research/fiscal-policy/policies-drive-public-pension-divestments.aspx.

and definition of fiduciary duties pose a challenge for such initiatives—recently, for instance, a state regulatory agency blocked Somerville, Massachusetts, from divesting from fossil fuels.[10] State-level policy can help here, by clarifying and expanding the latitude local pension funds have to embrace Environmental, Social, and Governance (ESG) criteria in their portfolios.

To date, *divestment*, while not by any means easy, has proven far less difficult than *reinvestment*. Similar policy questions around the definition of fiduciary duty abound. Local public funds need to go beyond screening investments to affirmatively target economic interventions advancing local economic well-being and equity as a whole. There is a growing trend toward "economically targeted investment," especially at the state level—an example would be allocating some public pension funds toward the support of businesses located in the same state. For instance, the Private Debt Program of the State of Wisconsin Investment Board has made $2 billion in financing available to local Wisconsin businesses since its inception in 1983.[11] But—under a strong definition of what counts as "impact"—it is important to distinguish investments designed to support and grow the current economy from those designed to begin economic transformation.

The latter goal can be seen in emergent efforts like a recent campaign in Boston. There a partnership has emerged between community-led initiatives like the Boston Ujima Project (an effort designed to democratize investment flows using a reparative logic of community control) and the city's robust private-sector impact investing infrastructure. This partnership recently succeeded in putting an ambitious proposal connecting sweeping divestment with reinvestment in community-sustaining enterprises before the city council. Ujima Director Nia Evans explains the divest/reinvest frame behind the demands for the hearing: "The city of Boston has an opportunity and a responsibility to invest in our communities, instead of the industries that are extracting our wealth and harming our livelihoods. It's time for full transparency and a process that is directly accountable to local residents."[12] Unfortunately, the same uncertainty in state law around pension fiduciary duty mentioned above has prevented this framework from advancing for the time being—although the organizing push did help encourage then Boston Mayor Marty Walsh to adopt some divestment guidelines for a much smaller but more flexible allocation of money in the city's operating funds.[13]

Adherence to public fiduciary duties is essential. Ultimately, both regulations and the culture of practice surrounding public fiduciaries must be shifted to emphasize the benefits of an investment frame which looks less at short-term profits in isolation and more at the total economic benefits that can be captured holistically by public entities. Insofar as investments in community can create more inclusive local economic prosperity, reduce demand

---

10. Katie Bowler, *Somerville Retirement Board and the Quest for Fossil Fuel Divestment*, Wicked Local (Mar. 8, 2018), https://www.wickedlocal.com/story/somerville-journal/2018/03/08/somerville-retirement-board-quest-for/64657014007/.

11. Lauren Dixon and Tom Woelfel, *The Pursuit of Financial Return and Societal Benefit: An Examination of Pension Fund Economically Targeted Investments*, Pacific Community Ventures (June 2017), https://www.pacificcommunityventures.org/wp-content/uploads/sites/6/2017/06/061417_Pension-Fund-ETI-Report.pdf.

12. Press release: Boston Residents Pack City Hall, Offering New Vision for City Investment Funds (Feb. 28, 2019), https://133258ba-5fd0-454f-8324-89e3dcdb1dde.filesusr.com/ugd/79496a_988c0c1605bc4405bcb9111658612598.pdf.

13. Sandra Larson, *Boston City Councilors Eye Pension Fund Divestment, Reinvestment*, Next City (Mar. 8, 2019), https://nextcity.org/daily/entry/boston-city-councilors-eye-pension-fund-divestment-reinvestment.

for services needed by the poor and housing insecure, grow the tax base, and so on, there is a powerful argument to be made that they are actually extremely wise investment decisions perfectly compatible with a broadly construed public fiduciary duty. Ambitious policies at the national level can begin to accelerate the adoption of such a perspective and the investment infrastructure to realize it. Notably, in France, so-called "solidarity-based funds" have been required to be offered in any regulated employee savings plan as a portfolio option since 2010. These funds, commonly called "90/10 funds," invest 90 percent of their capital in companies passing various social and ecological screens—but can deploy the remaining 10 percent to directly and indirectly support social enterprises of various sorts, accredited as "solidarity-based enterprises of social utility." As of 2018, these funds have over 9 billion euros under management.[14]

The city of Preston, in the United Kingdom, shows the impact that is possible when local public investment strategies are deployed in the context of a larger policy framework focused on inclusive local economic development. In the postindustrial city of Preston, a traditional cookie-cutter city center economic redevelopment scheme, premised on the attraction of large retail anchors and driven by private capital, collapsed in the wake of the 2007–2008 financial crisis. Faced with an urgent need for an alternative vision, Preston's local policymakers developed and implemented a comprehensive economic agenda centered in procurement policy and business development to stop the leakage of local economic resources from the community. As part of this broader strategy, the Preston City Council has worked to get the £5.5 billion+ Lancashire Pension Fund to invest £100 million in development targeting key projects in the city, including the reopening of a shuttered hotel and the construction of student housing.[15] This strategic use of local pension assets has, as part of Preston's overall community wealth-building strategy, led to it being named "most improved city in the UK" by PricewaterhouseCoopers.[16]

Public Participation in Investment Decisions

As impact investment of public funds becomes more common, a key decision point arises regarding how the "public" participates in investment decisions. Granting elected officials the authority to allocate significant sums of capital, especially with the expectation of below-market returns, creates significant opportunities for corruption. Two distinct (and potentially complementary) solutions have been developed to address this possibility, paralleling a larger conversation regarding public ownership more generally. On one hand, it is possible to depoliticize the deployment of investment capital by making it a technical matter, to be managed by experts operating semi-autonomously from elected political leadership, accountable to objective criteria contained in an institutional charter. There is a lot to recommend this model, especially for very large allocation of funds—expertise and efficiency are not matters to be taken lightly! However, while insulating the public from the

14. Frédéric Fourrier, *2019 Study on "90/10" Funds*, Finansol, https://www.finansol.org/_dwl/Study-On-2090-10-20Funds-20Finansol.pdf.
15. *Community Wealth Building in Action*, Preston City Council, https://www.preston.gov.uk/article/1599/Preston-and-Lancashire-City-Deal.
16. Richard Partington, *Preston Named as Most Improved City in UK*, The Guardian (Nov. 1, 2018), https://www.theguardian.com/politics/2018/nov/01/preston-named-as-most-most-improved-city-in-uk.

investments made on its behalf may make operations smoother and more professional, it does seem to short-circuit the promise of a more systemically democratic economy.

Boston Ujima's model—in which a combination of citywide and neighborhood assemblies are projected to make final decisions via vote about the fund's investments—is a pattern for this kind of democratization of control over capital. The alternative vision is to double down on democracy as the grounding for public accountability, opening up the processes of decision-making to participation at a popular level. Many emerging social and solidarity finance projects take this kind of directly democratic approach to the problem of oversight. Seed Commons, a national network of local loan funds organized to promote nonextractive investment in worker cooperatives, operates at a higher level of democratic control, with local funds, each themselves driven by grassroots participation from their respective communities, forming a council at the national level to steward the allocation of pooled capital.

Public policies guiding investment can also embrace this kind of intensive democratization as an alternative to more abstract and technocratic decision-making. A long and growing tradition of participatory planning—especially in Latin America and the Indian state of Kerala—provides a rich archive of practical experience. Starting in 1989, the city of Porto Alegre in Brazil, under the elected leadership of the Workers' Party, began allocating a portion of the city's budget to a process in which residents, engaging in a directly democratic process, would determine which projects to fund. Initial success of this model sparked a worldwide movement for "participatory budgeting." Likewise, in Kerala, the state-level government began a major experiment with decentralized and directly democratic planning in 1996, with over a third of the state's development budget expended following the results of a popular planning process grounded in discussions of hyperlocal assemblies.[17] In the United States, aside from a few experiments with participatory budgeting, there is less precedent to draw on, although there are some intriguing possibilities. One example is the Baltimore Children & Youth Fund, a new effort in public philanthropy, in which a $12 million annual allocation from city property taxes capitalizes a sizable grant-making fund. The project explicitly seeks to undo the model where philanthropy is something done for young people, with a goal of making it something that is managed with or even by them—something especially important in a city like Baltimore where white wealth is often deployed to help Black youth without their input or involvement. Practically, the Fund's commitment to racial equity and community democracy draws on broad participatory processes to identify the fund's priorities, combined with a representative board of community stakeholders who review and approve proposals.[18] See chapter 8 for more information about the Baltimore Children & Youth Fund.

Ultimately, the path forward may look like a blend of the two approaches—more traditional "insulated" management of large-scale pools of public capital, with smaller pools under participatory public control. Over time, as the institutional and experiential capacity of the public to engage in the processes afforded by the latter grows, more capital can be moved into fully democratized public funds.

---

17. Marta Harnecker and Jose Bartholome, *Planning from Below: A Decentralized Participatory Planning Proposal* (New York: Monthly Review Press, 2019).
18. Baltimore Children and Youth Fund, https://bcyfund.org/.

Operating Funds and Public Banks: Public Investment as Infrastructural Catalyst

Pension funds may possibly be the largest pools of capital under the control of local governments, but they are not the only ones. States and cities have other significant financial resources that can be redirected into impact vehicles. Operating funds—the money the state holds as it translates revenue into expenditures—can also be quite substantial. For instance, the State of New Jersey reported a year end general fund balance of $6.6 billion.[19] Currently, this balance sits in the large commercial banks servicing the state. This system of commercial banks holding state year-end balance funds is duplicated in forty-eight other states—with the exception of North Dakota. There populist farmers agitating for socialist policy a century ago secured the creation of a public bank designed to short-circuit this dependence of state finances on private banking—resulting in a durable institution that consistently returns a portion of its profits to the public, blocking the extraction of these profits to Wall Street.

A public bank is a vehicle for ensuring that public operating funds are used for investments with positive impact, with democratic oversight over priorities and processes. The Bank of North Dakota (BND), for instance, lends to agriculture and business in the state, as well as helping consumers directly with housing- and education-related lending. Revenue generated is partially returned to the state and partially retained to grow the Bank's capital, and has the ability to fund below-market programs for economic development. At the same time, the banking infrastructure also functions as a catalyst for preserving local banking. The services offered by the BND to other local financial institutions attenuate the need to rely on Wall Street megabanks. A dramatic example of the BND's impact was recently provided by the COVID-19 pandemic and the somewhat disastrous rollout of the Paycheck Protection Program loans. In many states—including notably the ones dominated by large banks—small businesses encountered significant hurdles trying to access this funding in a timely fashion. A study from the NY Federal Reserve, however, showed that North Dakota's banking ecosystem was able to connect the highest percentage of small businesses with emergency loans across the nation.[20]

Momentum around public banking is growing, notably in California, where a large statewide coalition, the California Public Banking Alliance, secured the passage of AB 857, authorizing the creation of public banks at the local level. As attorney and advocate Sushil Jacobs noted in his testimony in favor of the bill, the impact of public banks is manifold:

> First, public banks will allow California cities and counties to create sound investments that will save them money and allow them to invest their public deposits in fiscally, socially and environmentally responsible activities.
>
> Second, public banks can save taxpayer funds that are currently going to big banks and instead use those funds to finance public goods such as affordable housing,

19. *FY19 Comprehensive Annual Financial Report*, State of New Jersey, https://www.nj.gov/treasury/omb/publications/19cafr/NJCAFR2019%20Financial.pdf.

20. Haoyang Liu and Desi Volker, *Where Have the Paycheck Protection Loans Gone So Far?*, Liberty Street Economics: Federal Reserve Bank of New York (May 6, 2020), https://libertystreeteconomics.newyorkfed.org/2020/05/where-have-the-paycheck-protection-loans-gone-so-far.html.

transparent student loans, renewable energy, rebuilding after natural disasters, and local infrastructure projects such as schools, parks and roads.

Third, in partnership with local banks and credit unions, public banks can provide affordable loans and lines of credit to local small businesses and nonprofits, and provide a critical bulwark against displacement of community-serving anchor institutions. Public banks can increase the lending capacity of the local banking system through participation loans, by providing liquidity, and serving as regional bankers' banks.[21]

The public banking example shows clearly that the impact of public money can go beyond simply making investments in good projects that align with public goals. Used wisely, the strategic deployment of public capital can create new institutions and associated new patterns of capital flows, with the possibility of attenuating or eliminating the negative effects of more traditional flows of debt and equity.

Strategies and Examples: Catalytic Policies

State and local policies can accelerate and shape investments in social impact even when the capital being invested remains private. These are catalytic policies, designed to use the resources more traditionally associated with government, namely, expenditures, regulation, and management of economic development. These state and local policies create the conditions in which private capital more easily flows to impact investments. Such policies can remove barriers in existing regulations that prevent capital from being aggregated and deployed. For instance, as mentioned above, some states like Massachusetts may have regulations which block local jurisdictions from using pension funds as a source of social impact capital. Other catalytic policies can create new infrastructure for impact investment—creating new categories of funds, like France's 90/10 funds, or new institutions, like public banks. Catalytic policies can also accelerate impact investment by aligning existing pools of capital with community projects. Finally, catalytic policies can use public expenditures to support the pipeline of projects ripe for impact investment by funding things like ecosystems of technical assistance. Practitioners must stay abreast of these types of policies to understand how to devise solutions that meet their clients' needs in their geographic area.

Removing Barriers

One of the key barriers to impact investment is securities law. Designed, rightly, to protect the public from unscrupulous actors seeking to scam them into putting money into fraudulent investments, securities laws channel small-dollar investment toward the kind of publicly listed funds and companies which have the capacity to comply with the requirements and regulations around offerings and disclosure. However well meaning, for a small

21. Joint Informational Hearing on Public Banking, Testimony of Sushil Jacob, Lawyers' Committee for Civil Rights, Feb. 4, 2019, https://abnk.assembly.ca.gov/sites/abnk.assembly.ca.gov/files/hearings/Sushil%20Jacob%20 Testimony.pdf.

community enterprise with slim access to technical assistance, attempting to raise debt or equity from its community while dealing with the full weight of Securities and Exchange Commission (SEC) compliance is a terribly mismatched situation.

The federal Jumpstart Our Business Startup (JOBS) Act, passed in 2012, offered some relief, legalizing "crowdfunding"—the direct aggregation of capital from nonaccredited investors, subject to limits and accompanied by appropriate disclosures, using regulated platforms to substitute in part for the onerous disclosures required on other interstate public offerings.[22] But for many place-based community projects, the architecture of crowdfunding does not offer many advances over "direct public offerings" limited to residents of a specific state, which enjoy similar exemptions.[23]

Perhaps more interesting are the new community crowdfunding exemptions being enacted in the leading edge of new state cooperative incorporation statutes. In both California and Illinois, movement-driven legal efforts have succeeded in establishing new policies creating a class of investor-members in worker cooperatives, where investments from community investors, who by default have no legal right to make decisions for the cooperative, are exempt from state securities law. In California, this exemption comes with additional restrictions around investor rate of return and a relatively low cap ($1,000) on the amount of equity a community investor may provide—no such restrictions exist in the Illinois statute—which may as a consequence be a more significant tool for aggregating capital for worker cooperatives.[24]

The policies here provide a useful framework for impact investment—codifying and making recognizable a form of worker-controlled, community-based enterprises, and creating the pathway for these enterprises to raise capital from their communities without undoing the logic of workplace democracy that grounds their social impact in the first place. This is especially important, as advocates for both bills stressed, because workers in low-income communities and disinvested communities of color tend to not own significant capital they can risk in a business venture. Creating businesses that will be owned by low-income people these businesses are aiming to help requires a source of external capital. Examples of these kinds of thoughtful exemptions from securities law like California and Illinois state laws both facilitate such impact investments but also carefully circumscribe the rights this capital enjoys relative to the communities it is being deployed to serve.

Grow the Economic Pipeline, Grow the Investment Ecosystem

Impact investment is predicated on the existence of economic investment projects that can absorb these investments to provide the desired impact. In some cases, however, especially when new models of democratic economic development are moving from inspiring prototypes in a few places to wider deployment, the lack of suitable projects to absorb available capital may prove to be the true bottleneck. This results in a chicken-and-egg

22. *Regulation Crowdfunding: A Small Entity Compliance Guide for Issuers*, SEC (May 13, 2016), https://www.sec.gov/info/smallbus/secg/rccomplianceguide-051316.htm.
23. *Direct Public Offering*, Cutting Edge Capital, https://www.cuttingedgecapital.com/direct-public-offering/.
24. *CA Worker Cooperative Act*, Sustainable Economies Law Center, https://www.theselc.org/ca-worker-cooperative-act; Oscar Perry Abello, *Clearing the Legal and Financial Pathway for Worker Cooperatives in Illinois*, Next City (Aug. 27, 2019), https://nextcity.org/daily/entry/clearing-the-legal-and-financial-pathway-for-worker-coops-in-illinois.

problem—there may be impact capital ready for deployment, but it could be blocked because not enough projects exist to take on these investments, or the projects which exist are not sufficiently scaled up in size or sophistication to do so.

Worker cooperatives are a great example here. The model of the democratic workplace has enjoyed a good deal of (deserved) attention and enthusiasm in community development and equitable economic policy circles. Indeed, democratic workplace models have caught the attention of impact investors. But the number of worker cooperatives in the United States is quite small, in just the hundreds of businesses. Public policy in such a situation faces a challenge—how can capital be directed to invest in businesses that do not yet exist? An inadequate answer to this challenge for states and cities is to use limited public resources to fund the creation of individual businesses—a slow and uncertain process that will tie up and even risk significant amount of public funds, with results that will likely be disproportionate to the problems these efforts are intended to address. Mobilizing private capital would be a solution—if there were more worker cooperatives ready to absorb significant investments, which there are not. The best way for public resources to get out of this bind is to support the ecosystem of institutions capable of accelerating the growth of the sector.

This is essentially the strategy adopted by New York City in the NYC Worker Cooperative Development Initiative, in which the city council has allocated financial resources (currently over $3 million per year) to support the infrastructure of worker cooperative development in the city. This includes community-based cooperative development centers like the Center for Family Life, cooperative educational and advocacy projects like the Green Worker Coop Academy or the NYC Network of Worker Cooperatives, technical assistance providers like the ICA Group, and nonextractive nonprofit coop lenders like The Working World. In the period between 2017 and 2019, 113 worker cooperatives have been either formally created or otherwise soft-launched with the support of the initiative.[25] As the ecosystem of service providers and advocates has been able to draw on public funds to expand their operations, private impact capital has been able to find more opportunities to invest in a growing worker cooperative sector.

Public policymakers hoping to maximize impact of limited funds to spur impact investments should recognize that such catalytic investments in infrastructure and ecosystem development can help create the kind of businesses that most advance goals around equity and the democratic economy, creating opportunities for investment where none or few existed previously. For instance, a comparably small public expenditure for technical assistance, promotion, and ecosystem coordination in a state-level employee ownership center could create large opportunities for conversion of businesses to democratic ownership, with the opportunity to mobilize significant amounts of impact and nonimpact capital.[26] Moreover, even public authorities with the financial ability to deploy significant investment

---

25. 2017-2019 Working Together Addendum: A Report on the Last Three Fiscal Years of the Worker Cooperative Business Development Initiative (WCBDI), NYC Department of Small Business Services and Mayor's Office of Contract Services, https://www1.nyc.gov/assets/sbs/downloads/pdf/about/reports/worker_coop_report_fy17-19.pdf.

26. For a summary of the possible investment models here, *see* Andrea Armeni and Camille Kerr, *Investing in Employee Ownership: Financing Conversions through a Private Equity Fund Model*, Transform Finance (Nov. 2019), http://transformfinance.org/briefings/investing-in-employee-ownership-financing-conversions-through-a-private-equity-fund-model.

capital into impact vehicles should take into the account the need for simultaneously supporting the ecosystems of support that can create more attractive and effective targets for that investment. For instance, the federal Healthy Food Financing Initiative, authorized initially in 2009, works to expand food access and food security. This collaboration between the Treasury Department, Department of Health and Human Services, and Department of Agriculture provides both awards of capital through the Community Development Financial Institutions (CDFIs) Fund and grants to community developers through the Department of Health and Human Services, and, since 2014, through the U.S. Department of Agriculture. This type of public investment that invests in an ecosystem of support and incentivizes private capital has the potential to be catalytic in achieving short- and long-term impact goals.

Supporting Institutional Infrastructure and Aligning Private Capital

Government Incentives

Public funds can be invested or supplied as grants creating catalytic conditions for private impact investment, without regard to a direct return on this investment. A clear example of this is the "linked deposit"—here, a local public entity deposits funds in a private bank and forgoes some of the interest payments that it would otherwise expect. The bank, in turn, passes this savings on to businesses seeking loans that are satisfying impact criteria set by the public entity that made the deposit. For instance, Washington State authorizes up to $175 million in surplus operating funds for deposit in banks at below market interest rates in order to subsidize lower rates on loans to qualifying minority and women-owned businesses in the state.[27]

Another important use of public funds, common at both the state and federal levels, is loan guarantees, in which public authorities agree to cover all or a portion of default on a loan, allowing underwriting standards to be relaxed or interest rates pegged to perceived risk to be lowered. The Small Business Administration's 7(a) program is probably the most well-known loan guarantee, but others exist at the state and local levels, like California's California Capital Access Program (CalCAP). CalCAP provides loan guarantees to encourage lending institutions to provide capital to small businesses facing barriers to capital access, as well as investments in accessibility and sustainability.[28] Again, this is essentially a subsidy provided to private capital in order to persuade its deployment for public priorities—although in the best case the public authority spends nothing because the loans stay current.

Providing incentives to drive private capital into investments aligned with public needs can be especially powerful when the owners of that capital themselves have an interest in the investments beyond immediate financial return. For instance, in New Jersey, the New Jersey Housing and Mortgage Finance Agency's (NJHMFA) Hospital Partnership Subsidy Program matches state funds with hospitals that are interested in investing in building affordable housing. For the hospitals, such investments make sense even when the financial return is lower than other portions of their portfolios because access to housing is a key social determinant of health outcomes. Accordingly, spending to create housing in a local

27. Linked Deposit Loan Program, Washington State Office of Minority and Women's Business Enterprises, https://omwbe.wa.gov/small-business-assistance/money-loans/access-capital-access-money/linked-deposit-loan-program.
28. California Capital Access Program (CalCAP), CA State Treasurer, https://www.treasurer.ca.gov/cpcfa/calcap/.

community is a wiser investment in the health of a community than spending to treat the health consequences of homelessness and housing insecurity. By using state subsidies to close funding gaps between the cost of a housing project and what a hospital is willing or able to invest, NJHMFA can make sure the projects meet requirements around affordability and access requirements, while building more units than what could be accomplished with public funds alone.[29] This type of example also addresses core equity goals of addressing both housing and health inequities.

Government Requirements

Such partnership policies make a lot of sense for states and local governments constrained by tight budgets, on one hand, and radical change-making policy, on the other. "Win–win" approaches, where state resources subsidize private capital accumulation and thus make more resources available to solve social problems, are both easier sells politically and easier to integrate into narrow budgetary openings. But it is important to not let our political imagination be unduly circumscribed. The persuasive approaches outlined above can and should be complemented both by policies *requiring* private capital to be invested in ways which align with democratic priorities and by policies promoting alternative structures to aggregate capital in public or community hands. While radical in their implications, both of these financially prudent and radical change-making strategies can be realized as practical possibilities, even in the current political context.

An example of the "requirement" approach is the Community Reinvestment Act (CRA)—while far from perfect, the CRA, enacted in the face of social movements organizing against bank redlining policies, mandates that banks' loan making meet some basic criteria for racial equity, and gives communities standing to challenge the disparate impacts of the expansion and reorganization of the banking industry. Although threatened by the Trump administration, and marred by ineffective and lax application of its regulatory standards, the CRA is in principle an ambitious and far-reaching framework that mandates the "impact" that private bank lending produce. Indeed, the redlining the CRA attempted to remedy was itself in large part the result of public policies delivering a certain kind of retrograde and racialized inequitable impact from the deployment of private housing capital. The whole sordid history of redlining shows that it is a mistake to see the market for investment capital as a space which exists independent of government policy, which the state then has to enter in order to try and bend the flow of capital toward more beneficial outcomes. On the contrary, the investment market is already shaped and conditioned by a manifold of policy frameworks, regulations, and subsidies; however, the impact we get is not the one we might want if these policies were developed to actually reflect democratic and equitable priorities.

Developing Alternative Institutions

An "alternatives" strategy complements such regulatory approaches by recognizing that, no matter how constrained by rules and requirements, the market-driven allocation of capital in the service of private benefit will ultimately not be sufficient to deliver outcomes

29. Amanda Abrams, "NJ Pays Hospitals to Build Affordable Housing," *Shelterforce*, Nov. 2019, https://shelterforce.org/2019/11/04/nj-pays-hospitals-to-build-affordable-housing/.

compatible with equity and democracy. New institutions, with different sets of incentives and governance, are required to aggregate, steward, and deploy capital in a democratic economy—and state and local policies can play a catalytic role in developing or strengthening these institutions. Along with public banks (discussed above), CDFIs—especially nonprofit or member-owned ones—are a good example of this kind of alternative financial institution. While most support for CDFIs comes from the Department of the Treasury's CDFI Fund, New York State has moved to fund the NYS CDFI Fund, a state-level program designed to complement federal support that became law in 2008, but never received any appropriations, in large part due to the financial crisis. Over five years, the Fund is slated to receive a $25 million injection from the state, thanks to a provision in the enacted 2020–2021 state budget.[30]

Funding the NYS CDFI Fund—so it can provide grants and investments to the state's CDFIs as originally intended—is a key part of the NYS Community Equity Agenda, a framework developed by grassroots economic and racial justice organizations. In their policy brief supporting the fund, the New Economy Project singles out the impact of Community Development Credit Unions (CDCUs) in particular—these are member-owned CDFIs that provide both retail banking to consumers and business investment:

Community development credit unions (CDCUs), in particular, help low- and moderate-income families build assets by providing savings vehicles, consumer credit, home mortgages, and financial counseling. And because CDCUs are community-based financial cooperatives, they contribute to neighborhood economic security and preserve money and resources in the communities they serve, especially low-income communities of color and immigrant communities.[31]

When talking about impact "investment" and "investors," we can be blinkered by these words, which too often draw up connotations exclusively of individuals with significant and disproportionate wealth. An impact investment becomes something done by the wealthy to communities understood as lacking resources. Sometimes, especially when appropriate guardrails are in place to collect and honor community input, and to conceive and measure impact in thoughtful ways that center equity, the interests of investor and community can significantly and productively overlap. In other cases, like the "Opportunity Zones" discussed in chapter 4 of this book, broad, imprecise, and eminently gameable geographic targeting means that no such guarantee of mutual investor and community benefit exists.

But the demands of the NYS Equity Agenda demonstrate that such a view of impact investment, in which investors have all the capital and communities have all the need, is a limited and limiting one. CDCUs, at their best, allow low-income, disinvested communities to aggregate capital under explicitly democratic control, and use that aggregated capital to invest in businesses and projects that benefit the community. The impact of the investments being made here—deposits and loans—is a matter of both content (the benefits that

30. Oscar Perry Abello, "New York's Best Kept Secret to Support Community Financial Institutions" *Next City*, Jan. 14, 2020, https://nextcity.org/daily/entry/new-yorks-best-kept-secret-to-support-community-financial-institutions; "Governor Cuomo Announces Highlights of FY 2021 Budget," State of New York, Apr. 2, 2020, https://www.budget.ny.gov/pubs/press/2020/fy-2021-state-budget-highlights.html.

31. Support Cooperative and Community-Controlled Finance, NYS Equity Agenda, https://www.neweconomynyc.org/wp-content/uploads/2019/08/CDFI-Fund-2019.pdf.

accrue to a community, its residents, and businesses) and form (the creation of a democratic institution capable of building and holding community financial power).

While undoubtedly reparative justice demands, in the end, a transfer of financial resources from the extractors of wealth to the communities it was extracted from, it also demands the reconstruction of community capacity to hold and steward those resources. Effective, authentic, and equitable policies to support impact investment should be mindful of this dual mandate—on one hand, moving capital to places where the existing market logic would not, and on the other hand, making sure the communities in those places have the power and structures to control it once it is there. Public policy for impact investment—whether directly investing public funds or catalyzing the investment funds held elsewhere—cannot be content to merely move money against the current of our extractive, profit-maximizing economic system. It must view these currents as opportunities to reroute the course of the system itself.

Chapter 7
Community Capital Raising Strategies

Kim Y. Arnone

Introduction

A threshold concern for many impact enterprises is how to raise capital in alignment with their mission. More and more entrepreneurs are articulating social, environmental, and justice impact goals for their for-profit and nonprofit enterprises. Founders are embedding their values and vision for a better world into the fabric of their workplace, setting guidelines that they and their colleagues can rely on to make decisions on how to lead and grow their businesses and programs with integrity. For many, finding capital that supports both business planning and impact goals can be very difficult. Many social enterprises do not fit the profile of the type of company that venture capital firms are looking to fund as they may not have the right growth trajectory, as many options for sale or merger, or the possibility of extreme profits. While much is made of unicorn[1] businesses backed by venture capital, the reality is that very few businesses obtain venture capital funding and even fewer ultimately succeed.[2]

1. *Unicorn (finance)*, Wikipedia, https://en.wikipedia.org/wiki/Unicorn_(finance). A unicorn is a start-up valued at over $1 billion. *Id.*
2. Dileep Rao, *Why 99.95% of Entrepreneurs Should Stop Wasting Time Seeking Venture Capital*, Forbes (July 22, 2013), https://www.forbes.com/sites/dileeprao/2013/07/22/why-99-95-of-entrepreneurs-should-stop-wasting-time-seeking-venture-capital/#721afa0446eb.

Social enterprises,[3] like most conventional start-up and growing businesses, face dilemmas presented by traditional capital raise pathways. Do founders divert their time from working on the core business to focus on making connections to raise capital from traditional institutional and high-net-worth investors? Are enterprises willing to compromise vision, values, or impact goals to meet growth and profit requirements of new funders? Are businesses willing to cede some small or large measure of control of the company to outside investors who may not share an alignment with the entity's social impact values? Do enterprise leaders want their profits to benefit investors who neither share their values, come from their communities, nor want to secure the longevity of the enterprise?

If social enterprises aim not to make compromises expected by many providers of traditional[4] capital, what options are available? One set of solutions is found in the regulatory pathways that allow for-profit and revenue-based nonprofit enterprises to raise capital broadly and publicly from community members who share the same values, vision, and commitment to key principles as the enterprises themselves. It is this set of solutions that I refer to as "community capital raising." Unlike traditional capital sources, community capital is investment sourced from a broad spectrum of a community, including both wealthy and nonwealthy investors. While typically defined by geography (e.g., a city or county), it can also be based on a common interest (e.g., education or environment).[5]

These community capital approaches, discussed in detail below, serve a twofold purpose: They provide alternative funding avenues for mission-driven enterprises and allow community investors (of all wealth levels) to invest in businesses that they otherwise would not be able to under the prevailing private investment model, which model excludes all investors who are neither high net worth nor high salaried.

Community capital campaigns help democratize our economy by allowing more people to invest in who they know, what they know, values they believe in, and enterprises that are positively impacting their communities. These kinds of campaigns do not exclude wealthy or institutional investors (in fact, those investors are often necessary to the success of such raises), but they do level the playing field by having investors of all means invest together. These campaigns are transparent and give the enterprises the opportunity to put the entirety of their value proposition forward including both the potential monetary return on investment and the benefit of the impacts they create due to their adherence to social, environmental, and/or justice principles embedded in their businesses.

This chapter first discusses the term *community capital*, some of the advantages it can provide for certain social enterprises, and why it is important as a tool to democratize our economy. Next, the chapter provides some of the regulatory options available for enterprises to utilize community capital and the strengths and challenges of each. By looking at specific successful case studies, the chapter then further explains the range of regulatory options. Finally, this chapter ends with a review of some preparations social enterprises should make before embarking on a community capital raise.

---

3. *Social Enterprise*, Wikipedia, https://en.wikipedia.org/wiki/Social_enterprise. Social enterprises have both business goals and social goals and can be structured as for-profits and nonprofits.
4. By traditional capital, the author primarily refers to venture capital and lending by large commercial banking institutions.
5. *What Is Community Capital*, Cutting Edge Capital, https://www.cuttingedgecapital.com/what-is-community-capital/.

What Is Community Capital and Why Is It Important?

The term *community capital* is meant to encompass various legal strategies, each of which includes two key elements: (1) the issuer may raise capital broadly from community, both wealthy and nonwealthy investors; and (2) the issuer may advertise the investment offering broadly and generally solicit investors. In this way, community capital is raised through a wide cross-section of people and institutions, most of whom are within the issuer's network of supporters or customers, reside in the issuers' geographic community, or share an affinity for the product made, the service provided, and/or the method of production.[6] This chapter refers to this broad group of investors as "community investors" and defines the group as encompassing both accredited (wealthy) and nonaccredited (non-high net worth) investors.[7]

Community capital can be raised directly by social enterprises that run their own investment campaigns, or alternatively, community capital can be raised into a community investment fund (CIF) which then deploys that investment to a variety of community enterprises. CIFs are typically defined by geography (like regional business growth funds or a regional real estate revitalization fund), but they also can be based on a particular interest or industry (like renewable energy or education enterprises). The examples discussed in this chapter primarily focus on how individual businesses use community capital raising strategies, but the chapter also provides a short exploration of CIFs.

Community capital raises can be better solutions for social enterprises than other conventional capital raise strategies. In addition, such community-facing capital raises can offer broader impact on community members, communities, and local economies. One reason community capital offerings are appealing to social enterprises is that community members may be willing to accept more reasonable terms than are available from conventional lenders or institutional investors. Community members may be more willing to invest "patient capital," referring to when they realize the expected return on investment. This is often because they may recognize some intangible benefit they expect provided by the business or derived from joining in a community-serving venture. Intangible returns can include knowing that an investment supports businesses that create good jobs, source materials sustainably, help build and maintain community, keep local shopping districts vibrant, offer alternatives to big box store purchases, and so on.

In turn, having community investors in businesses has value beyond the money that they invest. Community investors are literally invested in the businesses' success and can be powerful sources of connection to a broader segment of community members and in turn help push growth. These relationships often mean that investors become these social enterprises' biggest evangelists proclaiming the advantages of their services or products,

---

6. While the "community" in community capital is most often a geographic community such as the town, region, or state served by the social enterprise, community investors do not have to be tied to where the business is located. For example, a renewable energy company building and financing wind farms may have its place of business in Florida, its projects in Illinois and Indiana, and most of its investors from California and New York. Investors in that example share an affinity for supporting renewable energy but are not geographically connected to the social enterprise.

7. Accredited investors are defined in 17 CFR 230.501 to include an individual or spouses with combined assets of $1,000,000 or more (excluding residence, cars, and furnishings); an individual with $200,000 in annual income in the past two years and expected in the current year; spouses with combined $300,000 in annual income in the past two years and expected in the current year; and entities with $5,000,000 in assets.

the strength of their mission, and community impacts. In short, investor relationships can, if nurtured, lead to additional business growth and overall community support.[8]

From the investors' perspective, the benefits of community capital include increased options for impact investment. Community capital offerings allow everyone to invest in alignment with their values. Currently, nonwealthy or community investors are not permitted to invest in most private enterprises, including social and environmental impact companies. Most people are limited to putting investment dollars into Wall Street offerings: publicly traded stocks, mutual funds, and money market accounts. Offerings that are open to community investors allow those people to invest in businesses, cooperatives, nonprofits, or other enterprises that offer innovative solutions; are committed to good environmental practices; and/or are supporting social justice missions. Many impact organizations make it a practice to include community viewpoints to help shape their missions and the focus of their work, products, and services. We need to ask ourselves: why do we leave those community members out of the investment opportunities in these organizations when it is time to grow the strategies the community members help define? The community capital raise strategies discussed in this chapter allow enterprises to choose methods that help provide a broader range of mission-driven investment options for all investors.

Community capital raises are not only beneficial to social enterprises and impact investors, these types of raises can have positive impacts on the greater community and economy. First is the benefit of local capital circulating locally. Every community investment means that dollars that could be flowing out of the community to Wall Street institutions remain in the local economy. If investors take even a small portion of their investable assets and invest locally or in alignment with values, that impact would be formidable.[9] These opportunities can create a cycle of investment that is nonextractive: investment, business growth, returns, reinvestment, and spending of returns can all take place within the local economy thus building wealth sustainably.

Community capital can also help address some of the issues we face in trying to increase equity and access to capital for women and people of color. To date, much of the focus has been on getting more women and people of color in front of venture capital investors, whose representatives are still mostly white and male.[10] However, the community

---

8. In terms of investment risk, it is important to note that the act of opening an offering to people of all wealth levels does not mean that everyone will have income to put toward a community investment, nor does it mean that any particular community investment fits everyone's risk level. The broader reach of community capital offerings means that more people can participate if they choose but the goal should not be that all risk is being placed on those investors who have the least amount of investment dollars or the least risk tolerance. This potential shifting of risk to community investors is, in part, mitigated by the fact that most community capital offering paths require significant disclosures and regulatory review and most of the community capital strategies discussed below have investor suitability requirements that are meant to limit the amount nonaccredited investors can invest.

9. 2020 Russell US Indexes Reconstitution, FTSE Russell (2021), https://content.ftserussell.com/sites/default/files/2021_russell_us_indexes_reconstitution_recap.pdf. As of May 2021, the total market capitalization of the U.S. stock market was approximately $47.7 trillion, according to the Russell 3000 Index. *Id.*

10. John Koetsier, *$1 Billion for 2,800 Startups: How Clearbanc Uses AI to Take Bias Out of Investing*, FORBES (June 27, 2020), https://www.forbes.com/sites/johnkoetsier/2020/06/27/1-billion-for-2800-startups-how-clearbanc-uses-ai-to-take-bias-out-of-investing/#4ff65e5551d0. In 2017, it was reported that only 2 percent of founders funded by venture capital were women. *Id.* Megan Corsano, *The Venture Capital Pipeline: Fixing Racial Disparities in Startup Funding*, THE BUSINESS JOURNALS: RICHMOND INNO (June 30, 2020), https://www.bizjournals.com/richmond/inno/stories/inno-insights/2020/06/30/the-venture-capital-pipeline-fixing-racial.html. Similarly, only one percent of venture capital investment reportedly goes to Black entrepreneurs. *Id.* Both of these articles also note that there are very few women and people of color in venture capital firms.

capital path can be another tool to help level the playing field. When a broader segment of a community is invited to invest, we are likely to see an increase in diversity of investors as compared to most existing high net worth investors and funding institutions. Entrepreneurs that receive funding will likely reflect the community that is investing in them. The expectation is that a diversity of community members will choose more diverse entrepreneurs that speak their language (literally and figuratively), reflect their values, and are committed to impacts that solve problems that affect them. In other words, if more women and people of color are investing, more women and people of color are likely to receive funding.

So, how do we achieve this? Investors (both accredited and community investors) should seek out community offerings and, when they do not find them, ask that investment offerings be open to community investors. Social enterprises, high net worth investors, and changemaking supporting organizations need to explore how to make investment opportunities open to all.

The current model for capital raising, even in most social and environmental impact enterprises, is to reach out to the wealthiest accredited and angel investors and large institutions when capital is needed. That model is not wrong, but choosing only that approach means that social enterprises are missing the opportunity to engage all supporters (regardless of their wealth) and missing out on the impacts that flow from doing so.

Several strategies exist that social enterprises may use in conducting a community capital raise. The next section details these strategies.

What Are the Primary Legal Strategies for Community Capital Offerings?

This section presents the primary strategies for community capital offerings and their basic legal requirements and restrictions. Each round to enlist investment capital is referred to as an offering, and there are a number of types.[11] Offering strategies for enterprises include direct public offerings (DPOs), regulation crowdfunding, and Regulation A. Social enterprises can also receive community capital investment indirectly through CIFs that use capital from community investors raised using one of the previously listed strategies. Community capital, like conventional capital, can be raised by the sale of securities to investors who provide funds to the company now in expectation of sharing in later returns on the company's growth.

A security is "an investment of money in a common enterprise with profits to come solely from the efforts of others."[12] All securities transactions, even exempt transactions, are regulated by provisions of the federal securities laws to protect the public against fraud from false or misleading statements by the issuer. The government enforces the federal securities laws through criminal, civil, and administrative proceedings.[13] The SEC enforces

11. Basically, an offering may consist of a securities offering, investment round, or funding round. Any investment round, pre-seed, seed, series A or otherwise, represents a singular investment or funding round and involves selling stocks, notes, or other securities to investors to generate capital.

12. *SEC v. Howey Co.*, 328 U.S. 293 (1946).

13. Private parties also can bring actions under certain securities laws. Also, if all conditions of the exemptions are not met, purchasers may be able to return their securities and obtain a refund of their purchase price.

federal securities laws, and each state has its own securities regulator. Any company selling securities must comply with both federal regulations and state securities laws and regulations in the states where securities are offered and sold (typically, the states where offerees and investors are based).

All securities offerings must first be cleared as either complying with or exempt from federal and state securities laws. For social enterprises seeking to raise community capital, the principal strategies, summarized below, include multiple forms of exempt Direct Public Offerings, state exemptions for particular types of entities (nonprofits, cooperatives), state crowdfunding regimes, federal Regulation Crowdfunding, and Regulation A offerings.

The examples below are grouped by the federal exemption, and applicable state regulations are also discussed.

Direct Public Offerings

A *Direct Public Offering (DPO)* refers to an offering of securities that may be offered by enterprises directly to their community or network, rather than through brokers, and that is open and can be advertised directly to community investors. Federal and state laws apply to DPOs. Generally, unless an offering is registered with the SEC, it must be *exempt* from registration under federal law. DPOs can take one of several regulatory pathways depending on the type of entity making them, the amount to be raised, and the location of the enterprise's network.

By using a DPO, a business or nonprofit can market and advertise its offering publicly by any means it chooses—through advertising in newspapers and magazines, at public events and private meetings, on the internet and through social media channels. DPOs can be focused on investors residing in a single state or multiple states. DPOs are available to many different entity structures, including corporations, LLCs, cooperatives, and revenue-generating nonprofit entities. Raising money through a DPO does not make the enterprise a publicly traded company and it does not require that the enterprise provide complicated ongoing reporting to securities regulators.

DPO legal strategies employ an exemption from federal securities registration law coupled with either an exemption under state law or a registration of the offering with state regulators. The most common federal regulatory exemptions utilized for DPOs are discussed below: (1) the intrastate exemption (Rule 147A), (2) small-offering or multistate exemption (Rule 504), and (3) the nonprofit exemption.[14] State compliance strategies include registration of the offering with state regulators or utilizing state exemptions from registration such as cooperative exemptions, state crowdfund exemptions, or state nonprofit offering exemptions.

Intrastate Exemption (15 U.S. Code § 77c(a)(11))

Federal securities law allows for single-state or intrastate DPOs conducted in compliance with Rule 147 or Rule 147A. Both Rules are for offerings made to investors in the offeror's home state with slightly different limitations, and both provide a "safe harbor" that ensures

14. Regulation A offerings can also be considered DPOs because they can be offered directly from an enterprise to investors, but as Reg A requires a detailed federal filing, I am addressing it separately below.

an offering would meet the requirements for the intrastate exemption in Section 3(a)(11) of the 1933 Act.[15] These types of DPOs permit residents from a single state to invest in the offering. Importantly for enterprises making an intrastate offering, this federal exemption is self-executing and does not require a federal filing.

This approach allows the issuer (the enterprise offering the investment) to use general solicitation and advertising to promote its offering.[16] There are, however, a number of requirements for use, and some limitations on the use, of this exemption.

Federal Prerequisites

Federal qualification turns on the contacts with the specific state: of the issuer, of the purchasers, and the duration the purchaser holds before reselling the investment security. After determining that federal requirements are met, then state law governs with respect to duties of disclosure.

First, the issuer has to be a resident of the state or territory meaning that it has to have its principal place of business in the state (it does not need to be organized in the state) and it has to be doing business in the state.[17]

Second, an issuer may only sell its securities to residents of the state in which the issuer is offering its security.[18] The issuer must reasonably believe, at the time of sale, that an investor is a resident of the state in which the offering is made.[19]

---

15. Rule 147A is substantially similar to the previous Rule 147 but allows for more liberal online offering rules and more flexible guidelines for issuers who are formed out-of-state, so long as the company satisfies the state's "doing business" requirement showing the in-state nature of the company's business; see 15 U.S. Code §77c(a)(11); 17 CFR §230.147; 17 CFR §230.147A. Rule 147 was retained primarily because many state crowdfunding laws were implemented explicitly requiring the use of Rule 147 as the federal exemption strategy. Unless an issuer is utilizing a state-level exemption requiring compliance with Rule 147, most issuers considering an intrastate DPO will choose to use the easier to comply with Rule 147A. This discussion primarily addresses the requirements related to Rule 147A.

16. 17 CFR §230.147A(b).

17. The issuer is considered doing business within a state or territory if the issuer satisfies at least one of the following requirements: (1) the issuer derived at least 80 percent of its consolidated gross revenues from the operation of a business or of real property located in or from the rendering of services within such state or territory; (2) the issuer had at the end of its most recent semi-annual fiscal period prior to an initial offer of securities in any offering or subsequent offering pursuant to this section, at least 80 percent of its assets and those of its subsidiaries on a consolidated basis located within such state or territory; (3) the issuer intends to use and uses at least 80 percent of the net proceeds to the issuer from sales made pursuant to this section (§230.147A) in connection with the operation of a business or of real property, the purchase of real property located in, or the rendering of services within such state or territory; or (4) a majority of the issuer's employees are based in such state or territory. 17 CFR §230.147A(c)(2).

18. 17 CFR §230.147A(d).

19. For individuals, state of residence is determined by where their principal residence is located and the investor must provide a representation that they are a resident of the state of the offering; this is usually included in the investment agreement. However, it is not sufficient to establish a reasonable belief of residency from a written representation alone. See Instruction to 17 CFR §230.147A(d). Additional information supporting a reasonable belief in residency of an investor can include personal knowledge based on a preexisting relationship with the investor, utility bill, tax return, driver's license or other government-issued document, directory listings, public records, and other reliable databases, such as credit bureaus. For businesses that are investing, residence is determined by where the entity has its principal place of business which means the location at which the officers, partners, or managers of the entity primarily direct, control, and coordinate its activities. 17 CFR §230.147A(d). For trusts that are not separate legal entities, residency is determined by that state of residence of its trustee or trustees. 17 CFR §230.147A(d).

Securities acquired in this type of offering may not be sold to an out-of-state investor until six months after the securities were purchased. This restriction must be included in a legend on the securities offered.[20]

State Law Compliance

Once the federal requirements for the exemption are addressed, an issuer must then look to state laws and regulations to determine the disclosures necessary to register or qualify the offering or to comply with any available state-level exemptions from registration.

Unless a specific state exemption also fits the offering (some examples are discussed below), the issuer must comply with the state laws and regulations in the state in which it wants to conduct the offering. Often this entails submitting offering materials to state regulators for review. Every state has regulations describing the required disclosures necessary to register an offering. This type of filing is often called a registration by qualification. Although each state has slightly different requirements, most require an offering memorandum that provides information on the business history and business plan of the issuer, its key management and ownership including their background and expertise, intended use of the funds to be raised, financial condition of the issuer, risk factors for investing in the security, the business and the industry, and a description of the terms of the security (equity, debt, or revenue-share descriptions; expected return on investment; voting or participation rights; liquidation preferences; etc.). Additionally, state regulations often require reviewed or audited financials but in some cases will accept financials certified by an officer as compliant with Generally Accepted Accounting Principles (GAAP).

For state-registered offerings, typically, there is no limit on how much can be raised by an issuer, but the offering is usually limited to a one-year offering period, unless renewed. State regulations usually also require the offering to include investor suitability requirements that limit the amount of securities investors can invest based on income and asset levels.[21]

Finally, for a Rule 147A offering, there are integration safe harbors available so that the offering can be run close in time to another offering using a different strategy which gives issuers flexibility in planning for investment.[22]

---

20. 17 CFR §230.147A(f).

21. Some states limit the investment amount to 10 percent of annual income or net assets while others have a formula that must be employed.

22. Offers or sales under the intrastate exemption will not be integrated with any of the following:
   (1) Prior offers or sales under any legal strategy
   (2) Subsequent offers or sales that are:
      (a) Registered with the SEC (except that in the thirty days before a registration statement is filed, the safe harbor only covers offers to institutional accredited investors)
      (b) Exempt under Regulation A
      (c) Exempt under Rule 701 (for securities-based compensation)
      (d) Under an employee benefit plan
      (e) Exempt under Regulation S (for offerings in other countries)
      (f) Exempt under section 4(a)(6) (commonly known as Title III crowdfunding)
      (g) Made more than six months after the completion of the intrastate offering

Under this intrastate DPO strategy, any kind of offering can occur up until the date immediately before the intrastate DPO begins and any capital raise strategy listed above can begin immediately after an intrastate DPO. 17 CFR §230.147A(g).

Who Uses Intrastate Offerings?

The intrastate offering strategy is often chosen by issuers that have a network of supporters or customers focused in a specific state or portion thereof. This strategy also has the benefit of not usually having an offering limit and allowing the issuer to sell the securities directly to investors without the use of an intermediary. Issuers considering this strategy must be prepared to work with counsel to draft a significant offering memorandum and have either internal or external marketing assistance to support the offering once approved. This approach is not easy but can be effective for social enterprises who have the capacity to directly reach out to a group of potential investors, such as existing customers.

Some examples of types of businesses that have successfully employed this approach include restaurants, food co-ops, local markets, and organic farms with community supported agriculture (CSA) programs.

Multistate or Limited Offering Exemption (17 CFR 230.504)

Federal Prerequisites

Federal regulations also permit multistate DPO offerings under Rule 504.[23] This small-offering exemption allows issuers to raise up to $10 million in a twelve-month period.[24] DPOs under Rule 504[25] may use general solicitation or general advertising as long as one of the following criteria is met:

(1) The DPO is offered exclusively in one or more states that provide for the registration of the securities, and require the public filing and delivery to investors of a substantive disclosure document before sale, and are made in accordance with those state provisions; or

(2) The DPO is made in one or more states that have no provision for the registration of the securities or the public filing or delivery of a disclosure document before sale, if the securities have been registered in at least one state that provides for such registration, public filing and delivery before sale, offers and sales are made in that state in accordance with such provisions, and the disclosure document is delivered before sale to all purchasers (including those in the states that have no such procedure).[26]

Finally, an issuer utilizing the Rule 504 exemption must file a Form D with the SEC within fifteen days of the first sale.[27]

State Law Compliance

A publicly offered multistate DPO must comply with state regulations in every state in which it plans to sell securities. Issuers can follow the qualification requirements or, in some cases, issuers may be able to utilize the "Small Corporate Offering Registration" (SCOR) process

23. *See* 17 CFR §230.504.
24. 17 CFR §230.504(b)(2).
25. Rule 504 is not available to certain types of issuers: those who are subject to the reporting requirements of section 13 or 15(d) of the Exchange Act, an investment company, or a development stage company that either has no specific business plan or purpose or has indicated that its business plan is to engage in a merger or acquisition with an unidentified company or companies. 17 CFR §230.504(b).
26. See 17 CFR §230.504(b)(i) and (ii), 17 CFR §230.502(c).
27. 17 CFR §230.503(a)(1).

whereby disclosures are done pursuant to a "North American Securities Administration Association" (NASAA) form instead of in an offering memorandum format.[28] Registration by qualification or use of the SCOR form both require disclosure materials covering similar topics albeit in different formats.

Registering an offering in multiple states can be onerous and expensive in that regulations and regulatory review processes vary from state to state and require responding to every state regulators' questions, comments, and requests for modifications. Some regions have agreed to coordinate state regulatory review of Rule 504 offerings which can ease registration hurdles.[29] However, the regions that do provide coordinated review include only thirty-one states; there is no coordinated review of New England states and some larger states, like California, do not participate in the coordinated review process.

Who Uses the Multistate Offering Strategy?

A multistate offering strategy is often used by issuers operating primarily within a particular region of the United States or for those with potential investors in a small number of states. Given the state-by-state nature of this approach, it is not usually cost-effective to take this approach to register in a large number of states, typically greater than five or six. For issuers seeking to reach residents of most or all states, Regulation Crowdfund or Regulation A, discussed below, may be more cost-effective approaches.

Some examples of types of businesses that have successfully utilized this approach include a regional meat/poultry CSA provider, a food cooperative on the border of two states, and a producer of food products in a region that include several states.

Nonprofit Exemption (Section 3(a)(4) of the Securities Act of 1933)

Federal Prerequisites

Nonprofits have their own federal exemption from securities registration.[30] This exemption applies to:

> Any security issued by a person organized and operated exclusively for religious, educational, benevolent, fraternal, charitable, or reformatory purposes and not for pecuniary profit, and no part of the net earnings of which inures to the benefit of any person, private stockholder, or individual, or any security of a fund that is excluded from the definition of an investment company under section 3(c)(10)(B) of the Investment Company Act of 1940 [15 U.S.C. 80a–3(c)(10)(B)].

The exemption is self-executing and thus does not require any federal filing.

Under this exemption, nonprofit organizations only need to look at regulations in the states they want to target for their capital raise. The federal rules do not place a limit on the amount that can be raised, and many states also do not impose a raise limit. Additionally, the federal exemption has no prohibition on general solicitation and advertising of the

---

28. Small Company Offering Registration (SCOR), NASAA, https://www.nasaa.org/industry-resources/securities-issuers/small-company-offering-registration-scor/ (providing information on the SCOR process can be found on the NASAA website).
29. Coordinated Review, http://www.coordinatedreview.org/ (providing information on the coordinated review process).
30. 15 U.S. Code § 77c.(a)(4).

offering so the issuer again looks to state law for any limitations, but typically a state-level exemption or registration process would also allow for general solicitation and advertising.

State Nonprofit Exemption Compliance

Approximately twenty-five states have exemptions from registration for securities offerings by charitable organizations which require little or no action on the part of the issuer. In an additional fifteen states, some type of notice filing is required to inform the state that the exemption is being utilized. The remainder of states have either a full registration requirement under their existing registration by qualification regulations or have a distinct registration requirement for charitable organizations.

Some examples: California requires nonprofits to fully register offerings with state regulators. Other states, like Massachusetts and Illinois, have full exemptions from state registration requirements. Because regulations and filing requirements can change, it is important to check all state regulations prior to starting the offering.

Because nonprofits do not have equity holders, they may only offer debt securities (investment notes). Nonetheless, nonprofits have design choices related to the offering such as interest rate, length of the payback period, frequency of payments, and structure of the payment (i.e., interest and principal paid annually, principal paid at maturity, etc.).

Who Uses the Nonprofit Exemption Strategy?

Nonprofits that consider a DPO are typically revenue-generating nonprofits that have service or product sales that will be able to support the debt service of the offering. Nonprofits that are exclusively grant and donation-based are not good candidates for a DPO.

Nonprofits that have used the federal exemption process coupled with state registration or the use of a state nonprofit exemption include independent schools, charitable loan funds, and community development financing institutions.

Common Ways to Pair State and Federal Exemptions

In addition to charitable exemptions, many states have specific exemptions for certain types of securities offerings, such as state crowdfunding, or for specific types of entities such as cooperatives.

State Crowdfund Exemptions

Many states have implemented their own investment crowdfunding exemption to provide a path for small businesses to raise capital in their home states. Often these exemptions are focused on relatively small offerings, usually $1 million or less. These state-level exemptions are not the same as Regulation Crowdfund, discussed below, which is a federal exemption that preempts state law. A state-level crowdfund exemption is usually coupled with the federal intrastate or charitable exemption for a single-state offering. If an issuer uses the federal intrastate exemption and the issuer's home state also has a state-level crowdfund exemption, the offering materials do not need to be registered with or reviewed by federal or state regulators to be offered in that state. This is the key difference between state registration and a state exemption.

State crowdfund exemption statutes usually impose limits on the raise amount and delineate what must be included in the offering materials. They often also require certain types of financial disclosures such as reviewed financials above certain raise levels. Some states require that you only advertise your offering on specific platforms that are registered with the state while others allow businesses to place their offerings on their own websites or any listing platform qualified to list DPOs.

Oregon is one example of a state that has an exemption that allows small businesses to raise up to $250,000. Issuers must use a state-approved platform to list the offering, which narrows the issuer's advertisement to potential investors.[31]

Massachusetts' exemption allows a Massachusetts issuer to raise up to $1 million or up to $2 million if the issuer supplies audited financials to investors. The exemption does not require that the raise be listed on any platform thus allowing the issuer greater leeway in how it can advertise and manage the offering. Massachusetts has a set of disclosure requirements which includes information similar to that of a registered offering and has a set of investor suitability requirements limiting the amount that nonaccredited investors can invest. Finally, Massachusetts has a requirement that issuers escrow investments until they reach thirty percent of their maximum offering amount.[32]

A third example of a state crowdfund exemption is Maryland. The Maryland statute requires that the issuer be organized or qualified to do business in Maryland and have its principal place of business there. All offers and sales must be to Maryland residents only. The issuer has the option of hosting its offering on its own website or on a third-party portal. The raise limit is $1 million in any twelve-month period and the state regulations impose investment limitations on investors based on income and asset levels. Specific disclosure requirements apply and a notice filing must be submitted to the state.[33]

Cooperative Exemptions

Several states have exemptions for offerings of specific types of cooperative securities. California allows cooperatives to offer investor memberships, using general solicitation, but limit the investment amount to $1,000 per person.[34] Illinois exempts any type of security issued by a bona fide agricultural cooperative and exempts membership stock in other types of cooperatives with a $10,000 limit per person.[35] Virginia has a very broad exemption for "[a]ny security issued by a cooperative association organized as a corporation under the laws of this Commonwealth."[36]

Charitable Exemptions

As noted above, there is a federal exemption for securities offerings by nonprofits and many states have exemptions too. For example, Massachusetts exempts registrations by "any security issued by any person organized and operated not for private profit but exclusively for religious, educational, benevolent, charitable, fraternal, social, athletic, or reformatory purposes, or as a chamber of commerce or trade or professional association."[37] Likewise, Illinois exempts securities "issued by a person organized and operated

31. See OAR 441-035-0070 et seq.
32. See 950 CMR 14.402(B)(13)(o).
33. *See In re* Maryland Crowdfund Exemption (Md. Sec. Comm., May 16, 2016), https://www.marylandattorneygeneral.gov/Securities%20Documents/Maryland_Crowdfunding_Order_5_16_16_final.pdf.
34. *See* Cal. Corp. Code § 25100(r).
35. *See* 815 ILCS 5/3(R).
36. *See* Va. Code § 13.1-514(A)(11).
37. Mass. Code § 402(a)(9).

not for pecuniary profit and exclusively for religious, educational, benevolent, fraternal, agricultural, charitable, athletic, professional, trade, social or reformatory purposes, or as a chamber of commerce or local industrial development corporation, or for more than one of said purposes and no part of the net earnings of which inures to the benefit of any private stockholder or member."[38]

In sum, state-level exemptions coupled with either the intrastate or nonprofit federal exemptions can provide a less onerous regulatory path for a social enterprise to follow. While disclosure materials are still required, utilizing both a federal and state exemption means that a regulatory review is not required, thus shortening the time to launch, saving costs, and removing the uncertainty that can come with a regulator's review.

Regulation Crowdfunding

Regulation Crowdfunding (also known as Regulation CF, Reg CF, or Title III) was part of the 2012 JOBS Act.[39] The JOBS Act was enacted to facilitate access to capital for start-ups and small businesses, and give a broader spectrum of people the ability to invest in start-ups and small businesses and to stimulate economic growth.

Reg CF is an exemption to the registration requirements under the Securities Act of 1933, so that a full registration of the security offering is not required.[40] Nonetheless, an issuer of securities under the Regulation CF exemption must meet certain disclosure requirements and must comply with regulations regarding, among others, the marketing of the securities and investment limitations. In addition, Reg CF has differing financial disclosure requirements depending on how much the issuer is raising and whether or not the issuer has utilized the exemption before.[41]

38. 815 ILCS 5/3(H).

39. 17 CFR § 227 et seq.

40. 17 CFR § 227.100.

41. For offerings that, together with all other amounts sold by the issuer under Section 4(a)(6) of the Securities Act (15 U.S.C. 77d(a)(6)) within the preceding twelve-month period, have, in the aggregate, the following target offering amounts:

(1) $124,000 or less, the amount of total income, taxable income and total tax, or the equivalent line items, as reported on the federal income tax returns filed by the issuer for the most recently completed year (if any), which shall be certified by the principal executive officer of the issuer to reflect accurately the information reported on the issuer's federal income tax returns, and financial statements of the issuer, which shall be certified by the principal executive officer of the issuer to be true and complete in all material respects. If financial statements of the issuer are available that have either been reviewed or audited by a public accountant that is independent of the issuer, the issuer must provide those financial statements instead and need not include the information reported on the federal income tax returns or the certifications of the principal executive officer.

(2) More than $124,000, but not more than $618,000, financial statements of the issuer reviewed by a public accountant that is independent of the issuer. If financial statements of the issuer are available that have been audited by a public accountant that is independent of the issuer, the issuer must provide those financial statements instead and need not include the reviewed financial statements.

(3) More than $618,000, financial statements of the issuer audited by a public accountant that is independent of the issuer; provided, however, that for issuers that have not previously sold securities in reliance on Section 4(a)(6) of the Securities Act (15 U.S.C. 77d(a)(6)), offerings that have a target offering amount of more than $618,000, but not more than $1,235,000, financial statements of the issuer reviewed by a public accountant that is independent of the issuer. If financial statements of the issuer are available that have been audited by a public accountant that is independent of the issuer, the issuer must provide those financial statements instead and need not include the reviewed financial statements. 17 CFR § 227.201(t).

One of the key features of Reg CF is that issuers may sell their securities in all fifty states and no state-level registration is required. However, an online intermediary must be used to market and sell the securities. Such intermediaries are permitted to take a success fee based on the amount raised in the offering which can increase costs.[42] Fees vary by platform, but most of the larger platforms charge approximately 7 percent.

Any type of entity may use the Reg CF exemption. The raise limit, in a 12-month period, is currently $5,000,000 but to offer that maximum amount an issuer must provide audited financial statements.[43] First time issuers with reviewed financial statements may raise $1,235,000 and thereafter may raise only $618,000 without providing audited, as opposed to reviewed, financials.[44]

For some enterprises, the offering limits may be insufficient to reach their capital raising goal. One way to raise more than the limit is to couple the Reg CF raise with a private offering under Regulation D, Rule 506(c).[45] These two types of raises can be run concurrently without being integrated as long as all other requirements of the two offerings are satisfied.

While Reg CF does include investment limitations, it allows almost anyone to invest in businesses that they know or support or in industries that align with their values. Any type of security can be offered (stock, notes, revenue-share interests) and while most marketing is limited to the portal website, the issuer can drive its community to the portal listing through e-mail, social media posts, and ads as long as its materials meet the Reg CF advertising rules.[46]

Accredited investors do not have a limit to how much can be invested in a Reg CF offering. Investors who are not accredited are limited as follows:

(i) The greater of $2,500, or 5 percent of the greater of the investor's annual income or net worth, if either the investor's annual income or net worth is less than $124,000; or

(ii) Ten percent of the greater of the investor's annual income or net worth, not to exceed an amount sold of $124,000, if both the investor's annual income and net worth are equal to or more than $124,000.[47]

Reg CF does not require a submission of an offering memorandum; however, it does require that specific disclosures on Form C be completed and submitted on the EDGAR (Electronic Data Gathering, Analysis, and Retrieval) system.[48] Many of the same categories of disclosures are required in Form C as with offering disclosures in DPOs. These include management and ownership information, planned uses of funds, financial condition, description of the features of the security, and material risk factors.

Almost all advertising must be done on the investment portal. Advertisements outside the portal can only include the following: (1) a statement that the issuer is conducting an offering and a link to their funding portal, (2) the terms of the offering, and (3) identifying facts like name, legal identity, location, phone, website, e-mail, and a brief description of

---

42. 17 CFR § 227.401.
43. 17 CFR § 227.100.
44. 17 CFR § 227.201(t)(3).
45. 17 CFR § 230.506.
46. 17 CFR § 227.204.
47. 17 CFR § 227.100(a)(2).
48. 17 CFR § 227.201.

the business.[49] The "terms of the offering" include the following: (1) the amount of securities offered, (2) the nature of the securities, (3) the price of the securities, and (4) the closing date of the offering period. Your ability to communicate directly with potential investors about matters outside the above-described facts is limited.[50]

Who Can Use This?

One of the strongest advantages of a Reg CF offering is that it is the most expedient way to make a national offering of securities for small businesses as it does not require review of offering materials by a regulator. Once the offering materials are complete and submitted to the SEC, the offering can begin. And, the wide reach of this exemption can be especially important to social enterprises that offer services or products across most or all of the United States or have broad appeal. Many portals are available to host these offerings and provide back-end support functions, including escrow accounts, payment processing, EDGAR filing services, marketing templates, and so on, which take some of the complexities and costs associated with a capital raise off of the enterprises. The challenges of this approach include that there is a significant cost to the portals in that they are paid through a percentage of the raise amount and other fees.

Regulation A

Regulation A (Reg A) was revised in March 2015 in order to implement Section 401 of the JOBS Act. Reg A is an exemption from registration for public offerings, but the disclosures required under this exemption are similar to those required in registered offerings, and those offering materials must be filed with the SEC. The revised Reg A includes two offering tiers: Tier 1 for offerings of up to $20 million in a twelve-month period, and Tier 2 for offerings of up to $75 million in a twelve-month period.[51]

Reg A is essentially a more expansive DPO in that it allows an issuer to publicly offer an investment opportunity directly to accredited and nonaccredited investors but does so on a grander scale than Reg CF. Reg A requires the filing of an offering circular or offering statement using a Form 1-A[52] with the SEC that requires more substantial disclosures than a state registration would if using a DPO strategy.[53] A Reg A offering has advantages over other DPO strategies in that, unlike the intrastate strategy, investors can reside in multiple states. Reg A has the advantage over Rule 504 in that it can be used to raise more than $10 million.

The differences between Tier 1 and Tier 2 of Reg A go beyond the difference in raise limits. Tier 2 offerings are nationwide, and issuers are not required to register or qualify their offerings with state securities regulators—Tier 2 preempts state securities registration laws.[54] Tier 1 offerings require companies to register or qualify their offering in any state

49. 17 CFR § 227.204.
50. *Id.*
51. See 17 CFR § 230.251 et seq.
52. Form 1-A, SEC, https://www.sec.gov/files/form1-a.pdf.
53. See 17 CFR Reg A § 230.252-230.253.
54. While Reg A Tier 2 preempts state securities registration requirements, states can and do impose notice filing and fee requirements. In addition, some states' broker and agent registration regulations make it impractical for an issuer to directly offer its securities and must either seek a broker's representation in those states or forego accepting investment from residents of those states. *See Issuer-Dealer and Agent Registration Requirements for*

in which they seek to offer or sell securities. Registration requirements vary by state as discussed above in the intrastate and multistate DPO sections.

Securities in a Reg A offering can be offered publicly, using general solicitation and advertising. In addition, if planning to use Tier 2 of Reg A, issuers may "test the waters" in advance of submitting material for qualification. Testing the waters allows companies to solicit interest in their contemplated securities offering before filing an offering statement with the SEC. This gives companies the chance to be able to determine whether enough market interest in their securities exists before they incur the full range of legal, accounting, and other costs associated with preparing and filing an offering statement with the SEC. Companies that "test the waters" under Reg A are required to include certain language, or legends, in their solicitation materials that generally notifies investors that no money for securities is currently being solicited or will be accepted, if sent, and that any indications of interest received by the company from potential investors are nonbinding. If the "test the waters" provision is used, issuers may only proceed under Tier 2, not Tier 1.[55]

Both accredited and nonaccredited investors may invest in Tier 1 and Tier 2 offerings.[56] However, there are federal limitations on the amount of money a nonaccredited investor may invest in a Tier 2 offering and state-level registrations will likewise impose investment suitability requirements. A company seeking qualification pursuant to Tier 2 is required to limit the amount of securities than a nonaccredited investor to no more than:

- 10 percent of the greater of annual income or net worth (for natural persons), or
- 10 percent of the greater of annual revenue, or net assets at fiscal year-end (for non-natural persons).[57]

Financial disclosures include that Tier 1 and Tier 2 issuers are required to provide balance sheets and other required financial statements for the two most recently completed fiscal years or for such shorter time that the company has been in existence. Issuers in Tier 2 offerings are required to have their financial statements audited. Issuers of Tier 1 offerings have minimal reporting requirements post-raise but issuers of Tier 2 offerings are required to file ongoing annual reports and semi-annual reports, current event updates, as well as a filing after the termination or completion of an offering.[58] The ongoing reporting requirements for a Tier 2 offering are additional time and cost commitments for an issuer and should be considered carefully before committing to this approach.

One of the updates to Reg A was the addition of several safe harbors so that a Reg A offering will not be integrated with any previously closed offerings, with a subsequent crowdfunding offering and in cases when the issuer can comply with the terms of both offerings independently, such as conducting a simultaneous Reg D, Rule 506(c) offering.[59]

Issuers Not Utilizing a Registered Broker-Dealer for Offers and Sales of Securities under Tier 2 of Regulation A, CrowdCheck (Aug. 2, 2019), https://www.crowdcheck.com/sites/default/files/Reg%20A%20Issuer-Dealer%20Memo%208.2.2019.pdf.

55. 17 CFR § 230.255.
56. 17 CFR § 230.251.
57. 17 CFR § 230.251(d)(2)(C).
58. 17 CFR § 230.257.
59. 17 CFR § 230.251(c).

Who Can Use This?

Reg A can be a very useful tool for larger social enterprises that want to reach investors across multiple or all states and raise a significant amount of capital. This approach is, however, quite expensive relative to other offering strategies because of the expansive filing process with the SEC and either the state filings needed for a Tier 1 offering or the audited financial statements and ongoing reporting required under Tier 2. Timing is also a consideration as this approach requires the most expansive offering disclosures and requires a review and qualification by the SEC. That process can take months to complete before an offering can be initiated.

Community Investment Funds: An Alternative Pathway for Community Capital

Community Investment Funds (CIFs) offer an alternative to direct investments for impact investors. Both accredited and nonaccredited investors may invest locally and in alignment with their values by investing in CIFs. This approach allows investors to fund community enterprise indirectly by investing in a purpose-designed fund that in turn invests with a particular set of values or parameters.[60] CIFs are regulated pursuant to the Investment Company Act of 1940 (1940 Act), and multiple forms may aggregate and deploy community capital. A CIF still has to comply with securities laws to raise capital for the fund to deploy and can do so using community capital strategies discussed in this chapter such as DPOs and Reg A offerings discussed above.[61]

Investment into CIFs can provide features that one-off investments cannot. These include the possibility to scale impact, create efficiencies, provide diversification, and offer potential for greater liquidity.

A CIF increases scalability because it can potentially raise an unlimited amount of money and finance an unlimited number of community enterprises. A fund offers some efficiency for investors, who only need to vet the fund and its investment criteria rather than vetting one enterprise at a time. A fund with multiple and growing investments also provides investors with some diversification from their very first investment. In addition, depending on how a CIF is structured and how it scales, it may have more exit options for investors.

The challenge with CIFs is twofold. First, funds are typically highly regulated which can be too burdensome and expensive for a new fund aiming to have impact on a community scale. Second, CIFs need qualified, committed managers to take the lead on starting and managing the funds.

As to the first, while most investment funds are regulated pursuant to the Investment Company Act of 1940 (1940 Act), there are several ways to structure CIFs that fit within an exemption from the regulatory burdens of the 1940 Act or do not meet the definition of an investment fund. These exemptions are not perfect for community scale funds and are sometimes complicated to navigate, but the exemptions make funds easier and more cost-effective to implement on a community scale.

60. For a comprehensive review of community investment funds, *see Community Investment Fund Handbook*, National Coalition for Community Capital, https://www.nc3now.org/uploads/1/4/0/1/140134350/community-investment-funds-final.pdf.

61. Note that Reg CF excludes investment funds from using the Reg CF offering strategy and also excludes enterprises that rely on certain exemptions to the 1940 Act, including the nonprofit fund exemption and the real estate fund exemption. 17 CFR § 227.100(b)(3).

As to the second challenge, because community-centered funds are not yet ubiquitous, more of us committed to social impact must learn about these possibilities and commit to start and build funds like these in our communities.

The following are a few examples of exempt CIF strategies.

Charitable Loan Fund (15 U.S. Code § 80a–3(c)(10)(A)(i))

This strategy is the most widely used model. Charities are exempt from both the 1940 Act and federal securities registration, which means that such funds need only register in states that do not have nonprofit offering exemptions. These types of funds are housed in and managed by nonprofits. As such, investment into the fund can only be through investment notes, whereby investors' return is limited to principal and interest. Because the charities managing these funds must meet the debt burden of the investment notes, typically the charities invest out into enterprises through notes too, because any other type of investment may make it difficult for the nonprofit to meet its debt obligations to investors. Any investment by the charity into social enterprises must also have a charitable purpose and align with the charity's IRS-approved purpose. Formation of the Charitable Loan Fund should follow thoughtful analysis, because the consequence of the investment not meeting the nonprofit's charitable purpose may mean a loss of tax-exempt status. There are numerous successful examples using this approach, including nonprofit funds managed by RSF Social Finance, Calvert Foundation, Community Vision, PV Grows, and Boston Ujima Project.

Real Estate Investment Fund (15 U.S. Code § 80a–3(c)(5))

This type of CIF takes advantage of an exemption from the Investment Company Act for real-estate-related investments.[62] This community fund type often has a goal of community revitalization (housing, neighborhood, main street, etc.). The fund can offer to investors equity, debt, or revenue-share securities. Capital raised can be used to purchase and revitalize real estate and then lease or sell it. Profits can be reinvested and/or be distributed to investors. The test to determine whether a fund meets the real estate exemption is that (1) at least 55 percent of its assets consist of mortgages and interests in real estate, (2) not more than 20 percent of its assets have no relationship to real estate, and (3) the rest of the fund's assets consist of real estate-type interests.[63] Examples of funds using this exemption include the Tulsa Real Estate Fund, Northeast Investment Cooperative, and Iroquois Valley Farmland REIT.

Supplemental Business Fund (15 U.S. Code § 80a–3(b)(1))

In this model, a fund can be exempted from registration under the Investment Company Act if it has some primary business other than the business of investing in securities. In

62. Additionally, a real estate investment business could also qualify under the supplemental business fund exemption. 15 U.S. Code § 80a–3(b)(1). If the criteria for a supplemental fund are met (see below), a real estate fund using that exemption would be able to utilize Reg CF to raise capital as an enterprise using the supplemental fund exemption not excluded from using the Reg CF securities strategy. 17 CFR § 227.100(b)(3).

63. *See Response of the Chief Counsel's Office Division of Investment Management*, SEC (Feb. 12, 2018), https://www.sec.gov/divisions/investment/noaction/2018/great-ajax-funding-021218-3c5.htm.

other words, there has to be an existing line of business that is distinct from managing the investment fund. A business running a supplemental business fund can in turn take equity positions—that is, acquire ownership stakes in other businesses (by purchasing ordinary shares, or securities) and any profits generated can be distributed to investors in the business. Although there are no current examples of this type of fund used for community impact and open to community investment, this structure has good potential as a tool and there is guidance in place as to how to structure a business/fund to comply with this exemption.

To Use This Exemption

The investment fund must be supplemental to another primary business. Business in this sense includes social enterprises. The SEC uses a multifactor legal test to determine whether a company relying on this strategy really is in a primary business other than investing.

No factor by itself is determinative. Two factors are considered the most objective and looked at first. The first is the nature of the company's assets. The more of a company's assets that are associated with its nonsecurities business, the more likely that the investment side will be considered its primary business. However, courts have recognized that some businesses are asset-light, and that fact should not by itself transform an operating company into an investment company. The second is the company's sources of income. Both net and gross income should be considered. An activity that produces a majority of both will likely be considered the primary business.[64] If the income and asset factors are not clear, the SEC will look at how the company described itself to investors and how it described the offering. For that reason, the marketing of the investment opportunity must be focused on the investment into the primary business and not primarily as a way to invest in the fund.

Some examples of how this might work in practice for social enterprises include:

(1) An advanced manufacturing facility that rents space to other enterprises, offers consulting services, rents the use of equipment, and runs an incubator could have a supplemental fund that invests in its incubated businesses.

(2) A co-working space whose primary business is a combination of renting space, renting facilities, and supplying-related services, and that also supports, incubates, or accelerates the businesses residing in its space, could develop a supplemental fund to invest in its resident businesses.

(3) A food co-op or community grocery that, in addition to their primary business, also supports new local food or farm businesses could have a supplemental fund to support the development of those food or farm businesses.

Such businesses that are well-positioned and connected to raise capital from their communities to support community wealth-building and well-being could well make use of

64. Additional factors in the test, established in *In re* Tonopah Mining Co., 26 S.E.C. 426 (1947), include: (1) *Company history*: A company with a history as an operating company in some primary business other than investing is less likely to be deemed an investment company subject to the 1940 Act registration; (2) *Self-Representation to the public*: If investors are likely to invest in the company because of the investment portfolio, investing is more likely to be considered its primary business; (3) *Activities of its officers and directors*: Whatever the officers and directors spend most of their time doing is likely to be considered the primary business.

the Supplemental Business Fund exemption from the registration requirements of the Investment Act. The Fund can aggregate community capital, with investment from those businesses' broad community of supporters.

Other types of exempt fund strategies

There are various other types of exemptions from the 1940 Investment Act that funds can utilize but are more difficult to implement on a community scale. Some of these other exemptions include the holding company exemptions,[65] a microfinance fund,[66] a receivables or seller financing fund,[67] and the intrastate fund.[68]

While social enterprises will continue to need community capital raise strategies to implement for themselves, many of these companies may be ready for investment but not ready to take on the heavy lift of a community capital raise. CIFs can fill that space for these enterprises while allowing communities to invest in a fund dedicated to the kind of impact they would like to see.

Imagine if every community had a charitable loan fund, real estate revitalization fund, and a type of supplemental fund. Community members would be able to invest in multiple funds that are working to solve community problems, support community entrepreneurs, and revitalize neighborhoods, all the while keeping investment dollars circulating within the community.

Examples of Community Capital Campaigns

Successful capital raising campaigns can come in many forms and can vary by the size of the businesses, the amount of the offering, and the geographic scope of the raise. Below are examples of enterprises with three different regulatory strategies and three different amounts of capital raised. Each was successful in highlighting their mission and rallying their communities to invest in their vision.

CERO Cooperative (Direct Public offering)

Cooperative Energy, Recycling, and Organics (CERO) is a worker-owned commercial composting company based in Dorchester, Massachusetts. CERO's mission is to keep food waste out of landfills by picking up clients' food waste and delivering it to local farms where the waste is converted to compost.[69]

At their start in 2012, the founders of CERO were working to find ways for working-class people and communities of color to both gain access to good green jobs and to have an ownership stake in those companies. CERO's founding worker-owners developed a business plan for a composting co-op company designed to meet the growing needs and legal requirements for composting food waste in the Boston area. To effectuate its plan, CERO needed to raise at least $100,000, but preferred to raise $350,000, for capital and equipment to get the business operating. However, as a start-up cooperative with no

---

65. 15 U.S. Code § 80a–3(a)(1) and 3(b)(2).
66. 5 U.S. Code § 80a–3(c)(4).
67. 5 U.S. Code § 80a–3(c)(5).
68. 5 U.S. Code § 80a–6(d).
69. Cero Cooperative, Inc., http://www.cero.coop/.

current operations, neither traditional bank financing nor venture capital investors were options for start-up capital. The company had no collateral available to secure commercial loans, and the growth trajectory and ownership structure of CERO were not appealing to venture investors. CERO knew it had community support for its idea but needed to turn that support into capital.

In 2014, the founding owners turned to a DPO process in Massachusetts to raise the capital CERO required by offering nonvoting preferred shares of stock to its supporters. No set annual dividend was promised to investors, but CERO set a target of providing dividends of four percent per year on investors' original investment amount. Typically, DPOs are difficult to market for new enterprises because they do not yet have a base of customers or supporters and have not yet built deep ties to the communities in which they are operating.

Once CERO decided how to structure its offering, it had to obtain state regulatory approval and, once approved, had to market its investment campaign. For CERO, marketing a capital raise prior to operations was the biggest challenge. CERO's approach was to connect with individuals and organizations who championed cooperatives, green jobs, or both. Working with other cooperative organizations was especially powerful. Most cooperatives adhere to a set of cooperative principles. These principles include the tenet of "cooperation among cooperatives" which means that cooperatives serve their members most effectively and strengthen the cooperative movement by working together through local, national, regional, and international structures. It was this network that helped spur CERO's capital campaign.

The founders networked through cooperative channels and worked to raise awareness within the communities they intended to serve. They used the public nature of the campaign to garner earned media to draw attention both to their cooperative model and their novel capital raise strategy.

Ultimately, CERO exceeded its goal amount and raised $370,000.[70] Using the DPO form of capital raising enabled working people across the Boston region to buy shares in CERO Cooperative. For many, this was a first-ever investment that allowed them to invest in their values, keep their money local, and share the pride of CERO's success. Since its DPO, CERO has continued to grow and thrive, and the equity raised through the DPO helped CERO to leverage additional sources of capital from community and cooperative lenders to spur additional growth.

Detroit City Football Club (Regulation CF)

Detroit City FC is a successful minor league soccer team located in downtown Detroit, Michigan. The team started in 2012 and grew out of a co-ed recreational league in the city. The club immediately embraced its community roots and fixed its club motto as "Passion for Our City, Passion for the Game."[71] The team has continued to build grassroots support over the years as it has grown its number of fans and expanded its community outreach.

In 2020, Detroit City FC was set to start its first professional season when the pandemic and related economic crisis suspended its inaugural season in the National Independent

70. *Our Community-Funded Roots*, Cero Cooperative, Inc., https://www.cero.coop/Community_Funding.

71. *Detroit City FC*, USL Network, https://www.detcityfc.com/.

Soccer Association (NISA). The team quickly turned to its fan base to help it weather this new set of challenges. Hoping to build on the success of its NISA league competitor, Chattanooga Football Club that had a successful fan ownership campaign in 2019,[72] Detroit City began exploring how to open team ownership to its fans.

Most professional American sports teams are owned and managed by a small number of high-net-worth individuals, but many lower tier or smaller market professional teams are exploring how to further connect with their community and supporters through fan ownership campaigns. Although most of Detroit City's network is in Michigan, a Reg CF offering was appealing over an intrastate DPO for several reasons rooted in the distinctions between the state DPO and federal Reg CF models: (1) there is a large network of soccer fans across all states; (2) the Reg CF offering material is filed with the SEC but is not reviewed by a regulator, as is done for state-registered offerings, thus making the time to launch significantly shorter; and (3) the Reg CF platform offered a user friendly interface and back-end payment processing, among other features, that Detroit City would have had to otherwise build out on their own website.

Detroit City offered approximately a 10 percent equity membership in the club to investors, if $1.2 million in investment capital was raised. The investment minimum was $125 and perks were offered at varying investment levels. The campaign launched at the end of July 2020 and was oversubscribed in less than two weeks.[73] With the use of a companion Rule 506(c) offering, Detroit City was able to raise approximately $1.5 million by selling equity interests to fans.

The team was able to accomplish this feat because of several key elements: (1) the team had both an energized fan base and an enticing offering to its soccer fans, (2) the club had prepared a strong marketing and public relations strategy in advance of the start of the offering and deployed it well, and (3) the team had a long and strong history of commitment to community and the fan ownership campaign reinforced the trust the team has already built.

TechSoup (Regulation A)

TechSoup is a global nonprofit that connects civil society organizations to technology resources to implement solutions that further its customers' missions.[74] TechSoup is a service provider and supplier of discounted technology tools and as such is a revenue-based nonprofit. It has a very large network that includes its customer nonprofit organizations, social impact companies, foundations, and individuals interested in the impact TechSoup makes. Each group of TechSoup's stakeholders is committed to TechSoup's and its customers' success.

---

72. *See CFC Adds Midfielder with Liga MX and USL Championship Experience: About Chattanooga Football Club*, SportsEngine (Apr. 28, 2022), https://www.chattanoogafc.com/news_article/show/1223118. In 2019, Chattanooga FC's Reg CF campaign raised over $800,000 from over 3,200 investors in just a few months. *Id.*
73. *See Detroit City FC Launches Public Campaign to Sell Portion of Club to Fans*, USL (July 30, 2020), https://www.detcityfc.com/news/2020/07/30/detroit-city-fc-launches-public-campaign-to-sell-portion-of-club-to-fans/. *See also Detroit City Football Club: Be an Owner of Detroit's Professional Soccer Team!*, WeFunder, https://wefunder.com/dcfc (demonstrating the public marketing and funding).
74. TechSoup, http://www.techsoup.org/.

To meet the growing and changing needs of its customers, TechSoup realized that it needed to increase the resources it distributes by more than double in a short period of time: from $1.995 billion (2019) to $4.8 billion (2021). TechSoup calculated that for every $100 invested, it would be able to distribute over $47,000 of additional resources to the nonprofit sector. By embarking on a capital raising campaign of $11.5 million over that three-year time frame, TechSoup projected it could increase its reach to serve 1.7 million organizations around the world.[75]

Choosing how to structure TechSoup's capital raise focused on two elements: (1) how to offer the investment opportunity publicly and simultaneously to both large institutional investors and nonaccredited community members, and (2) how to have the broadest geographic reach. Given that so many states require nonprofits to register their public offerings, TechSoup decided that using a nonprofit DPO strategy would not be expedient. Instead, TechSoup became the first nonprofit to use the Reg A Tier 2 offering strategy. The Reg A strategy, as discussed above, is robust and requires a thorough offering circular, audited financial statements and state-by-state notice filings (although not full state registrations). Reg A can be used as a DPO, which allowed TechSoup to offer investment opportunity directly to their whole community and not limit investors to only the wealthiest in their networks. This also allows issuing companies to advertise and market their offering to have the greatest potential reach. For TechSoup, a global social enterprise, Reg A had advantages over other DPO strategies: Unlike the intrastate strategy, investors can come from multiple states, and unlike Rule 504, it can be used to raise more than $10 million.

TechSoup offered investors three different five-year note options for investment designed to allow virtually every supporter to invest:

- Community Capital Notes: $50 minimum investment; 2.5 percent interest.
- Patient Capital Notes: $2,500 minimum investment; 3.5 percent interest.
- Risk Capital Notes: $50,000 minimum investment; 5 percent interest.

The value proposition that TechSoup was able to articulate with its capital campaign garnered significant investment. Over its three-year campaign, TechSoup raised its goal of $11.5 million in September 2021.[76] This amount is a combination of investment in the Reg A note offering plus other types of capital spurred by the marketing of the Reg A offering, including recoverable grants and commercial loans.

Preparing for a Community Capital Raise

Social enterprises can employ a variety of strategies to raise capital broadly and publicly from their community of supporters. Each strategy has benefits and challenges depending upon the amount of capital to be raised, where potential investors are located, and the type of entity doing the raise. In addition to deciding on a legal strategy to fit capital raise goals, enterprises need to be prepared for the offering.

---

75. *See The TechSoup Growth Capital Campaign*, TECHSOUP, http://www.techsoup.org/growth-capital-campaign.
76. See *Public Offering Fueling TechSoup's $11.5 Million Goal*, THE NONPROFIT TIMES (Aug. 14, 2021), https://www.thenonprofittimes.com/finance/public-offering-fueling-techsoups-11-5-million-goal/.

To have a successful community capital raise, an enterprise must have a compelling story connecting its vision and mission to the impact it is creating or will create with the proceeds of the capital raise. This necessarily means that the entity structure and business plan must be solid so that the strength of the enterprise can come through the offering materials. The issuer must also have its financials in order and statements ready per the requirements of the strategy chosen.

Finally, and most importantly, the enterprise must have a target set of potential investors—usually customers, partners, or those who share an affinity to the mission of the social enterprise. The issuer also needs ways to reach those investors with the offering's marketing materials and message. This outreach can take many forms, including being able to engage with a wide range of existing customers on a regular basis, having a strong and active social media following, utilizing a lengthy e-mail or newsletter list, and/or having a network of supporters that will use their own connections and network to support the raise. Simply having a network or access to a network of potential investors by itself is not enough. A thoughtful and well-crafted marketing plan is essential for a successful capital raise and time should be spent to map out the campaign in advance of obtaining regulatory approval.

While the legal aspects of preparing for a community capital campaign are important, no campaign can be successful without having a strong business and marketing plan.

Conclusion

To be successful, most social enterprises must engage their community of customers by showing how their product or service is valuable, furthers their mission, and has a positive impact. As their connections to community members grow, social enterprises open the possibility for community investors to become part of the capital solution for the growth of their businesses. Raising capital from community is not always the easiest path, but it does have potential for much greater impact than traditional capital.

Community capital raise strategies have the ability to significantly strengthen social enterprises as well as have important benefits for investors and the community as a whole. Through community capital campaigns, social enterprises not only raise capital but they gain another avenue to connect with supporters and further their mission. Community investors gain the opportunity to participate in their local economy or invest with their values in ways that only wealthy investors are usually permitted. There is significant impact in committing to opening the opportunity for all to participate, even while not all community members will participate. While not all investments will produce exceedingly high returns, intangible impacts can be significant—importantly, by keeping investment dollars circulating locally. Communities benefit too when impact businesses have the capital they need to grow because these thriving businesses can increase employment and contribute to the overall vibrancy of the local economy. The impacts that flow from community capital raising ultimately contribute to leveling the playing field for entrepreneurs and investors and working to democratize the economy.

Practitioners can help social enterprises understand both the challenges associated with community capital raise strategies and the ways in which choosing among these strategies can strengthen their business and further their impact.

Chapter 8
Role of Philanthropy in "Place-based" Community Investment Strategies

Susan D. Bennett, Danielle Torain, and James Wahls

In this chapter, the authors of two case studies write from their perspectives as innovative actors in separate grantmaking institutions, the Baltimore Children and Youth Fund (BCYF) and the Annie E. Casey (Casey) Foundation. The organizations direct grant funding and, in the case of the Casey Foundation, program-related investments (PRIs), to grassroots organizations and community development financial institutions (CDFIs), respectively.

Each program demonstrates the importance of effective place-based community investment that is locally targeted and democratically controlled. To different degrees, these initiatives are dedicated to building community assets and institutions in tandem with building community leadership, a focus that distinguishes them from other "place-based" efforts.

"Place-Based" versus "Place-Conscious" and "People-Based"

"Place-based" development encompasses multitudes of meaning. It has become the default term for the opposite of "top-down" mid-century urban development, with its highways to nowhere and destruction of Black communities. "Place-conscious" strategies are more targeted, putting people at the center of development and investments to restore disinvested communities while tapping into the "regional and market-wide systems" connecting people and communities to assets.[1] "People-based," in contrast to "place-based," development loosely describes antipoverty strategies that support the mobility of individuals from disinvested places of lesser opportunity to places of greater opportunity.[2]

Over a decade ago, scholars despaired of the persistence and generational impacts of concentrated poverty, embedded in racial segregation, and seemingly intractable, despite "place-based" and tax-credit-based strategies.[3] An Urban Institute study took part in this critical reevaluation of antipoverty strategies, prescribing "place-conscious" rather than "place-based" design of urban antipoverty programs. Indeed, the study recommends that programs address neighborhoods as "launch pads," providing safe housing, employment, and high-quality education sufficient to sustain residents in light of the reality that many move frequently, not often by choice.[4] It enumerates elements of programs that succeed in providing "collective impact:" consultation with residents regarding their needs and participation by residents in program design; coordination across resources in state, local, and private sectors to enhance outcomes and avoid useless replication; and holding projects accountable to carefully considered benchmarks for success.[5]

In the groundbreaking publication *Tackling Persistent Poverty in Distressed Urban Neighborhoods*, the Urban Institute recommends that philanthropies, a category of urban investors including BCYF[6] and Casey, strive to secure access to place-based assets of a conventional kind: capital and homeownership. BCYF also deliberately focuses on human capital, sometimes deemed less tangible, including skills in democratic management of place-conscious institutions.

Because Casey and BCYF are based in Baltimore, Maryland, some context on the city is useful.

Place When the Place Is Baltimore

"Place-based" only rarely means "place-conscious,".[7] One need look no further than the widely castigated Opportunity Zones program to define the antithesis of place-conscious and community-controlled development: not responsive to residents' articulations of

1. Margery Austin Turner and Mica O'Brien, *Place-Conscious Strategies to Restore Opportunity and Overcome Injustice*, Urban Institute (Feb. 2021), https://www.urban.org/sites/default/files/publication/103696/place-conscious-strategies-to-restore-opportunity-and-overcome-injustice.pdf.

2. Mobility strategies are most closely linked with the premise that the most effective way to attack poverty is to "de-concentrate," or move low-income residents away from, it. For a summary of the rationale and results of the Moving to Opportunity Program, which focused resources on relocating families from racially segregated public housing projects into more economically and racially integrated neighborhoods, see Raj Chetty et al., *The Effects of Exposure to Better Neighborhoods on Children: New Evidence from the Moving to Opportunity Experiment*, 106 Am. Econ. Rev. 855, 866 (2016).

3. *See, e.g.*, Patrick Sharkey, Stuck in Place: Urban Programs and the End of Progress Towards Racial Equality (2013).

4. Margery Austin Turner et al., Tackling Persistent Poverty in Distressed Urban Neighborhoods: History, Principles, and Strategies for Philanthropic Investment, Urban Institute, 11–12 (July 2014). https://www.urban.org/sites/default/files/publication/22761/413179-tackling-persistent-poverty-in-distressed-urban-neighborhoods.pdf (describing "place-conscious" antipoverty strategies and the concept of preserving urban neighborhoods as launch pads).

5. *Id.* at 11–15 (defining "collective impact" and articulating elements of "place-conscious" antipoverty strategies).

6. *Id.* at 27.

7. Margery Austin Turner et al., *supra* note 4.

community needs, not anchoring wealth within the community, and not building the capacity of residents to engage in decisions about development.[8] Other tax credit-compelled investment programs, such as the New Markets Tax Credit and the Low-Income Housing Tax Credit, operate under marginally more accountable regimes but share in these deficiencies.

As has often been the case for many legacy cities, Baltimore is publicly and stubbornly defined by its deficits. The death of Freddie Gray in police custody in 2015, and the resulting uprising manifested most visibly in poor Black areas of the city, drew attention to long-standing racial inequities, in policing and in economics.[9] Baltimore has an unenviable "first," as the first city to enact a racial zoning ordinance.[10] Its racially restrictive covenants, its twentieth-century three-tiered real estate market, and the reinforcement in the 1930s of these accumulated patterns of disinvestment by the Home Owners' Loan Act's mortgage insurance guides[11] all served to cement in place the "White L/Black Butterfly" geographic racial configuration along which so many indicia of inequality fall today.[12] Disparities in private capital investment, in construction, and in lending to homeowner households continue to follow the same geographical concentrations of race in the city established early in the previous century.[13]

Mobility strategies have received significant attention in Baltimore, as several of its public housing projects were demolished, their residents relocated, and the outcomes for children of those residents intensively studied.[14] Yet it is no surprise to the organizations that maintain a presence in or support institutions in Baltimore that place-conscious, "asset-based community development" is alive and well in the city. To illustrate, the Baltimore Roundtable for Economic Democracy (BRED) has incubated and launched several workers' cooperatives, promoting a vibrant culture of worker ownership.

---

8. For an assessment of the oversight of Opportunity Zone–funded projects, and of their fiscal or programmatic accountability, *see* U.S. Gov't Accountability Off., GAO 21-30, Opportunity Zones: Improved Oversight Needed to Evaluate Tax Expenditure Performance 6 (Oct. 2020), https://www.gao.gov/assets/gao-22-105526.pdf. The GAO further reported in November 2021 that nearly all funds under the program were invested in real estate.

9. There is a surfeit of coverage of Baltimore's deterioration in indicators of crime after Gray's death and after the execution of a consent decree between the city and the Justice Department to reform the Baltimore City Police Department's practice of brutality, corruption, and civil rights violations. For an overstated view that does give due credit to the efforts of Baltimore residents to reduce violence in their communities, see Alec MacGillis, *The Tragedy of Baltimore*, Pro Publica (Mar. 12, 2019), https://www.propublica.org/article/the-tragedy-of-baltimore.

10. See Garrett Power, Apartheid Baltimore Style: The Residential Segregation Ordinances of 1910-1913, 42 MD L. Rev. 289 (1983).

11. For an overview of the interplay over decades among many factors to reinforce segregation in Baltimore—formal local government action, federal funds for urban renewal, private residential covenants, social pressure, and the steering of Black, white, and Jewish homebuyers and sellers in the residential ownership and rental real estate market—*see, generally*, Antero Pietila, Not in My Neighborhood: How Bigotry Shaped a Great American City (2010). *See also* Lawrence Lanahan, The Lines Between Us: Two Families and a Quest to Cross Baltimore's Racial Divide 62-65 (2019) (describing Baltimore city's 1940s Post War Program to contain Black residents of public housing within a few inner-city locations).

12. Lawrence Brown, *Two Baltimores: The White L vs. the Black Butterfly*, Balt. City Paper (June 28, 2016), https://www.baltimoresun.com/citypaper/bcpnews-two-baltimores-the-white-l-vs-the-black-butterfly-20160628-htmlstory.html.

13. Lionel Foster, *"The Black Butterfly": Racial Segregation and Investment Patterns in Baltimore*, Urban Institute (Feb. 5, 2019), https://apps.urban.org/features/baltimore-investment-flows/.

14. *See* Stefanie Deluca et al., Coming of Age in the Other America (2016) (describing findings from longitudinal study based on interviews over ten years with 150 children, some relocated with their families from public housing complexes in Baltimore).

Baltimore is home to the Pleasant Hope Baptist Church and its signature project, the Black Church Food Security Network (Network), a nonprofit dedicated to the movement to promote "food sovereignty" in marginalized communities.[15] Although the Church grows and distributes vegetables to the hungry, its former pastor, the Rev. Dr. Heber M. Brown III, envisioned the Network as promoting social enterprise, not charity. The Network links consumers of fresh produce to Black farmers as far away as Texas and supports produce farming on Black church-owned land.[16] Of necessity, this list barely begins to describe how conditions in Baltimore are not only hospitable to place-conscious development but are already nurturing it.

The case studies' authors situate local philanthropic efforts within this context of place-conscious asset-based community development.

Case Study

The Founding of the Baltimore Children and Youth Fund

The Baltimore Children and Youth Fund (BCYF, or the Fund) is a $12 million nonlapsing fund dedicated to supporting Baltimore's children, youth, and young adults, ages twenty-four and under. BCYF was launched with two core purposes: (1) to deploy funding to Baltimore-based organizations that serve the children, youth, and young adult populations, and (2) to build the capacity of grassroots community-based organizations, particularly those led by people of color and working in disenfranchised neighborhoods. The early-stage concept of BCYF was founded upon the following driving values:

- Elevating authentic youth and community leadership;
- Increasing investment in historically under-resourced children and youth populations and communities;
- Increasing investment in grassroots leadership and leaders of color;
- Promoting Racial, Ethnic, and Intersectional Equity and Inclusion in practice; and
- Promoting greater transparency and accountability of process.

Conceptual and Legislative Origins

The initial idea that later became the BCYF initiative originated with former Baltimore City Council President Bernard C. "Jack" Young, who served as a long-standing advocate for establishing a dedicated municipal funding stream to support services and programming for children and young people.[17]

Young introduced the concept of a dedicated youth fund for Baltimore in 1996,[18] inspired by models in San Francisco and Oakland, California, which had amended their city charters to provide municipal funding for programs serving children and youth. He also

15. Edie Gross, *A Network of Black Farmers and Black Churches Delivers Fresh Food from Soil to Sanctuary*, Faith and Leadership (May 28, 2019), https://faithandleadership.com/network-black-farmers-and-black-churches-delivers-fresh-food-soil-sanctuary.
16. *Id.*
17. Marcia Kingslow, Baltimore Children & Youth Fund Process Evaluation Report.
18. Bakari Kitwana, *Baltimore Funding Model Challenges "Nonprofit Industrial Complex" Practices*, Colorlines (Aug. 30, 2018), https://www.colorlines.com/articles/baltimore-funding-model-challenges-nonprofit-industrial-complex-practices.

drew inspiration from Miami, Florida, which approved a $1 billion tax increase in order to sustain funding for children and youth programs in the midst of the Great Recession.[19]

Young first proposed a bill for the establishment of the fund in 2015.[20] The proposed legislation authorized an amendment to the Baltimore city charter, requiring three percent of the city's discretionary spending to be earmarked for children- and youth-serving programs.[21] More specifically, the amendment dedicated revenue representing three cents of every $100 of Baltimore's assessable property to resource the fund each year.[22] At the time of Young's proposal, the assessable base was estimated at roughly $38 billion, yielding $11 million per year in support of the youth-focused municipal fund.[23]

Then-Mayor Stephanie Rawlings Blake vetoed Young's legislative proposal, citing concerns around the city's fiscal health and a $75 million deficit.[24] She additionally cautioned that the new fund might tie the hands of future mayors, requiring cuts to core city services in tight budget years.[25]

In February 2016, the Baltimore City Council, for the first time since 1982, successfully overturned a mayoral veto through a unanimous vote of 15-0. This gave voters the ability to decide on the question of whether the city should create a special account to fund enrichment programs for children, youth, and young adults.[26] Of the motivations for their vote, members of the council cited the importance of putting the decision in the hands of local voters, empowering residents of the city to determine their preference and priority.[27]

In November 2016, Baltimore City voters approved the creation of BCYF with over 80 percent support.

The 2016 charter amendment,[28] which enabled the initiation of the fund's first-year planning effort, established the following scope for the fund:

- That the fund be structured as a continuing, nonlapsing funding source, to be used exclusively for the purposes of establishing new and augmenting existing programs for Baltimore City children and youth;
- That programs resourced through the fund be designed to:
    - Ensure that Baltimore's children and youth are healthy, are ready to learn and succeed in school, and live in stable, safe, and supportive families and communities;

19. *Id.*
20. *Id.*
21. Yvonne Wenger, *Baltimore City Council Overrides Mayoral Veto for First Time in a Generation*, Balt. Sun (Feb. 22, 2016), https://www.baltimoresun.com/maryland/baltimore-city/bs-md-ci-veto-override-20160222-story.html.
22. Colin Campbell, *Baltimore Voters Approve Youth Fund, All Other Ballot Questions*, Balt. Sun (Nov. 8, 2016), https://www.baltimoresun.com/maryland/baltimore-city/bs-md-ci-baltimore-questions-20161108-story.html.
23. Colin Campbell, *Baltimore Voters Approve Youth Fund, All Other Ballot Questions*, Balt. Sun (Nov. 8, 2016.), https://www.baltimoresun.com/maryland/baltimore-city/bs-md-ci-baltimore-questions-20161108-story.html.
24. Yvonne Wenger, *Baltimore City Council Overrides Mayoral Veto for First Time in a Generation*, Balt. Sun (Feb. 22, 2016), https://www.baltimoresun.com/maryland/baltimore-city/bs-md-ci-veto-override-20160222-story.html.
25. *Id.*
26. *Id.*
27. *Id.* "This is an opportunity for us to put this in the hands of the voters," Holton said. "It gives the people the opportunity to say what their preference and priority is."—Councilwoman Helen Holton, Chairwoman of the council's budget committee. *Id.*
28. Charter of Balt. City, Art. I, §13 (2021).

- Ensure that Baltimore City supports families as an important part of the City population and civic culture;
- Focus on the prevention of problems and on supporting and enhancing the strengths of children, youth, and their families;
- Complement the City's community development efforts;
- Strengthen community-based networks of recreation and after-school services in neighborhoods; and
- Ensure that children and youth with the highest needs receive maximum benefit from the Fund.

BCYF's enabling legislation[29] also provided that the fund be administered in accordance with:

- Best practices and successful and innovative models;
- Standards of equity in funding allocation across age groups—from infancy to transitional-aged youth;
- Principles of gender- and cultural-responsiveness; and
- The principle of collaboration, strengthening partnerships and working relationships among children, youth- and family-serving service providers, and public agencies.

The initial legislative framework for the fund provided that the resources could not be used to supplant funding provided by other agencies, except to the extent that federal, state, or private agency funds for those programs or services have been discontinued.[30]

Through the authorizing legislation, an additional $800,000 was allocated to support the delivery of capacity-building and technical support to prospective BCYF applicants and grantees.[31] Roughly $10 million in funds was to be deployed to community groups through local grants.

The Role of Activism in Shaping BCYF as a Model of Place-Based Community Investment

The overwhelming support of the Baltimore City Council and success of the 2016 legislative proposal was much the result of the work of grassroots activists and organizers who saw the fund as an opportunity to actively demonstrate ways of applying a racial justice and equity lens to place-based community investment practices in Baltimore. These leaders, most notably Dayvon Love and Adam Jackson of Leaders of a Beautiful Struggle, a grassroots policy think tank located in Baltimore, worked tirelessly to educate and onboard local public officials, neighborhood leaders, philanthropic leaders, and others to the notion of shaping the fund through a community-driven, equity-driven, and transparent process. They, together with local public officials and other stakeholders, saw a unique opportunity

29. Charter of Balt. City, Art. I, §13 (2021).
30. *Id.*
31. Authorizing legislation was required to designate a short-term intermediary as the entity that would be responsible for designing, launching, and administering the initial phases of the BCYF's operations. This authorizing legislation would grant the designated intermediary (fiscal agent) the ability to allocate up to ten percent of the BCYF's resources for administrative costs.

to organize and move the BCYF legislative proposal following the death of Freddie Gray, a young man who tragically died from injuries sustained while in police custody in 2015. For many, Gray represented countless young men and women in the city who have become casualties of gross underinvestment in low-income, Black neighborhoods and systematic economic and social injustice.

Following Gray's death, local frustrations regarding long-standing racial and structural inequities peaked and demands for sweeping reforms were high, providing an opportune moment to push for a radical shift in the city's approach to deploying public funds. With this lens, Love and Jackson forged collaborations with Samantha Mellerson and Danielle Torain, who were then national and place-based senior program officers of the Annie E. Casey Foundation, a national philanthropic institution headquartered in Baltimore, to aid in advising on the mechanics of the fund's early design, community engagement, and start-up effort. Together, Love, Jackson, Torain, Mellerson, and later, solidarity economies attorney Dorcas Gilmore explored a range of local, national, and international models of community participatory grantmaking and community capacity building. This partnership formed early segments of BCYF's first project team, and the concepts that resulted from these early conversations laid the foundational groundwork for BCYF's first-year planning and implementation effort.

In the first year, the intent and vision to have the fund designed and managed through a community participatory approach was most prominently reflected in three core components of the fund's design and launch effort. These were as follows:

(1) Initial Community Planning
(2) Community Design Sessions to Identify Pressing Needs; and
(3) Community Data Analysis Retreat to Determine the Fund's Priorities.

The following sections provide a brief overview of each.

Initial Community Planning

In 2017, Baltimore City Council President Jack Young convened the Children and Youth Fund Task Force, a body comprised of community leaders, youth program service providers, Baltimore City government representatives, and other key stakeholder representatives.[32] The Task Force was charged with providing policy recommendations to the Baltimore City Council concerning the design, governance, guiding values, and management of the Fund.[33] The Task Force was facilitated by the Council President's Office, staffed by then Deputy Chief of Staff Lester Davis, and co-chaired by Adam Jackson, CEO of Leaders of a Beautiful Struggle, and John Brothers, President of the Program for Charitable Giving at the T. Rowe Price Foundation.[34] Their partnership represented an intentional effort to ensure that the work of the Task Force be anchored in the voices and perspectives of residents and grassroots leaders, as well as other leaders of Baltimore's public and social sectors.

---

32. Bernard Young, *Baltimore City Council President Introduces Historic Youth Fund Legislation*, Baltimore City Council: Jack's Journal, Vol. 8, Issue 38 (Nov. 15, 2017), https://www.baltimorecitycouncil.com/jacksjournal/jacks-journal-vol-8-issue-38.
33. *Id.*
34. *Id.*

Community Leadership Role in Fund Design

Task Force members convened over a four-month period and worked together to make recommendations concerning the management of the Fund. Task Force members also undertook a community engagement effort, soliciting direct input and recommendations for shaping the fund from hundreds of community members across the city. The Task Force's resulting recommendations stressed that racial equity and community empowerment should guide BCYF's design. The Task Force developed the following guiding values for BCYF's work:

- That the work of the Fund be informed, driven, and led by youth voices;
- That the work of the Fund advance equity, and we welcome and support all races, classes, and gender identities;
- That the work of the Fund impact and be accountable to local communities, neighborhoods, and places where young people connect;
- That the work of the Fund not be politically driven, and earn confidence from the caring networks of Baltimore's young people;
- That the work of the Fund inspires new partnerships and approaches to philanthropy to advance Baltimore's young people;
- That the work of the Fund be focused, expedient, and conducted with urgency.

The Task Force's recommendations split into two categories[35]: (1) grantmaking parameters and criteria to guide the implementation of the Fund's resource deployment efforts and (2) organizational structure. The Task Force's proposed grantmaking criteria recommended that the Fund support:

- small pilot projects;
- small, grassroots organizations and those that have little or no prior grant experience (though, not to the exclusion of other organizations);
- the use of fiscal sponsors by non-501c3 organizations; and
- the availability of general operating funds and multiyear grants.

Relative to structure, the Task Force recommended that an intermediary anchor the Fund—at least in its early stages of development. The Task Force recommended that the chosen intermediary possess three core qualities:

(1) Experience working in disenfranchised communities in Baltimore,
(2) Experience in racial equity, and
(3) Experience with building the capacity of organizations serving disenfranchised communities in Baltimore.

The role of the initial intermediary would be to lead a process by which a permanent, independent organization, with an independent governing body, would be established to oversee the management of the Fund and ensure the initiation of the Fund's first round of grantmaking.

---

35. *Baltimore Children and Youth Fund Task Force Presentation to the Baltimore City Council President's Office*, http://lbsbaltimore.com/wp-content/uploads/2017/06/Children-and-Youth-Fund-Powerpointv4.pdf (last visited Sept. 16, 2022).

Impact Orientation

As a result of the Task Force's deliberations, the Associated Black Charities[36] (ABC), a public charity that advocates and facilitates the creation of measurably more prosperous communities, was appointed as the short-term intermediary to anchor the Fund's design and launch process.[37] ABC partnered with Frontline Solutions[38] and UPD Consulting,[39] two minority-owned consulting practices, to support the Fund's design and Year 1 implementation. Together, Frontline Solutions, UPD Consulting, and a team of local advisors served as the Fund's first-year "Planning Team."

As the first intermediary, ABC was responsible for the following short-term obligations[40]:

- fiscal management and fiduciary responsibility on behalf of the Fund,
- implementing a citywide capacity-building program targeted to community-based organizations located in underinvested and historically marginalized communities in Baltimore,
- conducting a community needs assessment to determine the grantmaking priorities of the Fund,
- producing an annual report on the activities and impact of the Fund, and
- executing external communication efforts to show the impact and efforts of grantees of the Fund.

Community Role in First-Year Grant Selection

To execute the first-year grant-selection effort, the Task Force provided that ABC set up an "assembly"—a body selected through a public process and comprised of residents representing local communities with the greatest need for investment in children- and youth-serving programming and resources. The Task Force provided that the Assembly be comprised of no less than 30 percent youth and young adults, ages thirty and under, representing both the in-school and out-of-school populations. The committee would be diverse in demographical representation, as well as represented sectors, lived experience, and local community geographies.

Community Design Sessions to Identify Pressing Needs

Baltimore City community members helped to set the Fund's Year 1 investment priorities during six community design sessions in March and April 2018. At the community design sessions, Baltimore City residents—young people, youth-serving mentors and practitioners, youth and community advocates, and concerned adults—helped determine which needs and issues the Fund should prioritize in its first year. In the sessions, community members

36. Associated Black Charities, http://www.abc-md.org/.

37. Ian Round, *ABC Tells City Council It Needs More Money to Manage Youth Fund*, BaltimoreBrew (Feb. 21, 2020). https://www.baltimorebrew.com/2020/02/21/abc-tells-city-council-it-needs-more-money-to-manage-youth-fund/.

38. Frontline Solutions, https://www.frontlinesol.com/.

39. UPD Consulting, https://www.updconsulting.com/.

40. *Baltimore Children and Youth Fund Task Force Presentation to the Baltimore City Council President's Office*, Leaders of a Beautiful Struggle, http://lbsbaltimore.com/wp-content/uploads/2017/06/Children-and-Youth-Fund-Powerpointv4.pdf.

shared the most pressing needs for children and young people in their neighborhoods, and then they brainstormed recommendations for how the Fund could best address those needs. The six community design sessions yielded about 1,400 recommendations.

Community Data Analysis Retreat to Determine the Fund's Priorities

Next, a team of twenty-six young leaders and concerned adults gathered in a one-day retreat managed by Frontline Solutions in partnership with Two Gems Consulting Services[41] to analyze the data and insights gathered from the six community design sessions. Two Gems Consulting Services is a Baltimore-based evaluation practice that designs custom information tools to help community stakeholders evaluate the effectiveness of their programs in the context of their unique situations.

Members of this team were recruited based on the following criteria:

- representation from diverse local geographies, gender identities, and racial and ethnic identities;
- representation of those who are most likely to benefit from the Fund (Baltimore City children, youth, and young adults, and the people who serve them);
- balance of youth and adult representation.

These youth and adult community representatives reviewed hundreds of insights and recommendations to fulfill a twofold charge:

(1) analyze and glean key insights from the community design sessions;
(2) work together to use the findings to inform the Fund's potential investment priorities in Year 1.

Next, the recommendations from the Data Retreat were submitted to the Planning Team, who used them to structure the Fund's Year 1 Request for Proposal (RFP).

Broader Philanthropic Context

The BCYF model was one of a series of place-based community investment platforms launched in the wake of the Baltimore Uprisings of 2015. The period birthed a series of collaborations between public, community, and philanthropic leaders who shared a desire to explore ways of facilitating a more equitable distribution of resources among local communities and historically underinvested populations. BCYF had a number of counterparts, including the Baltimore City Intergenerational Initiatives for Trauma and Youth (B-CIITY) and One Baltimore for Jobs (1B4J).[42]

Core Components of the BCYF Model in Year 1

Development of Year 1 Grantmaking Priorities

The grantmaking priorities of the Fund in Year 1 were developed by staff through the applied input of local community members. Staff used data from the local community design sessions and community participatory data analysis retreat (described above), complemented by supplemental research on the local funding landscape to craft the funding

41. Two Gems Consulting Services, https://www.twogemsconsulting.com/.
42. *See supra* Appendix (providing more information about each of these programs).

priorities which served as the anchor for the Fund's Year 1 RFP. The content of the Year 1 RFP was also shaped through the advisement of local thought partners with expertise in each respective content and investment area. The Year 1 priorities of the Fund were as follows:

- *Strengthening the Village*. This area focused on creating healthy, safe, supportive family and community environments that foster learning, growth, and empowerment of children and youth. Priority was given to community-based, youth-centered, multigenerational strategies that build organizational, community, and family capacity.
- *Fostering Authentic Youth Leadership, Empowerment, and Self-Actualization.* This area included strategies that foster the physical, mental, emotional, and spiritual growth of children, youth, and young adults. It emphasized life skills, leadership development, mentorships, health and wellness, and youth-centered arts.
- *Building Sustainable Bridges to Educational and Economic Advancement Opportunities and Pathways to Business Ownership.* This area focused on increasing access to job training, educational and supportive work experiences that help youth and young adults transition to college, vocational and career opportunities, including ownership of community-based enterprises.

BCYF structured funding opportunities into three categories. The three funding levels were intentionally designed to provide access to small-scale projects and emerging organizations as well as existing programs and organizations interested in scaling up and/or developing partnerships. The three funding levels in Year 1 were as follows:

- Level 1 grants in the range of $5,000 to $20,000—targeting small, new, and emerging programs and organizations without formal 501(c)(3) status.
- Level 2 grants in the range of $21,000 to $250,000—targeting established organizations experienced in work with children and youth populations
- Level 3 grants in the range of $251,000 to $500,000—targeting collaborations among community-based organizations, with an emphasis on partnering with youth-led organizations.

Year 1 Grant-Selection Committee Composition and Selection

As noted above, Council President Young's Children & Youth Fund Task Force recommended that the application scoring and selection process be anchored by local residents and community members representative of a diverse array of local neighborhood geographies, demographics, backgrounds, and points of view. The enabling legislation of the Fund mandated that a minimum of 30 percent of committee members be youth and young adults under the age of thirty, with youth over the age of 13 permitted to serve. Members of the Task Force also recommended that members of the committee (referred to above as an "assembly") be selected through an open application process. Nonresidents of Baltimore City as well as community members representing initiatives intending to apply for grant funds were restricted from serving on the grant-selection committee. The following factors were considered in the selection of committee participants:

- age, race, ethnicity, gender, languages spoken, and neighborhood of residence;
- community involvement;

- experience working with youth, young adults, and youth-serving programs;
- experience working with public, private, and nonprofit organizations;
- prior grant review experience;
- perspectives on racial equity and inclusion and collective, intergenerational decision making; and
- ability to devote the time required for the process.

As a result of the first-year selection process, a team of twenty-four Baltimore city community members with diverse backgrounds, ages, and grant review experience were invited to participate in the year one grant review panel. The panel had an emphasis on youth involvement and voice through intergenerational team building. Consistent with the vision of the Fund's initial Task Force, the panelists were chosen based on diverse representation of geography, age, race, and gender, as well as life, work, and youth programming experiences in Baltimore.

Grant Selection

The Year 1 grant-selection strategy drew on participatory decision-making models and models of shared power that emphasized transparency, intergenerational collaboration, public stewardship, and public accountability.

The grant-selection process consisted of the following elements:

- *On-Site Proposal Review and Support Process:* Two days of on-site review were held to help reviewers get acclimated to the review and scoring process. Staff were on-site to deliver 1-1 and group-based support, coaching, and technical assistance.
- *Independent Review and Scoring of Eligible Proposals:* Grant reviewers then independently read each assigned proposal and scored them using a thirty-point scale. Open office hours and support calls were hosted to provide reviewers with 1-1 coaching and technical assistance.
- *Participation in Group-Based Grant Deliberations:* Two days of in-person deliberations were held to provide review team members an opportunity to discuss proposals and determine recommendations for ABC. The initial deliberations were held by funding level, with reviewers discussing specific applications in levels 1, 2, and 3. A second phase of deliberations reviewed proposals across all funding levels to determine equitable distribution across geography, populations served, and priority areas for the Fund.
- *Submission of Final Recommendations to the interim intermediary, Associated Black Charities.* The recommendations of the grant-selection committee were accepted in full by Associated Black Charities (ABC).

Capacity-Building and Technical Assistance

The vision and mandate for BCYF set by members of Council President Young's Children & Youth Fund Task Force stressed the importance of community capacity building as a core tenant of the Fund's strategic framework and local contribution. Task Force members believed that organizational capacity support would prove crucial to enabling the Fund to fulfill its charge to reach providers with little or no prior history of receiving outside funding, and those with more modest administrative and operational infrastructure. The technical assistance strategy implemented by the BCYF team in Year 1 of the Fund's operation included provisions for support to prospective BCYF grant applicants to aid them in preparing for funding opportunities made available through the Fund, as well as targeted support to grant recipients.

Technical assistance resources made available to Year 1 applicants of the fund were organized and coordinated through a combination of in-house staffing, external partnerships, and hired consultative support. Technical support was delivered through one-on-one consultations, and small- and large-group sessions. Applicant-focused technical assistance covered topics such as grant-writing and technical proposal development, program design and planning, program evaluation, budget development, financial management, fiscal sponsorship, and program compliance issues.

BCYF's Year 1 technical assistance strategy for grantees focused on (1) delivering targeted support to organizations supported by BCYF to aid them in successful program implementation, and (2) addressing gaps in Baltimore's nonprofit technical assistance ecosystem by resourcing a team of technical assistance providers equipped with the skills, contextual understanding, and capacity to respond to the needs of grantees in a culturally responsive and effective manner.

Key areas of grantee-focused technical assistance included the following:

- Programmatic and general operational support
    - Start-up and planning support
    - Implementation and general operational support
    - Staff training, development, and technical assistance
    - Data tracking, evidence building, and evaluation
- Back office supports
    - Fiscal sponsorship
    - Independent audits
    - Financial management and reporting

The guiding values of BCYF heavily informed how members of its Technical Assistance Team were selected, supported, and held accountable by BCYF in its first year of operation. Within the course of the selection process for technical assistance partners, prospective providers were strongly encouraged to demonstrate an understanding of and sensitivity to

- the strengths, challenges, and perspectives of served leaders and their organizations;
- the unique social, political, economic, and cultural contexts in which they work;
- the ways in which issues of race, power, class, gender, and place-based discrimination show up at the interpersonal, organizational, and structural levels and impact the accessibility and provision of technical assistance services;
- effective approaches for customizing and adapting technical assistance approaches to match the needs of served leaders, organizations, and communities.

This guidance for prospective providers was based on the premise that a majority of the Fund's first-year grantees would be grassroots organizations and coalitions led by people of color who would employ a broad range of youth-led and youth-centered approaches and take on a diverse range of organizational structures. In their applications, prospective technical assistance partners were asked to show approaches that demonstrate an understanding of—and high level of responsiveness to—the needs and interests of clients who fit this general profile.

The Fund sought technical assistance partners who would work to ensure that services be delivered in a way that respects the expertise, ingenuity, and autonomy of the Fund's grantees and the communities from which they originate. The Fund additionally sought technical assistance providers that would uphold the value of racial equity both by identifying the ways that racism and other forms of structural oppression show up in the nonprofit/human service sector and in their method for providing tools for navigating these dynamics to the Fund's grantees.

Conclusion

The Baltimore Children & Youth Fund serves as an example of a grantmaking initiative that centers a range of community empowerment principles, including community-centered approaches to planning and design, community-participatory decision-making, community infrastructure development and investment in grassroots, community-serving institutions. Formed through historic action by the Baltimore City Council and a citywide voter referendum, the BCYF demonstrates the power of coordinated action across grassroots organizing and advocacy, legislative, philanthropic, capacity building and other domains. Philanthropic approaches anchored in democratic and community empowerment principles require intentional investment in and facilitated alignment across a range of institutional and community-level capacities including: community engagement, public education, data analysis, group facilitation and mediation, policy development, capital deployment and culturally-responsive technical assistance. BCYF's holistic approach to investing in organizations through technical assistance and direct grants reflects a place-based investment approach that centers community participation in the investment strategy and decision making to protect and invest in the City's most precious local resource, its youth.

Case Study

Private Foundations Are Equipped to Build Greater Race and Ethnic Equity within Community Small Business Ecosystems

Small business entrepreneurship has been identified as an opportunity to close the racial and ethnic wealth gap in communities in the United States.[43] Entrepreneurship is associated with higher levels of wealth as data show households where the head of the household

43. Joyce Klein, *Bridging the Divide: How Business Ownership Can Help Close the Racial Wealth Gap*, Aspen Institute 5 (Jan. 2017), https://www.aspeninstitute.org/wp-content/uploads/2017/01/Bridging-the-Divide.pdf?_ga=2.265469647.1397676862.1581866380-611808210.1581866380.

was self-employed had a median net worth five times that of households in which the head worked for someone else.[44] Data also show that Black entrepreneurs have higher wealth levels and mobility than Black workers, and that while Black entrepreneurs have levels of wealth mobility equal to those of white entrepreneurs, white workers have greater wealth mobility than Black workers.[45] Moreover, entrepreneurs of color are more likely to hire people of color.[46]

However, across the United States, small business entrepreneurs of color suffer from diminished capital access and business support due to systemic discrimination within local small business ecosystems.[47] Diminished capital access and business support are the result of generations of structural racism and ethnic discrimination embedded within public and private institutions.[48] Numerous reports have highlighted the effects of this result, including the Fed Small Business's 2019 Report on Minority-Owned Firms. This disparity has been exacerbated by the COVID-19 pandemic, especially for Black-owned business.[49]

Findings include that minority-owned firms suffer from lower revenues, greater reliance on personal funds and personal credit scores when applying for financing, worse outcomes when applying for financing, greater dissatisfaction and lack of trust with financial institutions, and greater use of higher interest financial products.[50]

Nonoperating private foundations possess the regulatory discretion, capital assets, and community influence to increase capital access and business support for entrepreneurs of color, thus contributing toward closing the racial wealth gap. This case study provides a brief overview of private philanthropy, highlights some of private foundations' funding tools, and discusses two approaches to how private foundations have catalyzed increased capital access and support for entrepreneurs of color in two American cities, Baltimore and Detroit.

Definition, Funding Tools, and Community Influence

The IRS provides a broad definition for private foundation, defining every organization that qualifies for tax exemption as an organization described in Section 501(c)(3) as a private foundation except for certain exclusions and exceptions.[51] The St. Louis Federal Reserve reports that private foundations, including nonoperating, exempt operating, and operating foundations, have an estimated $1,326 billion in total assets as of the first quarter

---

44. *Id.* at 6.
45. *Id.* at 6-7.
46. Among the 10 Most Populous Cities, African Americans Remain Underrepresented in Business Ownership, PolicyLink (June 26, 2019), https://www.policylink.org/taxonomy/term/2086.
47. Joyce Klein, *Bridging the Divide: How Business Ownership Can Help Close the Racial Wealth Gap*, Aspen Institute 10 (Jan. 2017), https://www.aspeninstitute.org/wp-content/uploads/2017/01/Bridging-the-Divide.pdf?_ga=2.265469647.1397676862.1581866380-611808210.1581866380.
48. Professor Tricia Rose, YouTube (Dec. 14, 2015), https://www.youtube.com/watch?v=X3KsVRkbnn4.
49. Press Releases: Committee Report Outlines COVID's Devastating Impact on Black-Owned Small Businesses, Committee on Small Business (Feb. 26, 2021), https://smallbusiness.house.gov/news/documentsingle.aspx?DocumentID=3578.
50. Mels de Zeeuw, Small Business Credit Survey: Report on Minority-Owned Firms, Federal Reserve Bank of Atlanta (Dec. 2019), https://www.fedsmallbusiness.org/medialibrary/fedsmallbusiness/files/2019/20191211-ced-minority-owned-firms-report.pdf.
51. *Private Foundations*, Internal Revenue Service (May 24, 2021), https://www.irs.gov/charities-non-profits/charitable-organizations/private-foundations.

of 2022.[52] However, many nontax professional and legal practitioners think of definitions similar to the Council on Foundations' definition when referring to private foundations:

> A nongovernmental, nonprofit organization with funds (usually from a single source, such as an individual, family, or corporation) and program managed by its own trustees or directors, established to maintain or aid social, educational, religious, or other charitable activities serving the common welfare, primarily through grantmaking. U.S. private foundations are tax-exempt under Section 501(c)(3) of the Internal Revenue Code and are classified by the IRS as a private foundation as defined in the code.[53]

A notable regulatory rule is that private nonoperating foundations are required by federal tax law to distribute a certain minimum amount each year for grants and other charitable qualifying distributions.[54] The required minimum amount is five percent of a foundation's assets.[55] The "payout rule" was created to prevent foundations from receiving assets but never actually making charitable distributions with them.[56] However, with charitable activities broadly defined by the tax code, private foundations have discretion in determining where to direct these significant resources.

Through laws and regulations, beginning with the Tax Reform Act of 1969, Congress authorizes private foundations to manage their assets primarily through grantmaking, traditional endowment management, and impact investing.[57] The IRS defines grants as the following types of expenditures: scholarships, fellowships, internships, prizes, and awards; loans for charitable purposes; program related investments (PRIs); and payments to exempt organizations to further the organizations' exempt purposes.[58] The goals of endowment management are to generally increase a private foundation's assets while meeting its spending needs or to facilitate a spend down of its assets in a prudent manner to avoid violating Section 4944(a) of the Code, the jeopardizing investment rule. If a private foundation invests in a manner that jeopardizes its exempt purposes, there is an excise tax imposed equal to ten percent of the amount so invested.[59]

---

52. Board of Governors of the Federal Reserve System (US), *Nonprofit Organizations; Total Financial Assets Held by Private Foundations, Level [BOGZ1FL164090015Q]*, Federal Reserve Bank of St. Louis, https://fred.stlouisfed.org/series/BOGZ1FL164090015Q.
53. *Foundation Basics*, Council on Foundations, https://www.cof.org/content/foundation-basics#what_is_private_foundation.
54. *See* Loren Renz, *Understanding and Benchmarking Foundation Payout*, Foundation Center 1 (Sept. 28, 2012), https://www.issuelab.org/resources/14076/14076.pdf.
55. *Id.*
56. *What Is the 5% Payout Rule*, National Center for Family Philanthropy (Oct. 15, 2008), https://www.ncfp.org/2008/10/15/what-is-the-5-payout-rule/.
57. Loren Renz, *Understanding and Benchmarking Foundation Payout*, Foundation Center 1, 4 (Sept. 28, 2012), https://www.issuelab.org/resources/14076/14076.pdf.
58. *Grant Defined*, Internal Revenue Service (Apr. 19, 2021), https://www.irs.gov/charities-non-profits/private-foundations/grant-defined.
59. IRC Section 4944(c)—Taxes on Investments Which Jeopardize Charitable Purpose—Exception for Program-Related Investments, Internal Revenue Service (June 26, 2021), https://www.irs.gov/charities-non-profits/irc-section-4944c-taxes-on-investments-which-jeopardize-charitable-purpose-exception-for-program-related-investments.

Impact investing, the process of investing with the intention to generate positive, measurable social and environmental impact alongside a financial return, is an important tool.[60] There are two primary types of impact investing, mission-related investing and program-related investing. Mission-related investments (MRIs) are risk-adjusted, market-rate investments made from a foundation's endowment.[61] In 2015, the IRS offered guidance encouraging private foundations to pursue MRIs with reasonable business care without violating the jeopardizing investments law.[62] MRI can be of any asset class, including cash, fixed income, public equity, private equity and venture capital, and real estate.[63] PRIs are a category of investments exempted from the jeopardizing rule.[64] For private foundations, PRIs are defined by the IRS tax code, and they are eligible to count against the five percent payout requirement.[65] Requirements include the following:

(1) The primary purpose is to accomplish one or more of the foundation's exempt purposes.
(2) Production of income or appreciation of property is not a significant purpose.
(3) Influencing legislation or taking part in political campaigns on behalf of candidates is not a purpose.[66]

The IRS provides further guidance through examples. Three of the relevant examples include:

(1) Low-interest loans to small businesses owned by members of economically disadvantaged groups, where commercial funds at reasonable interest rates are not readily available;
(2) Investments in businesses in low-income areas (both domestic and foreign) under a plan to improve the economy of the area by providing employment or training for unemployed residents; and
(3) Investments in nonprofit organizations combating community deterioration.[67]

PRIs can also be invested across all asset classes, including cash, fixed income, public equity, private equity and venture capital, and real estate.[68] Private foundations will often invest in CDFIs, U.S. Treasury certified community development financial institutions that take a market-based approach to supporting economically disadvantaged communities.[69]

---

60. *What You Need to Know about Impact Investing*, Global Impact Investing Network, https://thegiin.org/impact-investing/need-to-know/.
61. *Mission-Related Investment*, Mission Investors Exchange, https://missioninvestors.org/glossary.
62. I.R.S. Notice 2015-62, 2015-2 C.B. 411.
63. *What Is Mission Investing*, Mission Investors Exchange, https://web.cof.org/2013fall/docs/resources/Impact-Investing-Basics.pdf.
64. *Id.*
65. *Id.*
66. *Program-Related Investments*, Internal Revenue Service (Feb. 2, 2021), https://www.irs.gov/charities-non-profits/private-foundations/program-related-investments.
67. *Program-Related Investments*, Internal Revenue Service (Feb. 2, 2021), https://www.irs.gov/charities-non-profits/private-foundations/program-related-investments.
68. *What Is Mission Investing*, Mission Investors Exchange, https://web.cof.org/2013fall/docs/resources/Impact-Investing-Basics.pdf.
69. U.S. Department of the Treasury Community Development Financial Institutions Fund, https://www.cdfifund.gov/Pages/default.aspx.

Typically, these organizations rely on significant public and private philanthropic support and investments to be effective.

Private foundations can also provide recoverable grants and guaranties. Recoverable grants are grants as defined by the IRS used to finance charitable investment activities, where revenue generation and repayment are not as certain.[70] Repayment is only required if the activity generates repayment income.[71] Loan guaranties allow a foundation to extend its credit to a grantee without liquidating the foundation's current holdings or disbursing cash.[72] Guaranties provide a lifeline to organizations with limited access to reasonable, affordable capital because of a lack of credit history or investment uncertainty.[73]

Because private foundations' have capital assets and broad discretion to move those assets, they often have a disproportionate amount of community influence and power. This influence offers private foundations, especially large foundations, the ability to convene public and private institutions. It also gives private foundations the ability to leverage grants and investments into additional capital and develop strategies that influence or support local public policy agendas. Finally, private foundations can serve as an institutional advocate for community grantees and constituents that benefit from foundations' charitable activities.

Baltimore: Using Grantmaking and Influence to Build Investment Opportunity and Investor Interest

Entrepreneurs of color in Baltimore have suffered from underinvestment for decades resulting in limited small business and CDFI investment.[74] This limited access to capital and support has disproportionately affected Baltimore's entrepreneurs of color.[75] As a member of Casey's impact investment team, called Social Investments, the author designed an internal foundation strategy beginning in 2016 to help address this investment gap using each of the above-mentioned tools. Aligned with the foundation's commitment to increasing access to opportunity for children, families, and communities, the foundation sought to better understand what support and financing are available to the city's entrepreneurs of color.[76] The resulting strategy was summarized in the whitepaper, "Creating Equitable Opportunities for Baltimore Entrepreneurs of Color."[77]

---

70. Ranajoy Basu & Carl J. Fleming, *Innovative Finance Focus: Doing More with Less through Recoverable Grants*, 11 Nat'l L. Rev. (Jan. 12, 2021), https://www.natlawreview.com/article/innovative-finance-focus-doing-more-less-through-recoverable-grants.

71. *Id.*

72. *Program-Related Investment Loan Guarantees*, Foundation Source, https://foundationsource.com/resources/hub/resource/program-related-investment-loan-guarantees/.

73. *Id.*

74. Annie E. Casey Foundation, *More than $1.8 Million Raised to Address Barriers Faced by Entrepreneurs of Color in Baltimore* (Mar. 11, 2020), https://www.prnewswire.com/news-releases/more-than-1-8-million-raised-to-address-barriers-faced-by-entrepreneurs-of-color-in-baltimore-301021637.html.

75. Black entrepreneurs own 47 percent of the city's businesses, and only about ten percent of those firms have employees, an indicator of sustainability and growth. Moreover, black-owned businesses with employees generate disproportionately lower annual revenues than their white-owned counterparts ($789,222 compared with $2.9 million, respectively).

76. Creating Equitable Opportunities for Baltimore Entrepreneurs of Color, whitepaper on file with author.

77. *Id.*

The first strategy step was to analyze Baltimore's public and private institutions that catalyze, incubate, and assist small businesses, as well as the capacity of the city's CDFIs to provide financing to small businesses. Using grant funding, Casey commissioned two studies performed by consultants of color. The studies collectively included the execution of a local CDFI analysis and landscape review of available technical assistance programs, interviews with over thirty representatives, and analysis of data released by Opportunity Finance Network, the Baltimore Integration Partnership, ABC, Association of Enterprise Opportunity, U.S. Census Bureau, and Brookings Institution, among other sources.[78]

The consultants found that (1) Baltimore's small business system was fragmented, (2) public and philanthropic funding is needed, (3) CDFIs had underdeveloped lending portfolios, (4) available technical assistance failed to meet the unique needs of small businesses, (5) Baltimore entrepreneurs of color lacked trust in entrepreneurship ecosystems, and (6) technical assistance and business support providers were severely underfunded. In responses to these findings, Wahls created a strategy based on the following recommendations:

(1) build capacity of CDFIs and technical assistance providers to engage Black, Latino, and Native American businesses;
(2) coordinate philanthropic investments; and
(3) develop strategies that complement City of Baltimore small business strategies.[79]

In addition to using grant funding to commission the studies, philanthropic grant funding was used to build working relationships with local CDFI institutions and technical assistance partners to better understand their needs, identify potential funding opportunities, and signal to other funders that Casey was committed to this effort, which led to the development of the Baltimore Small Business Support Fund (Support Fund).

Casey designed and seeded the Support Fund through a $275,000 grant along with significant follow-on grants in collaboration with aligned local and national funders. With nearly $3 million in total commitments by 2021, the fund's initial purposes were to facilitate connections between CDFIs and small business support organizations, advance racial equity to improve outcomes for entrepreneurs of color, encourage philanthropic investment to support an inclusive ecosystem, and ensure alignment with other public and private small business initiatives in the city. The fund's design allowed for several elements:

- an efficient fundraising program through a donor-advised fund at the local community foundation,
- an investor-led advisory committee to collect philanthropic influence,
- a cohort collective learning model for grant recipients, and
- a partnership-designed selection process leading to selection of six initial organizations, five of which are led by leaders of color.

---

78. Creating Equitable Opportunities for Baltimore Entrepreneurs of Color, whitepaper on file with author.
79. *Id.*

Moreover, in response to the consultants' findings, Casey co-invested through a recoverable grant to support the only minority-depository institution (MDI) in Maryland that has successfully served Baltimore for decades. The patient grant capital offered the MDI additional capacity to provide affordable loan products and business support to emerging housing developers and other small businesses through a targeted entrepreneurs of color strategy. The loan products have been designed to address a marketplace gap and serve customers that are a higher credit risk than banks can traditionally accept and place those borrowers in a position to acquire more equity and track record. Finally, along with its own grantmaking efforts, the foundation used its community influence to assist with the development of Baltimore-dedicated impact investment strategies for local and national philanthropic and financial institutions.

However, as the COVID-19 pandemic ravaged the nation in 2020, the Support Fund shifted to crisis response mode. It did so by partnering with the Baltimore Development Corporation and the Mayor's Office of Minority and Women-Owned Business Development.[80] Casey reported the resulting strategy, the Small Business Technical Assistance Network (TA Network), as of August 2021, has helped more than 2,500 small businesses access financing—including an estimated $40 million in public recovery funding.[81] The TA Network was later re-envisioned as the Baltimore BASE (Business Assistance and Support for Equity) Network. The Support Fund, while not initially designed to as an emergency response vehicle, became the nexus point for Baltimore's COVID-19 small business response because of the fund's structural design and the funding discretion and societal influence its national and local philanthropic funders possessed.

In a continuation of its support of Baltimore entrepreneurs of color, in 2021, Casey used Support Fund lessons learned to invest millions through PRIs in a black-led CDFI that specializes in Small Business Administration–backed loans and a Latino-led and focused CDFI to provide additional small business capital to Baltimore entrepreneurs along with others nationally.

Comparison to Detroit Entrepreneurs of Color Fund Program-Related Investment

Lessons applied to the above-mentioned efforts in Baltimore stemmed from the author's lessons learned while executing the Detroit Entrepreneurs of Color Fund (Detroit EOC), a PRI the author designed beginning in 2013 in partnership with colleagues and a consultant team while working at the W.K. Kellogg Foundation (Kellogg). The author intentionally designed the Detroit EOC PRI to provide capital and technical assistance to Detroit small business owners of color as a response to the lack of capital flowing to Detroit's neighborhood businesses. Providing grants to fund research and a community landscape, the author used that data to design an investment approach that complemented established and emerging initiatives and community priorities. The resulting $3.5 million investment by Kellogg and equal co-investment by JPMorgan Chase in 2015 led to an initial $7.0 million

---

80. *See* Kingslow Associates, Evaluation of One Baltimore for Jobs: Job Opportunities for Disconnected Young Adults (Nov. 2018), https://aecfcraftstr01.blob.core.windows.net/aecfcraftblob02/m/resourcedoc/kingslow-evaluationofonebaltimoreforjobs-2018.pdf.

81. Annie E. Casey Foundation, *Blog: Baltimore Fund Backs Entrepreneurs of Color during the Pandemic*, AECF (Aug. 23, 2021), https://www.aecf.org/blog/baltimore-fund-backs-entrepreneurs-of-color-during-the-pandemic.

round of PRI, grant, and guaranty capital placed with the Detroit Development Fund, a neighborhood-focused CDFI.[82] As of 2019, the fund had grown to over $20 million from foundations and financial institutions, providing lending capital and customized pre- and post-loan technical assistance to entrepreneurs.[83] The model has served as a template for investment efforts nationally, including in California, District of Columbia, Georgia, Illinois, Michigan, New Mexico, New York, and other locations.

The Baltimore and Detroit strategies and investments were outcomes of internal analyses of the respective private foundations' impact investment portfolios and mission commitments to racial and ethnic equity. However, the Detroit model was built with the backdrop of at least $150-million-related grantmaking and PRIs by local and national foundations. This included grantmaking to Detroit-based CDFIs and the New Economy Initiative. Detroit Development Fund and other CDFIs like Invest Detroit benefitted from significant private and public support unlike Baltimore small business CDFIs. The Baltimore approach had to be designed with that factor in mind to address systemic flaws, capacity building, and gaps within the local ecosystem. This resulted in leading off with a capacity-building grant strategy while the Detroit investment was designed to increase efficient, intentional capital deployment to entrepreneurs.

Conclusion

The small business ecosystem efforts in Baltimore and Detroit show that intentional efforts focused on addressing systemic and institutional bias can be catalyzed when private foundations are willing to move beyond traditional grantmaking. The efforts discussed in this chapter highlight the risk-taking capability that foundations possess due to their capital assets, the federal regulatory framework, and their subsequent community influence. Foundations have the grantmaking tools to fund necessary pre-investment research and build a coalition of aligned institutions and community constituents. They also have the risk capital and flexibility to build sustainable investment solutions and leverage capital from a myriad of sources. Finally, foundations have access to all relevant institutions, including federal, state, and local governmental entities; other private foundations; regulated financial institutions; alternative financial providers; and small business development institutions. Collectively, these entities can develop legal, funding, and policy solutions that reduce systemic racial and ethnic discrimination for entrepreneurs of color.

Building Capacity by Training in the Arts of Participatory Philanthropy and Place-Conscious Community Control

While the philanthropic institutions described in this chapter seek to build community capacity, they approach that process differently by focusing on participatory grantmaking and organizational development for the BCYF and strengthening the ecosystem for community control of capital for Casey and Kellogg. As Danielle Torain describes, the BCYF

---

82. Nina Mendiolia, *Detroit's Entrepreneurs of Color Fund Receives $18M Investment*, DBusiness (Dec. 14, 2017), https://www.dbusiness.com/daily-news/detroits-entrepreneurs-of-color-fund-receives-18m-investment/.
83. *Id.*

was born of a fully democratic initiative: a citywide voters' referendum, conducted in the wake of the collective soul-searching in reaction to the death of Freddie Gray, to devote funds to improving conditions for youth in Baltimore. The enabling legislation that resulted from that referendum mandated that over thirty percent of the Year 1 Grant-Selection Committee consist of city residents between the ages of fourteen and thirty. That mandate, and the spirit of the legislation, drove BCYF from its beginnings to make its grants responsive to the community's articulation of the community's needs.

The inaugural Task Force for the Year 1 grant-selection round crafted an elaborate structure that delegated fact-finding and priority-setting to layers of community representatives. The decision makers who set the direction and process of dispensing BCYF's funds for its first year were wholly informed in that process by intense sessions of community-based information-gathering. This grounding of both process and knowledge in the community addressed from the beginning the many subtle sites at which irrevocable decisions may thwart the community's preferences for the services it receives and how it receives them.

Supporting parallel priorities, BCYF trained its community constituents in the mechanics and philosophy of transparent, participatory philanthropy. One of BCYF's goals was to address gaps in how Baltimore's culture of nonprofit philanthropy met the needs of those being served. These gaps included capacity building. How could potential recipients of grants gear up for those grants without knowing how to write grant applications? How could residents participate fully in determining priorities for grant-giving without learning about the importance of benchmarks? That assessment of needs for capacity resulted in training for potential grant recipients in the art of writing grants, and in training of the Grant-Selection Committee in grant review, including the design of a scale for scoring.

BCYF's principles for selection of grantees and grant levels of organizations followed priorities articulated in its community design meetings. A dedicated focus on small often volunteer organizations addressed a persistent challenge for organizations without tax exemption: they do not always present a risk that a grantor might find worth taking. To support these grantees meaningfully, BCYF committed Year 1 funds to back-office support and training in evaluation design. This training and support brought full circle the vision of the voters' referendum: through community-based representatives, community-driven processes, and community-articulated priorities, to enable community-serving organizations to succeed, and to build a lasting foundation for community voice in conversations about philanthropy.

For long-standing private foundations such as Casey and Kellogg, building community capacity begins with building access to capital for entrepreneurs of color. James Wahls describes how Casey and Kellogg, sometimes in partnership with major commercial national banks, deploy "program-related" and "mission-related" impact investments to strengthen the lending capacity of community-based and minority-focused lending institutions. The foundations have invested in key intermediaries, CDFIs and MDIs. They have seeded the Baltimore Support Fund and the Detroit Entrepreneurs of Color Fund, which support technical assistance, networking, and training for small business owners of color. Wahls highlights capacity building as a core rationale for the creation of the Support Fund and similar strategies to enable community-based and minority lenders and partners to better work in the communities in which they lend and serve.

Rejecting the "RECAP:"[84] Challenging the Dominant Narrative of Race, Opportunity, and Urban Poverty

The case studies presented in this chapter illustrate an important new direction in policy, practice, and scope, to set a new course to advance racial equity through community-directed investment strategies. The early decades of community economic development focused policy and capital delivery on building with bricks and mortar. For decades, one long-running debate within community economic development has been whether to invest in place-based or people-based strategies to redress community poverty and decline: If geography is destiny, is the better policy to rescue people, or places? Numerous governmental and philanthropic programs do some of each. And for those decades, the dominant narrative driving federal, state, and philanthropic investment has been "white proximity," guided by reliance among urban policy-setters on the concept of the "racially or ethnically concentrated areas of poverty" or "RECAP"[85] and, often, subsidy for mobility strategies. The "white proximity" model has centered areas of progress and opportunity in areas of whiteness.[86]

The white proximity model acknowledges an inconvenient truth: that centuries of overt and then systemic racism have concentrated privilege in white communities, whose constituent elements include housing and amenities, schools and education, health facilities and health care, secure employment, safe streets, and respectful policing. "Opportunity" policies that assist or expect families of color to move to whiter neighborhoods fail to recognize adequately that harm as well as good attends "mobility moves" out of communities, and that further harm is done by the consistent denigration of communities as devoid of opportunity These case studies reformulate the geography-is-destiny conundrum head-on.

This renunciation of the mobility premise of equitable development does indeed challenge the dominant current narrative of urban poverty remediation. The Opportunity Insights think tank, is home to the formidable body of empirical work by Raj Chetty, Nathaniel Hendren, and others,[87] who have posited links between neighborhoods and the life chances of those neighborhoods' children, finding significantly reduced economic outcomes for children correlating closely with geographical location.[88]

---

84. For a description of the reliance among urban policy-setters on the concept of the "racially or ethnically concentrated areas of poverty," see Edward G. Goetz et al., *Changing the Narrative and Playbook on Racially Concentrated Areas of Poverty*, Case Western Reserve University (2020), https://case.edu/socialwork/nimc/sites/case.edu.nimc/files/2020-09/Goetz.WWV_.Changing%20the%20Narrative.2020.pdf. Edward Goetz is the director of, and Anthony Damiano is a postdoctoral fellow at, the University of Minnesota's Center for Urban and Regional Affairs; Rashad A. Williams is a doctoral candidate at the University of Minnesota's Hubert H. Humphrey School of Public Affairs. This essay is one among an expansive collection of online essays published in the fifth volume of the San Francisco Federal Reserve's "What Works for America's Communities" series, available at https://case.edu/socialwork/nimc/resources/what-works-volume.

85. For a description of the reliance among urban policy-setters on the concept of the "racially or ethnically concentrated areas of poverty," or RECAP, see Edward G. Goetz et al., *Changing the Narrative and Playbook on Racially Concentrated Areas of Poverty*, Case Western Reserve University (2020), https://case.edu/socialwork/nimc/sites/case.edu.nimc/files/2020-09/Goetz.WWV_.Changing%20the%20Narrative.2020.pdf.

86. *Id.* at 8.

87. *Id.* at 4; *see* Opportunity Insights, https://opportunityinsights.org/, for links to research on concentration of poverty by ethnicity and race, and on ongoing initiatives to enhance improved life chances through mobility strategies.

88. *See, e.g.*, Raj Chetty et al., *Race and Economic Opportunity in the United States: An Intergenerational Perspective*, 135 Q. J. Econ. 711, 718 (2020) (finding that, despite poorer outcomes overall for Black than for white boys, ". . . that neighborhoods with low poverty rates, high rates of father presence among blacks, and low levels of racial bias, among whites have better outcomes for black boys and smaller racial gaps . . .").

While the Opportunity Insights website acknowledges the necessity of making neighborhoods safe and productive places to live in,[89] its research focuses overwhelmingly on assisting cities to develop mobility programs. The related interactive Opportunity Atlas[90] website allows the viewer to read a snapshot of demographic data and "outcome" data—income, educational attainment, mobility, life expectancy—of any city or any street address. The implication is that geography is destiny, one often best escaped.

The innovations showcased in this chapter reject that implication. Instead, they respond with energy, insight, and urgency: not to move residents out but to redouble efforts to transcend superficial "either-or" choices between mobility and place-conscious strategies. The PRIs of Annie E. Casey and grant and technical assistance investments of BCYF take the long view and reject white proximity as the basis for community development. Place-conscious, justice-seeking economic development requires ongoing identification, recruitment, and training of residents who feel committed to exercise control over the investment of funds and resources in their neighborhoods. That training encompasses knowledge of systems, processes, and industries. Only that knowledge yields meaningful "control": the ability to assess critically the mission and methods of development, and then ultimately to dictate what the mission and the methods should be.

Appendix

Baltimore City Intergenerational Initiatives for Trauma and Youth (B-CIITY)[91] (Excerpted from the Baltimore City Health Department's Office of Youth and Trauma Services website)

In September 2016, the Baltimore City Health Department (BCHD) was awarded a five-year, $5 million grant by the Substance Abuse and Mental Health Services Administration (SAMSHA) for the Resiliency in Communities After Street and Trauma (ReCAST) program.

The goal of ReCAST is to reduce the impact of trauma and build resilience in Central West Baltimore communities adversely impacted by the April 2015 unrest. The project empowers community organizations from West Baltimore to implement high-quality, trauma-informed services to promote connectedness and resilience in youth.

BCHD brought together a community coalition made up of several community organizations and community members that live and work in the Central West Baltimore communities of Sandtown/Winchester, Upton/Druid Heights, and Penn North. The Coalition supported the hiring of a Project Director and electing a community board.

The Coalition voted to rebrand itself as B-CIITY (Baltimore City Intergenerational Initiative for Trauma and Youth) to better represent the full scope and vision of the Coalition. The B-CIITY Community Board, made up of residents and stakeholders, serves in a leadership

89. *See Neighborhoods Matter: Children's Lives Are Shaped by the Neighborhood They Grow Up In*, Opportunity Insights, https://opportunityinsights.org/neighborhoods/ (stating, "Of course, helping families move can never be a scalable solution to improve upward mobility in and of itself; ultimately, we must make investments to make all communities areas of opportunity.").

90. The Opportunity Atlas, https://www.opportunityatlas.org/.

91. *Baltimore City Intergenerational Initiative for Trauma and Youth (B-CIITY) Supported by Recast*, Baltimore City Health Department, https://health.baltimorecity.gov/office-youth-and-trauma-services/baltimore-city-intergenerational-initiative-trauma-and-youth-b.

and advisory capacity to organizations that have and will receive grant funding to support their trauma-informed and resilience-based initiatives.

The stated mission of B-CIITY is to promote healing and thrive-ability through collaboration, resource generation, and network building for organizations that serve youth and their families experiencing trauma. B-CIITY prioritizes investment in initiatives that focus on (1) leadership, education, and workforce development; (2) mental, physical, and spiritual health; and (3) family, community, and cultural connectedness.

One Baltimore for Jobs[92] (Excerpted from the One Baltimore for Jobs Process Evaluation Executive Summary, by Kingslow & Associates)

In June 2015, following the uprising in response to the death of Freddie Gray while in police custody, the U.S. Department of Labor selected Baltimore as one of seven cities to receive a two-year, $5 million Urban Employment for Youth and Young Adults Demonstration grant. The aim of the demonstration was to develop innovative approaches to reengage disconnected youth and young adults, ages sixteen to twenty-nine, who live in distressed communities and increase their access to high-quality jobs in growing industries.

The Mayor's Office of Employment Development (MOED) implemented the Baltimore demonstration in collaboration with the Maryland Department of Labor, Licensing and Regulation (DLLR). Known as One Baltimore for Jobs (1B4J), the demonstration specifically focused on young adult black males who were unemployed or underemployed, lacked a high school credential, and/or had a criminal record. More broadly, 1B4J also sought to lay the groundwork for a stronger workforce system that brings together the public sector and training and service providers as partners to offer integrated services that better meet the needs of residents and employers.

1B4J was designed to connect young adults to potentially life-changing sector-based training programs that also provided critical support services to participants. These programs offer career pathways to middle-skilled jobs, but typically require that participants have a postsecondary credential, strong basic skills, and job readiness skills. Many of Baltimore's young adults, particularly people of color, cannot meet basic academic requirements and face other barriers to participation in these programs. 1B4J not only sought to connect young adults to specialized barrier removal and support services but to specifically align these programs with career pathway programs.

92. Kingslow Associates, *Evaluation of One Baltimore for Jobs: Job Opportunities for Disconnected Young Adults* (Nov. 2018), https://aecfcraftstr01.blob.core.windows.net/aecfcraftblob02/m/resourcedoc/kingslow-evaluationofonebaltimoreforjobs-2018.pdf.

Chapter 9
"Place-based" Cooperative Finance and Governance Models

Susan D. Bennett, Geoff Gilbert, Clark R. Arrington,
Andrea Armeni, and Curt Lyon

Introduction

The authors of this chapter's two case studies write about two lending institutions, Seed Commons and ROC USA. Each case study describes place-based community ownership and investment strategies, and visions of how most effectively to support equitable development in places that have seen too little of it. How the programs conceptualize "effectively" blurs conventional distinctions between investing, giving, and lending.

The case studies demonstrate the importance of the role of beneficiaries in dictating the destination and purpose of the lending.

Seed Commons and ROC USA put training and governance at the heart of their missions. A descendant of The Working World's (TWW) adaptation of the Argentinian *Empresas Recuperadas* movement, Seed Commons operates as a "non-extractive" lender, and as a contributor to and organizer of lenders.[1] Gilbert and Arrington characterize "non-extractive" lending as akin to investing, as lenders work from a truly "vested" interest in the success of the enterprises that they finance. Nonextractive lending limits repayment

1. The Working World, https://www.theworkingworld.org/us/peer-network/.

from borrowers to net earnings after payment of taxes and wages.[2] It also restricts lenders to collateralizing assets purchased with Seed Commons' funds or generated through Seed Commons' funds.[3]

Seed Commons works through its network of "Member Funds," nonprofit locally based lending institutions. Member Funds gain graduated access to capitalization from the Seed Commons Investment Fund, based on when they meet rigorous benchmarks for community lending, financial accountability, and associates' training. Training of the Member Funds entails training in the principles and mechanics of nonextractive lending, and coaching in the nitty-gritty of the process of issuing and tracking loans. In addition to extensive technical training, Seed Commons directs member funds to give priority to borrowers that organize as cooperative enterprises, that function as worker-owned enterprises, and that operate on principles of radical inclusion.

ROC USA also seeks to combat extractive lending. It consists of a national nonprofit LLC and Community Development Financial Institution (CDFI) with a financing arm, a nonprofit regional technical assistance network of nonprofit affiliates, and a nonprofit governance organization.[4] Its mission is to finance the conversion of affordable rental housing units to resident-owned cooperatives, with a focus on communities of manufactured homes.[5] In furtherance of that mission, its financing arm issues pre-development loans to tenants' groups that agree to governance by one member, one vote; and that reach a 40 percent threshold on a vote to convert. If the would-be housing cooperative fails in attaining the 40 percent, then ROC USA forgives the loan; if it achieves the threshold, then ROC USA folds the loan into acquisition lending, for which it will lend up to 60 percent of the cost.[6] Governance structures for the housing cooperatives include managing boards for budgeting and rent-setting, with co-op members voting on the budget and on capital improvements.

The primacy of co-op conversion for ROC USA responds to an acceleration of developers' strategies to buy unorganized tenants out of potentially lucrative housing sites. Seen from this perspective, it is extractive practice that drives ROC USA and Seed Commons to support cooperative governance as a bulwark against predation in both the housing and the lending industries. These institutions demonstrate the nuances of capacity building for sustainable place-conscious development.

Case Study

Seed Commons and Nonextractive Finance

This place-based investment strategy case example describes Seed Commons, a national network of locally rooted, nonextractive Member Funds that bring the power of big finance under community control.[7] The case example features two sections. The first sec-

2. Seed Commons, https://seedcommons.org/about-seed-commons/seed-commons-approach-to-non-extractive-finance/.
3. Seed Commons, https://seedcommons.org/about-seed-commons/seed-commons-approach-to-non-extractive-finance/.
4. *Mission & History*, ROC USA, https://rocusa.org/about-roc-usa/mission-history/.
5. *Id.*
6. *See infra* p. 17.
7. Seed Commons, https://seedcommons.org/.

tion describes the vision, history, and core principles of Seed Commons, the stages of membership of the Member Funds and Seed Commons' nonextractive approach to managing risk. The second section discusses some of the legal aspects of Seed Commons' organization and operations, including the entity type of Seed Commons and the Member Funds, the regulatory framework within which Seed Commons operates, the mechanics of nonextractive finance agreements, governance within the Seed Commons network, and the rights of Member Funds to access Seed Commons capital.

Section I: Seed Commons' Vision, History, Core Principles, and Stages of Fund Membership

Seed Commons' Vision

Seed Commons is an emerging national network of locally based nonextractive development finance organizations that seek to displace today's dominant financial model with a nonextractive and community-engaged financial infrastructure that supports community economic development and service needs, social justice, and environmental sustainability, particularly within communities that have faced the brunt of the extractive economy, deindustrialization, and systemic racial and gender discrimination.[8] The locally based nonextractive development finance organizations, which are called Member Funds, jointly control and govern the centralized Seed Commons Fund. By creating together, a national nonextractive finance infrastructure, the Member Funds are increasingly able to share information and resources and to access capital from socially responsive and social impact capital markets on the best possible terms.[9]

As Seed Commons grows, it will be introducing diverse new organizations into its membership, including both social justice organizations and financial and business development institutions. Seed Commons will drive resources to the cooperative and community-based enterprises that are supporting the movements that are shaping our world—including movements for racial justice, immigrant justice, indigenous land rights, and more. By taking guidance from the grassroots and sharing power and capital at the local level, Seed Commons aims to build the infrastructure necessary for a truly just, democratic, and sustainable new economy.

How Seed Commons Is Organized

As previously stated, Seed Commons consists of individual community-based Membership Funds and a centralized Membership controlled investment fund, the Seed Commons Investment Fund. The investment fund is a nonprofit corporation with IRC §501(c)(3) status and certified by the U.S. Department of the Treasury as a Community Development Finance Institution. The Membership Funds are organized as either unincorporated associations or nonprofit corporations. Some were organized specifically to become Membership Funds while others were existing community organizations that elected to join the Seed Commons network.

8. Seed Commons, https://seedcommons.org/about-seed-commons/.
9. *Id.*

Nonextractive Financing

As practiced by Seed Commons, nonextractive financing consists of the following elements:

- The repayment of Seed Commons financing is paid from after-tax earnings that are described as "Special Net Income." The exact formula is decided on a case-by-case basis but generally includes operational break even plus flexibility for increased worker compensation.[10]
- The financing is secured only by assets that are purchased with Seed Commons financing or were generated as a result of Seed Commons financing.
- The principal event default is nonpayment when Special Net Income is available to make the payment.[11]

Seed Commons' History

Seed Commons evolved from the Recovered Businesses Movement (*Empresas Recuperadas*) of Argentina in which after the financial collapse, workers reopened their abandoned factories and stimulated an economic recovery from the bottom-up.[12] In 2005, Brendan Martin, after earlier learning about the Movement from a film, The Take, by Avi Lewis left his Wall Street job and along with Avi Lewis started The Working World (TWW) in order to provide financing for resurrected worker-owned enterprises.[13] The Argentinian nonextractive financing prototype proved to be very successful and they expanded the model to Nicaragua in 2008.[14] In 2012, they launched a third fund in New York City.[15]

Shortly after TWW began operating in the United States, it became clear that scaling a nonextractive finance model across the United States would require the development of a network of locally based entities that could assess the readiness of potential borrowers and provide the close-at-hand technical assistance that had become a hallmark of TWW's practice of nonextractive finance. TWW, with assistance from other organizations with similar goals, began developing a network of regional finance affiliates in an effort to intensify job creation, job retention, and community-based enterprise development for residents of marginalized communities, both urban and rural.[16] The concept and infrastructure that developed, initially known as the Financial Cooperative, is now known as the Seed Commons.

Throughout the development of Seed Commons, TWW has served as the network's administrative anchor and as mentor to the Member Funds with respect to both the theory and practice of nonextractive finance. TWW has transitioned from a New York City fund to the Seed Commons Fund and has become the source of capital for Member Fund capacity building and for the financing of Member fund mission-aligned and community-based enterprises. At the same time, Member Funds are and have been working to develop their own capacities, both in lending and in the skills required to participate in the governance of Seed Commons.

---

10. Seed Commons, https://seedcommons.org/about-seed-commons/seed-commons-approach-to-non-extractive-finance/.
11. *Id.*
12. *Our History*, Working World, https://www.theworkingworld.org/us/about-us/ (last visited Aug. 29, 2022).
13. *Id.*
14. *Id.*
15. *Id.*
16. *Seed Commons*, Working World, https://www.theworkingworld.org/us/peer-network/.

Seed Commons' Core Principles

To ensure that the network continues to advance the core vision and mission of the Seed Commons, every Member Fund explicitly subscribes to the five core principles.[17]

(1) Building Cooperative, Democratic Ownership within Communities
Seed Commons aims to combat increasing inequality by moving resources to cooperatively owned and democratically controlled enterprises embedded in their communities. This ensures that the benefits of investment are widely distributed to more people, who in turn own and control these assets in ways that are accountable to their communities.

(2) Productive Sustainability
Investing Seed Commons' resources into financially sound and sustainable business projects is the foundation of its work. Long-term sustainability is key to achieving community self-determination and economic independence. Productive sustainability requires careful assessment of potential projects, high-touch training and technical assistance in democratic structure and business fundamentals, and ongoing support after investments are made.

(3) Maximizing Community Benefit
Seed Commons produces community benefit by increasing worker and community ownership, and supporting projects that address social, economic, and environmental justice. It accomplishes this by providing financing and technical assistance to local enterprises that distribute economic power as they distribute ownership.

(4) Radical Inclusion
Seed Commons seeks to be radically inclusive. This means that Seed Commons lends and facilitates lending to people from communities that have historically been excluded from access to economic stability: black and brown families, women and nonbinary people, immigrants and indigenous communities, low-income workers, and others who have faced the brunt of the extractive economy, deindustrialization, and systemic discrimination. This requires that technical assistance, key in assuring the success of investment projects, is provided to all projects to overcome historic lack of access to the resources that are prerequisites for a successful business enterprise.

(5) Nonextraction
Seed Commons strictly uses nonextractive financing. This means the repayment of financing comes only from an increase in revenues or profits stemming from Seed Commons investment. Repayment will not be extracted from prior existing business assets nor from the personal assets of those who make up the enterprise. Collateral will be restricted to items purchased with financing from Seed Commons.

17. *The Principles of Seed Commons*, Seed Commons, https://seedcommons.org/about-seed-commons/our-values/.

Seed Commons Stages of Fund Membership

There are currently over twenty Seed Commons Member Funds.[18] Ten Member Funds have reached the Full Member stage of membership: The Working World (New York, NY), Baltimore Roundtable for Economic Democracy (Baltimore, MD), L.A. Co-op Lab (Los Angeles, CA), Southern Reparations Loan Fund (Regional Network in the U.S. South), Co-op Cincy (Cincinnati, OH), Cooperation Richmond (Richmond, CA), Detroit Community Wealth Fund (Detroit, MI), Cooperation Buffalo (Buffalo, NY), PODER Emma (Asheville, NC), and the Climate Justice Alliance (National Network), which helps to run a cooperative loan fund project called Reinvest in Our Power that makes loans around the United States in projects that address inequity and democratize wealth by moving capital and governance from the extractive economy to the regenerative economy. Four Member Funds have reached the Lending Member stage of membership: Boston Ujima Project (Boston, MA), Co-op Hudson Valley (The Hudson Valley, NY), New Economy Works West Virginia (WV), and Philadelphia Area Cooperative Alliance (Philadelphia, PA). Eight Member Funds have reached the Apprentice Member stage of membership: Co-op Dayton (Dayton, OH), Cooperation New Orleans (New Orleans, LA), New Economy of Tennessee Loan Fund (Nashville, TN), Patchwork Cooperative Loan Fund (Lexington, KY), Repaired Nations (San Francisco Bay Area, CA), The Federation of Southern Cooperatives (U.S. South), The Wind River Food Sovereignty Project (Wind River Reservation, Wyoming), and Start.Coop, a cooperative incubator and accelerator that operates throughout the United States.

Recognizing that learning and enacting the principles of Seed Commons requires time and practice, membership in Seed Commons is staged across four levels, each with different rights and responsibilities: Pre-Apprentice Members, Apprentice Members, Lending Members, and Full Members.

Pre-Apprentice Member Funds are required to send prospective project officers to at least one rigorous four-day training, in which they are exposed to every aspect of the financing process and the tools that are available to them to do their jobs effectively, including Madeline, a library of shared online resources, which includes outlines for introducing a local fund into a community, annotated loan agreement templates, and more. A national training session is held at least annually. This training ends with an Annual Meeting of the membership. As Seed Commons grows, it will begin to hold regional gatherings in order to reach more people in more places. In addition to the face-to-face workshops, the Peer network also meets monthly for webinar-based conference calls.

Additionally, every Member Fund is assigned an experienced Project Officer, who has herself worked through multiple successful financing projects in the role of Loan Coach. At this time, most Loan Coaches are TWW staff, though a few of the other Member Funds at the Full Member stage have staff who are now experienced enough to play this role. The Loan Coach speaks regularly with the Member Fund Project Officer(s) as they work on their first financing projects. In addition, Loan Coaches ensure that Member Fund Project Officer(s) understand how to use Madeline to track potential projects and to prepare loan memos, how to evaluate whether a proposed project meets the values of radical inclusion and has potential to achieve productive sustainability, and how to work effectively with

18. *The Members of the Seed Commons Cooperative*, SEED COMMONS, https://seedcommons.org/peer-members/.

cooperative enterprises that may be struggling with their governance, management, or business model, among other tasks.

Managing Risk within Seed Commons

As described below in the subsection on the mechanics of nonextractive finance agreements,[19] Seed Commons includes in its nonextractive finance agreements with each enterprise that it finances two core nonextractive terms: (1) borrowers are not required to begin interest or principal repayments until they are able to cover their basic operating costs, including reasonable worker salaries; (2) financing agreements never name assets as security unless the collateralized asset has been purchased with the financing agreement proceeds or with the earnings generated from the financing agreement proceeds. These nonextractive terms change the way Member Fund financing organizations mitigate risk, as Member Funds enter into agreements with the borrowing enterprises that function more like investment agreements than lending agreements. Due to the absence of outside collateral to securitize financing within the nonextractive financing framework, Member Fund Project Officers mitigate risk by rigorously assessing the business plans of prospective borrowing enterprises, by improving business plans in conjunction with the prospective borrower, and by working with the borrower after the financing is extended to ensure that the borrower receives the technical assistance they require in order to succeed. This approach puts the borrower and the lender on the same side of the table, as both are deeply incentivized to do all they can to help the enterprise succeed. Aligning the incentives of borrower and lender in this manner upholds the principle of productive sustainability, as Member Funds are incentivized to invest Seed Commons resources in enterprises that can become financially self-sustaining within a reasonable but generally longer period of time than with which a traditional commercial lender would be comfortable.

The Working World developed this approach to nonextractive risk mitigation in its early years, and it continues to use the approach today. The Seed Commons Member Funds practice the following best practices at all stages of project financing to the Peers. These stages include:

- creating sustainable deal flows within a local fund's ecosystem;
- measuring the productive potential of potential financing agreements with the principle of radical inclusion;
- assisting enterprises in developing their business model and operational plans;
- assessing an enterprise's readiness to receive financing and to use the funds productively;
- monitoring closely an enterprise's progress after the financing is extended;
- providing ongoing technical assistance as needed (including helping the enterprise to pivot if needed); and
- following up on repayments once the enterprise has reached profitability.

---

19. *Seed Commons' Approach to Non-extractive Finance*, Seed Commons, https://seedcommons.org/about-seed-commons/seed-commons-approach-to-non-extractive-finance/.

When a Member Fund Project Officer, who is often working closely with a Loan Coach, believes a borrower is ready to receive financing and use it productively, the Loan Coach helps the Project Officer prepare to first present the details of the proposed financing agreement to the Member Fund's Local Sustainability Committee, which functions like a credit committee or loan committee at a more traditional lender. They present a detailed loan memo, which is produced by Madeline, based on the information that the Project Officer has provided over the life of the project. The Local Sustainability Committee asks questions, raises concerns, and may well instruct the Project Officer to do further work with the enterprise to strengthen its business model and plan or to adjust the terms of the proposed loan. Once the Local Sustainability Committee approves a loan, they refer the loan to the National Sustainability Committee, which is comprised of experienced Project Officers representing each of the Full Member Funds of Seed Commons. The same process is followed at the national level: questions, suggestions, cycles of improvement to the business model, and so on, before a loan is finally approved. The decision-making processes of the Local Sustainability Committees and of the National Sustainability Committee ensure that all loans are adequately vetted.

Section II: Seed Commons Legal Aspects: Entity Choice, Regulatory Framework, Nonextractive Finance Agreements, Governance, and Member Fund Rights to Capital

Entity Type: Seed Commons and the Member Funds

As indicated, Seed Commons is a nonprofit corporation that is recognized as a charitable organization pursuant to IRC §501(c)(3)[20] and that is certified by the U.S. Department of the Treasury as a CDFI.[21]

Member Funds are either organized as nonprofit corporations or as unincorporated associations. Some Member Funds have applied for and received 501(c)(3) recognition. Other Member Funds are fiscally sponsored by either Seed Commons or by a local 501(c)(3) organization that they trust.

An outstanding question is whether or not Member Funds can be organized as for-profit entities with individual shareholders or as for-profit subsidiaries of Seed Commons without jeopardizing Seed Commons' IRC §501(c)(3). If so, this would increase the options for local fund raising.

Regulatory Framework: Lending Law and Securities Law

Seed Commons and the Member Funds must engage lending laws and securities laws.

Lending Law

For a variety of reasons, Seed Commons and the Member Funds are exempt from lending laws in most jurisdictions. In some jurisdictions, nonprofit lenders are exempt from lending

20. *Exemption Requirements—501(c)(3) Organizations*, Internal Revenue Service (Mar. 4, 2021), https://www.irs.gov/charities-non-profits/charitable-organizations/exemption-requirements-501c3-organizations.
21. U.S. Department of the Treasury Community Development Financial Institutions Fund, https://www.cdfifund.gov/Pages/default.aspx.

laws. In other jurisdictions, Seed Commons and the Member Funds are not subject to lending laws due to a variety of reasons. For example, in New York, Seed Commons and the Member Funds are not required to receive a lending license because they do not provide financing of less than $50,000 at interest rates exceeding sixteen percent per year.[22] In some jurisdictions, such as California, Seed Commons and the Member Funds must comply with lending laws, including the California Financing Law,[23] which only exempts nonprofit lenders if the nonprofit lender makes no more than thirty-five loans during any given calendar year and if each of the loans: (1) are for $5,000 or more; (2) are for other than personal, family, or household purposes; and (3) are for the primary purpose of achieving one of the 501(c)(3) organization's exempt purposes as a public charity.[24]

Securities Law

Seed Commons, as a 501(c)(3) organization with a charitable purpose to promote economic development in marginalized communities, is exempt from the Securities Act of 1933 under Section 3(a)(4) of the Act, the nonprofit issuer exemption.[25] Any of the Member Funds raising their own capital through the sale of securities may also claim exemption under Section 3(a)(4) of the Securities Act of 1933, if the Member Fund is a 501(c)(3) organization with a charitable purpose to promote economic development in marginalized communities.[26] Seed Commons and the Member Funds must comply with State securities laws (Blue Sky Laws). Most Blue Sky Laws contain nonprofit issuer exemptions that mirror that of Section 3(a)(4) of the Securities Act of 1933. In States with Blue Sky Laws that do not contain a similar nonprofit issuer exemption, Seed Commons and the Member Funds must make use of other exemptions or register their securities.

Nonextractive Agreements with Cooperatives Receiving Financing

Seed Commons' commitment to nonextraction exists most powerfully in the details of the financing terms negotiated with borrowing enterprises, particularly as the terms apply to principal and interest repayment terms and security interests. While the Seed Commons makes many different types of investments (e.g., secured asset purchase loans, working capital loans, line of credit loans, and preferred share equity investments), each deal reflects both nonextractive terms and the needs and capacities of the borrower. Two core nonextractive terms included in all financing agreements are as follows: (1) borrowers are not required to begin interest or principal repayments until they are able to cover their basic operating costs, including reasonable worker salaries; (2) financing agreements never name assets as security unless the collateralized asset has been purchased with the financing agreement proceeds or with the earnings generated from the financing agreement proceeds.[27]

---

22. N.Y. Banking Law § 340 (Consol., 2021).
23. Cal Fin.Code § 22051.
24. Cal Fin.Code § 22064.
25. 15 U.S.C. § 77c(a)(4).
26. *Id.*
27. *Seed Commons' Approach to Non-extractive Finance*, Seed Commons, https://seedcommons.org/about-seed-commons/seed-commons-approach-to-non-extractive-finance/.

The first core term means that a borrowing enterprise enters into default only if it possesses the funds required to make a repayment and it does not do so. Nonextractive financing agreements between Seed Commons and borrowing enterprises define as "Special Net Income," the level of borrowing enterprise revenue beyond the borrowing enterprises' basic operating costs from which the borrowing enterprise is obligated to make repayments. Typically, borrowing enterprises are obligated to allocate a certain percentage of Special Net Income toward making repayments. If the borrowing enterprise does not possess sufficient funds to make a repayment during any given repayment period, the borrowing enterprise is not obligated to make a repayment during that period.

The second core term means that borrowing enterprises are not required to pledge collateral in order to receive nonextractive financing from Seed Commons. The requirement to pledge collateral is a huge barrier for receiving financing from mainstream lenders for many of the borrowing enterprises. Many of the borrowing enterprises are start-up or small enterprises with no assets or very limited assets, and many of the borrowing enterprises are owned by worker-owners who do not possess personal wealth or whose only assets are a house or a car. A core element of Seed Commons' practice of nonextractive finance is to not require borrowing enterprises and owners of borrowing enterprises to risk the limited assets that they possess in order to receive financing from Seed Commons.

An additional aspect of Seed Commons' nonextractive finance practice is that borrowing enterprises that are able to make full repayment of a loan to Seed Commons are expected to continue to make ongoing profit sharing payments to Seed Commons, typically around five percent, for a specified period of time following the completion of repayment of the loan. The profit sharing payments allow Seed Commons to extend its patient nonextractive capital to additional borrower enterprises.[28] Additionally, the hope is that profit sharing payments will eventually provide a main source of capital for the Seed Commons network so that Seed Commons and the Member Funds can become less and less reliable on raising capital from mainstream capital markets.

Nonextractive Investment Contracts with Investors Providing Capital

Seed Commons creates the opportunity for social impact investors to invest with lower risk and greater impact, as Seed Commons combines the heightened impact of community-based nonextractive financing with the reduced risk associated with the broad and diversified capital deployment of an aggregated national fund. Seed Commons raises the majority of its capital through the sale of Debt Notes to social impact investors. Thus far, Seed Commons Member Funds have deployed over $15.3 million nationwide, as of March 2021.[29] Seed Commons currently contains over $22 million in its fund,[30] most of which has been raised through the sale of Debt Notes to social impact investors, though some of Seed Commons' capital has been acquired through grants from social impact investors and from the U.S. Treasury Department's CDFI Fund.

28. *Seed Commons' Approach to Non-extractive Finance*, Seed Commons, https://seedcommons.org/about-seed-commons/seed-commons-approach-to-non-extractive-finance/.
29. *Transforming the Extractive Economy*, Common Future (Dec. 10, 2019), https://www.commonfuture.co/stories/something-is-happening-in-cleveland/.
30. *Impact Report 2020*, Seed Commons, https://seedcommons.org/impact-report-2020/.

To the extent that it can, Seed Commons tries to negotiate interest and default terms in its investment contracts with social impact investors that mirror the terms that Seed Commons provides to the borrowing enterprises. If social impact investors agree to extend nonextractive terms to Seed Commons, it makes it that much easier for Seed Commons to expand the amount of nonextractive financing that it can provide to borrowing enterprises. For example, Seed Commons seeks to negotiate investment contracts with investors that receive a floating rate of interest tied to the performance of the entirety of the Seed Commons portfolio that is capped at five percent and that possesses a floor of zero percent. This way, if Seed Commons, on the aggregate, does not receive interest from the borrowing enterprises, Seed Commons is not obligated to repay interest to its investors. In addition, Seed Commons seeks to negotiate investment contracts with socially conscious investors that contain a default provision that mirrors the Special Net Income provision in the financing agreements that Seed Commons enters into with borrowing enterprises. This provision requires Seed Commons to make repayments to investors during any given period only if Seed Commons has received sufficient repayments from the borrowing enterprises during that period.

Seed Commons' Governance

Seed Commons is governed cooperatively by the Member Funds.[31] The primary governance bodies within Seed Commons are the National Sustainability Committee and the General Assembly.

The National Sustainability Committee, which is elected by Full Members, serves as the primary credit committee for Seed Commons' capital placements that construct most of the Seed Commons investment portfolio. Full Member Funds each appoint a representative to the National Sustainability Committee.

The General Assembly provides for governance rights of one Full Member Fund, one vote. The General Assembly meets at least once each year and chooses representatives for the National Sustainability Committee and other needed committees and reviews and decides strategic directions for Seed Commons.

Member Fund Rights to Seed Commons Capital

Within the Seed Commons Network, Member Funds at various stages of membership possess different rights to access three distinct kinds of capital: Shared Capital, Allocated Capital, and Proprietary Capital.

Shared Capital

Peer Members at all stages of membership possess access to Shared Capital at the discretion of the National Sustainability Committee. As discussed above, a fundamental idea behind Seed Commons is that local Member Funds are more powerful acting together to access capital markets. Whereas a single loan fund, especially a start-up fund, would struggle to develop capital raising capacity, the Member Funds, by banding together, can deploy professionals to represent them and make national offerings that attract capital from multiple states. This kind of networking and national reach is especially needed to meet the capital

31. *Member Board and Sustainability Committee of Seed Commons*, Seed Commons, https://seedcommons.org/board-and-sustainability-committee/.

needs of rural and noncoastal communities that have little access to local capital because they have borne the brunt of extraction and systematic discrimination. Capital raised in this manner is called Shared Capital. All Member Funds in the network can access Shared Capital on a first-come, first-served basis once the loans that they seek to make have been approved by the National Sustainability Committee.

Allocated Capital

Full Member Funds, which have achieved Full Member status by demonstrating sufficient expertise at lending by having loans in active repayment for a certain period of time, are able to access a second pool of capital: Allocated Capital. As a Full Member Fund loans are repaid to Seed Commons, an Allocated Capital Account in the Member Fund's name is credited with the amount of principal repaid. These credits build the pool of allocated capital for the Full Member Fund. If a Full Member Fund wishes to make a loan from their Allocated Capital Account, they may do so at their own discretion, provided the capital is available, as allocated on a first-come, first-served basis. In practice, Member Funds have so far chosen to refer all of their loans to the National Sustainability Committee because they find the level of review extremely useful to their due diligence process. As Seed Commons continues to grow, however, the expectation is that more experienced Full Member Funds will make loans without deferring to the National Sustainability Committee. This will enable Full Member Funds to close deals at a rate that matches Seed Commons' growth plans, the achievement of which are important for ensuring that Seed Commons becomes a diversified fund that can provide lower risk opportunities for investors.

Proprietary Capital

Participating in the Shared Capital and Allocated Capital pools does not preclude any Member Fund from seeking to raise its own capital. In fact, a few Member Funds are already raising money on their own behalf. Capital raised locally is treated as the third form of capital within the Seed Commons network, Proprietary Capital. Member Funds possess sole direction to utilize the Proprietary Capital that they raise. As such, Member Funds may make loans from Proprietary Capital without referring them to the National Sustainability Committee, as long as the loans are consistent with both state and federal law and the mission of the Seed Commons.

Seed Commons uses a cooperative decision-making structure to grow capital in communities of color and low-income communities. The next case study of ROC USA uses cooperative ownership to address the urgent need in many communities for affordable housing.

Case Study

Resident-Owned Communities: ROC USA®

The supply of affordable housing is insufficient and declining in the United States.[32] About 2.7 million U.S. homeowners—two-thirds of which are low-income—live in communities of manufactured housing (sometimes called mobile homes). Manufactured housing

32. *The Problem*, National Low Income Housing Coalition, https://nlihc.org/explore-issues/why-we-care/problem.

is often described as the largest stock of unsubsidized affordable housing in the United States.[33] Until recently, these communities have been owned primarily by local or small-scale owners. But increasingly, corporate investors, including private equity and hedge funds, have purchased manufactured-housing communities, attracted by high returns, achieved by raising rents and fees; deferring maintenance; selling off the land for other uses; and sometimes engaging in predatory practices such as "rent-to-own" and aggressive repossessions.[34]

ROC USA®: History and Organizational Structure

The New Hampshire Community Loan Fund (NHCLF), one of the earliest CDFIs, was founded in 1984 with a pioneering approach to preserving affordable housing by financing conversion to cooperative, resident-owned communities (ROCs).[35] Cooperative ownership of communities makes housing *permanently affordable*, since shares in the co-op are fixed in value and do not appreciate, and the land is preserved forever as a community.

To scale this initiative nationally, in 2008 NHCLF joined with other investors to launch ROC USA® with the mission of making "quality resident ownership viable nationwide and to expand economic opportunities for homeowners in manufactured (mobile) home communities."[36] ROC USA, LLC is a nonprofit social venture that operates with two wholly-owned subsidiaries:

- *ROC USA® Capital* provides financing to cooperatively-owned and governed communities,[37] and
- *ROC USA® Network* includes twelve regional and statewide nonprofit affiliates that are certified to provide pre- and post-purchase training and technical assistance to local communities and to assist in developing local partners in twenty-one states.[38]

In addition, the ROC Association was established in 2013 "to increase customer involvement in the *governance* of ROC USA".[39] A separate nonprofit organization, ROC Association consists of co-op communities that are or have been under contract with ROC USA® Network affiliates.[40] The co-ops elect three representatives to serve s on the national fifteen-member ROC USA board of directors.[41]

---

33. U.S. Census Bureau/American FactFinder. *B25033: Total Population in Occupied Housing Units by Tenure by Units in Structure*. 2010-2014 American Community Survey, https://data.census.gov/cedsci/table?q=Total%20Population%20In%20Occupied%20Housing%20Units%20by%20Tenure%20by%20Units%20in%20Structure&tid=ACSDT5YAIAN2010.B25033https://rocusa.org/wp-content/executed-and-Certified-01.06.2020.pdf.
34. Sheelah Kolhatkar, *What Happens When Investment Firms Acquire Trailer Parks*, New Yorker (Mar. 8, 2021), https://www.newyorker.com/magazine/2021/03/15/what-happens-when-investment-firms-acquire-trailer-parks.
35. *In the Beginning*, Community Loan Fund, https://communityloanfund.org/about/history/beginning/.
36. *Mission & History*, ROC USA, https://rocusa.org/about-roc-usa/mission-history/.
37. *Financing*, ROC USA, https://rocusa.org/become-a-roc/financing/.
38. *Network Affiliates*, ROC USA, https://rocusa.org/about-roc-usa/network-affiliates/.
39. *ROC Association*, ROC USA, https://rocusa.org/about-roc-usa/roc-association-2/.
40. *Bylaws of ROC Association*, ROC USA, https://rocusa.org/wp-content/uploads/2022/02/ROC-Association-Bylaws-executed-and-Certified-01.06.2020.pdf.
41. *Id.*

Financial Structure and Investment History

Rare if not unique among CDFIs, ROC USA® LLC was launched in 2008 with $500,000 in *equity investments* from each the New Hampshire Community Loan Fund (NHCLF); Prosperity Now (formerly, the Corporation for Enterprise Development), and Capital Impact Partners.[42] These three organizations became members of the LLC. Other sources of equity have included the Ford Foundation ($3 million in 2007), NeighborWorks® America ($500,000 in 2008), JPMorgan Chase & Co. Foundation ($1.75 million), and an anonymous donor ($750,000 in 2020).[43]

ROC USA® Capital is a federally certified CDFI.[44] From 2010 through 2019, it received $5.1 million in grants from the U.S. Treasury Department's CDFI Fund. ROC USA® Capital has been profitable since 2011. In 2019, the three nonprofits that made original equity investments in the LLC each made second-round investments of $750,000. Beginning in 2019, ROC USA is paying five percent dividends on both rounds of LLC Member investments.

Key Accomplishments

Between May of 2008 and August of 2020, ROC USA® Capital financed more than $260 million for eighty-eight resident-owned communities, and preserved 7,886 homes.[45] In 2019 alone, ROC USA® Capital financed more than $50 million in project loans, helping co-ops to secure 1,242 homes in ten states.[46] In 2020, ROC USA Network represents 264 co-op communities and 18,000 Member-owners in 18 states.

Community Ownership and Governance

Manufactured-housing communities considering conversion to resident ownership typically must assess potential interest and study legal, financial, environmental, and other issues. If and when 40 percent of prospective owners express interest in cooperative conversion, they may apply to ROC USA® Capital for a forgivable loan to cover legal and due diligence costs and may contract with one of Network's affiliates that provides technical assistance. ROC USA® has standardized the ownership model so all co-ops in the Network function the same, providing ROC USA® with the ability to scale training and development services.

Only after receiving full due diligence and financing commitments do, the Member-owners of the co-op vote if it wants to purchase the community. If they vote no, ROC USA® forgives its loan and absorbs the cost; if there is a majority approval, the pre-purchase loan is folded into the acquisition financing package. ROC USA® Capital standard acquisition loan product covers 110 percent of the acquisition price to account for closing costs and reserves. The loan is then participated with banks, insurers and housing finance authorities. Capital retains the B tranche and services the loan. In some cases, communities secure other sub-debt or grants to fund the purchase or community improvements.

---

42. *Mission & History*, ROC USA, https://rocusa.org/about-roc-usa/mission-history/.
43. *Equity*, ROC USA, https://rocusa.org/equity/.
44. *Id.*
45. *Making Resident Ownership a Reality Nationwide*, ROC USA, https://rocusa.org/cms/assets/uploads/2018/05/ROC-USA-10-year-pdf-w_-linksFINAL.pdf4.
46. *Making Resident Ownership a Reality Nationwide*, ROC USA, https://rocusa.org/cms/assets/uploads/2018/05/ROC-USA-10-year-pdf-w_-linksFINAL.pdf4.

Co-op members elect a board to lead the purchase process and oversee management. The co-op assumes governance, from the start and eventually selects a management company. Members vote on the annual budget, including site fees, capital improvements, financing, bylaws, and community rules.

Benefits from Community Ownership and Governance

Reduced living costs for residents. ROC USA® data has shown that annual rent increases on ROC lots have averaged 0.9 percent, compared to 3.9 percent for commercially owned communities. Five years after co-op conversion, rents for lots in ROCs have on average been $30 a month lower than prevailing market rates.[47]

Increased home values. When commercial investors raise lot rents for residents, homes in a community become less attractive to potential buyers. By keeping rents lower than comparable properties, ROCs preserve or increase the value of homes owned by residents, thus building individual assets. (Shares in the community-owned land do not rise in price, which is essential to maintaining permanent affordability.)

Security of tenure: "When you're a renter, whether it be a park or a home, there's always the chance that could be taken away from you. When you own your own place and you're part of a co-op, you don't have to worry about that"[48] (Laurie Westendorf, Montana, quoted in ROC strategic plan).

Psychological benefits of ownership: Security of tenure and democratic governance bring important psychological benefits. "Knowing we're going to own it and run it the way we want to run it is such a relief. Now everyone is going to have a say"[49] (Nancy Froio, Massachusetts, quoted in ROC strategic plan).

Improved health and safety conditions: ROCs are highly motivated to address infrastructure, environmental, and maintenance issues that often are neglected by commercial owners who seek to maximize profit. "Things that need to be taken care of are now, and not let go like they used to be"[50] (Brian Miller, Delaware, quoted in ROC strategic plan). Over ten years, ROC USA calculated that ROCs had invested more than $49 million in health and safety improvements, including water, sewage, and drainage.

Community Empowerment: Governance and Capacity Building

Democratic and cooperative principles are embodied nationally in ROC USA and its affiliates. Resident-owner participation in governance is explicit and prominent in ROC's strategic plan: "ROC leaders and members will drive the national resident-ownership movement. . . . [R]aising up their voices matters. . . . ROC USA® is governed in part by the communities we serve, and [our] strategic plan engages ROC leaders even more deeply in the governance, strategy and programming [of ROC USA]."[51]

47. Independent Rent Study Shows ROCs Grow More Affordable Every Year, ROC USA, https://rocusa.org/stories/independent-rent-study/.

48. *Sustainability Scaling Resident Ownership: Leadership and Impact*, ROC USA: Strategic Plan July 2018-June 2021, 12, https://www.rocusa.org/wp-content/uploads/2018/08/ROC-USA-Strategic-Plan_FINAL.pdf.

49. *Id.*

50. *Id.*

51. *Id.* at 3.

The *ROC Association* is a nonprofit cooperative created in 2013 "to increase customer involvement in the governance of ROC USA®,"[52] and, specifically, to elect directors to the national board of directors of ROC USA®. Individuals are elected by their respective communities. ROC USA divides the country into three regions, each of which elects one representative for a two-year term.[53] To "strengthen the voices and skills of volunteers leaders from resident-owned communities," ROC USA®, in 2018, established the *ROC Leadership Institute*, a three-day national training program, and, in 2019, graduated a class of one hundred representing fifty communities.[54] A similar focus on empowering resident-owners is evident at the local level, as well: The NHCLF has developed a Community Leadership Program and a Policy Academy for ROC members.[55]

Sustainable Scaling: Challenges and Constraints

In its strategic plan adopted in 2018 titled "Sustainably Scaling Resident Ownership," ROC USA® set the ten-year goal of increasing the number of ROCs preserved from 220 to 500, thereby increasing the number of homes preserved from 14,443 to 30,000.[56]

Financial challenges

CDFIs—like other financial institutions—grow their balance sheets by increasing their equity (net worth), thus enabling them to raise additional debt to fund their growing loan volume. While all CDFIs need equity, ROC USA® is distinctive in that it incurs potential costs when it must forgive loans to communities that decide not to convert after borrowing for initial feasibility studies. The CDFI Fund has been a key source of substantial equity grants for ROC USA® as for hundreds of other CDFIs, but the fund's equity grants must be matched with nonfederal equity. However, the sources and supply of equity donations are limited.

Cost of funds is an important concern for CDFIs, which pass on their own cost of capital to borrowers. In order to keep ROCs as affordable as possible for residents, ROC USA® needs access to loan capital at *concessionary rates*. Donors can maximize their impact on communities by providing loans to CDFIs at the lowest possible cost and, where possible, coupling loans with equity donations.

Long-term financing is a challenge for ROC USA® and for other CDFIs engaged in housing finance. Financing typically available to and through ROC USA® typically has a ten-year term, after which loans must be refinanced. By providing loans with terms of fifteen years or longer, investors can reduce administrative burdens on CDFIs and communities; help ensure stable, favorable rates; and enhance the stability of tenure for residents.

---

52. *ROC Association*, ROC USA, https://rocusa.org/about-roc-usa/roc-association-2/.
53. *Bylaws of ROC Association*, ROC USA, https://rocusa.org/wp-content/uploads/2022/02/ROC-Association-Bylaws-executed-and-Certified-01.06.2020.pdf.
54. *Leadership Institute Empowers ROC Leaders*, ROC USA, https://rocusa.org/about-roc-usa/roc-leadership-institute/.
55. *Community Leadership*, Community Loan Fund, https://communityloanfund.org/focus/roc-nh/training/leadership/.
56. *Sustainability Scaling Resident Ownership: Leadership and Impact*, ROC USA: Strategic Plan July 2018-June 2021, 2, https://www.rocusa.org/wp-content/uploads/2018/08/ROC-USA-Strategic-Plan_FINAL.pdf.

Marketplace challenges

The drive to expand community ownership faces aggressive competition from private equity and hedge funds, which currently control a significant market share, have vast resources, and, in some cases, are aggressively seeking to expand. *Opportunity to Purchase* (or, *Right of First Refusal*) laws help level the playing field, since they provide manufactured-housing communities with notice of pending sales and the right to match investors' purchase offers. These laws make it possible for ROC USA® present homeowners with a viable opportunity to choose resident ownership, but they have been adopted in only five states. Otherwise, ROC USA® undertakes market development to find local community owners interested in offering their community to the homeowners. Donors can advance the cause of resident ownership by supporting advocacy efforts to change the laws. Moreover, they can support organizing and educational campaigns of ROC USA®, its affiliates, and other allies.

Recommendations for Philanthropy

Apart from addressing investment challenges—the need for donated equity, concessionary rates, longer terms—philanthropies can increase their impact through other means.

The field can benefit from increased support for data-gathering and documentation. In various ways, the experience of cooperative ownership suggests positive impacts on health. There is considerable anecdotal reporting that *becoming owners* enhances residents' sense of personal security and reduces stress, especially—although not only—among older residents. Additional research may be able to demonstrate *improved health outcomes*. Similarly, research may demonstrate the public health benefits of ROC improvements in *physical infrastructure and/or environmental conditions*, such as water quality. *Reducing displacement* through cooperative ownership may also improve the well-being of health of residents: Forced relocation is stress-inducing and often a health-altering event for individuals.

Funding of "soft" costs may help expand community ownership and deepen participant engagement. Conversion to cooperative ownership requires substantial *education and training*, not only in the pre-purchase phase but also in the ongoing management and governance of ROCs. Dedicated funding for these costs can help to keep down the costs of financing, which otherwise are covered by interest on loans charged to communities. *Resident participation* in advocacy and policymaking—locally, statewide, and nationally—may be expanded by funding travel or other expenses.

Chapter 10

Beyond Impact: Shifting the Field of Impact Investment to Achieve Economic Justice and Racial Equity

Dorcas R. Gilmore

> "Capitalism does not permit an even flow of economic resources. With this system, a small privileged few are rich beyond conscience, and almost all others are doomed to be poor at some level. That's the way the system works. And since we know that the system will not change the rules, we are going to have to change the system."
>
> —Dr. Martin Luther King, Jr.[1]

National and global events since the dawn of this new decade—the killing of George Floyd in 2020 and subsequent global protests against racial violence, ticking of the climate clock with more severe weather catastrophes, and widening income inequality—show pervasive and persistent racial, environmental, and economic inequities. As the American public has

1. Harry Belafonte, My Song: A Memoir of Art, Race, and Defiance (Knopf, 2011).

focused attention on these inequities through protests and a variety of corporate campaigns, investors have taken note.[2] In June 2020, Confluence Philanthropy, a membership organization of "private, public and community foundations; family offices; individual donors; and their values-aligned investment advisors representing more than $92 billion in philanthropic assets under management, and over $3.5 trillion in managed capital,"[3] asked its members to commit to discussing racial equity at their investment meetings. By October 2020, sixty-seven institutional investors with a combined $1.9 trillion in assets under management made this commitment.[4]

Increasingly, the American public demands social equity goals and accountability from corporations. Generational changes demonstrate the need for alignment between business practices and the impact of those choices on Main Street and in communities most excluded from the economy. Consumption patterns of Generation Z, those born between the mid-1990s and early 2010s, are more driven by a company's ethics, practices, and social impact than those of any other generation before them.[5] Societal and generational shifts call for change in the field of impact investing to deliver greater social impact that achieves economic justice and racial equity. These bold goals necessitate challenging the underlying inequities in the market.

This chapter is a report from the leading edge of transformative finance and reveals how individual and institutional investors can address systemic inequities in the structure and deployment of impact investments. Based on interviews with nine leaders deploying specific transformative finance approaches,[6] this chapter demonstrates that fundamental changes in the investment field are possible, and that there is a breadth of investment strategies that advance racial and economic equity. This chapter provides lessons and approaches from investors at one end of the impact investing spectrum, framed by the Global Impact Investing Network (GIIN)[7] using below-market investments of grants, equity, and subordinated loans, to investors on the other end, seeking market-rate returns along with impact outcomes. The chapter concludes by considering the import of such practices for lawyers representing impact investor clients committed to shifting the status quo.

---

2. *See Top of Mind: Investing in Racial Economic Equality*, Global Macro Rpt. (Goldman Sachs), July 16, 2020, https://www.goldmansachs.com/insights/pages/investing-in-racial-economic-equality-f/report.pdf; *see also* Press Release, Council of Institutional Investors, Leading Investor Group Calls for Action on Racism (June 9, 2020), https://www.cii.org/calltoaction.

3. Confluence Philanthropy, https://www.confluencephilanthropy.org/ (last visited Mar. 3, 2022).

4. Morgan Stanley, Racial Equity Investing 3 (2020), https://www.giarts.org/sites/default/files/2021-06-24-racial-equity-investing.pdf.

5. Tracy Francis & Fernanda Hoefel, *The Influence of Gen Z—the First Generation of True Digital Natives—Is Expanding*, McKinsey & Company (Nov. 12, 2018), https://www.mckinsey.com/industries/consumer-packaged-goods/our-insights/true-gen-generation-z-and-its-implications-for-companies.

6. *See infra* pp. 215–220. The interviews that led to this chapter asked a series of questions that focused on the (1) most useful investment tools/approaches to achieving social and economic equity, (2) most promising practices or innovations in the field of investing for social and economic equity, (3) key trends and challenges in the field of investing for social and economic equity, (4) necessary shifts the field of investing for social and economic equity needs to make to achieve equitable outcomes in the most under-resourced/disinvested communities, and (5) recommendations for lawyers serving these investors.

7. *What You Need to Know about Impact Investing: Elements of Impact Investing*, Global Impact Investing Network (GIIN), https://thegiin.org/impact-investing/need-to-know/#what-is-impact-investing (presenting a spectrum of eight forms of impact investing sorted by risk and return, from below-market investments to market investments).

Racial and Economic Equity in Impact Investing

The twenty-first century's movements for racial and economic equity have fueled a new generation of changemaking investors, intermediaries, and social entrepreneurs promoting the advancement of impact investing, with the goal of creating more just and equitable outcomes for all communities. These changemaking investors and intermediaries are transformative capital visionaries, central to ensuring that investments for social and economic equity meaningfully achieve their long-term goals in low-income communities and communities of color.

These transformative capital visionaries emphasize that investments must not only aim to have impact, but they must also work to undo structural inequities and remake the economy. They assert that the economy must significantly change to create economic justice and racial equity in communities of color and low-income communities. Just as large-scale public policies and concerted private actions created the present matrix of interconnected social and economic inequities,[8] these investors and financial intermediaries assert that remaking the economy to be fair and equitable also requires public policy and public finance changes at all levels, along with private sector mindset shifts and private investment changes. They believe large-scale change is possible, and that this systemic, societal scale of change requires a transformative finance approach to imagine and use a range of private investments.

Transform Finance[9] identifies three core principles of a transformative finance approach: "1) it meaningfully engages communities in the design and governance of investment processes; 2) it adds more value than it extracts; and 3) it fairly balances risk and return between investors and non-investors."[10]

Investor Mindsets and Behaviors Must Change and Their Investment Decisions Must Address Structural Inequities

Investment for racial and economic equity requires key changes in thought and action. A shift in power and control over investment structure and measurement from traditional investors to the intended beneficiaries of investment—low-income communities and communities of color—is imperative. Realizing this shift in power and control demands a deep understanding and analysis of the roles of racial capitalism, "the process of deriving social and economic value from the racial identity of another person,"[11] and of economic extraction in wealth creation across asset classes. This structural approach takes a broader

8. *See* Melvin Oliver & Thomas Shapiro, Black Wealth, White Wealth: A New Perspective on Racial Inequality (Routledge, 2nd ed. 2006); Richard Rothstein, The Color of Law: A Forgotten History of How Our Government Segregated America (Liveright, 2018); Ira Katznelson, When Affirmative Action Was White: An Untold History of Racial Inequality in Twentieth Century America (W. W. Norton & Comp., 2006).

9. Transform Finance, http://transformfinance.org/ (last visited Mar. 3, 2022). Transform Finance is a nonprofit research and action organization that works with investors and social entrepreneurs to "challenge legacy investment approaches, seed transformative investment models, and build movement power." *Id.*

10. Andrea Armeni & Curt Lyon, Grassroots Community Engaged Investment: Redistributing Power Over Investment Processes as the Key to Fostering Equitable Outcomes, Transform Finance at 2 (Apr. 2021), https://static1.squarespace.com/static/54cfca5be4b06d2d0d7c0f1d/t/6065dc5d38b2ae3f783b1df6/1617288341085/Transform+Finance+Grassroots+Community+Engaged+Invesment+2021-04-01.pdf.

11. *See* Nancy Leong, *Racial Capitalism*, 126 Harv. L. Rev. 2151 (2013).

and deeper view of the impacts of an investment: "The negative side of economic inequity is not always clear on its face. We have to ask structural questions of: 'What is the quality of jobs? What is this doing to the tax base? Is this displacing a historically public investment?' We must look at the second layer of effects" (Andrea Armeni).

Understand the Root Causes of Inequities: History and Present of Racial Capitalism

The history of economic extraction from communities of color in the United States is well documented.[12] Settler colonialism in Indigenous lands and the enslavement of Africans are the historical foundations of the American economy.[13] Racial capitalism continued with racialized exclusion from various aspects of economic opportunity—education,[14] employment,[15] housing,[16] credit,[17] and business capital.[18] Not until the 1950s through 1970s with *Brown v. Board of Education*,[19] the Civil Rights Act of 1964,[20] the Voting Rights Act of 1965,[21] the Fair Housing Act of 1968,[22] and the 1976 amendments to the Equal Credit

12. *See* Janelle Jones, *The Racial Wealth Gap: How African-Americans Have Been Shortchanged Out of the Materials to Build Wealth*, Economic Policy Institute: Working Economics Blog (Feb. 13, 2017), https://www.epi.org/blog/the-racial-wealth-gap-how-african-americans-have-been-shortchanged-out-of-the-materials-to-build-wealth/; Christian E. Weller et al., *The State of Communities of Color in the U.S. Economy*, CAP (Jan. 21, 2011), http://cdn.americanprogress.org/wp-content/uploads/issues/2011/01/pdf/comm_of_color.pdf?_ga=2.152568560.878212577.1664247401-2126491866.1664247401; Jeremie Greer, *Wealth Building Won't Work While Wealth Extraction Continues*, ShelterForce (Feb. 14, 2022), https://shelterforce.org/2022/02/14/wealth-building-wont-work-while-wealth-extraction-continues/; Ericka Taylor, *A New Online Educational Tool on the History of U.S. Wealth Extraction*, Inequality.org (Sept. 9, 2021), https://inequality.org/research/educational-tool-history-of-wealth-extraction/.

13. Natsu Taylor Saito, Settler Colonialism, Race, and the Law: Why Structural Racism Persists (2020). *See, generally*, Colonial Racial Capitalism (Susan Koshy et al., eds., 2002).

14. *See* Nataliya Braginsky, *Not an "Achievement Gap," A Racial Capitalism Chasm*, Law and Political Economy Project (Nov. 18, 2020), https://lpeproject.org/blog/not-an-achievement-gap-a-racial-capitalist-chasm/. *See also* Jay Shambaugh, Ryan Nunn, & Stacy A. Anderson, *How Racial and Regional Inequality Affect Economic Opportunity*, Brookings (Feb. 15, 2019), https://www.brookings.edu/blog/up-front/2019/02/15/how-racial-and-regional-inequality-affect-economic-opportunity/. "*Public education*, which has often been underfunded in African-American majority schools, limiting skill acquisition and upward mobility for black Americans." *Id.*

15. *See* Jay Shambaugh, Ryan Nunn, & Stacy A. Anderson, *How Racial and Regional Inequality Affect Economic Opportunity*, Brookings (Feb. 15, 2019), https://www.brookings.edu/blog/up-front/2019/02/15/how-racial-and-regional-inequality-affect-economic-opportunity/. "Employment discrimination, which makes it more difficult for black families to escape from poverty or build wealth in their community." *Id. See also* Danyelle Solomon, Abril Castro, & Connor Maxwell, *Systematic Inequality and Economic Opportunity*, CAP (Aug. 7, 2019), https://www.americanprogress.org/article/systematic-inequality-economic-opportunity/.

16. *See* Danyelle Solomon, Abril Castro, & Connor Maxwell, *Systematic Inequality: Displacement, Exclusion, and Segregation*, CAP (Aug. 7, 2019), https://www.americanprogress.org/article/systemic-inequality-displacement-exclusion-segregation/.

17. *See Community Development Innovation Review: The Racialized Roots of Financial Exclusion*, Federal Reserve Bank of San Francisco (Aug. 19, 2021), https://www.frbsf.org/community-development/publications/community-development-investment-review/2021/august/the-racialized-roots-of-financial-exclusion/.

18. *America 2021: The Opportunity to Advance Racial Equity*, McKinsey & Company (Feb. 17, 2021), https://www.mckinsey.com/featured-insights/diversity-and-inclusion/america-2021-the-opportunity-to-advance-racial-equity (providing that the average starting capital for Black-owned businesses is $35,000, relative to $107,000 for white-owned businesses).

19. Brown v. Board of Education, 347 U.S. 483 (1954).

20. Civil Rights Act of 1964, 42 U.S.C. §§ 2000e (1964).

21. Voting Rights Act of 1965, 52 U.S.C. § 10101 (1965).

22. Fair Housing Act of 1968, 42 U.S.C. §§ 3601-19 (1968).

Opportunity Act[23] did the United States meaningfully address racial exclusion in the economy post-Reconstruction.

However, whether measured by median household income, poverty, or wealth, the United States' stark, racialized economic inequality persists, particularly between white and Black and Indigenous people, who bear the brunt of growing income and wealth disparities in the United States.[24] As of 2019, the median yearly household income of Black people, at approximately $45,000, is about 60 percent the median income for white households, $76,000. This gap is wider than the gap in median income that was measured between white and Black households in 1975.[25] A racialized pattern of poverty also continues with the rates of poverty for Black and Hispanic people being 2.5 and 2 times higher, respectively, than the rate for non-Hispanic white people.[26] Unemployment rates also evidence this racialized trend, with the rate for Black people and American Indians and Alaska Natives being almost double the rate for whites and 1.3 times greater than the rate for Hispanic people.[27] In addition to the present economic disparities of income, poverty, and unemployment, racialized wealth disparities indicate long-standing and multigenerational impacts. Unlike income, wealth is a key indicator of long-term economic stability.[28]

According to the Federal Reserve, there is an enormous disparity in wealth in the U.S., with non-Hispanic white people holding 83.5% of the country's wealth in the third quarter of 2021[29] compared to being 59.3% of the population according to the U.S. Census Bureau as of July 2021.[30] The percentage of wealth held by non-Hispanic white people has remained disproportionate for at least 30 years, ranging from 90-82% since 1990.[31] This

23. Equal Credit Opportunity Act, 15 U.S.C. § 1691 (1974) (amended 1976).

24. Juliana Menasce Horowitz, Ruth Igielnik, & Rakesh Kochhar, *1. Trends in Income and Wealth Inequality*, Pew Research Center (Jan. 9, 2020), https://www.pewresearch.org/social-trends/2020/01/09/trends-in-income-and-wealth-inequality/.

25. Jessica Semega et al., *Income and Poverty in the United States: 2019-Current Population Reports*, U.S. Census Bureau (Sept. 2020), https://www.census.gov/library/visualizations/2020/demo/p60-270.html.

26. *Figure 8: Poverty Rate and Percentage Point Change by Selected Characteristics: People*, U.S. Census Bureau, https://www.census.gov/content/dam/Census/library/visualizations/2020/demo/p60-270/Figure8.pdf. The 2019 poverty rate for Whites was 9.1, for non-Hispanic Whites was 7.3, for Blacks was 18.8, for Hispanics was 15.7, and for Asians was 7.3. *Id.*

27. BLS Reports: Labor Force Characteristics by Race and Ethnicity, Bureau of Labor Statistics (Dec. 2020), https://www.bls.gov/opub/reports/race-and-ethnicity/2019/home.htm. "In 2019, the unemployment rate averaged 6.1 percent for Blacks, 6.1 percent for American Indians and Alaska Natives, 5.3 percent for people of Two or More Races, 3.3 percent for Whites, 3.2 percent for Native Hawaiians and Other Pacific Islanders, and 2.7 percent for Asians. The unemployment rate was 4.3 percent for Hispanics." *Id.*

28. *See Prototype Measures of Economic Well-Being and Growth*, U.S. Dep't of Comm.: Bureau of Econ. Analysis, https://apps.bea.gov/well-being/ (describing that "[a]nother key measure of the economic well-being of a nation is its wealth. Wealth increases economic welfare by supplementing income for large purchases, unemployment, emergencies, retirement, education, and bequests to heirs.").

29. *DFA: Distributional Financial Accounts*, Board of Governors of the Federal Reserve System, https://www.federalreserve.gov/releases/z1/dataviz/dfa/distribute/chart/#quarter:126;series:Net%20worth;demographic:race;population:1,3,5,7;units:shares;range:1989.3,2021.1.

30. *QuickFacts: United States*, U.S. Census Bureau, https://www.census.gov/quickfacts/fact/table/US/PST045219.

31. Ana Hernández Kent & Lowell Ricketts, *Has Wealth Inequality in America Changed Over Time? Here Are Key Statistics*, Federal Reserve Bank of St. Louis (Dec. 2, 2020), https://www.stlouisfed.org/open-vault/2020/december/has-wealth-inequality-changed-over-time-key-statistics.

can be attributed to the inheritance of generational wealth and a lack of economic mobility for people of color, particularly Black and Hispanic populations.[32]

These present and multigenerational economic disparities are also connected to a range of health disparities.[33] Disparities in access to and quality of healthcare as well as disparate exposure to health risks across racial and ethnic groups in the United States are well established.[34] One current example can be found in the statistics of COVID-19 cases, hospitalizations, and deaths in the United States. The Centers for Disease Control and Prevention highlighted Black, Native American, and Hispanic and Latinx populations' higher rates of COVID cases, hospitalizations, and deaths than the national average.[35] Native Americans are at more than triple the risk of hospitalization, and more than double the risk of death.[36] Health disparities are one important example of the community and individual impacts of racialized disparities in community investment. To address these racialized disparities in health, wealth, and well-being, communities across the country continue to organize and demand investment shifts to structurally change long-standing inequities.[37] These demands have led to some investors and social entrepreneurs leading the way with intentional approaches that advance racial and economic equity.[38]

---

32. *DFA: Distributional Financial Accounts*, Board of Governors of the Federal Reserve System, https://www.federalreserve.gov/releases/z1/dataviz/dfa/distribute/chart/#quarter:126;series:Net%20worth;demographic:race;population:1,3,5,7;units:shares;range:1989.3,2021.1; Neil Bhutta et al., *Disparities in Wealth by Race and Ethnicity in the 2019 Survey of Consumer Finances*, Board of Governors of the Federal Reserve System (Sept. 28, 2020), https://www.federalreserve.gov/econres/notes/feds-notes/disparities-in-wealth-by-race-and-ethnicity-in-the-2019-survey-of-consumer-finances-20200928.htm.

33. *See* The Root Causes of Health Inequity, NIH (Nat'l Academic Press, 2017), https://www.ncbi.nlm.nih.gov/books/NBK425845/ (identifying that a root cause of health inequity is an unequal allocation of power and resources manifested in unequal social, economic, and environmental conditions). *See also* Nambi Ndugga & Samantha Artiga, *Disparities in Health and Health Care: 5 Key Questions and Answers*, KFF (May 11, 2021), https://www.kff.org/racial-equity-and-health-policy/issue-brief/disparities-in-health-and-health-care-5-key-question-and-answers/ (explaining that health outcomes and disparities are driven by social and economic inequities).

34. *See* The Root Causes of Health Inequity, NIH (Nat'l Academic Press, 2017), https://www.ncbi.nlm.nih.gov/books/NBK425845/ (providing examples of the impact of structural inequities). "African American women are more likely to give birth to low-birthweight infants, and their newborns experience higher infant death rates that are not associated with any biological differences." *Id.*

35. Hospitalization and Death by Race/Ethnicity, CDC, https://www.cdc.gov/coronavirus/2019-ncov/covid-data/investigations-discovery/hospitalization-death-by-race-ethnicity.html (Feb. 1, 2022).

36. *Id.*

37. *See Advocate for Social and Economic Justice*, AFL-CIO, https://aflcio.org/what-unions-do/social-economic-justice (last visited Dec. 13, 2021). "One of the ways we work to restore balance to our economy is by changing corporate practices through shareholder-driven reforms that are designed to increase corporate accountability." *Id. See also NCRC, Morgan Stanley Announce $15 Billion Plan to Increase Lending and Investments in Lower-Income Communities*, NCRC (Sept. 10, 2020), https://ncrc.org/ncrc-morgan-stanley-announce-15-billion-plan-to-increase-lending-and-investments-in-lower-income-communities/ (explaining that the National Community Reinvestment Coalition expects Morgan Stanley's lending and investments in low- and moderate-income communities and communities of color to increase by 43 percent annually over previous years); *The NAACP Minority Empowerment ETF: Overview*, Impact Shares, https://www.impactetfs.org/NACP-etf/ (last visited Mar. 4, 2022) (providing an index, which is designed to provide exposure to companies in the United States with strong racial and ethnic diversity policies in place).

38. *See infra* pp. 12–17 (describing a range of communities and individuals striving to demand equitable investment shifts). *See, e.g.*, The Racial Equity Asset Lab, https://racialequityassetlab.org/; Common Future, https://www.commonfuture.co/; Transform Finance, http://transformfinance.org/; Kataly Foundation, https://www.katalyfoundation.org/; Impact America Fund, https://www.impactamericafund.com/; SOC Investment Group, https://www.socinvestmentgroup.com/.

Act Intentionally to Achieve Racial and Economic Equity

An understanding of racial capitalism and shift in mindset must also be followed by intentional actions that address racial and economic inequities. Intentionality, a core characteristic of impact investing, includes identifying investment opportunities, structuring investments, and working with communities to ensure investments achieve racial and economic equity goals. Intentionally focusing on racial and economic equity requires investors and the impact investing community to:

(1) Change mindsets that are primarily focused on returns, even concessionary returns, to prioritize racial and economic equity through community investment;
(2) Challenge assumptions about communities who are the intended beneficiaries and the types of capital that communities need;
(3) Engage with communities who are the intended beneficiaries of the investment capital as co-investors of capital, instead of passive recipients of capital;
(4) Commit to measurable shifts of investor power to communities;
(5) Re-imagine investment risk and risk analysis to consider risks to communities that might result from the failure of the investment;
(6) Focus on communities' visions and goals for resilience and well-being as measurements of investment impact;
(7) Think creatively beyond specific investment tools to holistic investment approaches that incorporate leveraging investors' full spectrum of investment resources, including financial capital, social capital, and human capital, to achieve racial and economic equity;
(8) Leverage investments to achieve bold, transformational societal change;
(9) Connect across issue areas and build in an intersectional approach to investment decision making; and
(10) Understand, embrace, and invest in community-led initiatives at all stages of capital raising and invest in ecosystems of support for community-led initiatives that advance racial and economic equity.

This intentional approach centers community control, community wealth building and economic mobility, and access to capital in a range of asset classes. To achieve measurable community-defined results along with systems change, investors must first be willing to learn and appreciate the extent of structural inequalities and adopt a mindset that prioritizes community impact and greater community control of investment decision-making over investor returns and control. This transformative finance approach questions the role of investor return in investment decision making and calls for community return as a co-equal to, and in some instances higher priority than, that of the financial investor.

Concessionary returns, or below-market-rate returns, are an established part of the impact investing landscape. Intentional transformative finance investors and investment intermediaries call for investors to move beyond concessionary returns and commit to understanding the root causes of social inequalities and make investment decisions that address those structural inequalities through restructuring investment governance models, goals, and measurements.

Promising Practices in the Field

With this intentionality of approach, transformative investors and financial intermediaries interviewed for this chapter highlighted several promising practices and trends in the field of impact investing to grow, replicate, and innovate for larger field shifts to directly address racial and economic inequities. These promising practices signal the possibilities for shifts in investment mindset and approach in the larger field. This section focuses on ten promising practices in the field of impact investing that have the potential to address structural inequities and/or shift power and control of investment decision making and outcomes to communities of color and low-income communities.

(1) Using Race and Gender Lenses in Environmental, Social, and Governance (ESG) Investing
Applying a racial equity lens in ESG investing[39] has become a more prominent approach.[40] Similarly, the consideration[41] and use[42] of a gender lens have increased.[43] These increases are demonstrative of a shift in the focus in ESG investing.

(2) Gathering Better Data on Quantifying Social and Economic Risks
An increase of data access and sharing can create positive direct and indirect social and economic benefits.[44] There is a strong link between better data and better business decision-making, and many organizations are working to implement these data collection measures.[45]

---

39. *See* Press Release: SEC Announces Enforcement Task Force Focused on Climate and ESG Issues, U.S. Securities and Exchange Commission (Mar. 4, 2021), https://www.sec.gov/news/press-release/2021-42. The SEC created a Climate and ESG Task force in the Division of Enforcement which will develop initiatives to proactively identify ESG-related misconduct. "Climate risks and sustainability are critical issues for the investing public and our capital markets," said Acting Chair Allison Herren Lee. "The task force announced today will play an important role in enhancing and coordinating the efforts of the Division of Enforcement, the Office of the Whistleblower, and other parts of the agency to bolster the efforts of the Commission as a whole on these vital matters." *Id.*

40. *See* Sarah Brodsky, *Investing through a Racial Equity Lens*, Impactivate (Mar. 19, 2019), https://www.theimpactivate.com/investing-through-a-racial-equity-lens/ (providing three examples of how investors have applied a racial equity lens to their portfolios). *See also* Examining Existing and Potential Investments with a Racial Equity Lens, Mission Investors Exchange: Tools and Resources (Jan. 2022), https://missioninvestors.org/resources/examining-existing-and-potential-investments-racial-equity-lens *citing* Sharlene Brown & Athena Owirodu, *Capital at a Crossroads: Accelerating Racial Equity Investment across Asset Classes* (Croatian Inst. Racial Equity, Econ., Fin. and Sustainability, 2021), https://croataninstitute.org/wp-content/uploads/2021/10/10_18_21_REEFS_TPA_Public-Final.pdf (defining and describing a framework for racial equity investing).

41. David Uzokie, *Integrating a Gender Lens in Sustainable Investing*, IISD (Jan. 31, 2021), https://www.iisd.org/articles/gender-lens-sustainable-investing.

42. Investing to Advance Women: A Guide for Investors, US SIF, https://www.ussif.org/files/Publications/Investing%20to%20Advance%20Women_US%20SIF.pdf (last visited Mar. 3, 2022).

43. Id.

44. Enhancing Access to and Sharing of Data: Reconciling Risks and Benefits for Data Re-use across Societies: 3. Economic and Social Benefits of Data Access and Sharing, OECD iLibrary, https://www.oecd-ilibrary.org/sites/90ebc73d-en/index.html?itemId=/content/component/90ebc73d-en (last visited Mar. 3, 2022). "Data access and sharing can help generate social and economic benefits worth between 0.1 and 1.5 percent of gross domestic product (GDP) in the case of public-sector data, and between 1 and 2.5 percent of GDP (in few studies up to 4 percent of GDP) when also including private-sector data." Id.

45. *See, e.g.*, *Measuring the Social Impact of Corporate Investments*, Deloitte, https://www2.deloitte.com/us/en/pages/consulting/solutions/corporate-social-impact-measurement-metrics.html (last visited Mar. 3, 2022). Deloitte created Social Impact Measurement Model (SIMM) which seeks to bring data-backed insights on the social impact of corporate investments. *Id.*

(3) Embedding Economic Justice and Racial Equity into Corporate Governance
Embedding economic justice and racial equity into corporate governance can contribute to structural change in organizations and improved outcomes.[46] An increasing number of corporations and public entities are considering amending and imbedding a framework of economic justice and racial equity into corporate charter documents and approaches to decision-making to address systematic racism.[47]

(4) Increasing Initiatives for Greater Racial and Gender Diversity of Asset Managers
Many companies have established clear targets to measure corporate progress toward racial equity,[48] and an important measure is the diversity of the asset managers determining how and where investments are directed. Major foundations have committed to shifting assets to women and people of color asset managers,[49] recognizing that diversity and inclusion in endowment investments are critical to mission alignment.[50]

(5) Creating Investment Committees that Include Community Stakeholders
Engaging community stakeholders in community investment strategies can add value by building local ownership and synergy around shared interests.[51] Some organizations and their investment committees have included community members and granted them special voting rights.[52]

---

46. *See* Ron S. Berenblat et al., *Racial Equity Audits: A New ESG Initiative*, Harvard Law School Forum on Corporate Governance (Oct. 30, 2021), https://corpgov.law.harvard.edu/2021/10/30/racial-equity-audits-a-new-esg-initiative/#16b (providing an example that the 2021 proxy season saw an influx in proposals for companies to conduct Racial Equity Audits under Rule 14a-8 of the Securities and Exchange Act of 1934).

47. *See, e.g.*, NYC for Racial Justice: An Interim Report from the Racial Justice Commission Staff, NYC Racial Justice Commission, https://racialjustice.cityofnewyork.us/wp-content/uploads/2021/10/RJC_NYC4RC_PrelimRept_FIN.pdf (recommending changes to the New York City Charter); The 2021 CEO Blueprint for Racial Equity, Policy Link (2021), https://corporateracialequityalliance.org/sites/default/files/2021%20CEO%20Blueprint%20for%20Racial%20Equity%20070121-1.pdf.

48. Melisande Schifter, *7 Ways Companies Are Advancing Racial Justice in Business*, World Economic Forum (June 18, 2021), https://www.weforum.org/agenda/2021/06/7-ways-companies-are-advancing-racial-justice-in-business/. ". . . PepsiCo set the target to expand the representation of Black managers to 10% of its workforce by 2025 and as of first quarter of 2021, PepsiCo. Reported to increase its Black managerial representation to 8%, including adding 28 Black associates to its executive ranks." *Id.*

49. Juan J. Martinez & Ashley Zohn, *Knight Diversity of Asset Managers Research Series*, Knight Foundation, https://knightfoundation.org/topics/diverse-asset-managers/ (last visited Apr. 25, 2022); *see, e.g.*, Roy Swan & Darren Walker, *Capital for Justice: Spurring on Impact Investing for Racial Equity*, Stanford Social Innovation Review (Apr. 29, 2019), https://ssir.org/articles/entry/capital_for_justice_spurring_on_impact_investing_for_racial_equity (providing an example that "the Kresge Foundation to move 25 percent of its assets under the control of women and firms led by people of color by 2025").

50. *Diversity in Asset Management: Research and Practice*, Mission Investors Exchange (Oct. 2019), https://missioninvestors.org/resources/diversity-asset-management-research-and-practice.

51. Strategic Community Investment: A Quick Guide 4 (IFC 2010), https://www.ifc.org/wps/wcm/connect/4e313b34-a5d2-477f-8fde-5f422a28815b/IFC_com_inv_handbook_2.pdf?MOD=AJPERES&CACHEID=ROOTWORKSPACE-4e313b34-a5d2-477f-8fde-5f422a28815b-jqeEYVL.

52. *See Frequently Asked Questions*, Candide Group, https://candidegroup.com/olamina-faqs (last visited Mar. 3, 2022) (describing that Olamina Fund seeks to honor all stakeholders through "community participation in profits" and a "Community Advisory Board" where the "Community Advisory Board members have a veto vote in that no loans can be made without their consent").

(6) Redefining Investor Capacities and Qualifications
Understanding the intended impact and community beneficiaries is a critical capacity for investment decision-making. Some investors are now not only focusing on what happens *before* investments are made but also what happens *after*—creating more opportunities for stakeholders or the intended beneficiaries to advise on investment design, implementation, and evaluation.[53] Transformative investment approaches are being led by low-income communities and communities of color, who are often the stakeholders in impact investments.[54]

(7) Defining Scale: Community-by-Community Approaches, Not One-Size-Fits All
Creating a smaller, more local scale of solutions and applying those to a few different communities can often be more efficient and effective than creating large-scale solutions and applying them to a sprawling set of communities. There are several examples of successful localized approaches involving small groups, which could help other groups move forward with strategies applicable to their own local communities.[55]

(8) Increasing Shareholder Coalitions and Advocacy Campaigns
Asset owners, investment managers, and financial advisors are deploying shareholder advocacy to promote socially responsible investing.[56] Additionally, there has been an increase in advocacy campaigns and support for programs that provide community benefits.[57]

(9) Organizing Wealthy Individuals Focused on Redistributing Their Wealth
Some high net worth individuals have committed to donating their wealth in their lifetimes.[58] Some of these wealthy individuals and their advisors are specifically

---

53. *Impact Due Diligence: Emerging Best Practices*, Pacific Community Ventures (July 2, 2019), https://www.pacificcommunityventures.org/2019/07/02/impact-due-diligence-emerging-best-practices/.
54. *See infra* note 57.
55. *See* Michael H. Shuman, Creating a Community Investment Fund: A Local Food Approach, Cutting Edge Capital (June 2013), https://www.cuttingedgecapital.com/wp-content/uploads/Creating-a-Community-Investment-Fund-A-Local-Food-Approach.pdf (describing a process by which a small group of local food advocates who began creating an investment fund in the Pioneer Valley of Western Massachusetts).
56. Deborah Nason, *Shareholders Challenge the Companies They Invest in to Promote Good in the World*, CNBC (Nov. 30, 2020), https://www.cnbc.com/2020/11/30/shareholders-challenge-firms-they-invest-in-to-promote-good-in-the-world.html. *See also Shareholder Advocacy*, AFL-CIO, https://aflcio.org/what-unions-do/social-economic-justice/shareholder-advocacy (last visited Dec. 13, 2021). "One of the ways we work to restore balance to our economy is by changing corporate practices through shareholder-driven reforms that are designed to increase corporate accountability." *Id.*
57. *See, e.g.*, *Opioid Settlement Priorities: Recommendations from the Addiction Solutions Campaign*, Legal Action Center (May 17, 2018), https://www.lac.org/assets/files/Opioid-Settlement-Priorities_5.17.18.pdf. The Addiction Solutions Campaign has provided three impact areas to change the trajectory of the opioid crisis, which has disproportionately impacted low-income communities. One proposed solution is to promote and financially incentivize integration of addiction care with the rest of healthcare. *Id.*
58. *See* Jonathan Pociano, *Warren Buffett Donates Another $4.1 Billion and Resigns from Gates Foundation*, Forbes (June 23, 2021), https://www.forbes.com/sites/jonathanponciano/2021/06/23/warren-buffett-donates-another-41-billion-and-resigns-from-gates-foundation/?sh=4003b0141bc9 (explaining that Warren Buffet donated $4.1 billion to charity in 2021). *See also Pledge Signatories*, The Giving Pledge, https://givingpledge.org/pledgers (last visited Mar. 3, 2022) (providing a list of individuals who joined the Giving Pledge with letters explaining their decision to make a public commitment, their reasons for engaging in philanthropy, and the causes that motivate them). *Id.*

dedicating their efforts to addressing racial inequities.[59] For example, the Good Life Pledge is a commitment by wealthy individuals to donate one-third of their assets to Black, Brown, and Native communities "toward building critical infrastructure in these communities, and unlocking capital investments for those who have historically suffered, and who still suffer redlining, disinvestment, institutional racism, and environmental injustice."[60]

(10) Developing Funds Focused on Nonextraction and Community Control
Several funds are community-controlled and emphasize value creation for communities as the principal objective.[61] For example, Seed Commons, a fund devoted to cooperative development, focuses on nonextraction, where the returns to the lender will not exceed the wealth created by the borrower.[62]

Transformative investors and intermediaries are heeding low-income communities' and communities of color's demands and visions of justice and equity by creating and growing models of investment, investment opportunities, and tools that support community-driven solutions. Led by a range of visionary changemakers across asset classes, these promising practices support changes in impact investing that are already underway.

Visionary Changemakers: Investing for Social Impact, Economic Justice, and Racial Equity

This section highlights how the interviewees for this chapter, nine visionary changemakers in impact investing, are advancing the field shifts necessary to achieve economic justice and racial equity.

Focusing on Racial Equity as a Linchpin of Change—Erika Seth Davies, the Racial Equity Asset Lab

> "Do we serve money or do we use money to serve some other need? What serves what? Our capitalism is predicated on exploitation of bodies and labor and land through theft, there is not much this kind of system won't do for profit. Until we get honest about this, then we are not going to be able to really address this."

Erika Seth Davies is the founder of the Racial Equity Asset Lab (REAL), which "centers racial equity in impact investing and works to shift capital to close the persistent racial

---

59. *See, e.g.*, Nicholas Kulish and David Gelles, *MacKenzie Scott Gives Away Another $2.74 Billion Even as Her Wealth Grows*. NY Times (June 15, 2021), https://www.nytimes.com/2021/06/15/business/mackenzie-scott-philanthropy.html; chordata capital, https://chordatacapital.com/ (last visited Apr. 8, 2022).
60. The Good Life Pledge, https://www.goodlifepledge.com/ (last visited Mar. 3, 2022).
61. *Community-Controlled Capital and Participatory Investing*, Mission Investors Exchange (May 2020), https://missioninvestors.org/resources/community-controlled-capital-and-participatory-investing (providing the Heron Foundation, Boston Ujima Fund, The REAL People's Fund, Fresno DRIVE Initiative, The Buen Vivir Fund by Thousand Currents, and Seed Commons as examples of impact investors at the forefront of action that puts decision-making power in the hands of community members).
62. *Seed Commons' Approach to Non-extractive Finance*, Seed Commons, https://seedcommons.org/about-seed-commons/seed-commons-approach-to-non-extractive-finance/ (last visited Mar. 1, 2022).

wealth gap,"[63] and CEO of Rhia Ventures, a venture capital fund for early- and growth-stage companies across the reproductive and maternal health landscape. As a consultant to a range of investors from community development financial institutions and foundations to a faith-based endowment fund, REAL has advised investors with over $9 billion in assets under management. REAL identifies the ways a racial equity approach is catalytic for investments to achieve transformative goals and works closely with an investment team to develop a roadmap to operationalize the plan. For example, REAL has worked with foundations to develop the racial equity framework and accountability measures for evaluating their endowment management, including training investment committee members and staff, creating specific plans to move from intention to action, assessing manager diversity, enhancing investment committee selection criteria, and revising organizational policies to prioritize diversity, equity, and inclusion goals.

Building a Shared Vision and Models for an Equitable Economy—Rodney Foxworth, Common Future

> "There continues to be a dangerous trend of calling an investment a social and economic equity investment because it is an educational platform that produces positive outcomes for Black and Brown kids. That's good, but are we investing in things that would fundamentally ensure that the communities in which those children come from are actually economically viable and have a sense of empowerment?"

Rodney Foxworth is the CEO of Common Future, a national intermediary and network of frontline leaders, impact investors, and philanthropists working to build an equitable and inclusive economy. A recipient of the 2022 Skoll Award for Social Innovation, Common Future has been a leader in directly addressing the need for racial and economic equity focus and clarity in investment decision making and highlighting the importance of people of color leadership in this work. Specifically, Mr. Foxworth has called on foundations to include communities of color and low-income communities in the grant decision-making process, giving communities more power to control investment funds. Focusing on community control and trusting community decision-making, in 2021, Common Future forged a collaboration with its network and launched a $800,000 character-based loan pool for people of color businesses. Character-based lending is based on community ties, instead of credit scores. This character-based loan pool, launched in mid-2021, is providing below-market-rate loans to Black and Indigenous businesses.[64]

Uplifting Practices that Are Transforming the Economy—Andrea Armeni, Transform Finance

> "If we are serious about this, then it is not a top to bottom effort. Communities are placed at the center of decision-making and given asset building opportunities, and they are key in deciding how the investment occurs."

---

63. The Racial Equity Asset Lab, https://racialequityassetlab.org/.

64. *See* Chris Winters, *Lending on Character, Not Credit Scores*, Yes! Solutions Journalism (Nov. 15, 2021), https://www.yesmagazine.org/issue/a-new-social-justice/2021/11/15/banking-bipoc-businesses.

Andrea Armeni is co-founder and Executive Director of Transform Finance. Transform Finance is a research and implementation partner that supports investors and social change actors to challenge legacy investment approaches, seed transformative investment models, and build movement power. To provide concrete examples and a framework for community-centered investment, Mr. Armeni with Curt Lyon developed the Grassroots Community Engaged Investment (GCEI) framework. In *Grassroots Community Engaged Investment: Redistributing Power Over Investment Processes as the Key to Equitable Outcomes*,[65] they highlight eight examples of GCEIs across the United States. The GCEI framework assesses and offers models of investments "with meaningful input, decision-making power, and/or ownership from grassroots stakeholders." The locus of control in investment decisions distinguishes GCEIs from impact investments generally: "Projects that feature GCEI are unified by the notion that investment efforts should not happen 'to' communities, but 'with' them; they should respond to, address, and be accountable to the visions, needs, and aspirations of the community itself."[66]

Using the Range of Investment Tools to Drive Catalytic Change—Nwamaka Agbo, Kataly Foundation and Restorative Economies Fund

> "How are we in full integrity with our values and our pocketbooks? How do we really hold values of justice? How do we grow capacity and change systems?"

Nwamaka Agbo is the CEO of the Kataly Foundation and Managing Director of the Restorative Economies Fund (REF). The Kataly Foundation is an approximately $500 million sunsetting foundation dedicated to supporting the economic, political, and cultural power of Black and Indigenous communities and all communities of color. To guide her own work and to answer the questions Ms. Agbo posed to the sector, she developed the Restorative Economies framework that "centers on healing and restoration of vulnerable communities who have been marginalized and oppressed by a polluting and extractive economy, by investing in strategies that create shared prosperity and self-determination for a just transition to the next economy."[67] In alignment with this framework, REF pursues healing and restoration through investing in community-owned and governed projects and using a nonextractive, integrated capital approach.[68] She challenges the field of philanthropy to utilize all of its tools to support the dreams communities have for their own resilience and well-being.

---

65. Andrea Armeni & Curt Lyon, Transform Finance, https://static1.squarespace.com/static/54cfca5be4b06d2d0d7c0f1d/t/6065dc5d38b2ae3f783b1df6/1617288341085/Transform+Finance+Grassroots+Community+Engaged+Invesment+2021-04-01.pdf.
66. *Id.*
67. *What Is Restorative Economics?* Nwamaka Agbo, https://www.nwamakaagbo.com/restorative-economics.
68. RSF, Integrated Capital Approach, https://rsfsocialfinance.org/vision/how-we-work/integrated-capital/ (defining an integrated capital approach as "the coordinated use of different forms of financial capital and non-financial resources to support an enterprise that's working to solve complex social and environmental problems"). *Id.*

Ceding Power to Grow Community Ownership—Lynne Hoey, formerly with Olamina Fund at Candide Group; currently with Kataly Foundation

> "How do [investors] create the conditions for people to succeed, feel like they can dream, and feel like they can articulate what they need?"

Lynne Hoey is the former Managing Director of the Olamina Fund at Candide Group and currently Chief Investment Officer at Kataly Foundation. The Olamina Fund is a $40 million fund devoted to addressing access to capital for communities bearing the brunt of economic extraction, particularly Black and Native communities.[69] The Olamina Fund itself models shifting control of investment decisions to trusted institutions in communities of color and low-income communities. These trusted institutions include women and people of color-led community development financial institutions and cooperative loan funds. Through its Community Advisory Board, community stakeholders are a part of the determinations of investment strategy and investment decisions as members of the Credit Committee.[70] The Community Advisory Board has meaningful decision-making power with a "veto vote in that no loans can be made without their consent."[71] Another means of ceding power is Olamina's commitment to hiring and developing fund managers of color, which included hiring Leslie Lindo to succeed Lynne Hoey as Managing Director. This dual approach shifts control of investment decisions, builds community wealth, and grows the pool of fund managers who are people of color.

Leveraging Venture Capital to Grow More People of Color Businesses—Stefanie Thomas, Impact America Fund

> "We need to get real about power and control, who has it and who doesn't. What does community-centered design look like from beginning to end? Everything from how we figure out who is in need and what we need to ultimately cutting the check and putting the resources together to the said beneficiary."

Stefanie Thomas is Senior Investment Associate at the Impact America Fund. Impact America Fund provides venture capital investments in high promise businesses that will yield significant community returns narrowing the racial and gender equity gap. Ms. Thomas's call to be intentional about power, racial equity, and returns to communities of color is central to the work of the Impact America Fund. Impact America Fund invests in ventures like Mayvenn, a website platform for independent hairstylists to connect with customers and enhance their businesses. Mayvenn was built for and by hairstylists. To date, Mayvenn has paid out $20 million in commissions and fees to hairstylists who are disproportionately Black women. Impact America Fund builds its portfolio from deeply understanding the catalytic potential of enterprises led by people of color to build supply chains, create jobs, and

69. *Olamina Fund: About*, Candide Group, https://candidegroup.com/olamina-fund (last visited Mar. 3, 2022).
70. *Olamina Fund: Ecosystem Partners*, Candide Group, https://candidegroup.com/olamina-partners (last visited Apr. 16, 2022).
71. *Frequently Asked Questions*, Candide Group, https://candidegroup.com/olamina-faqs (last visited Apr. 16, 2022).

increase incomes in their communities and knowing the racially exclusionary investment practices that have starved these businesses of capital. This investment approach centers the skills and experiences of entrepreneurs of color.

Organizing Institutional Investors to Advance Corporate Social Responsibility—Tejal Patel and Richard Clayton, SOC Investment Group

> "[Our role is to] figure out a way to use the interest and authority that we have as shareholders to influence what the company is focusing on . . . and moving substantiative changes like fair wages, equal opportunity for training, hiring, and promotion, childcare, or flexible schedules."
>
> —Tejal Patel

> "[Our goal is that] shareholders would be in more of a position to ask whether ahead of time they should be giving companies the benefit of the doubt, just because they're running big profits, or whether they should be insisting that the company has clear standards of how it's going to operate and value certain constituencies within the company while also adhering to high standards for conduct."
>
> —Richard Clayton

Tejal Patel and Richard Clayton are, respectively, Corporate Governance Director and Research Director of SOC Investment Group. SOC Investment Group "works with pension funds sponsored by unions affiliated with the Strategic Organizing Center (SOC), a coalition of unions representing more than four million members, to enhance long-term shareholder returns through active ownership."[72] They educate and advocate for broader understanding of investor risk and alignment of workplace practices with the fiduciary duty of officers to protect against investor risks. This understanding of investor risk incorporates short- and long-term social risks of corporate actions. SOC Investment Group supports investors to translate social risks into financial risks that can be evaluated through risk reports and equity audits. These risk reports and other governance accountability tools assess the impacts of human capital decisions like fair wages and equitable leave policies, as well as the structure of executive compensation. SOC Investment has advanced civil rights audits, executive clawback proposals, and highlighted a range of unsafe consumer and workplace practices by some public companies.[73]

Highlighting the Importance of Racial and Gender Inclusion for Fund Managers—Renaye Manley, SEIU Capital Stewardship and formerly Council of Institutional Investors Director

> "Investments should not be thought of as a form of charity. It is a way to build power and sustainability in our communities. People of color have to be able to be at the table and determine what it looks like on both sides of the table."

---

72. *About SOC Investment Group*, SOC Investment Group, https://www.socinvestmentgroup.com/.
73. *Id.*

Renaye Manley is Deputy Director of Strategic Investments at Service Employees International Union (SEIU), and a former Board member of the Council of Institutional Investors. SEIU represents over two million service sector workers across the country with investments in more than fifty public pension funds and nineteen Taft Hartley funds.[74] SEIU's Capital Stewardship Program has been demanding accountability for investment decision making and focusing on the diversity of asset managers for many years. In its 2016 report, *Casting a Wider Net: Increasing Opportunities for Minority and Women Owned Asset Managers in Institutional Investments*, with the Roosevelt Institute and ReFund America Project, SEIU called for investment consulting firms to develop goals, policies, practices, and tracking mechanisms to ensure greater diversity of emerging asset managers.[75] This long-standing advocacy, combined with the organizing of investors with over $1.2 trillion in assets, led to a collaboration with BlackRock and a commitment from the world's largest investment firm to investigate the racial impacts of its policies and practices.[76]

These practitioners are driving change in the investment landscape, and represent the kinds of potential clients that lawyers must be able to serve to support shifts that advance racial and economic equity.

Lawyers' Roles in Shifting Investment Mindset and Behavior for Economic Justice and Racial Equity

As legal counsel to investors representing clients in a wide range of investment transactions, business lawyers have important roles to play in creating a more equitable economy. The changemakers interviewed for this chapter offered important recommendations for business lawyers to consider in changing their mindsets and behaviors with respect to advising clients, some of whom are the impact investing changemakers mentioned above.

Shifting Legal Frameworks and Default Legal Theories

In August 2019, the Business Roundtable announced that 181 CEOs signed on to its statement of the need for a new purpose of the corporation that includes stakeholders, not only shareholders: "Each of our stakeholders is essential. We commit to deliver value to all of them, for the future success of our companies, our communities and our country."[77] These leaders began their statement with a commitment to a more equitable economy: "Americans deserve an economy that allows each person to succeed through hard work

74. *All about Retirement Security*, SEIU, https://seiu.org/cards/all-the-educational-resources-you-need-to-be-a-leader (last visited Apr. 25, 2022).

75. Casting a Wider Net: Increasing Opportunities for Minority and Women Owned Asset Managers in Institutional Investments, SEIU (2016), https://d3jpbvtfqku4tu.cloudfront.net/img/28927_capstewd_reportv7b.pdf.

76. *See, e.g.*, *SEIU and Change to Win's investment funds pushing for racial diversity in financial institutions*, SEIU, https://www.seiu.org/blog/2021/4/seiu-and-change-to-wins-investment-funds-pushing-for-racial-diversity-in-financial-institutions (last visited Dec. 13, 2021). "[A] group of investors consisting of over $1.2 trillion in assets—the [SEIU] Capital Stewardship Program and the Change to Win Investment Group—have been demanding that leading investment firms examine how their plans and policies impact communities of color." *Id.*

77. *Business Roundtable Redefines the Purpose of a Corporation to Promote "An Economy that Serves All Americans,"* Business Roundtable (Aug. 19, 2019), https://www.businessroundtable.org/business-roundtable-redefines-the-purpose-of-a-corporation-to-promote-an-economy-that-serves-all-americans.

and creativity and to lead a life of meaning and dignity."[78] Since that statement, the COVID-19 global pandemic, rise in racialized violence across the globe, and decline of democratic institutions have made the need for this change more urgent.

As business leaders have voiced a desire to achieve fundamental corporate shifts that balance the interests of profit maximization with the needs of communities and workers, there are a range of corporate law changes that are needed to mitigate and address current domestic and international social, economic, and racial equity crises. Traditional legal frameworks and approaches to assessing and balancing risk and return impede shifting the legal and policy landscape for transformative finance. These transformative finance practitioners offered a few specific areas of change to legal theories and business practice:

- the business judgment rule and its deference to corporate officers,
- existing legal limits of director and officer's fiduciary duties that prioritize profit maximization in traditional corporate forms,
- default contractual provisions that attempt to mitigate investor risk at all costs,
- thresholds for shareholder derivative suits, and
- limits of risk assessments and models that do not account for the environmental and social devastation caused by destructive corporate practices.

To create a national economy "that allows each person to succeed through hard work and creativity and to lead a life of meaning and dignity,"[79] corporate law and business practices must change in a number of ways. Business lawyers have crucial roles to play in the shifts needed to achieve this audacious and important goal.

Shifting Mindsets and Approaches to Client Counseling and Advice

In addition to these fundamental shifts in corporate law and business frameworks, interviewees shared this overriding message: lawyers interested in serving clients who are pursuing transformative investment for racial and economic equity must challenge themselves in thought and action.

Lawyers Must Be Creative, Move Outside of Their Comfort Zone, and Collaborate with Other Lawyers

In every interview, these changemakers recounted experiences of working with lawyers who posed challenges to their objectives, who continually questioned the wisdom of the investment approach, and who were unwilling to shift from the traditional lender–borrower, grantor–grantee, or investor–investee relationship mindset. While investors and practitioners appreciated the due diligence of lawyers they encountered and worked with, they emphasized the importance of the lawyer thinking creatively about the possibilities for systems change and the options to build models of change through individual transactions.

The most effective experiences that interviewees had with lawyers were with lawyers who supported co-design of the transaction and were able to effectively collaborate with other lawyers to translate and negotiate transformative finance goals.

78. *Id.*
79. *Id.*

Lawyers Must Think Bigger about the Possibilities for Change and See the Client's Vision of Transformation

Investors and intermediaries talked about looking for lawyers who could not only support their visions for change with the required knowledge and technical skills, but also lawyers who can be partners in envisioning how legal structures and tools could advance communities' demands for economic justice and racial equity. Every interviewee spoke about experiences of lawyers uplifting only risks and challenges inherent in transformative change, instead of placing those important risk considerations and barriers alongside possibilities to create new tools and approaches to achieving racial and economic equity through investment. These changemakers emphasized the importance of the need for a mindset shift that includes thinking bigger and more imaginatively about the possibilities for large-scale change.

Interviewees were looking for, and some had experience with, lawyers who could implement their visions of societal change and work hand-in-hand to use various legal tools and relationships to support the client's visions. These changemakers saw this mindset shift as a major role that lawyers could play in changing investment approaches and facilitating transformative finance deals.

Lawyers Must Collaborate with Their Clients to Redefine Risk and Assess Risk from the Perspectives of the Most Impacted Communities

In envisioning the transformation these transformative finance clients seek to achieve, lawyers need to understand risk differently. This involves seeing and taking seriously the risks to communities of investments failing or falling short of their promised goals, along with traditional risks of financial and/or reputational loss to lenders, grantors, and equity investors. Many of the interviewees are doing this in their work through a range of strategies, including shifting the understanding of shareholder risk of publicly traded companies' workplace practices, incorporating community risk into loan agreements, and taking the most subordinate positions in financing community development projects.

Lawyers Must Collaborate with Other Professionals to Create Transformative Investment Approaches

As interviewees talked about their legal needs and experiences with lawyers, they also discussed the significance of lawyers being ready and willing to collaborate with accountants, lenders, and other finance and tax professionals who can work as a part of the client's investment team. One example of this need for collaboration and shared approaches is with community-controlled and/or cooperatively owned projects. The need for collaboration was particularly highlighted in relationships between lawyers and finance professionals: "We need legal and financial practices that recognize and support community ownership and multiple owners with various governance structures. Practices need to be rooted in the history of an oppressed people in a particular place and not a process that does not address the realities of communities" (Nwamaka Agbo).

Lawyers Must Use Their Social Capital and Voices to Change the Investment Landscape to Achieve Economic Justice and Racial Equity

Finally, to support shifting the field, lawyers must also be willing to use their social capital and voices to support the kinds of shifts in the investment landscape that are required to achieve economic justice and racial equity. The prevailing message was that lawyers must lead and take their leadership potential seriously. This leadership includes educating about and advocating for transformative finance models. As legal counsel to a range of investors, business lawyers are uniquely poised to serve as catalysts for policy and practice changes that build an equitable and fair economy.

Conclusion

This chapter focuses on the shifts occurring in the investment landscape that address the present and long-standing racial and economic inequities in American society. Through interviews with a group of innovative investors, advocates, and intermediaries leading the way for transformative investments, the chapter offers promising practices in the field of investment for racial and economic equity and key lessons for lawyers serving these clients. The work of lawyers is an essential component in building the legal infrastructure for fair and just economic practices—from regenerative finance, a concept at the intersection of impact investing and ESG investments that aim to use money to solve problems and support healthy communities, to nonextractive finance, which requires a lender's return on investment and the cost of capital will never exceed the wealth created by the borrower.

Ultimately, for lawyers as well as investment practitioners, such shifts in the field of transformative social-impact investing require changes in mindset and approach to aggregating and deploying investments. Lawyers have a range of important roles to play that foster transformative change. The changes needed to shift the landscape require business lawyers to lead by using their platforms and social capital to transform the economy through individual transactions, corporate law changes, and public policy reforms.

Index

About the Editors

Dorcas R. Gilmore is a racial and economic justice attorney and consultant with over twenty years of experience working with national, regional, and local organizations across the United States. She is a principal of Gilmore Khandhar, LLC, a solidarity economies law firm representing social ventures, investors, and community enterprises that create a more just and equitable economy. She began her legal career as a Skadden Fellow and Staff Attorney at the Community Law Center, where she developed a youth business legal services program and represented communities fighting anti-gentrification efforts. She was an Assistant General Counsel for the National Association for the Advancement of Colored People (NAACP), serving as corporate counsel and economic and environmental and climate justice advocacy counsel for the national office and over 2,200 state and local affiliates. She received the NAACP Staff Attorney of the Year Award for her work. She was a Wasserstein Public Interest Fellow at Harvard Law School. She is a Past Chair of the ABA Business Law Section's Community Economic Development Committee and former Governing Committee member of the ABA Forum on Affordable Housing & Community Development Law. She is currently on the Board of Directors of Black Lives Matter Grassroots, Global Boatworks Holdings, Inc., and Baltimore Action Legal Team. She was a founding Advisory Committee member of the Shriver National Center on Poverty Law's Racial Justice Institute and Board of Directors of the National Black Worker Centers. Committed to building the field, she has directed community equity development law clinics and trained law students as a Practitioner in Residence at American University Washington College of Law and Visiting Associate Professor at George Washington University Law School and University of Maryland Carey School of Law. Prior to her legal career, she worked abroad on international economic development efforts as a part of the Dominican Republic's Presidential Plan Against Poverty. She graduated from Rollins College and the University of Maryland Carey School of Law, where she was a Gilbert & Jaylee Mead Public Interest Scholar.

Lisa Green Hall brings thirty years of expertise in economic justice, social impact, and community development finance. Using the tools of impact investing and philanthropy, she has served in executive roles across multiple sectors in the United States and abroad.

She previously served as a Fellow and Fair Finance Lead at the Beeck Center for Social Impact and Innovation (Beeck Center). In this capacity, she was Professor of Practice and a member of the Georgetown faculty. Her area of focus at the Beeck Center was the inclusive economy. She is currently Impact Chair and a member of the leadership team for Apollo Global Management's impact investing platform and the Apollo Impact Mission (AIM) fund. In this capacity, she chairs the Advisory Committee for impact investing and partners with the investment team on impact management, strategy, and oversight of the platform. She also serves on the Investment Committee for the AIM fund. She also served as Managing Director at Anthos Asset Management, headquartered in Amsterdam, the Netherlands, where she was based for three years. She was President and CEO of Calvert Impact Capital following her tenure as head of the investment portfolio. She served in the Clinton Administration as a policy advisor at the National Economic Council where she worked on the creation of the New Markets Tax Credit program. She currently sits on the board of Habitat for Humanity International, Natural Resources Defense Council, and Community Development Trust and was previously a member of the Investment Committee of the Nathan Cummings Foundation. She was also previously a member of the Board of Overseers for the University of Pennsylvania Graduate School of Education. She is a graduate of the Leadership Greater Washington class of 2008 and participated in the Marshall Memorial Fellowship in 2003. She earned an MBA from Harvard Business School and a BS in Economics from the Wharton School at University of Pennsylvania.

Susan R. Jones is a Professor of Clinical Law and a member of the full-time faculty at The George Washington University Law School in Washington, DC, where she is the Director & Supervising Attorney of the Small Business & Community Economic Development Clinic (SBCEDC). She is an active member of the District of Columbia Bar having served as Vice-Chair to the DC Bar CED Pro Bono Project Advisory Committee (now known as the Nonprofit and Small Business Legal Assistance Program). She was a Distinguished Visiting Professor at the University of Maryland School of Law and the Haywood Burns Visiting Chair in Civil Rights at the City University of New York School of Law at Queens College. A leader in clinical legal education, she chaired the Association of American Law Schools (AALS) Section on Clinical Legal Education and she served on the executive committee of that section and as chair of the Section on Africa. She was a member of the AALS Standing Committee on Clinical Legal Education, chair of the AALS Section on Poverty Law, a member of the Executive Committee of the AALS Section on Transactional Law and Skills, and as cochair of the Transactional Clinics Committee of the AALS Clinical Section. In addition to her work with the AALS, she has held numerous leadership positions in the American Bar Association (ABA) including vice-chair of the Economic Justice Committee, Section of Civil Rights and Social Justice, service on the governing committee of ABA Forum on Affordable Housing and Community Development Law, editor-in-chief and senior editor of the ABA Journal of Affordable Housing and Community Development Law, and co-chair of the Forum's Legal Educators' Practice Division. She is a co-founder and past co-chair of the Community Economic Development Committee of the ABA Section on Business Law and she served on the ABA Business Law Education Committee as well as on the ABA Commission on Homelessness and Poverty. She is a Fannie Mae Foundation Fellow, Harvard University Kennedy School of Government (2002); a member of Leadership Washington

(1997); and an elected member of the American Law Institute. Her scholarly pursuits include numerous published articles in the field of entrepreneurship and the law, small and microbusiness, and community economic development (CED). She is the author of *A Legal Guide to Microenterprise Development* (ABA Publishing) and co-editor of *Building Healthy Communities: A Guide to Community Economic Development for Advocates, Lawyers, and Policymakers* (ABA Publishing). She was awarded Washington Area Lawyers for the Arts (WALA) Lifetime Achievement Award for distinctive service to the greater Washington, DC, creative community and for twenty years of service on the WALA Board of Directors. Her scholarship, practice, and interests include impact investing, solidarity economies lawyering, transactional small business, CED, microbusiness development, social entrepreneurship, international/comparative CED, nonprofit organizations and charitable giving, microbusiness and entrepreneurship in underrepresented communities, worker cooperatives, arts and entertainment, and the creative economy. She is a graduate of Brandeis University BA and Antioch Law School, JD and MA in Clinical Legal Education.

About the Contributors

Carolyn Kim Allwin is the head of ESG in the United States for Capco, a global technology and management consultancy specializing in driving digital transformation in the financial services industry. She has a specific sector focus in helping companies navigate regulatory changes and implement efficient cross-border tax planning strategies. She also serves as a venture partner for Clearstone, a collaborative venture fund led by venture partners to identify, assess, invest in, and actively add value to impactful start-ups and reducing upward mobility barriers for low-income populations. Before Capco, she served as chief sustainability officer for Recap Investing and as tax counsel for both GoldenTree Asset Management and Ernst & Young. She is also an adjunct professor at Bard Graduate Programs in Sustainability and serves as chair of the board of directors and Thought Leadership at Impact Capital Forum. She earned her Bachelor of Arts degree at Johns Hopkins University, a Master of Arts degree from New York University, a Juris Doctor degree from Boston College Law School, and a Master of Business Administration degree from The Wharton School. She resides in New York with her husband and two children.

Andrea Armeni is the Co-Founder and Executive Director of Transform Finance, a research, education, and implementation partner that supports investors and social change actors to challenge legacy investment approaches, seed transformative investment models, and build movement power. A corporate lawyer by training, he has spent the last decade exploring how capital can be made more just and equitable and helping activists and grassroots groups reclaim power over it. He is an adjunct faculty member at New York University, where he teaches in the Masters program; his course on finance and social justice received the 2021 Award of Excellence from the Financial Times and the Impact Finance Faculty Consortium. He is the co-author, most recently, of "Grassroots Community Engaged Investment: Redistributing Power over Investment Processes as the Key to Fostering Equitable Outcomes" and "Addressing Capital's Effects on Racial Justice: How Investments Drive Injustice and What Investors Can Do about It." He served as a Senior Investment Advisor to the Secretariat of the United Nations Joint SDG Fund, is a steering committee member of the Racial Equity Economics Finance Sustainability (REEFS) initiative, and is a board member of the impact investing arm of CARE International. He holds a BA in analytic philosophy from Columbia University and a Juris Doctor from the Yale Law School.

Kim Y. Arnone is Managing Partner at the law firm of Cutting Edge Counsel and a principal in its practice group, Cutting Edge Capital. She specializes in developing community- and impact-centered capital raise strategies for investment funds, social enterprises, cooperatives, and nonprofits. She has assisted a wide range of businesses in successful campaigns, including the first-of-their-kind Regulation A offerings by a revenue-driven tech nonprofit and a cooperative community development financing institution; private offerings for investment funds supporting people of color, women, and LGBT entrepreneurs; crowdfund campaigns for multiple fan-owned professional sports teams and leagues; direct public offerings for impact businesses and funds from multiple industries, including the farm/food/restaurant/composting ecosystem; and innovative cooperative business investment campaigns. She lives with her wife and son in Oakland, California.

Clark R. Arrington is an experienced attorney and educator with degrees from Pennsylvania State University (BA Sociology) and the University of Notre Dame Law School. He currently serves as General Counsel to Obran Cooperative LCA, a conglomerate of companies controlled by a worker-owned holding company and he is a Senior Fellow with Seed Commons, a national network of community-based cooperative finance organizations. He also coordinates the 40 Acres and a Mall Legal Team that represents Downtown Crenshaw Rising, a Los Angeles–based community development group uniquely funded by an array of community and social impact investors. He is a 2021 inductee into the Cooperative Hall of Fame and recent recipient of the Malcolm X Black Unity Award. He lives in Philadelphia with his wife and teenage daughter.

Navjeet Bal is Managing Director and General Counsel at Social Finance. She is responsible for working with the Social Finance team to develop and execute innovative financings that bring together the public, private, and nonprofit sectors to promote solutions to social needs. She brings over twenty-five years of experience as a public finance attorney and a public official to Social Finance. As bond counsel to the Commonwealth of Massachusetts and many public authorities throughout Massachusetts and New England, she was responsible for structuring innovative bond financings to address critical infrastructure needs, including the first issue of Green Bonds issued in the municipal market in 2013. She served as the Commissioner of Revenue in Governor Deval Patrick's administration from 2008 through 2011. She has held many leadership positions in legal, community, and professional organizations. She currently serves on the boards of the Boston Public Library, the Williams College Gaudino Fund, and the Massachusetts Nonprofit Network, among other organizations.

Susan D. Bennett is Professor of Law Emerita at American University Washington College of Law, where she founded and directed the Community and Economic Development Law Clinic. She held the position of Director of Clinical Programs for the Washington College of Law from 2003 to 2006. She is the co-recipient of the Association of American Law Schools' 2021 William Pincus Award, conferred on a professor of law for outstanding career achievement in clinical teaching and scholarship. Before coming to WCL, she specialized in housing and consumer litigation as a staff attorney at the Maryland Legal Aid Bureau. She has written on community economic development, the ethics of group representation, and federal housing programs. She has consulted as a Fulbright Senior Specialist with Universidad Católica de Chile in Santiago concerning the development of its small business clinic and held positions chairing the Advisory Board of the D.C. Bar's Community Economic Development Project, co-chairing the Legal Educators' Division of the ABA Forum on Affordable Housing and Community Development Law and the Board of Directors of the National Law Center on Homelessness and Poverty, and serving as a member of the American Bar Association's Commission on Homelessness and Poverty. She is a current and founding board member of the D.C. Reduced Fee Lawyer and Mediator Referral Service. She received her BA from Yale University and her JD from Columbia University.

Deborah Burand is a professor of clinical law at NYU School of Law where she directs the International Transactions Clinic, a law clinic where law students work on cross-border transactions for clients that are bringing business solutions to some of the world's most pressing problems. She also is a Faculty Co-Director of the Grunin Center for Law and Social Entrepreneurship, the first center of its kind at a law school. She writes and lectures on issues related to social entrepreneurship, sustainable finance, impact investing, social finance innovations, microfinance, microfranchising/social franchising, and innovations in legal experiential education. In 2021, the Financial Times and the Impact and Sustainable Finance Faculty Consortium recognized her and her colleague Professor Scott Taitel (Wagner Graduate School of Public Service at NYU) for innovation and creativity with respect to teaching materials created for sustainable finance education. She currently sits on the boards of the MicroBuild Fund (a proof-of-concept fund launched by Habitat for Humanity International that is aimed at growing the housing microfinance sector while expanding decent housing for the poor), Calvert Impact Capital (a nonprofit investment firm that works with investors to move capital into communities around the world), and the Library of the Great Lakes (a nonprofit organization that inspires and supports exploration of the science, history, literature, arts, and cultures of the Great Lakes region). Outside of academia, her career has spanned in nearly equal parts—the private sector (global law firm), the nonprofit sector (microfinance and conservation organizations), and the public sector (U.S. Federal Reserve Board, U.S. Treasury Department, and, during the Obama Administration, General Counsel of the U.S. government's development finance institution—the DFC [then called OPIC]).

Leslie Cornell is a Vice President of Policy and Deputy General Counsel at Social Finance, Inc., a national impact finance nonprofit, where she advises on sourcing and structuring innovative, first-of-their-kind impact finance transactions to support results-focused social programs across various issue areas, including homelessness, workforce development, and criminal justice. She advises cross-functional project teams across a wide range of transactions, including complex debt financings, equity impact investments, private funds, fund of funds, and other pooled investment vehicles. Her work supports the development of innovative financing strategies with state and local governments, institutional and philanthropic investors, and nonprofit service providers that directly and measurably improve the lives of those in need. She is also part of the Social Finance legal team that was awarded the 2019 Grunin Prize by the New York University School of Law's Grunin Center for Law and Social Entrepreneurship. She holds a BS in Media Arts and Sciences and an MA in Political Science from the University of Illinois at Urbana–Champaign, where she was a Civic Leadership Fellow and President of the Illini Union Board. She is a cum laude graduate of Loyola University Chicago School of Law, where she served as editor-in-chief of the Consumer Law Review.

John Duda is Executive Director of The Real News Network, a nonprofit multimedia newsroom focused on amplifying voices from the frontlines of movements fighting for economic and racial justice. Before joining The Real News in 2020, he worked for nine years at The Democracy Collaborative, an international research institute working to develop practical models for a postcapitalist economy, where he served as Director of Communications. During his tenure, the organization's staff grew by a factor of five, developing into an essential transatlantic think tank advancing democratic economic alternatives. He is a founding worker-owner at Red Emma's, Baltimore's largest worker cooperative, created in 2004, where his work focuses on developing the project's extensive event and programming platform. He holds a PhD in Intellectual History from Johns Hopkins University for his work on the intersections of radical social movements, digital media makers, and the sciences of complexity and self-organization; a Master of Logic from the Universiteit van Amsterdam; and a BA from the University of Pennsylvania. He has written extensively on left organizing, history, and economic alternatives, and lives in Baltimore.

Geoff Gilbert is an organizer, attorney, and writer, and an Ashkenazi Jew. He lives and is building community in Washington, DC on land that belongs to the Piscataway, Pamonkey, and Conoy Nations. He leads the Beloved Community Incubator's (BCI) provision of legal and technical assistance to roughly fifteen DC-area cooperatives, collectives, and nonprofit movement organizations, including the high-touch cooperatives that BCI is incubating. He is also a committed mutual aid organizer who organizes and writes in support of all people reckoning with the United States' historical and present practices of settler colonialism, imperialism, patriarchy, and white supremacy and all people building solidarity economies around the world rooted in real, lived justice for all. Previously, he worked for Seed Commons as a Staff Attorney for three years and earned a JD from the Georgetown University Law Center in 2018.

Hilary Jackler serves as the Managing Partner of the Washington, DC and Richmond, VA offices of Kutak Rock LLP. She has supported federal, state, and local government clients to accomplish billions of dollars of public–private partnership projects, develop thousands of acres of governmentally owned real estate, and establish programs and policies. She has also supported governmental, nonprofit, and private sector clients working on pay-for-success projects and creating and implementing grant programs. She received a BA from the University of Maryland, cum laude, and a JD from the University of Maryland School of Law, magna cum laude.

Curt Lyon is the Deputy Director at Transform Finance, where he advocates for a more just economy at the intersection of finance and social movements. In this role, he manages research, educational opportunities, and organizational direction on a wide range of topics within finance. Before Transform Finance, he became activated by solidarity economy movements and provided operational support for several organizations in the Boston area, including the Boston Ujima Project and New Economy Coalition. He considers himself an active learner of investment structures that redistribute wealth and power, as well as movement strategies that build a more equitable economy. He lives in Queens, New York City.

Chintan Panchal is the co-founder of RPCK Rastegar Panchal LLP, a mission-aligned global boutique law firm focused on fund formation, finance, and M&A transactions. He leads RPCK's impact investing practice and counsels family offices, fund sponsors, and entrepreneurs on structuring and executing multiple bottom-line transactions and building social enterprises. His theory of change is that capitalism, as a powerful tool for harnessing human effort, can be a highly effective force for driving positive change in the world when properly aligned. Prior to founding RPCK, he practiced law at Allen & Overy LLP and clerked for the Honorable Judith M. Barzilay (Ret.) of the U.S. Court of International Trade. He has a law degree from Emory University and is a member of the bar in New York and the District of Columbia.

Perry Teicher is Impact Finance Counsel at Orrick Herrington & Sutcliffe LLP. He leads Orrick's global Impact Finance & Investment practice, advising impact-oriented clients globally, and serves as a leader of Orrick's ESG initiatives. He represents and advises entrepreneurs, fund sponsors, family offices, and tax-exempt organizations across a wide range of transactions, including corporate legal matters, cross-border mergers and acquisitions, private fund formation matters and portfolio transactions, and private placements. He has served as co-chair of the NYU Law Grunin Center/Impact Investing Legal Working Group's annual conference on Legal Issues in Social Entrepreneurship and Impact Investing and is involved in other sector building initiatives. He served as a Peace Corps Volunteer in Kazakhstan, where he supported the development of businesses aiming to create mobility and opportunity for people with disabilities in the region. He received a joint JD from the University of Michigan Law School, MBA from the University of Michigan, and a BA in Organizational Studies and Political Science from the University of Michigan.

Danielle Torain is a proud Baltimore native and the director of Open Society Institute-Baltimore, with over a decade's experience in the public, nonprofit, and philanthropic sectors. A graduate of the University of Richmond and the University of Maryland Francis King Carey School of Law, she worked in the Baltimore Mayor's Office of Criminal Justice, leading a citywide initiative to strengthen systems of support for incarcerated youth, and worked on local jobs programs with the Mayor's Office of Employment Development. She was senior director of strategy and development at the Center for Urban Families and spent four years at the Annie E. Casey Foundation's Baltimore Civic Site, leading its place-based strategies in workforce development and economic inclusion, community capacity building, and resident leadership. In the aftermath of Baltimore's 2015 uprising following the death of Freddie Gray, she helped launch several initiatives to connect emerging activists with the philanthropic resources needed to carry out their work. In 2016, she helped plan OSI-Baltimore's Solutions Summit and led a panel discussion about jobs and economic development. Her work has been recognized through numerous honors and awards, including being named one of the Maryland Daily Record's "Leading Women," a

"Maritime Magic Rising Star of Baltimore" by the *Baltimore Business Journal*, and receiving a "Spirited Women Award" in recognition of "everyday women who are making extraordinary contributions to their community and those around them."

Etienne C. Toussaint is an Assistant Professor of Law at the University of South Carolina School of Law where he teaches contracts, secured transactions, business associations, and other courses related to business law, political economy, and critical theory. His interdisciplinary scholarship on housing, community economic development, economic and environmental justice, human rights law, and legal education has appeared or is forthcoming in the *California Law Review*, the *Harvard Environmental Law Review*, the *Columbia Human Rights Law Review*, the *Michigan Journal of Law Reform*, the *Utah Law Review*, and the *Houston Law Review*, among other journals. Prior to entering legal academia, he worked as a Project Finance Associate with international law firm Norton Rose Fulbright and subsequently as a Law & Policy Fellow with the Poverty & Race Research Action Council in Washington, DC. He previously served as Board Member of the Washington Council of Lawyers in Washington, DC, an Assistant Professor of Law at the University of the District of Columbia David A. Clarke School of Law, and a Visiting Associate Professor of Clinical Law and Friedman Fellow at The George Washington University Law School. In 2021, he was elected as a term member of the American Bar Association Commission on Homelessness and Poverty, and in 2022, he was awarded the Society of American Law Teachers Junior Great Teacher Award. He received a JD from Harvard Law School, MSE in Environmental Engineering from the Johns Hopkins University, and a BS in Mechanical Engineering from MIT.

James Wahls is the senior vice president of Mission Investors Exchange, the leading impact investing network for philanthropic asset owners dedicated to deploying capital for social and environmental change. He also serves as the managing director of Revolve Fund, a philanthropic initiative that provides interest-free, recoverable capital to support black/African American, Latinx, Native American, and other people of color-led businesses, nonprofits, and financial intermediaries. He brings more than fifteen years of experience in the philanthropic, impact investing, and legal sectors. With stints at the Annie E. Casey Foundation in Baltimore, Maryland and the W.K. Kellogg Foundation in Battle Creek, Michigan, he has managed or co-managed $240+ million in impact investing allocations comprised of grant, equity, debt, and direct investments. Notable strategies designed or led by him include the Baltimore Small Business Support Fund and the Detroit Entrepreneurs of Color Fund. He also executed investments in affordable housing, financial inclusion, quality job creation, and community development.